Why You Need This New Edition?

7 good reasons why you should buy this new edition of *Thinking Socratically: Critical Thinking About Everyday Issues*

1. Nine new readings.
2. Applications of critical thinnking to such topics as 9/11, racial profiling, and a Yale campus murder.
3. New and expanded exercises, especially for deductive reasoning.
4. Eight new sections—more about consensus, belief, evidence and patterns.
5. Application of critical thinking to specific disciplines such as history and science.
6. An alternative to the current strident pattern of contemporary discourse.
7. Greater emphasis on the power of language to influence everyday thought and critical thinking.

Third Edition

THINKING SOCRATICALLY
CRITICAL THINKING ABOUT
EVERYDAY ISSUES

Sharon Schwarze

Harvey Lape
Cabrini College

Pearson

Boston   Columbus   Indianapolis   New York   San Francisco   Upper Saddle River
Amsterdam   Cape Town   Dubai   London   Madrid   Milan   Munich   Paris
Montreal   Toronto   Delhi   Mexico City   Sao Paulo   Sydney   Hong Kong
Seoul   Singapore   Taipei   Tokyo

Editorial Director: Craig Campanella
Editor in Chief: Dickson Musslewhite
Executive Editor: Ashley Dodge
Editorial Project Manager: Kate Fernandes/Carly Czech
Vice President, Director of Marketing: Brandy Dawson
Senior Marketing Manager: Laura Lee Manley
Marketing Assistant: Paige Patunas
Manager, Rights and Permissions: Charles Morris
Image Permission Coordinator: Ben Ferrini
Media Director: Brian Hyland
Digital Media Editor: Rachel Comerford
Production Manager: Pat Brown
Full-Service Project Management: Mohinder Singh/Aptara®, Inc.
Composition: Aptara®, Inc.
Printer/Binder: Courier Companies, Inc.
Cover Printer: Courier Companies, Inc.
Text Font: Times Lt Std

Credits and acknowledgments borrowed from other sources and reproduced, with permission, in this textbook appear on appropriate page within text.

Library of Congress Cataloging-in-Publication Data
Schwarze, Sharon.
  Thinking Socratically: critical thinking about everyday issues/Sharon Schwarze, Harvey Lape.—3rd ed.
    p. cm.
  Includes index.
  ISBN-13: 978-0-205-09801-9
  ISBN-10: 0-205-09801-0
  1. Critical thinking.   2. Reasoning.   3. Socrates.   I. Lape, Harvey.   II. Title.
  BC177.S36 2012
  160—dc23

                                                                              2011031596

10 9 8 7 6 5 4 3 2 1

ISBN-10: 0-205-09801-0
ISBN-13: 978-0-205-09801-9

Dedication

To our students, past, present, and future. We hope your critical thinking skills bring you productive, happy, and pleasant lives.

CONTENTS

PREFACE

As this edition goes to press, the need for *Thinking Socratically* is clearer than ever. The model of critical thinking of open rational dialogue with friends that this text proposes is sorely needed in the United States and the world. Open rational dialogue stresses working together to overcome differences and come to agreement, whether those differences are differences of political viewpoint, arguments about the historical record, the future direction of scientific research, or the morally appropriate stance on a public or private issue. Americans are all too aware that the public dialogue has been rather shrill of late with many people very entrenched in their beliefs, rather than listening and talking with others who may disagree.

Thinking Socratically can help readers understand how each person's web of belief functions and how it shapes his or her acceptance and rejection of new ideas. It explains why it is hard to have open rational dialogue and how we must *work* to be open like Socrates and less like dogmatic like Euthyphro. Our view of critical thinking emphasizes the lack of certainty that characterizes our knowledge of the world and stresses the role that consensus plays in the development of knowledge, thus leading away from dogmatism and toward the openness and listening which make room for better critical thinking and resolution of differences.

In an age when almost everyone has access to the Internet and people can speak their minds on a blog whether they have anything wise to say or not, it is important that people are good critical thinkers. There is an awful lot of information out there available to those who want and need it, but there is also much noise. Critical thinking is needed more than ever to guide students in this Internet age. We hope that *Thinking Socratically*, edition 3, can help students sort the warranted claims from the unwarranted claims they will find and consequently help them lead happier and more productive lives.

To this end, we have made the following improvements:

1. Eight new sections
2. Updated readings to reflect recent issues and events such as racial profiling and the 2010 Yale campus murder
3. Longer readings trimmed
4. Outdated readings removed
5. New and additional Exercises, especially for deductive reasoning
6. Central concept of web of belief placed more prominently and connected to consensus and personal belief
7. Clearer explanation of traces and patterns in inductive reasoning
8. Greater emphasis on the power of language to influence everyday thought and critical thinking

We think these changes and new readings will help students grasp the important concepts of critical thinking we have articulated. The emphasis on language and how it shapes our world and our belief systems, the discussion of how we try to warrant our beliefs to other people, and how we then build consensus to arrive at claims we consider factual make clear that critical thinking is a continual process and that we are always involved in warranting and rewarranting—through language. Yelling, bumper stickers, and fighting are not forms of warranting nor are they forms of critical thinking.

We have also added nine new readings while removing some that might appear dated to undergraduates. The new readings bring up such contemporary issues as racial profiling, Thomas Jefferson's illegitimate children, and a murder on the Yale campus. Readers should find these entertaining as well as challenging to their critical thinking skills. Many users asked for more Exercises, and we have added in this category as well. We think we have made our user-friendly text still more user friendly.

In the end, we write for the same reason we teach: so our readers and students can live more productive, happier, and more pleasant lives and so the world we live in will be a better world for all.

ACKNOWLEDGMENTS

We wish to acknowledge all those thinkers, critical and non-critical, whose patterns of reasoning inspire us to try to improve the thinking of future readers. We particularly want to thank those faculty who have used our text in the past and have made specific suggestions for the current edition, especially Ben Gorman and Andrew Beckerman. We have tried to incorporate their suggestions. Thanks also to those students who have called or e-mailed their questions to us. Their queries have shown us where we needed to be clearer!

We would also like to thank the various editors who have contributed to putting this text together. For the current edition: Maggie Barbieri, Nicole Conforti, Kate Fernandes, Ted Knight, and Marianne Peters-Riordan. Our greatest debt we owe to our very first editor, Ted Bolen, who realized the potential of our unique approach to improve the critical thinking of college students. His insight is responsible for this Third Edition.

PART I

Connections

You might be surprised by the title of this section of a textbook on critical thinking. What does "Connections" have to do with critical thinking? But that is the purpose of critical thinking—to help us connect. To help us connect our ideas of the world and make sense out of them **and** to help us connect with other people!

Critical thinking, first and foremost, helps us organize our ideas about the world and connect them together in various patterns such as the patterns of deductive and inductive reasoning (discussed in Parts II and III). These patterns help us make sense out of the world, making our lives richer, fuller, and more comfortable. Otherwise the world is a jumble of perceptions, and it would be very confusing. By applying critical thinking to our perceptions, we make *connections* between our experiences, creating order. This helps us anticipate the future, explain the past, and understand, in part, how the world works. We are all engaged in critical thinking all our lives. The point of this book is to help be better at it so that we can live still better.

The second connection that critical thinking makes is between people. A good way to think of critical thinking is as an open rational dialogue among friends. Our friends are important to us. They listen to us. They respond. They correct our mistakes. Together, we arrive at conclusions that we think are justified. Our friends can be our classmates, our family, our baseball team, or our fellow citizens. Our dialogues with our friends influence our beliefs and the way we look at the world. And we influence their beliefs. We generally arrive at some consensus. If we do not, we continue the dialogue. When the rational dialogue stops, the connection can turn unfriendly or worse—we could fight. That is why rational dialogue/critical thinking is so important. It is the best way to connect with other people. Part I is about this ***connection***.

1

Why Be a Critical Thinker?

CRITICAL THINKING AND THE IMPORTANCE OF OPEN DIALOGUE

This book is about becoming a better critical thinker. People who are good critical thinkers have the habit of good reasoning and have well-developed reasoning skills. All of us use critical thinking at times, for instance when we are trying to decide what kind of car to buy or how to win our next soccer game against the team that always beats us. Some people are better critical thinkers than others, however. They have good critical thinking skills and have the habit of using them. We hope that our leaders are such people: good critical thinkers who will use their thinking skills to govern well. Employers, when asked what they would like to see in an employee, more often than not say the most important skills an employee can have are good critical thinking skills. This is because critical thinking is needed for every job or profession. The skills are the same no matter what your walk of life, from being a CEO of a company to being a CEO of a room full of children.

While all people think, most people can become better thinkers by improving their skills of critical thinking. Becoming a better critical thinker is a bit like being a player on the basketball team. Everyone on the team can play basketball, usually quite well. But everyone on the team can benefit from having a coach who drills on the fundamentals, sets out what to practice, and suggests ways to be successful in particular game situations. That is what this book does for critical thinking. It takes the skills we all have and makes them better by drilling the fundamentals, setting up practices, and showing how to analyze situations from our ordinary experience that can be enhanced by good critical thinking skills.

WHAT IS CRITICAL THINKING?

Critical thinking is open rational dialogue among friends. It's as simple as that. We all do it. But we could all do it a bit better. Sometimes people think a critical thinker is a person who acts and responds like a computer or one who is so cerebral (like Spock in "Star Trek") that no ordinary person can talk with her. That is not our idea. We have a different model in mind. We think a critical thinker is someone like the teacher Socrates, for whom this book is named and about whom you will soon read. Socrates is known for asking so many questions that you may find Socrates' repeated questioning somewhat tedious. What is important about his example, though, is that he is always willing to discuss the matter further. The discussion is always open. **We think that this willingness to keep the discussion open is the hallmark of being a critical thinker.** The person who thinks critically is *not* the person who is always right or the person who never makes a mistake. Nor is the critical thinker that person who goes around being critical of everyone else. (You know the type.) Rather, the person who is a critical thinker is always willing to examine her own beliefs, to entertain alternate possibilities, and to talk with other people about those beliefs and possibilities. As we see it, critical thinking is a form of reasoning and reasoning is a dialogue, so good critical thinking means having a rational dialogue, both with yourself and with others, about an issue and keeping that dialogue **open.**

The best kind of critical thinking is an open dialogue with friends. *Friends* are people who are willing to listen and respond. Someone is a friend because she is willing to stay and discuss, not vice versa. That is, the hallmark of a friend is her willingness to engage in rational open dialogue and to keep this dialogue open as long as there is an opportunity for rational resolution.

Sometimes, of course, no friend is available. Then we must carry on the open dialogue with ourselves—through thinking. This is sometimes hard to do. We often fail to question our own beliefs the same way someone else might question them, but it is a very important aspect of being a rational person and a critical thinker. Thinking is like talking, a kind of talking to ourselves. When the "talking" stops, the thinking stops. Clearly, there are better and worse ways of thinking. The better ways of thinking, of course, are the preferred ways. Good critical thinkers tend to be more successful at meeting their goals and therefore live more productive and happier lives.

Much of the rest of this book is about learning the difference between the good critical thinking and thinking that isn't so good. But the most important aspect of being a good critical thinker is to **do** the thinking—to think! Just like the basketball player who needs to play basketball to get better, the critical thinker must play the game. This means to carry on the dialogue as far as possible and not to stop because one is too stubborn or too lazy or too tired to continue. Socrates always said he was a seeker after wisdom, not a wise person and, as a seeker, he was always willing to continue the discussion.

So, the goal we seek is open rational dialogue with friends, using the skills of critical thinking. This sounds simple. Most people believe that they are open to other's ideas and are good listeners, willing to consider alternative points of view. Too often in a dialogue, however, the person who is "listening" is thinking about what she is going to say next, not about what the other person is saying. The dialogue is complicated by the fact that we do not all experience the world in the same way. We do not all share the same view of what is real and/or important in the world. It is hard to carry on a dialogue with someone who does not share our view of the world. We usually think that our view is the right one and the other person must be wrong. How can we settle this? We could settle this by going to war—and nations often do! But there is a better way: open rational dialogue. Open rational dialogue cannot tell us this person is right and that person is wrong. What it can tell us is that some ways of looking at the world **work better** than others, thereby enabling us to live happier and healthier lives. Since most of us would like to live happy and healthy lives, we want to know more about those ways of looking at the world. The purpose of this book is to provide you with the tools of critical thinking that can guide you in your use of rational dialogue and how to get the most out of it.

While many people agree that critical thinking and rational dialogue generally "work better" than nonrational thought and dialogue, explanations as to why this is the case vary. Philosophers of many different schools have offered a wide variety of answers to this question, which we will not recount here.[1] We think the best way to support this claim is to warrant it with statements that most people would accept and which do not require any appeal to controversial assumptions that many people might question.

We see three reasons why rational approaches work better in our lives than nonrational approaches. First, rational approaches work better because human beings are animals with purposes and plans. They may live in the present, but they have intentions and plans for the future. For these plans to be successful, their expectations about what will happen must be accurate. So, they use reason and past experience to form their expectations about the future. This kind of critical thinking enables them to anticipate what is likely to happen and, consequently, to be successful in fulfilling their intentions.

In his account of the investigations of the *Challenger* shuttle disaster, Richard Feynman, physicist and Nobel Prize recipient, presents a clear example of the need to use reason and critical thinking to anticipate what will happen and to plan accordingly.[2] As a member of the disaster investigation team, Feynman refused to accept NASA safety estimates without also being shown the evidence and the reasoning necessary to support them. NASA estimated the chance of engine failure at 1 in 100,000, which would lead to the expectation that a shuttle could fly every day for 300 years without failure. Feynman's reexamination of the data revealed the actual probability to be 1 in 200, which would not make the *Challenger*'s failure a surprise.

---

[1]Two popular views are those of Plato and Thomas Aquinas. Plato claimed that there was a *logos* or natural logical order in the world that matched the logical order of human reason or critical thinking. Thomas Aquinas, on the other hand, claimed that the world was created by a first cause or first mover that itself was rational, namely, God. So, according to both of these views, rational thought and critical thinking work better than irrational thought because they match the world better. Our Socratic approach tries to avoid claims about the nature of the world and to suggest that the likeliest explanation for the success of reason and critical thinking is its insistence on giving a hearing to all sides of an issue and to keeping the dialogue going. At the end of the *Euthyphro,* when Euthyphro has tired of trying to give a rationally adequate account of piety, Socrates almost begs him not to abandon the task. We agree with Socrates more than with Plato and Aquinas. Rationality, whatever its shortcomings, is the best game in town.

[2]Richard Feynman, *What Do You Care What Other People Think?* (New York: W.W. Norton & Company, 1988).

A second reason why we claim that rational approaches work better than nonrational ones is that when other people figure in our plans and purposes, the best way to include them or bring them along is by giving them reasons. Of course, other people are not always persuaded by reason or by the reasons we give. This does not mean that there are not some reasons that might be persuasive that we have not given—either because we choose not to give them or because we do not think of them at the time. Even Socrates, facing a death sentence when he was on trial for impiety, was not able to persuade the Athenian jury of his innocence despite his considerable powers of reason.[3] There are times, unfortunately, when we are convinced the other side will not listen to reason, as when dealing with a political or religious fanatic or a thug in the street. Then it might be reasonable to become unreasonable, at least for the moment! Anger and other emotional responses can be successful, if used carefully, with reason. In general, however, unreasonableness begets further unreasonableness and violence begets violence. Since the collective experience of the human race testifies to this pattern, lapses into unreason should be infrequent.

Keeping the dialogue open not only keeps us from using force but it has the added benefit of keeping us engaged. It means that we must make an **effort.** To continue the dialogue, we must make an effort to find reasons that are persuasive, to understand the other person's point of view, and to rethink our own point of view. A problem with "agreeing to disagree" is that it makes us powerless with regard to the future. It cuts off our opportunity of persuading others to join us in our plans. It leaves us standing alone.

Finally, we would like to have pleasant experiences, not unpleasant ones. Having pleasant experiences is connected to being able to anticipate future events, making plans, and having friends to share our plans. It is also about being able to remember and recreate the pleasant experiences through dialogue with friends. Enjoying and savoring life necessitates being open to new possibilities and avoiding potential unpleasant experiences.

Becoming a critical thinker is a dynamic process, one that takes time and effort on your part, just as becoming a better basketball player takes time and effort no matter how good a player you might already be. During this process you will be questioning some of your firmly held assumptions, improving your reasoning skills, and learning some new concepts that will help you think critically. You will have to practice the skills you are learning and to be open to some different ways of thinking about the world. An open rational dialogue takes work. It is actually hard to be open to new ways of thinking, but critical thinking skills will help you anticipate and have the pleasant experiences you seek.

Throughout this text, we will present readings from everyday life, from popular publications, from newspapers, and from the history of philosophy, to illustrate the concepts and skills of critical thinking we expect you to acquire. You will see how the concepts of critical thinking and good reasoning work in our everyday lives, and you will learn how to apply them in familiar contexts. The first reading is a very famous dialogue called *Euthyphro,* written by the philosopher Plato in the fourth century B.C.E. Socrates and Euthyphro are discussing what they think piety is and who is a pious

---

[3]Plato's account suggests, however, that part of Socrates' failure was due to his unwillingness to offer the kind of "reasons" which were usually persuasive with Athenian juries, namely, to parade his wife and children before them and to do other things that would appeal to their sympathies.

person. This is a very important question because Socrates is on his way into court where he has been accused of impiety, a charge which will eventually lead to his death. If you think the word *piety* sounds too old-fashioned, substitute the word *good* in its place. As you read this dialogue, think about the characters in the dialogue, not just the words. Think about how they exemplify or fail to exemplify what you think is open rational dialogue. Also consider the kind of person Socrates is. And the kind of person Euthyphro is. Do you know people like Euthyphro? How would you describe them?

EUTHYPHRO

Plato

Characters

Socrates

Euthyphro

SCENE The Hall of the King

EUTHYPHRO.   What in the world are you doing here in the king's hall,[1] Socrates? Why have you left your haunts in the Lyceum? You surely cannot have a suit before him, as I have.

SOCRATES.   The Athenians, Euthyphro, call it an indictment, not a suit.

EUTH.   What? Do you mean that someone is prosecuting you? I cannot believe that you are prosecuting anyone yourself.

SOCR.   Certainly I am not.

EUTH.   Then is someone prosecuting you?

SOCR.   Yes.

EUTH.   Who is he?

SOCR.   I scarcely know him myself, Euthyphro; I think he must be some unknown young man. His name, however, is Meletus, and his district Pitthis, if you can call to mind any Meletus of that district—a hook-nosed man with lanky hair and rather a scanty beard.

EUTH.   I don't know him, Socrates. But tell me, what is he prosecuting you for?

SOCR.   What for? Not on trivial grounds, I think. It is no small thing for so young a man to have formed an opinion on such an important matter. For he, he says, knows how the young are corrupted, and who are their corrupters. He must be a wise man who, observing my ignorance, is going to accuse me to the state, as his mother, of corrupting his friends. I think that he is the only one who begins at the right point in his political reforms; for his first care

[1]The anachronistic title "king" was retained by the magistrate who had jurisdiction over crimes affecting the state religion.-Ed.

is to make the young men as good as possible, just as a good farmer will take care of his young plants first, and, after he has done that, of the others. And so Meletus, I suppose, is first clearing us away who, as he says, corrupt the young men growing up; and then, when he has done that, of course he will turn his attention to the older men, and so become a very great public benefactor. Indeed, that is only what you would expect when he goes to work in this way.

EUTH.   I hope it may be so, Socrates, but I fear the opposite. It seems to me that in trying to injure you, he is really setting to work by striking a blow at the foundation of the state. But how, tell me, does he say that you corrupt the youth?

SOCR.   In a way which sounds absurd at first, my friend. He says that I am a maker of gods; and so he is prosecuting me, he says, for inventing new gods and for not believing in the old ones.

EUTH.   I understand, Socrates. It is because you say that you always have a divine guide. So he is prosecuting you for introducing religious reforms; and he is going into court to arouse prejudice against you, knowing that the multitude are easily prejudiced about such matters. Why, they laugh even at me, as if I were out of my mind, when I talk about divine things in the assembly and tell them what is going to happen; and yet I have never foretold anything which has not come true. But they are resentful of all people like us. We must not worry about them; we must meet them boldly.

SOCR.   My dear Euthyphro, their ridicule is not a very serious matter. The Athenians, it seems to me, may think a man to be clever without paying him much attention, so long as they do not think that he teaches his wisdom to others. But as soon as they think that he makes other people clever, they get angry, whether it be from resentment, as you say, or for some other reason.

EUTH.   I am not very anxious to test their attitude toward me in this matter.

SOCR.   No, perhaps they think that you are reserved, and that you are not anxious to teach your wisdom to others. But I fear that they may think that I am; for my love of men makes me talk to everyone whom I meet quite freely and unreservedly, and without payment. Indeed, if I could I would gladly pay people myself to listen to me. If then, as I said just now, they were only going to laugh at me, as you say they do at you, it would not be at all an unpleasant way of spending the day—to spend it in court, joking and laughing. But if they are going to be in earnest, then only prophets like you can tell where the matter will end.

EUTH.   Well, Socrates, I dare say that nothing will come of it. Very likely you will be successful in your trial, and I think that I shall be in mine.

SOCR.	And what is this suit of yours, Euthyphro? Are you suing, or being sued?
EUTH.	I am suing.
SOCR.	Whom?
EUTH.	A man whom people think I must be mad to prosecute.
SOCR.	What? Has he wings to fly away with?
EUTH.	He is far enough from flying; he is a very old man.
SOCR.	Who is he?
EUTH.	He is my father.
SOCR.	Your father, my good man?
EUTH.	He is indeed.
SOCR.	What are you prosecuting him for? What is the accusation?
EUTH.	Murder, Socrates.
SOCR.	Good heavens, Euthyphro! Surely the multitude are ignorant of what is right. I take it that it is not everyone who could rightly do what you are doing; only a man who was already well advanced in wisdom.
EUTH.	That is quite true, Socrates.
SOCR.	Was the man whom your father killed a relative of yours? But, of course, he was. You would never have prosecuted your father for the murder of a stranger?
EUTH.	You amuse me, Socrates. What difference does it make whether the murdered man were a relative or a stranger? The only question that you have to ask is, did the murderer kill justly or not? If justly, you must let him alone; if unjustly, you must indict him for murder, even though he share your hearth and sit at your table. The pollution is the same if you associate with such a man, knowing what he has done, without purifying yourself, and him too, by bringing him to justice. In the present case the murdered man was a poor laborer of mine, who worked for us on our farm in Naxos. While drunk he got angry with one of our slaves and killed him. My father therefore bound the man hand and foot and threw him into a ditch, while he sent to Athens to ask the priest what he should do. While the messenger was gone, he entirely neglected the man, thinking that he was a murderer, and that it would be no great matter, even if he were to die. And that was exactly what happened; hunger and cold and his bonds killed him before the messenger returned. And now my father and the rest of my family are indignant with me because I am prosecuting my father for the murder of this murderer. They assert that he did not kill the man at all; and they say that, even if he had killed him over and over again, the man himself was a murderer, and that I ought not to concern myself about such a person because it is impious for a son to prosecute his father for murder. So little, Socrates, do they know the divine law of piety and impiety.

SOCR. And do you mean to say, Euthyphro, that you think that you understand divine things and piety and impiety so accurately that, in such a case as you have stated, you can bring your father to justice without fear that you yourself may be doing something impious?

EUTH. If I did not understand all these matters accurately, Socrates, I should not be worth much—Euthyphro would not be any better than other men.

SOCR. Then, my dear Euthyphro, I cannot do better than become your pupil and challenge Meletus on this very point before the trial begins. I should say that I had always thought it very important to have knowledge about divine things; and that now, when he says that I offend by speaking carelessly about them, and by introducing reforms, I have become your pupil. And I should say, "Meletus, if you acknowledge Euthyphro to be wise in these matters and to hold the correct belief, then think the same of me and do not put me on trial; but if you do not, then bring a suit, not against me, but against my master, for corrupting his elders—namely, myself whom he corrupts by his teaching, and his own father whom he corrupts by admonishing and punishing him." And if I did not succeed in persuading him to release me from the suit or to indict you in my place, then I could repeat my challenge in court.

EUTH. Yes, by Zeus! Socrates, I think I should find out his weak points if he were to try to indict me. I should have a good deal to say about him in court long before I spoke about myself.

SOCR. Yes, my dear friend, and knowing this I am anxious to become your pupil. I see that Meletus here, and others too, seem not to notice you at all, but he sees through me without difficulty and at once prosecutes me for impiety. Now, therefore, please explain to me what you were so confident just now that you knew. Tell me what are righteousness and sacrilege with respect to murder and everything else. I suppose that piety is the same in all actions, and that impiety is always the opposite of piety, and retains its identity, and that, as impiety, it always has the same character, which will be found in whatever is impious.

EUTH. Certainly, Socrates, I suppose so.

SOCR. Tell me, then, what is piety and what is impiety?

EUTH. Well, then, I say that piety means prosecuting the unjust individual who has committed murder or sacrilege, or any other such crime, as I am doing now, whether he is your father or your mother or whoever he is; and I say that impiety means not prosecuting him. And observe, Socrates, I will give you a clear proof, which I have already given to others, that it is so, and that doing right means not letting off unpunished the sacrilegious man, whosoever he may be. Men hold Zeus to be the best and the most just of the gods; and they admit that Zeus bound his own father, Cronos, for wrongfully devouring his children; and that Cronos, in his turn, castrated his father for similar reasons. And yet these same men are incensed with me because I proceed against my father for doing wrong. So, you see, they say one thing in the case of the gods and quite another in mine.

SOCR.   Is not that why I am being prosecuted, Euthyphro? I mean, because I find it hard to accept such stories people tell about the gods? I expect that I shall be found at fault because I doubt those stories. Now if you who understand all these matters so well agree in holding all those tales true, then I suppose that I must yield to your authority. What could I say when I admit myself that I know nothing about them? but tell me, in the name of friendship, do you really believe that these things have actually happened?

EUTH.   Yes, and more amazing things, too, Socrates, which the multitude do not know of.

SOCR.   Then you really believe that there is war among the gods, and bitter hatreds, and battles, such as the poets tell of, and which the great painters have depicted in our temples, notably in the pictures which cover the robe that is carried up to the Acropolis at the great Panathenaic festival? Are we to say that these things are true, Euthyphro?

EUTH.   Yes, Socrates, and more besides. As I was saying, I will report to you many other stories about divine matters, if you like, which I am sure will astonish you when you hear them.

SOCR.   I dare say. You shall report them to me at your leisure another time. At present please try to give a more definite answer to the question which I asked you just now. What I asked you, my friend, was, What is piety? and you have not explained it to me to my satisfaction. You only tell me that what you are doing now, namely, prosecuting your father for murder, is a pious act.

EUTH.   Well, that is true, Socrates.

SOCR.   Very likely. But many other actions are pious, are they not, Euthyphro?

EUTH.   Certainly.

SOCR.   Remember, then, I did not ask you to tell me one or two of all the many pious actions that there are; I want to know what is characteristic of piety which makes all pious actions pious. You said, I think, that there is one characteristic which makes all pious actions pious, and another characteristic which makes all impious actions impious. Do you not remember?

EUTH.   I do.

SOCR.   Well, then, explain to me what is this characteristic, that I may have it to turn to, and to use as a standard whereby to judge your actions and those of other men, and be able to say that whatever action resembles it is pious, and whatever does not, is not pious.

EUTH.   Yes, I will tell you that if you wish, Socrates.

SOCR.   Certainly I do.

EUTH.   Well, then, what is pleasing to the gods is pious, and what is not pleasing to them is impious.

SOCR.   Fine, Euthyphro. Now you have given me the answer that I wanted. Whether what you say is true, I do not know yet. But, of course, you will go on to prove that it is true.

EUTH.   Certainly.

SOCR.   Come, then, let us examine our statement. The things and the men that are pleasing to the gods are pious, and the things and the men that are displeasing to the gods are impious. But piety and impiety are not the same; they are as opposite as possible— was not that what we said?

EUTH.   Certainly.

SOCR.   And it seems the appropriate statement?

EUTH.   Yes, Socrates, certainly.

SOCR.   Have we not also said, Euthyphro, that there are quarrels and disagreements and hatreds among the gods?

EUTH.   We have.

SOCR.   But what kind of disagreement, my friend, causes hatred and anger? Let us look at the matter thus. If you and I were to disagree as to whether one number were more than another, would that make us angry and enemies? Should we not settle such a dispute at once by counting?

EUTH.   Of course.

SOCR.   And if we were to disagree as to the relative size of two things, we should measure them and put an end to the disagreement at once, should we not?

EUTH.   Yes.

SOCR.   And should we not settle a question about the relative weight of two things by weighing them?

EUTH.   Of course.

SOCR.   Then what is the question which would make us angry and enemies if we disagreed about it, and could not come to a settlement? Perhaps you have not an answer ready; but listen to mine. Is it not the question of the just and unjust, of the honorable and the dishonorable, of the good and the bad? Is it not questions about these matters which make you and me and everyone else quarrel, when we do quarrel, if we differ about them and can reach no satisfactory agreement?

EUTH.   Yes, Socrates, it is disagreements about these matters.

SOCR.   Well, Euthyphro, the gods will quarrel over these things if they quarrel at all, will they not?

EUTH.   Necessarily.

SOCR.	Then, my good Euthyphro, you say that some of the gods think one thing just, the others another; and that what some of them hold to be honorable or good, others hold to be dishonorable or evil. For there would not have been quarrels among them if they had not disagreed on these points, would there?
EUTH.	You are right.
SOCR.	And each of them loves what he thinks honorable, and good, and just; and hates the opposite, does he not?
EUTH.	Certainly.
SOCR.	But you say that the same action is held by some of them to be just, and by others to be unjust; and that then they dispute about it, and so quarrel and fight among themselves. Is it not so?
EUTH.	Yes.
SOCR.	Then the same thing is hated by the gods and loved by them; and the same thing will be displeasing and pleasing to them.
EUTH.	Apparently.
SOCR.	Then, according to your account, the same thing will be pious and impious.
EUTH.	So it seems.
SOCR.	Then, my good friend, you have not answered my question. I did not ask you to tell me what action is both pious and impious; but it seems that whatever is pleasing to the gods is also displeasing to them. And so, Euthyphro, I should not be surprised if what you are doing now in punishing your father is an action well pleasing to Zeus, but hateful to Cronos and Uranus, and acceptable to Hephaestus, but hateful to Hera; and if any of the other gods disagree about it, pleasing to some of them and displeasing to others.
EUTH.	But on this point, Socrates, I think that there is no difference of opinion among the gods: they all hold that if one man kills another unjustly, he must be punished.
SOCR.	What, Euthyphro? Among mankind, have you never heard disputes whether a man ought to be punished for killing another man unjustly, or for doing some other unjust deed?
EUTH.	Indeed, they never cease from these disputes, especially in courts of justice. They do all manner of unjust things; and then there is nothing which they will not do and say to avoid punishment.
SOCR.	Do they admit that they have done something unjust, and at the same time deny that they ought to be punished, Euthyphro?
EUTH.	No, indeed, that they do not.
SOCR.	Then it is not the case that there is nothing which they will not do and say. I take it, they do not dare to say or argue that they must not be punished if they have done something unjust. What they say is that they have not done anything unjust, is it not so?
EUTH.	That is true.

SOCR.	Then they do not disagree over the question that the unjust individual must be punished. They disagree over the question, who is unjust, and what was done and when, do they not?
EUTH.	That is true.
SOCR.	Well, is not exactly the same thing true of the gods if they quarrel about justice and injustice, as you say they do? Do not some of them say that the others are doing something unjust, while the others deny it? No one, I suppose, my dear friend, whether god or man, dares to say that a person who has done something unjust must not be punished.
EUTH.	No, Socrates, that is true, by and large.
SOCR.	I take it, Euthyphro, that the disputants, whether men or gods, if the gods do disagree, disagree over each separate act. When they quarrel about any act, some of them say that it was just, and others that it was unjust. Is it not so?
EUTH.	Yes.
SOCR.	Come, then, my dear Euthyphro, please enlighten me on this point. What proof have you that all the gods think that a laborer who has been imprisoned for murder by the master of the man whom he has murdered, and who dies from his imprisonment before the master has had time to learn from the religious authorities what he should do, dies unjustly? How do you know that it is just for a son to indict his father and to prosecute him for the murder of such a man? Come, see if you can make it clear to me that the gods necessarily agree in thinking that this action of yours is just; and if you satisfy me, I will never cease singing your praises for wisdom.
EUTH.	I could make that clear enough to you, Socrates; but I am afraid that it would be a long business.
SOCR.	I see you think that I am duller than the judges. To them, of course, you will make it clear that your father has committed an unjust action, and that all the gods agree in hating such actions.
EUTH.	I will indeed, Socrates, if they will only listen to me.
SOCR.	They will listen if they think that you are a good speaker. But while you were talking, it occurred to me to ask myself this question: suppose that Euthyphro were to prove to me as clearly as possible that all the gods think such a death unjust, how has he brought me any nearer to understanding what piety and impiety are? This particular act, perhaps, may be displeasing to the gods, but then we have just seen that piety and impiety cannot be defined in that way; for we have seen that what is displeasing to the gods is also pleasing to them. So I will let you off on this point, Euthyphro; and all the gods shall agree in thinking your father's action wrong and in hating it, if you like. But shall we correct our definition and say that whatever all the gods hate is impious, and whatever they all love is pious; while whatever

	some of them love, and others hate, is either both or neither? Do you wish us now to define piety and impiety in this manner?
EUTH.	Why not, Socrates?
SOCR.	There is no reason why I should not, Euthyphro. It is for you to consider whether that definition will help you to teach me what you promised.
EUTH.	Well, I should say that piety is what all the gods love, and that impiety is what they all hate.
SOCR.	Are we to examine this definition, Euthyphro, and see if it is a good one? Or are we to be content to accept the bare statements of other men or of ourselves without asking any questions? Or must we examine the statements?
EUTH.	We must examine them. But for my part I think that the definition is right this time.
SOCR.	We shall know that better in a little while, my good friend. Now consider this question. Do the gods love piety because it is pious, or is it pious because they love it?
EUTH.	I do not understand you, Socrates.
SOCR.	I will try to explain myself: we speak of a thing being carried and carrying, and being led and leading, and being seen and seeing; and you understand that all such expressions mean different things, and what the difference is.
EUTH.	Yes, I think I understand.
SOCR.	And we talk of a thing being loved, of a thing loving, and the two are different?
EUTH.	Of course.
SOCR.	Now tell me, is a thing which is being carried in a state of being carried because it is carried, or for some other reason?
EUTH.	No, because it is carried.
SOCR.	And a thing is in a state of being led because it is led, and of being seen because it is seen?
EUTH.	Certainly.
SOCR.	Then a thing is not seen because it is in a state of being seen: it is in a state of being seen because it is seen; and a thing is not led because it is in a state of being led: it is in a state of being led because it is led; and a thing is not carried because it is in a state of being carried: it is in a state of being carried because it is carried. Is my meaning clear now, Euthyphro? I mean this: if anything becomes or is affected, it does not become because it is in a state of becoming: it is in a state of becoming because it becomes; and it is not affected because it is in a state of being affected: it in a state of being affected because it is affected. Do you not agree?
EUTH.	I do.
SOCR.	Is not that which is being loved in a state either of becoming or of being affected in some way by something?

EUTH.   Certainly.

SOCR.   Then the same is true here as in the former cases. A thing is not loved by those who love it because it is in a state of being loved; it is in a state of being loved because they love it.

EUTH.   Necessarily.

SOCR.   Well, then, Euthyphro, what do we say about piety? Is it not loved by all the gods, according to your definition?

EUTH.   Yes.

SOCR.   Because it is pious, or for some other reason?

EUTH.   No, because it is pious.

SOCR.   Then it is loved by the gods because it is pious; it is not pious because it is loved by them?

EUTH.   It seems so.

SOCR.   But, then, what is pleasing to the gods is pleasing to them, and is in a state of being loved by them, because they love it?

EUTH.   Of course.

SOCR.   Then piety is not what is pleasing to the gods, and what is pleasing to the gods is not pious, as you say, Euthyphro. They are different things.

EUTH.   And why, Socrates?

SOCR.   Because we are agreed that the gods love piety because it is pious, and that it is not pious because they love it. Is not this so?

EUTH.   Yes.

SOCR.   And that what is pleasing to the gods because they love it, is pleasing to them by reason of this same love, and that they do not love it because it is pleasing to them.

EUTH.   True.

SOCR.   Then, my dear Euthyphro, piety and what is pleasing to the gods are different things. If the gods had loved piety because it is pious, they would also have loved what is pleasing to them because it is pleasing to them; but if what is pleasing to them had been pleasing to them because they loved it, then piety, too, would have been piety because they loved it. But now you see that they are opposite things, and wholly different from each other. For the one is of a sort to be loved because it is loved, while the other is loved because it is of a sort to be loved. My question, Euthyphro, was, What is piety? But it turns out that you have not explained to me the essential character of piety; you have been content to mention an effect which belongs to it—namely, that all the gods love it. You have not yet told me what its essential character is. Do not, if you please, keep from me what piety is; begin again and tell me that. Never mind whether the gods love it, or whether it has other effects: we shall not differ on that point. Do your best to make clear to me what is piety and what is impiety.

EUTH.   But, Socrates, I really don't know how to explain to you what is in my mind. Whatever statement we put forward always some-how moves round in a circle, and will not stay where we put it.

SOCR.   I think that your statements, Euthyphro, are worthy of my ances-tor Daedalus.[2] If they had been mine and I had set them down, I dare say you would have made fun of me, and said that it was the consequence of my descent from Daedalus that the state-ments which I construct run away, as his statues used to, and will not stay where they are put. But, as it is, the statements are yours, and the joke would have no point. You yourself see that they will not stay still.

EUTH.   Nay, Socrates, I think that the joke is very much in point. It is not my fault that the statement moves round in a circle and will not stay still. But you are the Daedalus, I think; as far as I am concerned, my statements would have stayed put.

SOCR.   Then, my friend, I must be a more skillful artist than Daedalus; he only used to make his own works move, while I, you see, can make other people's works move, too. And the beauty of it is that I am wise against my will. I would rather that our statements had remained firm and immovable than have all the wisdom of Daedalus and all the riches of Tantalus to boot. But enough of this. I will do my best to help you to explain to me what piety is, for I think that you are lazy. Don't give in yet. Tell me, do you not think that all piety must be just?

EUTH.   I do.

SOCR.   Well, then, is all justice pious, too? Or, while all piety is just, is a part only of justice pious, and the rest of it something else?

EUTH.   I do not follow you, Socrates.

SOCR.   Yet you have the advantage over me in your youth no less than your wisdom. But, as I say, the wealth of your wisdom makes you complacent. Exert yourself, my good friend: I am not asking you a difficult question. I mean the opposite of what the poet[3] said, when he wrote:

"You shall not name Zeus the creator, who made all things: for where there is fear there also is reverence."

Now I disagree with the poet. Shall I tell you why?

EUTH.   Yes.

SOCR.   I do not think it true to say that where there is fear, there also is reverence. Many people who fear sickness and poverty and other such evils seem to me to have fear, but no reverence for what they fear. Do you not think so?

EUTH.   I do.

---

[2]Daedalus' statues were reputed to have been so lifelike that they came alive.-Ed.

[3]Stasinus

SOCR.	But I think that where there is reverence there also is fear. Does any man feel reverence and a sense of shame about anything, without at the same time dreading and fearing the reputation of wickedness?
EUTH.	No, certainly not.
SOCR.	Then, though there is fear wherever there is reverence, it is not correct to say that where there is fear there also is reverence. Reverence does not always accompany fear; for fear, I take it, is wider than reverence. It is a part of fear, just as the odd is a part of number, so that where you have the odd you must also have number, though where you have number you do not necessarily have the odd. Now I think you follow me?
EUTH.	I do.
SOCR.	Well, then, this is what I meant by the question which I asked you. Is there always piety where there is justice? Or, though there is always justice where there is piety, yet there is not always piety where there is justice, because piety is only a part of justice? Shall we say this, or do you differ?
EUTH.	No, I agree. I think that you are right.
SOCR.	Now observe the next point. If piety is a part of justice, we must find out, I suppose, what part of justice it is? Now, if you had asked me just now, for instance, what part of number is the odd, and what number is an odd number, I should have said that whatever number is not even is an odd number. Is it not so?
EUTH.	Yes.
SOCR.	Then see if you can explain to me what part of justice is piety, that I may tell Meletus that now that I have been adequately instructed by you as to what actions are righteous and pious, and what are not, he must give up prosecuting me unjustly for impiety.
EUTH.	Well, then, Socrates, I should say that righteousness and piety are that part of justice which has to do with the careful attention which ought to be paid to the gods; and that what has to do with the careful attention which ought to be paid to men is the remaining part of justice.
SOCR.	And I think that your answer is a good one, Euthyphro. But there is one little point about which I still want to hear more. I do not yet understand what the careful attention is to which you refer. I suppose you do not mean that the attention which we pay to the gods is like the attention which we pay to other things. We say, for instance, do we not, that not everyone knows how to take care of horses, but only the trainer of horses?
EUTH.	Certainly.
SOCR.	For I suppose that the skill that is concerned with horses is the art of taking care of horses.
EUTH.	Yes.
SOCR.	And not everyone understands the care of dogs, but only the huntsman.

EUTH.	True.
SOCR.	For I suppose that the huntsman's skill is in the art of taking care of dogs.
EUTH.	Yes.
SOCR.	And the herdsman's skill is the art of taking care of cattle.
EUTH.	Certainly.
SOCR.	And you say that piety and righteousness are taking care of the gods, Euthyphro?
EUTH.	I do.
SOCR.	Well, then, has not all care the same object? Is it not for the good and benefit of that on which it is bestowed? For instance, you see that horses are benefited and improved when they are cared for by the art which is concerned with them. Is it not so?
EUTH.	Yes, I think so.
SOCR.	And dogs are benefited and improved by the huntsman's art, and cattle by the herdsman's, are they not? And the same is always true. Or do you think care is ever meant to harm that which is cared for?
EUTH.	No, indeed; certainly not.
SOCR.	But to benefit it?
EUTH.	Of course.
SOCR.	Then is piety, which is our care for the gods, intended to benefit the gods, or to improve them? Should you allow that you make any of the gods better when you do a pious action?
EUTH.	No indeed; certainly not.
SOCR.	No, I am quite sure that this is not your meaning, Euthyphro. It was for that reason that I asked you what you meant by the careful attention which ought to be paid to the gods. I thought that you did not mean that.
EUTH.	You were right, Socrates. I do not mean that.
SOCR.	Good. Then what sort of attention to the gods will piety be?
EUTH.	The sort of attention, Socrates, slaves pay to their masters.
SOCR.	I understand; then it is a kind of service to the gods?
EUTH.	Certainly.
SOCR.	Can you tell me what result the art which serves a doctor serves to produce? Is it not health?
EUTH.	Yes.
SOCR.	And what result does the art which serves a shipwright serve to produce?
EUTH.	A ship, of course, Socrates.
SOCR.	The result of the art which serves a builder is a house, is it not?
EUTH.	Yes.
SOCR.	Then tell me, my good friend: What result will the art which serves the gods serve to produce? You must know, seeing that you say that you know more about divine things than any other man.
EUTH.	Well, that is true, Socrates.

SOCR.   Then tell me, I beg you, what is that grand result which the gods use our services to produce?

EUTH.   There are many notable results, Socrates.

SOCR.   So are those, my friend, which a general produces. Yet it is easy to see that the crowning result of them all is victory in war, is it not?

EUTH.   Of course.

SOCR.   And, I take it, the farmer produces many notable results; yet the principal result of them all is that he makes the earth produce food.

EUTH.   Certainly.

SOCR.   Well, then, what is the principal result of the many notable results which the gods produce?

EUTH.   I told you just now, Socrates, that accurate knowledge of all these matters is not easily obtained. However, broadly I say this: if any man knows that his words and actions in prayer and sacrifice are acceptable to the gods, that is what is pious; and it preserves the state, as it does private families. But the opposite of what is acceptable to the gods is sacrilegious, and this it is that undermines and destroys everything.

SOCR.   Certainly, Euthyphro, if you had wished, you could have answered my main question in far fewer words. But you are evidently not anxious to teach me. Just now, when you were on the very point of telling me what I want to know, you stopped short. If you had gone on then, I should have learned from you clearly enough by this time what piety is. But now I am asking you questions, and must follow wherever you lead me; so tell me, what is it that you mean by piety and impiety? Do you not mean a science of prayer and sacrifice?

EUTH.   I do.

SOCR.   To sacrifice is to give to the gods, and to pray is to ask of them, is it not?

EUTH.   It is, Socrates.

SOCR.   Then you say that piety is the science of asking of the gods and giving to them?

EUTH.   You understand my meaning exactly, Socrates.

SOCR.   Yes, for I am eager to share your wisdom, Euthyphro, and so I am all attention; nothing that you say will fall to the ground. But tell me, what is this service of the gods? You say it is to ask of them, and to give to them?

EUTH.   I do.

SOCR.   Then, to ask rightly will be to ask of them what we stand in need of from them, will it not?

EUTH.   Naturally.

SOCR.   And to give rightly will be to give back to them what they stand in need of from us? It would not be very skillful to make a present to a man of something that he has no need of.

EUTH.	True, Socrates.
SOCR.	Then piety, Euthyphro, will be the art of carrying on business between gods and men?
EUTH.	Yes, if you like to call it so.
SOCR.	But I like nothing except what is true. But tell me, how are the gods benefited by the gifts which they receive from us? What they give is plain enough. Every good thing that we have is their gift. But how are they benefited by what we give them? Have we the advantage over them in these business transactions to such an extent that we receive from them all the good things we possess, and give them nothing in return?
EUTH.	But do you suppose, Socrates, that the gods are benefited by the gifts which they receive from us?
SOCR.	But what *are* these gifts, Euthyphro, that we give the gods?
EUTH.	What do you think but honor and praise, and, as I have said, what is acceptable to them.
SOCR.	Then piety, Euthyphro, is acceptable to the gods, but it is not profitable to them nor loved by them?
EUTH.	I think that nothing is more loved by them.
SOCR.	Then I see that piety means that which is loved by the gods.
EUTH.	Most certainly.
SOCR.	After that, shall you be surprised to find that your statements move about instead of staying where you put them? Shall you accuse me of being the Daedalus that makes them move, when you yourself are far more skillful than Daedalus was, and make them go round in a circle? Do you not see that our statement has come round to where it was before? Surely you remember that we have already seen that piety and what is pleasing to the gods are quite different things. Do you not remember?
EUTH.	I do.
SOCR.	And now do you not see that you say that what the gods love is pious? But does not what the gods love come to the same thing as what is pleasing to the gods?
EUTH.	Certainly.
SOCR.	Then either our former conclusion was wrong or, if it was right, we are wrong now.
EUTH.	So it seems.
SOCR.	Then we must begin again and inquire what piety is. I do not mean to give in until I have found out. Do not regard me as unworthy; give your whole mind to the question, and this time tell me the truth. For if anyone knows it, it is you; and you are a Proteus whom I must not let go until you have told me. It cannot be that you would ever have undertaken to prosecute your aged father for the murder of a laboring man unless you had known exactly what piety and impiety are. You would have feared to risk the anger of the gods, in case you should be doing wrong, and you would have been afraid of

what men would say. But now I am sure that you think that you know exactly what is pious and what is not; so tell me, my good Euthyphro, and do not conceal from me what you think.

EUTH. Another time, then, Socrates. I am in a hurry now, and it is time for me to be off.

SOCR. What are you doing, my friend! Will you go away and destroy all my hopes of learning from you what is pious and what is not, and so of escaping Meletus? I meant to explain to him that now Euthyphro has made me wise about divine things, and that I no longer in my ignorance speak carelessly about them or introduce reforms. And then I was going to promise him to live a better life for the future.

STUDY QUESTIONS

1. Who is more pious, Euthyphro or Socrates? Why?
2. Some people believe that an act is good because God wills it. From your reading of *Euthyphro,* what is problematic about this claim?
3. What characteristics of friendship are displayed in the dialogue?
4. Why is the definition of piety important? In the dialogue? In life in general?

REASON AND CULTURE

All this talk about being reasonable seems to ignore a very important aspect of what it means to be a human being, namely, having feelings or emotions. Emotion, not reason, seems to be responsible for most of the excitement of life, the highs and lows that make our lives richer and more fun. What would life be like without falling in love, without shedding tears watching a sentimental movie, without cheering passionately for your favorite sports team? People who are incapable of having such feelings seem to be missing something in their lives. Mystery, not reason, is exciting. We wait with bated breath while the magician saws into two the box with the lady in it. And most cultures have their "Halloweens" when people pay tribute to spooks and goblins.

Some people have argued that favoring reason over mystery is simply a result of our "overly rational" Western heritage and that in trying to promote the use of reason we are just promoting Western culture at the expense of cultures that favor mystery. According to this view, we "Westerners" do not accept emotion and mystery because they do not fit in with our beliefs, and our beliefs are, in part, the product of our culture. People born into another culture may be more comfortable with mystery and find reliance on reason narrow and hard to accept.

Clearly there are differences among cultures, and it may be that people reared in one culture sometimes do not understand another culture or are prejudiced against it only because it is "different." However, it does not follow that our preference for reason over emotion, feeling, and mystery is a merely prejudice and without justification. It may be that our partiality toward rational judgment is a cultural bias, but this bias is warranted by the fact that rational inquiry **works for us**. Reason, not mystery, is much better at helping us fulfill **our** purposes and achieve our goals. One must remember that rational dialogue means keeping the dialogue **open**. That includes keeping the dialogue open to other cultures, open to other ideas, and even open to mysteries. It does not mean imposing one culture's values on another. There is room for reason *and* mystery in the world. But keeping the dialogue open does not mean that we must convert to or accept the offerings of every cultural alternative. And, indeed, when that alternative dismisses open dialogue, we must resist. The problem with a cultural view that puts a high value on mystery is that often it itself is not sufficiently open to difference and consequently to rationality. Simply to accept something as a mystery is not to know what will happen in the future or why. One cannot know what to expect. We are then at the mercy of whatever happens. We cannot avoid events we would prefer to avoid nor bring about events that make us happy or satisfied.

The openness of the dialogue is the critical factor here. Because the dialogue is continuous and never closed, it is always open to revision. If we do not get the results we anticipate, then we revise our reasoning or our expectations. We continue our dialogue with each other and with the world until our results match up with our expectations and we are able to fulfill our purposes. As human beings we are continuously revising our expectations on the basis of the evidence we gather. The believer in mystery is generally not open to revising her beliefs. Since the result is a product of mystery, there are no guidelines for revision. In the "mystery" view, when one's beliefs fail to work or they lead to inaccurate predictions, one can only say that the times were not right or that the gods were unwilling. And one can only hope to get the desired result the next time, since it is entirely a mystery as to what will happen. This view clearly, then, makes us powerless with regard to the future.

Obviously we are not going to be able to anticipate everything that is going to happen. Sometimes, in fact, we would rather not know. Life would be deadly dull if we knew exactly what was about to happen to us. We like the idea of some mystery in the world. On the other hand, we like to avoid pain and suffering when we can. Some people have the attitude that reason can resolve every problem. This is not the case. Sometimes there is no right answer, and we must make a forced choice between unattractive alternatives. Examples like this are common, for instance, in the practice of medicine. But the mode of rational inquiry and of open dialogue has a very good track record in helping humans fulfill their plans and goals.

The following two stories present the contrast between reason and mystery. The first is a short story written by the famous Yiddish storyteller Isaac Bashevis Singer. As you read it, notice how Singer captures this complex issue about reason and mystery in a very simple autobiographical tale about a boy, his parents, and some shrieking geese. The boy is obviously in awe of the apparent mystery advocated by his father, but at the same time he finds comfort in his mother's reasonable reassurance that "Dead geese don't shriek." The second story is about a naturalist, Mr. Ruschi, and the efforts of two Brazilian shamans to save his life. Mr. Ruschi's purpose is to live, and modern medicine does not seem able to help him. He may fulfill his purpose by taking the shamans' cure even though he does not understand it. It is a mystery both to him and to modern science.

WHY THE GEESE SHRIEKED

Isaac Bashevis Singer

In our home there was always talk about spirits of the dead that possess the bodies of the living, souls reincarnated as animals, houses inhabited by hobgoblins, cellars haunted by demons. My father spoke of these things, first of all because he was interested in them, and second because in a big city children so easily go astray. They go everywhere, see everything, read nonreligious books. It is necessary to remind them from time to time that there are still mysterious forces at work in the world.

One day, when I was about eight, he told us a story found in one of the holy books. If I am not mistaken, the author of that book is Rabbi Eliyahu Graidiker, or one of the other Graidiker sages. The story was about a girl possessed by four demons. It was said that they could actually be seen crawling around in her intestines, blowing up her belly, wandering from one part of her body to another, slithering into her legs. The Rabbi of Graidik had exorcised the evil spirits with the blowing of the ram's horn, with incantations, and the incense of magic herbs.

When my brother Joshua questioned these things, my father became very excited. He argued: "Was then the great Rabbi of Graidik, God forbid, a liar? Are all the rabbis, saints, and sages deceivers, while only atheists speak the truth? Woe is us! How can one be so blind?"

Suddenly the door opened, and a woman entered. She was carrying a basket with two geese in it. The woman looked frightened. Her matron's wig was tilted to one side. She smiled nervously.

Father never looked at strange women, because it is forbidden by Jewish law, but Mother and we children saw immediately that something had greatly upset our unexpected visitor.

"What is it?" Father asked, at the same time turning his back so as not to look upon her.

"Rabbi, I have a very unusual problem."

"What is it?"

"It's about these geese."

"What's the matter with them?"

"Dear Rabbi, the geese were slaughtered properly. Then I cut off their heads. I took out the intestines, the livers, all the other organs, but the geese keep shrieking in such a sorrowful voice. . ."

Upon hearing these words, my father turned pale. A dreadful fear befell me, too. But my mother came from a family of rationalists and was by nature a skeptic.

"Slaughtered geese don't shriek," she said.

"You will hear for yourself," replied the woman.

She took one of the geese and placed it on the table. Then she took out the second goose. The geese were headless, disemboweled—in short, ordinary dead geese.

A smile appeared on my mother's lips. "And *these* geese shriek?"

"You will soon hear."

The woman took one goose and hurled it against the other. At once a shriek was heard. It is not easy to describe that sound. It was like the cackling of a goose, but in such a high, eerie pitch, with such groaning and quaking, that my limbs grew cold. I could actually feel the hairs of my earlocks pricking me. I wanted to run from the room. But where would I run? My throat constricted with fear. Then I, too, shrieked and clung to my mother's skirt, like a child of three.

Father forgot that one must avert one's eyes from a woman. He ran to the table. He was no less frightened than I was. His red beard trembled. In his blue eyes could be seen a mixture of fear and vindication. For my father this was a sign that not only to the Rabbi of Graidik, but to him too, omens were sent from heaven. But perhaps this was a sign from the Evil One, from Satan himself?

"What do you say now?" asked the woman.

My mother was no longer smiling. In her eyes there was something like sadness, and also anger.

"I cannot understand what is going on here," she said, with a certain resentment.

"Do you want to hear it again?"

Again the woman threw one goose against the other. And again the dead geese gave forth an uncanny shriek—the shriek of dumb creatures slain by the slaughterer's knife who yet retain a living force; who still have a reckoning to make with the living, an injustice to avenge. A chill crept over me. I felt as though someone had struck me with all his might.

My father's voice became hoarse. It was broken as though by sobs. "Well, can anyone still doubt that there *is* a Creator?" he asked.

"Rabbi, what shall I do and where shall I go?" The woman began to croon in a mournful singsong. "What has befallen me? Woe is me! What shall I do with them? Perhaps I should run to one of the Wonder Rabbis? Perhaps they were not slaughtered properly? I am afraid to take them home. I wanted to prepare them for the Sabbath meal, and now, such a calamity! Holy Rabbi, what shall I do? Must I throw them out? Someone said they must be wrapped in shrouds and buried in a grave. I am a poor woman. Two geese! They cost me a fortune!"

Father did not know what to answer. He glanced at his bookcase. If there was an answer anywhere, it must be there.

Suddenly he looked angrily at my mother. "And what do you say now, eh?"

Mother's face was growing sullen, smaller, sharper. In her eyes could be seen indignation and also something like shame.

"I want to hear it again." Her words were half pleading, half commanding.

The woman hurled the geese against each other for the third time, and for the third time the shrieks were heard. It occurred to me that such must have been the voice of the sacrificial heifer.

"Woe, woe, and still they blaspheme. . . . It is written that the wicked do not repent even at the very gates of hell." Father had again begun to speak. "They behold the truth with their own eyes, and they continue to deny their Maker. They are dragged into the bottomless pit and they maintain that all is nature, or accident . . ."

He looked at Mother as if to say: You take after *them*.

For a long time there was silence. Then the woman asked, "Well, did I just imagine it?"

Suddenly my mother laughed. There was something in her laughter that made us all tremble. I knew, by some sixth sense, that Mother was preparing to end the mighty drama being enacted before our eyes.

"Did you remove the windpipes?" my mother asked.

"The windpipes? No . . ."

"Take them out," said my mother, "and the geese will stop shrieking."

My father became angry. "What are you babbling? What has this got to do with windpipes?"

Mother took hold of one of the geese, pushed her slender finger inside the body, and with all her might pulled out the thin tube that led from the neck to the lungs. Then she took the other goose and removed its windpipe also. I stood trembling, aghast at my mother's courage. Her hands had become bloodied. On her face could be seen the wrath of the rationalist whom someone has tried to frighten in broad daylight.

Father's face turned white, calm, a little disappointed. He knew what had happened here: logic, cold logic, was again tearing down faith, mocking it, holding it up to ridicule and scorn.

"Now, if you please, take one goose and hurl it against the other!" commanded my mother.

Everything hung in the balance. If the geese shrieked, Mother would have lost all: her rationalist's daring, her skepticism, which she had inherited from her intellectual father. And I? Although I was afraid, I prayed inwardly that the geese *would* shriek, shriek so loud that people in the street would hear and come running.

But, alas, the geese were silent, silent as only two dead geese without windpipes can be.

"Bring me a towel!" Mother turned to me.

I ran to get the towel. There were tears in my eyes. Mother wiped her hands on the towel like a surgeon after a difficult operation.

"That's all it was!" she announced victoriously.

"Rabbi, what do you say?" asked the woman.

Father began to cough, to mumble. He fanned himself with his skullcap.

"I have never before heard of such a thing," he said at last.

"Nor have I," echoed the woman.

"Nor have I," said my mother. "But there is always an explanation. Dead geese don't shriek."

"Can I go home now and cook them?" asked the woman.

"Go home and cook them for the Sabbath." Mother pronounced the decision. "Don't be afraid. They won't make a sound in your pot."

"What do you say, Rabbi?"

"Hmm . . . they are kosher," murmured Father. "They can be eaten." He was not really convinced, but now he could not pronounce the geese unclean.

Mother went back to the kitchen. I remained with my father. Suddenly he began to speak to me as though I were an adult. "Your mother takes after your grandfather, the Rabbi of Bilgoray. He is a great scholar, but a cold-blooded rationalist. People warned me before our betrothal. . ."

And then Father threw up his hands, as if to say: It is too late now to call off the wedding.

THE SHAMAN AND THE DYING SCIENTIST

A BRAZILIAN TALE

Alan Riding

The story began with a front-page report Jan. 12 in the Rio de Janeiro daily *Jornal do Brasil* that carried the headline, "Nature condemns a man who protected her." It recounted how Mr. Ruschi was dying as a result of having touched poisonous Dendrobates toads while carrying out research in the Amapá region of the Amazon in 1975.

The Power of a Poet

Other papers immediately caught onto the story, but it was three days later that President José Sarney was reportedly moved by a newspaper column written by a prominent Brazilian poet, Alfonso Romano de Sant'Anna. The column took its title from a novel *Chronicle of a Death Foretold* by the Colombian Nobel laureate, Gabriel García Márquez.

In it, the poet appealed to the president to order a search for an antidote not only in the United States and the Soviet Union but also among the Indian tribes of the Xingu National Park. "Brazil cannot afford to lose a man of Ruschi's stature just because some shameless toads declared him to be their enemy," Mr. Sant'Anna wrote.

Mr. Sarney immediately told his Interior Minister, Ronaldo Costa Couto, to contact Raoni, the middle-aged cacique, or chief, of the 4,000-strong Txucarramae tribe, who is also recognized as a spokesman for Brazil's 180,000 surviving Indians. And a few days later, an unusual sight in his feathered headdress and with the huge protruding lower lip that members of his tribe develop through wearing a disk, Raoni was received by the President in his office in Brasilia.

Raoni told Mr. Sarney that he had dreamed of Mr. Ruschi struggling with toads and, after looking at photographs of the naturalist, he proclaimed: "He already has the face of a toad. He has become a toad. We have to take the toad from inside or he will soon die."

The Treatment Begins

A Brazilian Air Force plane flew to the Xingu, 500 miles northwest of Brasilia, to collect herbs as well as Sapaim, a shaman from the nearby Caimura tribe. And, in the middle of last week, in the presence of newspaper reporters and television crews, Raoni and Sapaim met Mr. Ruschi in Rio de Janeiro.

The naturalist recounted that for more than a year he had suffered intense pain, nausea, fevers and nose bleeding and could rarely sleep for more than two or three hours at a stretch. Further, reporters noted, he was barely able to climb a short stairway and his eyes and mouth looked swollen and red.

The treatment, which was witnessed by a reporter from Jornal do Brasil and by Mr. Ruschi's wife, Marilande, first involved Raoni and Sapaim smoking 10-inch hallucinogenic herbal "cigars" and exhaling over the patient while chanting.

Raoni then massaged Mr. Ruschi's body and appeared to extract a green strong-smelling pasty substance that he identified as the toad poison. While blowing smoke, the Indian chief rubbed it between his palms and it disappeared, the reporter said. Finally, the naturalist took a herbal bath.

He Is Pronounced Cured

For three days, with the entire nation's attention focused on the house where the treatment was taking place, the ritual was repeated, with Mr. Ruschi claiming that he was feeling steadily better. By last Saturday, Raoni said all the poison had been removed and Mr. Ruschi was pronounced cured.

Before completing the ritual, though, Raoni indicated that tradition required he be given a present by the person who had called on him—in this case, President Sarney. The present could be a clay pot or, he added more pointedly, land for the Indians. Raoni and Sapaim then went on a shopping spree in Rio de Janeiro and, with Interior Ministry officials paying the bills, acquired $800 worth of beads and trinkets.

The final act will take place in Brasilia when President Sarney presents his gift to Raoni in the presence of Mr. Ruschi, with all three expected to use the occasion to appeal for greater preservation of the natural and native patrimony of this vast land. Then only an epilogue will still have to be written, describing whether Mr. Ruschi was indeed permanently cured.

Not surprisingly, some skepticism has already been heard from physicians. Wallace Magalhães, who treated Mr. Ruschi last year, said his liver was poisoned from excessive self-medication taken to combat chronic malaria. Haity Moustatche, a scientist at the Fundação Oswaldo Cruz medical research center, said, "We have to determine whether, in all the ritual, there was also some treatment."

But, for the moment at least, with patient and shaman as well as public and press delighted with the present happy ending, Mr. Ruschi seemed to offer the best closing words for the fairy tale. He said that, when he died, he wished to be buried in the rain forest near his home. "And I have the hope," he added, "that the hummingbirds will lead me to the Kingdom of God."

STUDY QUESTIONS

1. Put yourself in the place of the child narrator of Singer's story. With which parent do you identify? Why?

2. What can we learn from the shamans? The article says that after treatment by the shamans Mr. Ruschi felt better. What are some possible reasons for why Mr. Ruschi was feeling better after the treatment?

3. How would you respond to someone who asked you, "Why be reasonable?"

THE LIMITS OF REASON

We have argued that using reason and the skills of critical thinking can make our lives more pleasant and happy. It helps us know what to expect and make plans and to have friends to share them with. But reason does have its limits. We can only reason *from* one thing *to* another. So our reasoning must begin by assuming something. This might be the axioms of mathematics, a set of scientific laws in physics or chemistry, or the Constitution in United States law. Usually we agree on some set of fundamental assumptions. That is what enables us to talk to each other and that is what enables mathematicians to talk to each other, or scientists, or Americans. Americans, for example, believe that "all . . . (people) are endowed by their Creator with certain inalienable rights, namely, life, liberty and the pursuit of happiness." This assumption then guides further agreements or disagreements they might have.

Sometimes, however, our disagreements are rooted in different ideas about where to start. Two scientists who agree on the "laws of nature" might disagree about the existence of God. While one may believe that the world would not exist at all if there was no God to create it, the other may think the assumption of God's existence unnecessary to explain anything in science. What they both, probably, will admit is that the principles of physics (which they both consider to be fundamental to good scientific reasoning) will not settle their disagreement.

The short story of the shrieking geese illustrates the power of reason to solve problems and make lives happier. The woman who owns the geese is very upset because her expectation is that properly slaughtered geese do not shriek and she wants to eat the geese. She is a poor woman and does not want to have to throw out the geese (or bury them in a grave). Since her expectations are reasonable based on previous experience, it is also reasonable to assume that there is an explanation for the fact that the geese are now shrieking. Taking the approach of reason advocated by the mother, and not the approach of awe at the apparent mystery taken by the father, enables her to confirm that her expectations were reasonable and to fulfill her intention to eat the geese.

The inability of medicine to cure Mr. Ruschi and Socrates' failure to convince Euthyphro to continue the dialogue about the nature of piety, on the other hand, indicate the limits of reason and of "thinking Socratically." The application of reason does not always solve our problems. Even when we make our best effort, the open dialogue, which is the hallmark of rationality, is not always successful. It does not always lead to agreement. Even friends may not agree, not even in the long run! They may begin from different assumptions or fail to have the same goals. The greater the difference in initial assumptions or in goals, the greater the difficulty of coming to agreement. Intercultural dialogues often display this difficulty.

Another limitation on the open dialogue is that we do not always have enough time to resolve differences and find agreement, or solve the puzzle or problem. Circumstances may be overwhelming, demanding immediate action. For instance, the immanence of death in Mr. Ruschi's case rules out waiting for medicine to discover a cure for his diseased body. Ruschi must act, not talk. There are certainly situations in life where we cannot delay and still achieve the goals we seek. We must act on the best information available and hope to continue the open dialogue at a later time.

Finally, the open rational dialogue is limited by the values we hold. While we believe that all human beings share the general goals of being able to anticipate and plan for the future and of having friends and pleasant experiences, they do not always place the same value on the same specific experiences as ways of meeting these general goals. Our values act as a constraint on our exercise of reason, directing it to the ends we set. Reason both helps us decide what ends we should value and achieve those we value while avoiding the ones we do not.

Our claim, then, in behalf of reason and open rational dialogue is warranted but limited. Reason cannot answer **all** our questions or fulfill **all** our purposes. Sometimes the answers defy human reason, and sometimes reason is not persuasive of others. Sometimes our purposes even lie outside the realm of reason as when we choose the sloppy sentimentality of a romantic movie or give ourselves goose bumps by reading a horror story. In general, however, rational thinking and rational behavior is what enables us to meet our goals and expectations. It helps us to have friends who share our outlook on the world. Trying to be rational and to make rational decisions helps us enjoy the pleasant and avoid the unpleasant.

Because the rational dialogue is open, it means that we can learn from our experience and from the experience of others. If we reason well, we get better at fulfilling our goals and purposes. In the following chapters, we will give you some concepts and skills that will improve your reasoning skills. But in a very important sense, we have already given you the most important tip we can give you, which is always to be **open** to further discussion and to make the **effort** that the open dialogue demands.

The problem with shamans, witch doctors, and others who work in mysterious ways is that the end of the explanation comes too soon. We are stopped by "mystery" from asking precisely the questions that might be helpful in the future. We are forced to discontinue the dialogue before we begin to understand how we might affect that future.

Despite the limitations of reason, we find the advantages of being reasonable persuasive. It is difficult to argue otherwise. Indeed, you might notice something rather peculiar going on here. It is hard to make a case for being nonrational without seeming to contradict yourself. Making a case for a position means giving arguments or reasons in support of it. The person arguing against the use of reason is placed in the awkward position of giving reasons for not giving reasons, or of making an argument for not making arguments. Although not contradictory, it is clearly self-defeating behavior. That is, the harder you try to convince someone with reasons that she should not pay attention to reasons, the more successful you are, the more you will fail. It's like a child's trying to convince her parent that she is sufficiently mature to stay up to watch a late night television show while crying like a baby because the parent is saying no. Usually when a person asks a question, she wants a reasonable answer, not a shower of tears or a punch on the jaw. Although we may be coerced by power, we prefer to be persuaded by argument and evidence. It seems a much better fit with our sense of what it means to be a person and a human being.

Summary

To begin our open rational dialogue, we must begin somewhere. The alternative would be to reason "backward" forever and never come to an end/beginning. We must choose between reasoning on and on, never coming to a conclusion or we must begin to reason from some claim for which we give no reasons. Neither alternative is very satisfactory. One is endless and the other is arbitrary. The "Big Bang" theory about the origins of the universe discussed by Lewis Thomas, which you will read about in Chapter 2, exemplifies this age-old problem. If you want to know what there was in the universe before the big bang, physicists cannot tell you. The laws of physics as we know them began with the big bang. One is left to wonder: If reason is so limited, then why try so hard to be rational?

This philosophical puzzle led the nineteenth-century Danish philosopher Kierkegaard to claim that all choices rest ultimately on "a leap of faith." What Kierkegaard meant by this is that if all reasoning begins from some initial claim, then it would seem that no choice is wholly rational for each choice rests on an initial assumption that is not itself justified. Each choice is, therefore, taken on "faith." Kierkegaard concluded from this that people should choose a life of faith, not reason. We disagree. While Kierkegaard's point about the limits of reason is well taken, it does not follow from these limitations that people should choose a life of faith and mystery, not reason. People are still usually better off trying to be reasonable. Open rational dialogue and critical thinking lead to more successful anticipation of future events and happier outcomes than does assuming that the world is a mystery and unknowable.

The rational open dialogue also has the advantage of being a good way of persuading others to join us in our plans. It is less likely to have the unpleasant consequences attendant on the use of force, or threats of force, which historically have often been used to persuade others to accept or believe mystery. These uses of force include excommunication from the "tribe," burning at the stake, threats of death by lightning, etc. and so on. The rational dialogue invites, but does not force, agreement. It relies solely on the power of evidence. It allows—and even encourages—the other party to think critically and to respond critically to that evidence.

To put the matter another way, the way Socrates would put it: **Rational dialogue is the essence of friendship**. The people we talk to and who talk with us are our friends. When we are friends, we are willing to listen; we are willing to change our minds when persuaded; we are willing to go an extra mile to find a common ground. Most people would agree that being a friend means sharing. And what could be more important to share than our thoughts and beliefs? To do this we must talk—together. There is more than irony in Socrates' words when he refers to Euthyphro as his friend each time Euthyphro wants to go away and end the dialogue.

Exercises

1–I

1. What is the hallmark of the rational person?
2. What are the five limitations of human reason?

3. Give three reasons why rational approaches generally work better than nonrational approaches.
4. How would your explanation differ if:
    a) you were explaining to your best friend why your computer was not performing as you expected?
    b) you were explaining to your best friend why you just bought a new Corvette?

1–II

1. Find an example in a recent newspaper of an event attributed to mystery, that is, something that *cannot* be known. Give an explanation of why it is considered a mystery.
2. Bring in two different accounts of the same event, which are told from very different cultural perspectives. You could use the Internet for this.
3. Why do you love your girlfriend/boyfriend? Is this an example of reasonable behavior or an affair of the heart? Explain.
4. Mr. Ruschi died soon after his session with the shamans. Does that information change your earlier interpretation of that event? If so, how?
5. Do you think there are events for which there are no rational explanations? Why or why not?

2

Language

THE PRIORITY OF LANGUAGE

We all know how to use language. Otherwise we couldn't have written this, and you couldn't be reading it. We simply *use* language without thinking about how important language is to us. It is important to recognize that critical thinking could not take place without language. When we reason, make decisions, offer an explanation, or describe our moods and feelings, we use language. It's our main mode of communication with others. It can be used to convey information, to express feelings, to give orders, to ask questions, or to entertain. It's also how we think and communicate with ourselves. Language has its limitations, as we will see, but it is our basic tool when it comes to critical thinking. So, our investigation of the skills and concepts of critical thinking must begin with a discussion of language.

We generally use language to accomplish some purpose. For example, we may use it to order a salad or discuss politics or sing a song. Our uses of language may be successful or not. Success is usually judged by how clearly we communicate our thoughts to someone else, or how much closer we have moved to our goals. With some oversimplification, the goals when we use language usually fall into one of the three following categories:

- to understand, predict, and control the world around us so that we can survive and prosper,
- to maintain and improve our relationships with those around us so that we have more friends and fewer enemies and can love and be loved,
- to have pleasant rather than unpleasant experiences and to enjoy as much of our lives as we possibly can.[1]

---

[1]These divisions of human concern have a long and honorable history from Plato to Freud.

Language which is successful at prediction and control is often considered the most powerful use of language and therefore taken as a model for other language uses. If we stop to think about it, however, it is much easier to predict and control the objects and other non-human aspects of our lives than it is to control our human relationships. Just consider how difficult it has proven to be to negotiate a peace treaty or to make a plan to control global warming or to convince a friend that the music you like is better than the music he likes. Clearly language which is successful in maintaining and improving our relationships with other people is more sophisticated and more complicated than the language of prediction and control of physical things. We will consider the uses of language with **all three** of these goals in mind; however, the language of human relationships is the most important understanding we could have for getting along in the world.

LANGUAGE AND THE WORLD

Do you ever think about how language relates to the world? To put the matter another way, why do you hold the beliefs about the world that you hold? For instance, why do you believe that Chicago is located in Illinois or that an electric current makes the lights work? Probably the most common answer to this question is "Because that's the way the world is," implying that it would be foolish to believe otherwise. Of course, we are not so sure of all our beliefs, and sometimes we choose other responses like "My mother told me that when I was ten" or "I just can't help being afraid of dogs; I was bitten by a dog when I was six" or "I've never liked the taste of lima beans." That is, we generally think that we have two kinds of beliefs: (1) beliefs which we hold because we think they are accurate pictures of the world and (2) beliefs which are particular to us as individuals, to our upbringing, and to our tastes and preferences. We often refer to the first kind of belief as objective and the second as subjective.

Consider the following two descriptions of the houses of nineteenth-century New York City:

> I was much pleased with New York. The new houses are palaces. They are very large and built in a rich . . . ornate style of architecture. The material is brown sandstone which has a fine effect.
>
> (Letter quoted by John Maass in
The Victorian Home in America)

> . . . the intolerable ugliness of New York ... the narrow houses so lacking in dignity. . . . This little low-studded. . . . New York, cursed with its universal chocolate-colored coating of the most hideous stone ever quarried. . . .
>
> (Edith Wharton, *A Backward Glance*)

How could they differ so much? After all, there could be only one "objective reality" which is New York. But, there are two different authors or subjects. Perhaps each author has created his or her own "subjective reality." So, just what is the connection between language and the world?

At this point we might take either of two tacks, and both philosophers and non-philosophers have a long history of having done this. We could say that one of the two descriptions is better than the other because it comes closer to describing the objective reality which is New York City. That is, the language of the better description "mirrors" or "corresponds" to the world in ways that the lesser one does not. We might even go so far as to call the better description "right" or "true" or "objective." Or rather than saying that one of the descriptions is better than the other, we could say that the two passages describe two different realities, realities which are created by the two different narrators. On this view, reality or the world is simply a product of our individual subjective experience. No wonder we disagree so often.

There is a third alternative that we—the authors—think is preferable to the objectivist or subjectivist accounts of the relationship between language and the world, and this is the "Socratic" account. There are many good reasons for adopting what we have called the Socratic point of view, but we will not review all of them here. What you should know is that this Socratic viewpoint enables us to clarify some cloudy issues and to avoid getting bogged down by unsolvable puzzles about the relationship between language and the world.

What is this Socratic account? According to the Socratic account, no belief about the world should be evaluated solely by itself. Rather beliefs should be evaluated as parts of larger sets or *systems of beliefs*. For example, the two descriptions of New York City are both part of larger systems of belief—beliefs about size and scale in architecture, about the attractiveness of brown sandstone exteriors, and so on. Some systems of beliefs work well; some don't work or work very poorly in terms of helping us reach the general goals of human beings mentioned above. To put it another way, some systems work up to our expectations for them, and others do not. When a set or system of beliefs fails to work up to expectation, we begin to replace it with a set that works better. For example, if you have always been afraid of dogs (having been bitten in the past), but recently you have become friends with the cutest little beagle, you will probably replace your original set of beliefs about all dogs being mean with one that includes cute friendly little beagles. Our systems of beliefs can be about anything in the world—the architecture of New York City, the parts of the atom, the nature of dogs, or the taste of lima beans.

Our sets of beliefs are evaluated by how well they work for us as individuals and by how well they work for us as members of the larger community. This means that our belief systems are continuously open because they are continuously being tested by our experience of the world and in our dialogues with our friends and others. For example, suppose you believe you see a spider on the wall. You get closer to the wall and find a smudge of dirt. Then you will revise your set of beliefs, throw out the spider, and put in dirt on the wall, or dirty wall. Or suppose you think you see a spider and all the rest of the people around you insist that it's a fly, not a spider. Your belief about a spider has not "worked very well," and since everyone else sees a fly, you are likely to change your set of beliefs. Sometimes, we have to discard whole sets of beliefs. For instance, when the Iron Curtain crumbled across Eastern Europe and the Cold War came to an end, the United States' beliefs about its role in the world had to change. Or in the sixteenth century when astronomers began to doubt that the earth was the center of the universe, they began to create new a completely new set of beliefs about a sun-centered universe.

One young man finds a need to revise his set of beliefs.

Used by permission of Atlantic Feature Syndicate.

Now, if you think you see a connection between this Socratic account of language and our earlier account (in Chapter 1) of critical thinking as open rational dialogue, you are correct. It is our belief that a good critical thinker or a rational person is someone who is open to this continuous "dialogue" between beliefs and the world, who understands why this openness is important, and who is continually testing his systems of beliefs against experience. As you seek to improve your reasoning skills, you need to keep in mind the two dialogues that shape our beliefs: the dialogue between ourselves and the world and the dialogue between ourselves and our friends.

To illustrate how our descriptions of the world are embedded in systems of belief about the world, we have provided two readings from two twentieth-century authors, both of whom are generally credited with being "Renaissance men," individuals who are proficient in a wide variety of areas. Both are open to dialogue—with others and with the world. The first piece is by Lewis Thomas. Thomas was a medical doctor, a biologist, a writer, and an administrator. For many years, he was the chief executive officer of the Memorial Sloan-Kettering Cancer Center, one of the best specialized hospitals in the United States. As you will see in this reading, he had the ability to use his detailed knowledge of science to muse about the human condition and our place in the cosmos. The second author is Stephen Jay Gould, who was a paleontologist,

Harvard professor, and prolific author. Gould was well known for his expertise on the fossils of snails. Here, he describes his experiences looking for the bones of prehistoric hominids.

Both readings also show something very important about experience, namely, that our experience is not neutral but rather is influenced by the systems of beliefs we hold. To a larger extent than we usually appreciate, what we perceive is dependent on what we are prepared to perceive or what we expect we are going to perceive. If we have been seeing spiders on the wall, then the next black spot that moves on the wall we are likely to take to be a spider. Whereas if there have been lots of flies buzzing about the room, then we are more likely to take the black spot on the wall to be a fly. We actually *see* spiders or we *see* flies. Our minds organize the experience according to a pattern, one that is familiar or one that we may be expecting. (This is why witnesses at the scene of a crime are not always accurate reporters of what happened.)

We have all had that happen to us. Perhaps you have been waiting on the street corner for a friend, when you suddenly see him coming around the corner. When the person you see gets closer, you realize it is not your friend but someone who looks like your friend—or maybe even someone who does not look like your friend at all. We tend to find what we are looking for! As a consequence, says Thomas in the piece below, we fail to recognize something very important, namely, that the most surprising thing about the universe is the earth. We are just so used to its being here and our being a part of it. And Gould is very frank about his inability to see the bones he is looking for but has not been trained to see. What he does see are snails because he has been trained to see snails! These are two very good examples of how *Our belief systems influence what we see and what we see influences our belief systems.*

Experience can even vary not just from person to person, but for the same person, from moment to moment. To see this, consider the following well-known example:

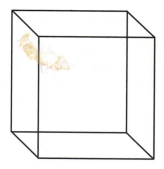

You probably see a cube protruding either down toward the right or up toward the left. Of course, the figure is not really a cube. It is just 12 lines on a flat surface. But you see it as a cube. Now look at it again. If you saw it as protruding down toward the right, look at how it now protrudes up toward the left. Or vice versa. The figure hasn't changed—but your perception has. Seeing, when we think about it, turns out to be a complex process, greatly influenced by our previous experience (e.g., Gould's training in snail fossils) and our systems of beliefs. Lewis Thomas urges us to get beyond the somewhat limiting effects of previous experience and look to the periphery of our sight—to see what we can see with "the corner of the eye."

THE CORNER OF THE EYE

Lewis Thomas

There are some things that human beings can see only out of the corner of the eye. The niftiest examples of this gift, familiar to all children, are small, faint stars. When you look straight at one such star, it vanishes; when you move your eyes to stare into the space nearby, it reappears. If you pick two faint stars, side by side, and focus on one of the pair, it disappears and now you can see the other in the corner of your eye, and you can move your eyes back and forth, turning off the star in the center of your retina and switching the other one on. There is a physiological explanation for the phenomenon: we have more rods, the cells we use for light perception, at the periphery of our retinas, more cones, for perceiving color, at the center.

Something like this happens in music. You cannot really hear certain sequences of notes in a Bach fugue unless at the same time there are other notes being sounded, dominating the field. The real meaning in music comes from tones only audible in the corner of the mind.

I used to worry that computers would become so powerful and sophisticated as to take the place of human minds. The notion of Artificial Intelligence used to scare me half to death. Already, a large enough machine can do all sorts of intelligent things beyond our capacities: calculate in a split second the answers to mathematical problems requiring years for a human brain, draw accurate pictures from memory, even manufacture successions of sounds with a disarming resemblance to real music. Computers can translate textbooks, write dissertations of their own for doctorates, even speak in machine-tooled, inhuman phonemes any words read off from a printed page. They can communicate with one another, holding consultations and committee meetings of their own in networks around the earth.

Computers can make errors, of course, and do so all the time in small, irritating ways, but the mistakes can be fixed and nearly always are. In this respect they are fundamentally inhuman, and here is the relaxing thought: computers will not take over the world, they cannot replace us, because they are not designed, as we are, for ambiguity.

Imagine the predicament faced by a computer programmed to make language, not the interesting communication in sounds made by vervets or in symbols by brilliant chimpanzee prodigies, but real human talk. The grammar would not be too difficult, and there would be no problem in constructing a vocabulary of etymons, the original, pure, unambiguous words used to name real things. The impossibility would come in making the necessary mistakes we humans make with words instinctively, intuitively, as we build our kinds of language, changing the meanings to imply quite different things, constructing and elaborating the varieties of ambiguity without which speech can never become human speech.

Look at the record of language if you want to glimpse the special qualities of the human mind that lie beyond the reach of any machine. Take, for example, the metaphors we use in everyday speech to tell ourselves who we are, where we live, and where we come from.

The earth is a good place to begin. The word "earth" is used to name the ground we walk on, the soil in which we grow plants or dig clams, and the planet itself; we also use it to describe all of humanity ("the whole earth responds to the beauty of a child," we say to each other).

The earliest word for earth in our language was the Indo-European root *dhghem*, and look what we did with it. We turned it, by adding suffixes, into *humus* in Latin; today we call the complex polymers that hold fertile soil together "humic" acids, and somehow or other the same root became "humility." With another suffix the word became "human." Did the earth become human, or did the human emerge from the earth? One answer may lie in that nice cognate word "humble." "Humane" was built on, extending the meaning of both the earth and ourselves. In ancient Hebrew, *adamha* was the word for earth, *adam* for man. What computer could run itself through such manipulations as those?

We came at the same system of defining ourselves from the other direction. The word *wiros* was the first root for man; it took us in our vanity on to "virile" and "virtue," but also turned itself into the Germanic word *weraldh*, meaning the life of man, and thence in English to our word "world."

There is a deep hunch in this kind of etymology. The world of man derives from this planet, shares origin with the life of the soil, lives in humility with all the rest of life. I cannot imagine programming a computer to think up an idea like that, not a twentieth-century computer, anyway.

The world began with what it is now the fashion to call the "Big Bang." Characteristically, we have assigned the wrong words for the very beginning of the earth and ourselves, in order to evade another term that would cause this century embarrassment. It could not, of course, have been a bang of any sort, with no atmosphere to conduct the waves of sound, and no ears. It was something else, occurring in the most absolute silence we can imagine. It was the Great Light.

We say it had been chaos before, but it was not the kind of place we use the word "chaos" for today, things tumbling over each other and bumping around. Chaos did not have that meaning in Greek; it simply meant empty.

We took it, in our words, from chaos to cosmos, a word that simply meant order, cosmetic. We perceived the order in surprise, and our cosmologists and physicists continue to find new and astonishing aspects of the order. We made up the word "universe" from the whole affair, meaning literally turning everything into one thing. We used to say it was a miracle, and we still permit ourselves to refer to the whole universe as a marvel, holding in our unconscious minds the original root meaning of these two words, miracle and marvel—from the ancient root word *smei*, signifying a smile. It immensely pleases a human being to see something never seen before, even more to learn something never known before, most of all to think something never thought before. The rings of Saturn are the latest surprise. All my physicist friends are enchanted by this phenomenon, marveling at the small violations of the laws of planetary mechanics, shocked by the unaccountable braids and spokes stuck there among the rings like graffiti. It is nice for physicists to see something new and inexplicable; it means that the laws of nature are once again about to be amended by a new footnote.

The greatest surprise of all lies within our own local, suburban solar system. It is not Mars; Mars was surprising in its way but not flabbergasting; it was a disappointment not to find evidences of life, and there was some sadness in the pictures sent back to earth from the Mars Lander, that lonely long-legged apparatus poking about with its jointed arm, picking up sample after sample of the barren Mars soil, looking for any flicker of life and finding none; the only sign of life on Mars was the Lander itself, an extension of the human mind all the way from earth to Mars, totally alone.

Nor is Saturn the great surprise, nor Jupiter, nor Venus, nor Mercury, nor any of the glimpses of the others.

The overwhelming astonishment, the queerest structure we know about so far in the whole universe, the greatest of all cosmological scientific puzzles, confounding all our efforts to comprehend it, is the earth. We are only now beginning to appreciate how strange and splendid it is, how it catches the breath, the loveliest object afloat around the sun, enclosed in its own blue bubble of atmosphere, manufacturing and breathing its own oxygen, fixing its own nitrogen from the air into its own soil, generating its own weather at the surface of its rain forests, constructing its own carapace from living parts: chalk cliffs, coral reefs, old fossils from earlier forms of life now covered by layers of new life meshed together around the globe, Troy upon Troy.

Seen from the right distance, from the corner of the eye of an extraterrestrial visitor, it must surely seem a single creature, clinging to the round warm stone, turning in the sun.

EIGHT LITTLE PIGGIES

Stephen Jay Gould

There are no great secrets to success, no unusual basis for "Leakey's luck," beyond hard work and experience. . . .

Leakey [a famous paleontologist well-known for his discoveries of very important early-human fossils] maintains a staff of trained Kenyan observers. He provides a long course in practical mammalian osteology (study of bones)—until they can distinguish the major groups of mammals from small scraps. The main ingredient of Leakey's luck is unleashing these people in the right place.

Kamoya Kimeu supervises this exploration. He has found more important fossils than anyone else now alive. One night in camp, he told me his story. As a boy, he tended goats, sheep, and cattle for his father. He attended school for six years and then went to work for a farmer. His employer urged him to return to school and study to become a veterinary paramedic. Kamoya then walked for several days back to Nairobi, where his uncle told him that Louis Leakey, Richard's father, was recruiting people to "dig bones." His mother gave him only cautious approval, telling him to quit and come home if the task involved (as he then suspected) digging up human graves. But when he saw so many bones from so many kinds of creatures, he knew that nature had strewn these burial grounds. The sediments of West Turkana are, if anything, even more profuse.

When I arrived on January 16, Kamoya's team had just found a new and remarkably well-preserved ape skull (in a profession that usually works with fragments, mostly teeth, a skull more than half complete, and with a fully preserved dentition, is cause for rejoicing). The next day, we studied and mapped the geological context and then brought the specimen back to camp. I wrote in my field book: "Everyone is very excited because they have just found the finest Miocene ape skull known from Africa. It is quite new—with a long face, inflated nasal region, incisors worn flat with a diastema [gap] a finger wide to the massive canine—almost like a beaver among apes."

Research is a collectivity, and we all have our special skills. Kamoya's workers are the world's greatest spotters; Richard also has a hawk's eye, the intuition of a geologist who has lived with his land, and the organizational skills of a Washington kingpin; his wife, Meave, has an uncanny spatial sense and can beat any jigsaw champ in putting fossil fragments together; yours truly, I fear, is good for one thing only— seeing snails.

All field naturalists know and respect the phenomenon of "search image"—the best proof that observation is an interaction of mind and nature, not a fully objective and reproducible mapping of outside upon inside, done in the same way by all careful and competent people. In short, you see what you are trained to view—and observation of different sorts of objects often requires a conscious shift of focus, not a total and indiscriminate expansion in the hopes of seeing everything. The world is too crowded with wonders for simultaneous perception of all; we learn our fruitful selectivities.

I couldn't see bone fragments worth a damn—and Richard had to direct my gaze before I could even distinguish the skull from surrounding lumps of sediment. But could I ever see snails, the subject of my own field research—and no one else had ever found a single snail at that site. So I rest content with my minuscule contribution, made in character, to the collective effort. At the top right of page 143 in the November 13, 1986, issue of *Nature*—the article that describes the new skull— a few snails are included in the faunal list of the site, some added by my search image. (I also found, I believe, the first snails at the important South African hominid site of Makapansgat in 1984—where I also couldn't see a bone. I think I am destined to be known in the circle of hominid exploration as "he who only sees the twisted one.")

STUDY QUESTIONS

1. "I may call a chair 'a chair' and someone else may call it 'a bed.' Who can say who is right? We're both right."
   What's wrong with this claim?
   What's right about this claim?
2. In what way does Lewis Thomas share a point of view about words with Plato?
3. Why must we look at the world "from the corner of the eye"?
4. What does Gould mean by the phenomenon of search image? Describe a time when *you* experienced search image, successfully or unsuccessfully.

WORDS, STATEMENTS, AND BELIEFS

Words are the smallest pieces of language. We seldom use them one at a time, although we sometimes do. "Sit," we say sternly to the disobedient dog. "July," we say in response to the question "What month were you born in?" But most of the time, our words are strung together into larger multiword pieces of language like statements, questions, orders, and exclamations.

If we do not know what a particular word means, there are ways of finding out. To consider an extreme case, imagine that we're the sole survivors of a shipwreck, washed onto an island where the natives speak a language unknown to us. We notice that the word *gavagai* is frequently uttered. In this case (an example made famous by the philosopher W.V. Quine), we would likely try to determine whether the utterance of the word *gavagai* coincided in any regular way with some obvious feature of the world. Suppose the natives uttered *gavagai* when two or more white rabbits were playing in the morning sunshine. We might then reasonably believe that *gavagai* was the plural form of our word *rabbit* (or perhaps means white rabbits or even *white rabbits playing in the sunshine before noon*). Although few of us will ever be marooned on a strange island where we need to build a language from scratch, we all behave somewhat like castaways when we hear or read an unfamiliar word in our own language. In this case, however, we are familiar with most of what was said before or after the unfamiliar word. We have a context to help us define the word. If that does not do the trick, we may fall back on the castaway technique and see if the use of the word coincides with some feature of the world around us.

The process of assigning meanings to words is, of course, called **defining**, and there are at least three ways of defining words. In the first and simplest, we define a word by pointing at some part of the world (or at some part of the world in a picture or other representation). This is called an **ostensive definition** from the Latin word meaning "to point." We have already glimpsed ostensive definition in the example of the castaways. As castaways, we hope that the natives' use of *gavagai* will point out some feature of the world for us and thus define *gavagai*.

Another way of defining a word is to survey contemporary users of the word (often a panel of expert users) and ask them what the word means. These **lexical definitions** are then collected into the dictionaries we use to look up unfamiliar words. The notion of lexical definition allows for and assumes change. So, what *horse* meant to our ancestors (say, *the predominant means of transportation, fueled by hay and oats*) it may not mean to us.

Finally a third sort of definition, the **stipulative definition**, attempts to isolate a fixed meaning of a word for particular purposes. For instance, a rocket scientist might define *force* as the product of the mass of a body multiplied by its acceleration whereas the non-scientist might use *force* as a synonym for *power*. Often stipulative definitions catch on and become part of our general usage and then show up later in the dictionary as lexical definitions.

A statement is a group of words which is used to assert something. Usually we assert something we believe. For example, the statement "This is my book" asserts that this is my book. It would be unusual to assert "This is my book" unless I believe that this is my book. A statement is not the same thing as a sentence which may contain one statement ("This is my book"), more than one statement ("This is my book and it has a blue cover"), or no statements at all ("Is this my book?"). Except for so-called rhetorical questions, questions do not assert anything at all.

"When you're on their flowers, you're a snail. When they want to eat you, suddenly you're an escargot."

Words even influence taste!

When we think about things, we generally make statements about them to ourselves. If you think the kitten is cute, you probably say to yourself (or whoever will listen), "That little kitten is cute." Or maybe you just say some sort of shorthand, "Cute little kitten." As we said above, thinking is like talking to yourself. When you are thinking, you make statements to yourself, some short, some perhaps very complex or some even running together with other statements. These statements are expressions of your beliefs. **A belief is an opinion, a claim, or a thought that you have.** Beliefs are not generally held individually. They are part of systems, some of which may be very large. For instance, you probably have a large system of beliefs about kittens, from what it is for something to be a kitten, to how you enjoy being around kittens, or to how they bother your allergies. This large system of beliefs about kittens is connected to other systems of beliefs, maybe about cats, or large cats like tigers, and so on. Your belief about this particular kitten is also connected to your beliefs about what makes things little and cute.

We express our beliefs when we talk. As noted above, it sounds rather foolish for someone to say, "This little kitten is cute, but I don't believe it." Of course, people do lie about what they believe, but then we have a name for those kinds of statements. We call them lies! We also express our beliefs sometimes by saying, "I believe that the little kitten is cute." When a belief is expressed this way, it is called a **belief statement**. So beliefs can be expressed either as statements or as belief statements. When we are thinking, we are more likely to use simple statements; but when we talk to others, we might use belief statements. A belief statement, our stated belief that something is the case, should not be confused with statements about faith or trust. This latter kind of belief is best thought of as a *belief in something*, as in the claim, "I believe in you" or "I believe in the United States of America" or "I believe in the tooth fairy." While statements of faith are important, they are not major components of critical thinking and reasoning.

WARRANTED STATEMENTS

Critical thinking is thinking about our belief statements. In particular it is about supporting or *warranting* our belief statements and separating the warranted belief statements from those that are not warranted or that might not be warrantable. To warrant a statement is to make other statements in support of it—as in an open rational dialogue. No statement is self-warranting; that is, no statement offers more than trivial support for itself. We are unconvinced by someone who argues "I'm right because I'm right" or "The sky is blue; therefore, the sky is blue." Since no statement is self-warranting, the process of warranting our statements could be endless. Clearly there must be practical limits. We usually try to warrant our statements using other statements which, though not self-warranting, are not likely to raise demands for further warranting.

Warranting Statements

How would someone try to make an assertion self-warranting? Consider the following possible dialogue between an interviewer and an ice skating judge:

INTERVIEWER:	The second skater didn't get as good a score as the first.
JUDGE:	No, she didn't skate as well.
INTERVIEWER:	Why do you say she didn't skate as well?
JUDGE:	Well, clearly, because she didn't get as good a score as the first skater.
INTERVIEWER:	Then she made some mistakes?
JUDGE:	Yes, she must have made some mistakes. You can see that from her scores. If she hadn't made mistakes, she would have gotten a higher score.

Efforts to make statements self-warranting are very unsatisfying, either repetitious or viciously circular!

For example, consider what it would take to warrant the statement "That is my book." Suppose, for instance, you notice that the woman with the red hat who has been sitting next to you on the bus picks up your copy of *Thinking Socratically,* puts it in her handbag, and begins to stand up as the bus slows to stop. Your immediate goal is the recovery of your book and to move toward that end you say, "Excuse me but that is my book." If the lady then hands you the book saying, "I'm so sorry; I mistook it for a similar looking one I've been reading," your statement "That is my book" would not need warranting.

If, however, the red-hatted lady clutched the book to her side and said, "I'm sorry but you must be mistaken—this is *my* copy of *Thinking Socratically* and I have my receipt from the bookstore to prove it," then your statement would need warranting, since it did not accomplish its goal. It did not get your book back.

If you were still convinced that the book was yours, not hers, you might reply by using the following warranting statements: "But I'm sure that it is *my* book. I always write my name on the first page of all my books. Let's look at the first page to settle it." The lady agrees and opens the book to the first page where to your great surprise is, written in unfamiliar script, a stranger's name! Now your attempt to warrant seems to need warranting itself and your initial statement "That is my book" seems less warranted than ever. Of course, things might have happened differently. The flyleaf might have revealed your name, enabling you to say "My name is on the flyleaf," thus warranting your set of warranting statements and, retroactively, your first statement— "That is my book."

You may be thinking here that calling a statement "warranted" is an awful lot like calling a statement "true." The ordinary notion of truth, however, tends to carry the implication that the individual statements we make can somehow be compared to the real world and then dubbed true if they match it or false if they don't. For example, if one utters the statement "The sky is blue," he then verifies or confirms that statement by comparing it to reality; that is, he looks out the window and sees that the sky is blue. But what we actually do is more like this: We look out the window, see a blue sky, and think or say "The sky is blue." Now, the only way we can check the truth of this second belief statement is to look again and see if we are prompted to think or say again "The sky is blue." What we are comparing are not a statement and a part of the world, but rather just our two statements—our two belief statements—one with the other. This is a subtle but an important point about warranting. We warrant one statement with another statement or one belief statement with another belief statement. "The world" is something we only know through perception. Our perceptions are expressed as belief statements which form parts of larger systems of beliefs. These systems influence how we experience the world, and our experience influences these belief systems.

For instance, think about the point Stephen Jay Gould made about his fossil search. He perceives snails. He perceives snails because he has a large belief system about snails and how they appear, which tells him that the fossil he has just found is a snail fossil. Similarly, we have a large system of beliefs about that thing we see when are outside and look up that we call "the sky" and which often has the same color as the things we call "blue." One does not *simply* see a blue sky any more than one *simply* sees hominid fossils or snail fossils. Seeing is a very complicated and com-

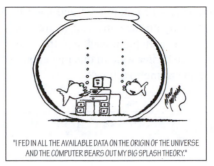

"I FED IN ALL THE AVAILABLE DATA ON THE ORIGIN OF THE UNIVERSE
AND THE COMPUTER BEARS OUT MY BIG SPLASH THEORY."

The corner of *whose* eye also makes a difference!

Copyright © Scott Arthur Masear 1993. Reprinted by permission Scott Arthur Masear.

plex process despite the fact that we do it so quickly and without awareness of this process. What we see is what we have been "trained" to see. Our beliefs or systems of beliefs influence our experience, and our experience helps to create our systems of beliefs!

Since this comparison between statements and the world cannot be carried out in the way usually intended by most users of the word *true*, we prefer to talk about statements as **warranted** or **unwarranted**; that is, we prefer to talk about statements that either are or are not supported by other statements. (If you prefer, you can substitute the words plausible and implausible for warranted and unwarranted.) We will continue to develop the distinction between warranted and unwarranted statements throughout this text.[2]

There are several ways that people try to warrant their statements by using other statements. Some of these ways are better than others. We have just discussed one of these: using perception and the other belief statements it generates to warrant our beliefs. Open rational dialogue using the skills of critical thinking is another. In the next reading, the narrator tries to warrant her statements by repeating them, over and over with slight variation. Many of us do this. If you listen to the conversations going on around you, you will hear people repeating themselves, trying to make sure that their listener accepts their belief as warranted. It will be obvious to you that warranting statements demands more than mere repetition. The author of the piece, Gertrude Stein, has a very good ear for the way we often do talk. Sometimes we even read this way, going over and over the material. After reading this piece, you will want to learn better ways of warranting statements! Perhaps you have heard of Stein. She is famous for having said, "Rose is a rose, is a rose." Stein was an American expatriate living in France in the first half of the twentieth century. Her house was a salon where artists and writers such as Picasso, Matisse, Hemingway, and Fitzgerald gathered. She

---

[2]Sometimes we say, "It's true that . . ." or "I'm telling the truth when I say that . . ." What we generally mean when we use these expressions is that we believe what we are saying. We are not lying or trying to deceive. Sometimes we might mean that we are very committed to the belief we have just uttered or are about to utter. These uses of "true" and "truth" are useful and not confusing, What we want to avoid is the idea that we can somehow compare our linguistic utterances with some nonlinguistic entity like "the world" or "a fact."

was one of the earliest collectors of modern art and tried to do with language what modern visual artists were doing on the canvas. Just like Picasso, she took apart her subject matter, scrambled it, and then put it back together—her own way. You may be rather puzzled or even annoyed by her style in this piece, but ask yourself **why** she has adopted this style. What is she trying to tell us?

Making of Americans

Gertrude Stein

Sometimes in listening to a conversation which is very important to two men, to two women, to two men and women, sometimes then it is a wonderful thing to see how each one always is repeating everything they are saying and each time in repeating, what each one is saying has more meaning to each one of them and so they go on and on and on and on and on repeating and always to some one listening, repeating is a very wonderful thing. There are many of them who do not live in each repeating coming out of them but always repeating is interesting. Repeating is what I am loving. Sometimes there is in me a sad feeling for all the repeating no one loving repeating is hearing, it is like any beauty that no one is seeing, it is a lovely thing, always some one should be knowing the meaning in the repeating always coming out of women and of men, the repeating of the being in them. So then.

Every one is a brute in her way or his way to some one, every one has some kind of sensitiveness in them.

. . .

I am thinking very much of feeling things in men and women. As I was saying every one is a brute in her way or his way to some one, every one has some kind of sensitiveness in them. Mostly every one has some inner way of feeling in them, almost every one has some way of reacting to stimulus in them. This is not always the same thing. These things have many complications in them.

I am beginning now a little a description of three women, Miss Dounor, Miss Charles and Mrs. Redfern. I am beginning now a little a realisation of the way each one of them is in her way a brute to some one, each one has in her way a kind of sensitiveness in being. This is now some description of each one of the three of them Miss Dounor, Miss Charles and Mrs. Redfern.

In listening to a conversation, as I was saying, repeating of each one and the gradual rising and falling and rising again of realisation is very interesting. This is now some description of the three women and as I was saying of the sensitiveness in each one of them to some things and the insensitiveness to other things and the bottom nature in them and the kinds of repeating in them and the bottom nature and the other natures mixed with the bottom nature in each one of them.

Sensitiveness to something, understanding anything, feeling anything, that is very interesting to understand in each one. How much, when and where and how and when not and where not and how not they are feeling, thinking, understanding. To begin again then with feeling anything.

Mostly every one is a brute in her way or his way to some one, mostly every one has some kind of sensitiveness in them.

Mostly every one can have some kind of feeling in them, very many men and very many women can have some understanding in them of some kind of thing by the kind of being sensitive to some kind of impression that they have in them.

. . .

As I was saying some men and some women have very much of sensitive being in them for something that can give to them real feeling. They can then, some of these of them, when they are filled full then of such feeling, they can then be completely loving, completely believing, they can then have a trembling awed being in them, they can have then abundant trembly feeling in them, they can then be so full up then with the feeling in them that they are a full thing and action has no place then in them, they are completely then a feeling, there are then men and women, there are then women and men who have then this finely sensitive completed feeling that is sometime all them and perhaps Cora Dounor was one of such of them. Perhaps she was one of them and was such a one in loving Phillip Redfern. Perhaps that was the whole being she had in her then.

Each one as I am saying has it in them to feel more or less, sometime, something, almost certainly each one sometime has some capacity for more or less feeling something. Some have in them always and very little feeling, some have some feeling and much nervous being always in them, some have as a bottom to them very much weakness and eagerness together then and they have then such of them some sensitiveness in them to things coming to them but often after they are then full up with nervous vibrations and then nothing can really touch them and then they can have in them nervous vibratory movement in them, anxious feeling in them and sometimes stubborn feeling then in them and then nothing can touch them and they are all this being then this nervous vibratory quivering and perhaps Mrs. Redfern was such a one Mrs. Redfern who had been Martha Hersland and was married now to Phillip Redfern and had come to Farnham and had there seen Phillip Redfern come to know Miss Dounor and had been then warned to take care of him by the dean of Farnham Miss Charles. She never knew then, Mrs. Redfern never knew then that she would not ever again have him, have Redfern again. This never could come to be real knowledge in her. She was always then and later always working at something to have him again and that was there always in her to the end of him and of her. There will be a little more description of her written in the history of the ending of the living in her father, in the history of the later living of her brother Alfred Hersland who now just when her trouble was commencing was just then marrying Julia Dehning, in the history of her brother David Hersland her younger brother. More description of her will be part of the history of the ending of the existing of the Hersland family. There will be very much history of this ending of all of them of the Hersland family written later. . . .

STUDY QUESTIONS

1. Why is this excerpt from Gertrude Stein included in this text?
2. What did you learn from this reading about how we form our impressions of other people? Why is it difficult to know who other people are?
3. In view of the Stein you just read, how is a typical show on television, such as a made-for-television movie or a soap opera, unrealistic?
4. Consider this quotation from an old stump speech by Hillary Rodham Clinton who has generally been noted for being an articulate public speaker: "I think it's appropriate to take a few minutes to reflect on some of the issues that people of faith have in common, and from my perspective, as I have travelled extensively now through New York and been in the company of so many different New Yorkers from so many different walks of life, I agree that the challenges before us, as individuals, as members and leaders of the community of faith, as those who already hold positions of public responsibility and those who seek them that we do all share and should be committed to an understanding of how we make progress, but we define that progress broadly, deeply, and profoundly." (Reported in *The New Yorker*.)
   Is Stein's portrayal really so bizarre?

FACTUAL STATEMENTS

Those statements which have been found to be the most warranted—those for which support is seldom asked—we call factual statements. These are the statements that we ourselves and the people who share our belief systems accept without further warranting. To put it another way, factual statements are those belief statements about which there is consensus among us that these belief statements are warranted or could be warranted if they were questioned.

Let us apply this account of factual statements, as those which have been found to be the most warranted, to the saga of the book on the bus: Suppose that even after examination of the flyleaf reveals a stranger's name, you still believe that the book is yours. In desperation you yell, "Driver, stop the bus! Call the police! This woman is trying to steal my book!" The driver stops the bus and calls the police to investigate. The lady—true to her word—pulls a receipt for a copy of *Thinking Socratically* from her handbag and shows the police her name written on the first page. What would be the point of your claiming that it is a **factual statement** that the book is yours if no statement you have made supports that claim? If the statement "That is my book" is ever to be accepted as factual, then it, or some other statement which supports it, must first be warranted.

To emphasize this point: Suppose that despite all your setbacks you persist, and finally one or more of your statements begin to offer support. For example, suppose that you say, "Microscopic analysis of the hair found between pages 100 and 101 will reveal a match with hair taken from my cat Fred, a member of a breed so rare that he is the sole North American example." And, further suppose that somewhat later a laboratory technician says, "The hair taken from Fred matches perfectly the hair found between pages 100 and 101 of the disputed copy of *Thinking Socratically*." At that moment, your initial statement "That is my book" becomes plausible because the statements about Fred's hair warranted it. That is, the statement "That is my book" can only be regarded as a factual statement if those statements that support it cease to be called into question (perhaps because the results of the microscopic analysis of Fred's hair have become widely known). **Factual statements, after all, are just those statements which for whatever reason are seldom called into question.**[3]

One final note about the warranting of statements. As the above example shows, statements are not warranted individually, but rather as members of a group or set of statements which "lean" on each other for support. Considered as isolated individual statements, none of the group is capable of standing on its own if called into question. The red-hatted lady, the bus driver, and the police can only come to accept your statement expressing your belief that the book is yours if it is part of a larger system or set of claims, some of which they accept as factual. Thus, the way to begin the process of warranting a statement is by making another statement. Statements—or beliefs—are accepted as members of groups of statements, and the relation of a statement to the other statements in the group is what makes it a factual statement.

WEB OF BELIEF

Just as statements are parts of larger systems of statements, our individual beliefs are part of larger systems of beliefs. These larger systems are often referred to as **webs of belief**. Each of us has a huge web of belief that has many hundreds of thousands of belief "threads" woven into it, making connections with each other along different pathways—just like a spider web does. When we acquire a new belief, we attach it to the web in the appropriate spot. Sometimes acquiring a new belief means we have to weed out some old belief(s). Sometimes a new idea will seem so new that there doesn't seem to be a place for it in our web. This is one reason why learning something that is totally new to you, like calculus for example, is hard. It has few connections to other beliefs in your web of belief. People often reject ideas or beliefs that don't "fit" into their webs.

At the center of our webs of belief are the beliefs that hold the web together or are fundamental to the other beliefs in the web. For many people, these beliefs are about their personal identity: who they are, who their parents were, where they live—the kinds of beliefs we don't even think about unless a story or a movie about someone suffering from amnesia causes us to reflect on what it would be like to lose all those beliefs! Some of our beliefs are on the periphery of our webs of belief. These are the beliefs that are easily given up if our experience should contradict them. For example, you might believe that Sammy's is the best deli in town. You've been there several times and every pastrami sandwich you ate was first rate. But then you have a bad experience at Sammy's or you have a superior pastrami sandwich across the street at Geno's. Your web of belief will change, accommodating this new experience.

---

[3]People often just use the word "facts" instead of "factual statements" when they intend to refer to those statements which are thought to be so well accepted as to be beyond doubt. Or they say, "It's a fact" to indicate that they find a statement so warranted that no one else should question it. We prefer the phrase **factual statements** to avoid suggesting that there are things in the world called facts. There is only the world of our experience—a world of sky and kittens and books, not of "facts."

Webs of belief are generally coherent. That is, the beliefs within them are consistent with one another. We tend to weed out contradictions. You cannot believe both that Sammy's is the best deli and that Geno's is the best deli, so you give up one belief and replace it with the one that fits better. We use these webs of belief to guide us in our daily lives and in our future lives. You can think of a web of belief as a "world view" which helps us create a coherent picture of the world around us. This world view is a huge collection of interconnected beliefs, some of which are central to our thinking and our ability to get along in the world and some of which are easily abandoned without much affect on the other beliefs in the web.

The following two readings illustrate how webs of belief and world views influence our day-to-day experience of events in the world. The first reading is about how some people in the Arab world understand the event known as 9/11. Their web of belief/world view suggests a completely different view of what occurred that day than does the world view shared by most Americans. It shows how much a person's web of belief shapes new beliefs as they are added to it. The second reading is on a much lighter note! Be sure to pay attention to how the narrator's new belief at the end of the story forces him to reconstruct his web and throw out several previous beliefs.

9/11 RUMORS THAT HARDEN INTO CONVENTIONAL WISDOM

Michael Slackman

CAIRO—Seven years later, it remains conventional wisdom here that Osama bin Laden and Al Qaeda could not have been solely responsible for the attacks of Sept. 11, 2001, and that the United States and Israel had to have been involved in their planning, if not their execution, too.

This is not the conclusion of a scientific survey, but it is what routinely comes up in conversations around the region—in a shopping mall in Dubai, in a park in Algiers, in a café in Riyadh and all over Cairo.

"Look, I don't believe what your governments and press say. It just can't be true," said Ahmed Issab, 26, a Syrian engineer who lives and works in the United Arab Emirates. "Why would they tell the truth? I think the U.S. organized this so that they had an excuse to invade Iraq for the oil."

It is easy for Americans to dismiss such thinking as bizarre. But that would miss a point that people in this part of the world think Western leaders, especially in Washington, need to understand: That such ideas persist represents the first failure in the fight against terrorism—the inability to convince people here that the United States is, indeed, waging a campaign against terrorism, not a crusade against Muslims.

"The United States should be concerned because in order to tell people that there is a real evil, they too have to believe it in order to help you," said Mushairy al-Thaidy, a columnist in the Saudi-owned regional newspaper Asharq al Awsat. "Otherwise, it will diminish your ability to fight terrorism. It is not the kind of battle you can fight on your own; it is a collective battle."

There were many reasons people here said they believed that the attacks of 9/11 were part of a conspiracy against Muslims. Some had nothing to do with Western actions, and some had everything to do with Western policies.

Again and again, people said they simply did not believe that a group of Arabs—like themselves—could possibly have waged such a successful operation against a superpower like the United States. But they also said that Washington's post-9/11 foreign policy proved that the United States and Israel were behind the attacks, especially with the invasion of Iraq.

"Maybe people who executed the operation were Arabs, but the brains? No way," said Mohammed Ibrahim, 36, a clothing-store owner in the Bulaq neighborhood of Cairo. "It was organized by other people, the United States or the Israelis."

The rumors that spread shortly after 9/11 have been passed on so often that people no longer know where or when they first heard them. At this point, they have heard them so often, even on television, that they think they must be true.

First among these is that Jews did not go to work at the World Trade Center on that day. Asked how Jews might have been notified to stay home, or how they kept it a secret from co-workers, people here wave off the questions because they clash with their bedrock conviction that Jews are behind many of their troubles and that Western Jews will go to any length to protect Israel.

"Why is it that on 9/11, the Jews didn't go to work in the building," said Ahmed Saied, 25, who works in Cairo as a driver for a lawyer. "Everybody knows this. I saw it on TV, and a lot of people talk about this."

Zein al-Abdin, 42, an electrician, who was drinking tea and chain-smoking cheap Cleopatra cigarettes in Al Shahat, a café in Bulaq, grew more and more animated as he laid out his thinking about what happened on Sept. 11.

"What matters is we think it was an attack against Arabs," he said of the passenger planes crashing into American targets. "Why is it that they never caught him, Mr. bin Laden? How can they not know where he is when they know everything? They don't catch him because he hasn't done it. What happened in Iraq confirms that it has nothing to do with bin Laden or Qaeda. They went against Arabs and against Islam to serve Israel, that's why."

There is a reason so many people here talk with casual certainty—and no embarrassment—about the United States attacking itself to have a reason to go after Arabs and help Israel. It is a reflection of how they view government leaders, not just in Washington, but here in Egypt and throughout the Middle East. They do not believe them. The state-owned media are also distrusted. Therefore, they think that if the government is insisting that bin Laden was behind it, he must not have been.

"Mubarak says whatever the Americans want him to say, and he's lying for them, of course," Ibrahim said of Hosni Mubarak, Egypt's president.

Americans might better understand the region, experts here said, if they simply listen to what people are saying—and try to understand why—rather than taking offense. The broad view here is that even before Sept. 11, the United States was not a fair broker in the Arab-Israeli conflict, and that it then capitalized on the attacks to buttress Israel and undermine the Muslim Arab world.

The single greatest proof, in most people's eyes, was the invasion of Iraq. Trying to convince people here that it was not a quest for oil or a war on Muslims is like convincing many Americans that it was, and that the 9/11 attacks were the first step.

"It is the result of widespread mistrust, and the belief among Arabs and Muslims that the United States has a prejudice against them," said Wahid Abdel Meguid, deputy director of the government-financed Al Ahram Center for Political and Strategic Studies, the nation's premier research center. "So they never think the United States is well intentioned, and they always feel that whatever it does has something behind it."

Hisham Abbas, 22, studies tourism at Cairo University and hopes one day to work with foreigners for a living. But he does not give it a second thought when asked about Sept. 11. He said it made no sense at all that bin Laden could have carried out such an attack from Afghanistan. And like everyone else interviewed, he saw the events of the last seven years as proof positive that it was all a United States plan to go after Muslims.

"There are Arabs who hate America, a lot of them, but this is too much," Abbas said as he fidgeted with his cellphone. "And look at what happened after this—the Americans invaded two Muslim countries. They used 9/11 as an excuse and went to Iraq. They killed Saddam, tortured people. How can you trust them?"

COOKIES

Douglas Adams

This actually did happen to a real person, and the real person is me. I had gone to catch a train. This was April 1976, in Cambridge, U.K. I was a bit early for the train. I'd gotten the time of the train wrong. I went to get myself a newspaper to do the crossword, and a cup of coffee and a packet of cookies. I went and sat at a table. I want you to picture the scene. It's very important that you get this very clear in your mind. Here's the table, newspaper, cup of coffee, packet of cookies. There's a guy sitting opposite me, perfectly ordinary-looking guy wearing a business suit, carrying a briefcase. It didn't look like he was going to do anything weird. What he did was this: he suddenly leaned across, picked up the packet of cookies, tore it open, took one out, and ate it. Now this, I have to say, is the sort of thing the British are very bad at dealing with. There's nothing in our background, upbringing, or education that teaches you how to deal with someone who in broad daylight has just stolen your cookies. You know what would happen if it had been South Central Los Angeles. There very quickly would have been gunfire, helicopters coming in, CNN, you know. . . . But in the end, I did what any red-blooded Englishman would do: I ignored it. And I stared at the newspaper, took a sip of my coffee, tried to do a clue in the newspaper, couldn't do anything and thought, What am I going to do?

In the end I thought, Nothing for it, I'll just have to go for it, and I tried very hard not to notice the fact that the packet was already mysteriously opened. I took out a cookie for myself. I thought, That settled him. But it hadn't because a moment or two later he did it again. He took another cookie. Having not mentioned it the first time, it was somehow even harder to raise the subject the second time around. "Excuse me, I couldn't help but notice . . ." I mean, it doesn't really work.

We went through the whole packet like this. When I say the whole packet, I mean there were only about eight cookies, but it felt like a lifetime. He took one, I took one, he took one, I took one. Finally, when we got to the end, he stood up and walked away. Well, we exchanged meaningful looks, then he walked away, and I breathed a sigh of relief and sat back.

A moment or two later the train was coming, so I tossed back the rest of my coffee, stood up, picked up the newspaper, and underneath the newspaper were my cookies. The thing I particularly like about this story is the sensation that somewhere in England there has been wandering around for the last quarter-century a perfectly ordinary guy who's had the same exact story, only he doesn't have the punch line.

STUDY QUESTIONS

1. What are some of the beliefs in parts of the Arab world that are central to the story that is being told there about what happened on 9/11?
2. How does the narrator's web of belief change when he discovers his cookies under his newspaper? Describe the web of belief of "the other guy" walking around England somewhere.
3. How much and in what ways do you think you could revise your web of belief before:
   your friends and/or your family noticed the change?
   you began to lose your friends?
   you become a different person?

Summary

Warranted statements are statements that have gone through the process of warranting: Other statements have been offered in support and at least some people have ceased questioning them. The people who have ceased questioning then regard these statements as "warranted." The support process is the open rational dialogue among friends described in Chapter 1. **Unwarranted statements** are those for which no support has been offered or the support offered has failed to convince the others in the dialogue. An unwarranted statement might be accepted by someone but its acceptance is hit or miss. When the support offered for a statement has been so successful that the statement becomes warranted for almost everyone, that statement is a **factual statement**, one that is so well accepted that it goes unquestioned. A factual statement today may not be a factual statement tomorrow. For example, if we were Europeans of the fourteenth century, we would probably believe that "The earth is flat" is a factual statement. This is why it is so important to keep the dialogue open. We warrant statements to ourselves and with our friends so that we can accomplish our general goals of anticipating the future, having friends, and enjoying pleasant experiences while avoiding the unpleasant.[4]

---

[4]This account of warranting has led some philosophers (Bertrand Russell and others) to claim that "truth" has been confused with what is useful or with what "works" in a particular context. Our point is that believing the world to be a certain way (e.g., that the sky is blue) makes sense just so long as it **does** work, that is, just so long as it is supported by descriptions of our experience and by others' experience—which they share with us in open rational dialogue. To add that the statements so warranted are also *true* is to say nothing more than " . . . and we believe them."

The selections you have read illustrate very clearly the way we use language as a tool to accomplish our goals. Language is best used in open rational dialogue where we try to warrant our claims with factual statements that demand no further warrant. Probably as you read the selection from Gertrude Stein, you were put off by the constant repetition of the description of the characters by the narrator who is not sure she has been successful in her communication. Like many of us at times, she is not sure her statements have **worked**. Although no statements are self-warranting, we sometimes try to make them self-warranting by repeating them until (we hope) they are no longer questioned. Listen to the people around you. Do you find them repeating themselves to make sure that their statements are accepted or at least understood?

Or consider the essay from Lewis Thomas. Thomas suggests that we may be on the verge of adopting both a new way of looking at the world and a new set of statements to describe and make meaningful what we see. Our planet earth, according to Thomas, is perhaps most plausibly viewed not "straight on," as a collection of separate interacting life-forms, but rather from "the corner of our eye," as one complex living organism "clinging to the warm stone, turning in the Sun." Such a revolutionary statement as this one, which asks us to rethink our place in the universe, would clearly require a great deal of warranting before it became accepted. Stephen Jay Gould, on the other hand, reminds us of the dialogue between ourselves and the world. The world, he points out, is not seen in the same way by all competent and careful people. We tend to see what we are trained to see. Therefore, it is very important that we keep our dialogue with the world as open as we can.

The *Euthyphro* of Plato which you read in Chapter 1 reveals how we often fail to warrant our statements. Socrates asks Euthyphro to support his claim that he knows what *piety* is. Euthyphro's very assurance makes him unwilling to engage in this task. Euthyphro is at first so sure that he knows all about piety that he is willing to bring a charge of murder against his own father. When Socrates questions him, however, he is unable to supply a single warranting statement. That is, he does not offer any statement which is unlikely to be called into question. The Socratic dialogue form lets us see how we use language in our relationships with others and how difficult it sometimes is to be successful in those relationships. Even though Euthyphro has not been able to provide Socrates with a single warranting statement for his claims, he is still convinced that he knows what piety is and that putting his own father on trial is a pious act. Notice that Euthyphro makes other unwarranted claims, such as his claim that Socrates will win his case! Certainly Euthyphro's claim was not widely accepted by his fellow countrymen, who were soon so convinced of Socrates' impiety that they put him to death. Paradoxically Plato's dialogue called *Euthyphro* and the statements in it made by Socrates have been accepted in the world and have introduced countless numbers of students to philosophy for two thousand years!

The statements we take to be warranted form a web, a web of belief. This web of belief is very large and contains thousands of beliefs that are supportive of one another. Some are crucial to holding up the web, and some are quite unimportant. Together they form a view of the world which shapes our perception of experience and gives rise to new beliefs about the world. Understanding how webs of belief function helps us understand how people from different countries around the world see the world so differently and why we often have such difficulty getting along with one another. Knowing about our own web of belief can help us as individuals understand why we are sometimes so stubborn and unwilling to participate in open rational dialogue. We do not like it when someone challenges our beliefs, especially the ones in the center of our webs. It is hard to reweave one's web of belief, but sometimes it is necessary to avoid holding inconsistent or unwarranted beliefs.

Exercises

2–I

1. Words are often used differently in different generations. List 10 words you and your friends might use whose meanings your parents might find puzzling.
2. Is "Columbus discovered America in 1492" a warranted statement? Defend your answer.
3. How can it happen that two people who attend the same event later give two very different descriptions of it?
4. *Piety* is a very important word for Socrates. His life depends on how it is defined. What are some more contemporary words whose definitions can have very significant consequences for people's lives?

2–II

1. We have seen that perceptions are not neutral. Not only does how we describe our experiences vary, but even the experiences themselves can vary and not just from person to person, but for the same person, from moment to moment. You have probably seen this familiar example of this phenomenon. What two different perceptions do you experience? How can you account for your having two different experiences of one physical image?

2. Explain how you would teach a child the definition of *horse*.
3. Are you familiar with the book called *Magic Eye* (N.E. Thing Enterprises, 1993)? How does Gould's concept of "search image" relate to the illustrations in this book and its sequels?
4. Draw a picture of part of your web of belief. Be sure to show in your picture how the beliefs in it are connected to each other and which beliefs are more important and central and which are more peripheral.
5. Suppose you found out that you are not the biological child of your parents but that you were adopted as a toddler from Russia. What new beliefs would you add to your web of belief? Which beliefs currently in your web of belief would you discard? Are these beliefs near the center or the periphery of your web of belief?

3

Knowledge and Certainty

BELIEF AND KNOWLEDGE

We have seen that our beliefs are best thought of as parts of a web—a web each of us has constructed and continues to construct in order to link together the statements which express our beliefs.[1] We build our webs, not like spiders to catch flies, but rather to have some sort of coherent system, a world-view adequate to guide us through the rest of the day and through the rest of our lives. The center of this web is occupied by our most entrenched belief statements, that is, those it would be hardest to give up. To abandon one of these center-of-the-web belief statements, we would have to adjust or even abandon the many other belief statements linked to it in the web. The periphery of the web is composed of our belief statements of which we are least sure and which we could give up with minimal readjustment of the web.

We warrant our belief statements to ourselves by fitting them into our web of other belief statements. If a statement meshes with few or none of the other belief statements in our web of belief, then that statement is hard to fit in. We do not have a place where it fits. And if a new statement contradicts one or more of the beliefs in our web, it is likely to be rejected. Those new statements which mesh with some of the other belief statements already in our web may be retained in our webs as beliefs. Statements, however, which fit very well into our web which mesh with many of the other belief statements in our web—these "well meshed" statements we regard as **knowledge**. When we say that we *know* something we are not claiming to be infallible. Rather we are indicating that we would be amazed if these things

---

[1]*The Web of Belief,* by Quine and Ullian, shares many of the same ideas expressed here.

we claim to *know,* which we have warranted to ourselves and which fit securely in our web, couldn't be warranted to others as well.[2]

For example, the statement "Abraham Lincoln was the author of the Gettysburg Address" will be warranted for you if it fits together with other belief statements from your web such as "The Gettysburg Address was written by the U.S. president who held office during the Civil War," "Abraham Lincoln was the U.S. president during the Civil War," and so on. Hence, you say you **know** that Lincoln was the author of the Gettysburg Address.

When we wish to warrant one of our statements to some other person, the best way of doing so is to begin an open dialogue with that person. In this dialogue, we express those statements from our web which we think offer the greatest amount of support for the statement we wish to warrant. For example, if the statement you want to warrant is your claim "Abraham Lincoln was the author of the Gettysburg Address," you might begin by uttering the two warranting statements from your web of belief just mentioned (i.e., "The Gettysburg Address was written by the U.S. President who held office during the Civil War" and "Abraham Lincoln was the U.S. President during the Civil War").

As noted above in Chapter 2, if the statements which express our knowledge claims are accepted by almost everyone around us, we regard them as **factual statements**. The statement about Abraham Lincoln is one that you do regard as factual. In the first place, it fits well into your web of belief—so well that you would be amazed if you could not warrant it to others if asked to do so. In the second place, this statement is accepted by virtually everyone around you. From our discussion about the **open dialogue**, **warranting for ourselves**, **warranting for others**, and **factual statements**, we can describe the goal of critical thinking in the following way: The critical thinker is someone who makes the effort to warrant as many of her beliefs as is possible, and who attempts to test and share her knowledge with everyone who is willing to participate in an open dialogue. The result of this goal of critical thinking is something clearly beneficial to all—factual knowledge which has been tested in the arena of open dialogue and found to be warranted. This is clearly preferable to what often passes for factual knowledge, namely, something uncritically accepted on the basis of authority, or prejudice, or some combination of the two.

KNOWLEDGE AND CERTAINTY

Discussions of knowledge are sometimes confusing (to both philosophers and non-philosophers). On the one hand, most of us are pretty modest about our claims to knowledge. If asked, "Are you infallible?" most of us would likely reply, "Of course not." On the other hand, when we try to make clear what the difference is supposed to be between knowledge and belief, the idea that comes to mind is that to know something is somehow to be unable to be wrong about it while a belief is something we could be mistaken about.

---

[2]A similar account of what it means to say that we *know* something, as opposed to merely saying that we *believe* it, is offered by the well-known Austrian philosopher Ludwig Wittgenstein. See his *On Certainty* #355.

For example, suppose that your teacher arrives 10 minutes late for class looking very disheveled and upset and announces to the class, "I apologize for being so late but I ran into Santa Claus in the stairwell, and he dropped his big bag of toys, spilling toy trains, and dolls, and other toys all over the stairs. By the time we picked them all up, I was late for class." The class might well respond to this story with incredulous or skeptical looks. Suppose that the teacher, somewhat irritated by the skeptical attitude of the class, responds in the following way, "Look, I know that my story seems to be a strange one, but I really did run into Santa Claus. I *know* that the person I ran into was Santa Claus." By claiming to *know* that she ran into Santa Claus, the teacher seems to be saying that she cannot be mistaken about this matter.

Suppose that in order to counter their skepticism the teacher asks the class to search the buildings and grounds of the college, hoping that they will find either Santa himself or some trace of his having been there—perhaps parts of broken toys in the stairwell or reindeer tracks on the roof. Further suppose that the search for Santa Claus evidence turns up no trace of any Santa Claus having been anywhere near the classroom building at the time in question. "I am very sorry to have sent you on a wild goose chase," the teacher might then tell the class. "I *know* that I saw Santa Claus, but I must have been *mistaken*." But wait. This sounds strange. Would she *really* say, "I *know* . . . but I must have been *mistaken*."? She would be more likely to say, "I *thought* I knew but I must have been wrong." But suppose she did say, "I *know* that I saw Santa Claus, but I must have been *mistaken*." Why does this seem such a strange thing for the teacher to say? If before the "Santa search" the teacher had merely claimed to *believe* that she saw Santa Claus, there would be no strangeness. There is nothing odd or paradoxical about later saying we must have been mistaken about something we earlier said that we believed. It happens to all of us all the time. When we say we know something, however, there is definitely something odd about later saying we were mistaken about it.

It has been the dream of philosophers, scientists, and theologians to rule out this possibility of being mistaken. They have sought an account of knowledge—unlike our web of belief account of knowledge described above—in which knowledge could be regarded as certain or perhaps even infallible. Generally, two different approaches have been taken in pursuit of this dream. The first is that taken by those thinkers called **empiricists** (from the ancient Greek word for experience, *empeirei*). Empiricists claim that we can be virtually certain about at least some of the statements we make because some of them are warranted directly by experience and by the things we see, touch, hear, smell, and taste. On close examination, however, we see that this approach is flawed. The only access we have to experience or to any other of our thoughts is through the expression of those thoughts in language, either to ourselves or to others. Hence, the only thing which can support or warrant a statement is another *statement*. It is certainly tempting to think that we could have an experience or a thought without also having any *linguistic expression* of that experience or thought, but when we actually try to do so we see that it cannot be done.[3] On further reflection,

---

[3]The Austrian philosopher Ludwig Wittgenstein mentioned above relates the following amusing anecdote on this subject: "A French politician once wrote that it was a peculiarity of the French language that in it words occur in the order in which one thinks them." (*Philosophical Investigations,* #336.) Is it likely that our politician, when he noticed this fortuitous similarity between thought and French, was thinking in anything other than French?

it is difficult even to imagine in what form these unexpressed experiences and thoughts would exist. The only way to express our thoughts, to ourselves or to others, is by making statements.[4]

Consider, for instance, the statement "Koala bears are warm and cuddly." This statement is warranted, not by some collection of raw visual data which look brown and raw tactile data that feel soft, but rather by statements which you make, either to yourself or to others, statements such as "This is a koala bear," "It's brown," "It's cuddly," and so on. That is, the statements we make are not warranted directly and individually by unarticulated experiences but rather by other statements, some of which may be about what we are now experiencing and others of which are about the various things we need to assume in order to make any statements about our present experiences. So your statement about koala bears needs as warrant not merely other statements like the ones above about your present experience, but a whole "supporting cast" of other statements, for instance, statements about the general reliability of your memory (e.g., that you didn't call this fuzzy thing in front of you a kangaroo last time round), and about the accuracy of your senses (that this is not an illusion nor are you dreaming or drunk). Most of this supporting cast of statements, of course, remains unuttered except in unusual situations. The point is that it is not immediate experience but statements—groups or whole "webs" of statements—that we use to warrant statements, which we want to warrant or which are called into question by others.

The traditional alternative to empiricism with respect to the problem of how knowledge could be certain or infallible is the one used by the French mathematician and philosopher René Descartes. A short excerpt from his *First Meditation* is a reading for this chapter. Descartes claims that all knowledge has to be either certain or based on something certain. Philosophers usually call approaches like Descartes' **foundational** views of knowledge because of their requirement that each piece of knowledge be based or founded on something certain.

This approach, like that of the empiricists, is also flawed. The problem with this view of knowledge—with its architectural image of pieces of knowledge resting on foundations consisting of other pieces of knowledge—is that the foundation can't go down forever. It must have at its most basic level something which it is impossible to doubt, something absolutely certain. What would be required, then, at the very bottom of the foundation would be statements which somehow warrant themselves. This self-warranting, according to Descartes, would take place through our "clearly and distinctly" perceiving that a particular statement cannot possibly be doubted. But, as Descartes himself shows in the reading, virtually none of our statements are free from doubt. We cannot even be sure that we are awake and not asleep and only dreaming that we are awake. The only statement which, according to Descartes, meets this high standard is the statement "I exist" since in order to doubt I exist, I would need to assume that I exist, for if I didn't exist I couldn't possibly do anything and I certainly could not doubt.

So the question for Descartes is: "Can we plausibly base all of human knowledge on our absolute certainty about our own existence?" In all fairness to Descartes,

---

[4]This point is also made in Chapter 2 in the discussion of **factual statements** and the microscopic analysis of Fred's hairs. See Chapter 2.

he makes a valiant attempt to do so. But only the most sympathetic critic could label his attempt a success. Descartes needs, just to indicate *one* of his difficulties, the services of a benevolent non-deceiving God just to guarantee that when we are certain about anything other than our own existence, we cannot be wrong. His idea here is that a benevolent, non-deceiving God would not let us live in a cruel world of deception. So Descartes' foundationalist demand for certainty leads ultimately to a theological basis for all of human knowledge, a view about which there is generally more doubt than certainty!

It should be pointed out that there is one class of statements, which might be called definitional statements, which could be regarded as self-warranting. For instance, if a triangle is defined as "a closed geometrical figure having three sides," then the statement "A triangle has three sides" could be seen as self-warranting. This is because it would then amount to the statement "A closed geometrical figure having three sides has three sides." This, we believe, is as close as we ever get to statements which are self-warranting or absolutely certain. This kind of self-warranting statement is disappointing and trivial, since it repeats in the predicate all or part of its subject. Such statements seem unlikely candidates for the role of foundation stones for all the rest of knowledge.

What can we say about the results of these historical attempts to link knowledge and certainty? We have seen that empiricism goes wrong by assuming that statements can be warranted by such things as collections of visual, audible, and tactile data, while Descartes (and others with foundational views of knowledge) goes wrong by assuming that some statements *warrant themselves* in a nontrivial way. If both of the classical attempts to show that some knowledge is absolutely certain have failed, where does this leave us? Is there any difference between merely believing and actually knowing? Must knowledge be infallible?

Rather than ask how knowledge can be certain or infallible, let us reconsider the account of knowledge given above. Clearly our knowledge, in our everyday world, is made up of those statements which are warranted to the point where we do not call them into question. If asked to warrant them, we warrant them by uttering other statements. These statements are well entrenched in our web of belief such that it would be very difficult to give them up. Taking them out or giving them up would cause a large section of the web to unravel or fall apart. When a web unravels, it has to be rewoven. New beliefs and connections have to be created. Our knowledge, then, is not infallible. We ourselves can be mistaken, and we can think of many examples of things that other people have claimed to know but which later turned out to be unwarranted. However, we do not need infallibility to distinguish knowledge and belief. They are distinguished, on our view, by the entrenched nature of the statements we claim to know in our web of belief and by our ability to warrant our knowledge claims to ourselves and to others. We will look at some cases of this below. First, by way of example, we will look at two efforts of foundationalism, one classic and one rather humorous.

The first reading for this section is a very famous selection from René Descartes' *Meditations on First Philosophy*. Descartes was a seventeenth-century thinker who was impressed with the certainty he found in mathematics and suspected that everything else he had been taught was capable of being doubted. So, he set out to determine what he could know beyond a shadow of a doubt. You are probably familiar with the answer he gave to his own question. The one thing he found he could not doubt was his own existence. He expressed his proof for his existence in a now famous argument, the conclusion of which is: *cogito, ergo sum*. I think, therefore I am.

Descartes' overall approach to knowledge, it will be recalled, is a foundational one. That is, Descartes thought that in order to have firm and lasting knowledge, each "piece" of knowledge must be based on another piece of knowledge, which is either completely free from doubt or based on a piece completely free from doubt. This model of knowledge is very like a house—with the roof resting on the walls and the walls resting on the firm foundation. In this section's second reading from cosmologist Stephen Hawking (a cosmologist is a scientist who studies the origin of the universe), Hawking relates a story about the philosopher Bertrand Russell who, while giving a public lecture, was himself lectured to by a member of his audience—a woman with her own foundational view. In this amusing account of the universe, we glimpse a foundation for the universe which, she claims, goes on forever.

MEDITATIONS ON FIRST PHILOSOPHY IN WHICH THE EXISTENCE OF GOD AND THE DISTINCTION OF THE SOUL FROM THE BODY ARE DEMONSTRATED

René Descartes

Meditation One: Concerning Those Things That Can Be Called into Doubt

Several years have now passed since I first realized how many were the false opinions that in my youth I took to be true, and thus how doubtful were all the things that I subsequently built upon these opinions. From the time I became aware of this, I realized that for once I had to raze everything in my life, down to the very bottom, so as to begin again from the first foundations, if I wanted to establish anything firm and lasting in the sciences. But the task seemed so enormous that I waited for a point in my life that was so ripe that no more suitable a time for laying hold of these disciplines would come to pass. For this reason, I have delayed so long that I would be at fault were I to waste on deliberation the time that is left for action. Therefore, now that I have freed my mind from all cares, and I have secured for myself some leisurely and carefree time, I withdraw in solitude. I will, in short, apply myself earnestly and openly to the general destruction of my former opinions.

Yet to this end it will not be necessary that I show that all my opinions are false, which perhaps I could never accomplish anyway. But because reason now persuades me that I should withhold my assent no less carefully from things which are not plainly certain and indubitable than I would to what is patently false, it will be sufficient justification for rejecting them all, if I find a reason for doubting even the least of them. Nor therefore need one survey each opinion one after the other, a task of endless proportion. Rather—because undermining the foundations will cause whatever has been built upon them to fall down of its own accord—I will at once attack those principles which supported everything that I once believed.

Whatever I had admitted until now as most true I took in either from the senses or through the senses; however, I noticed that they sometimes deceived me. And it is a mark of prudence never to trust wholly in those things which have once deceived us.

But perhaps, although the senses sometimes deceive us when it is a question of very small and distant things, still there are many other matters which one certainly cannot doubt, although they are derived from the very same senses: that I am sitting here before the fireplace wearing my dressing gown, that I feel this sheet of paper in my hands, and so on. But how could one deny that these hands and that my whole body exist? Unless perhaps I should compare myself to insane people whose brains are so impaired by a stubborn vapor from a black bile that they continually insist that they are kings when they are in utter poverty, or that they are wearing purple robes when they are naked, or that they have a head made of clay, or that they are gourds, or that they are made of glass. But they are all demented, and I would appear no less demented if I were to take their conduct as a model for myself.

All of this would be well and good, were I not a man who is accustomed to sleeping at night, and to undergoing in my sleep the very same things—or now and then even less likely ones—as do these insane people when they are awake. How often has my evening slumber persuaded me of such customary things as these: that I am here, clothed in my dressing gown, seated at the fireplace, when in fact I am lying undressed between the blankets! But right now I certainly am gazing upon this piece of paper with eyes wide awake. This head which I am moving is not heavy with sleep. I extend this hand consciously and deliberately and I feel it. These things would not be so distinct for one who is asleep. But this all seems as if I do not recall having been deceived by similar thoughts on other occasions in my dreams. As I consider these cases more intently, I see so plainly that there are no definite signs to distinguish being awake from being asleep that I am quite astonished, and this astonishment almost convinces me that I am sleeping.

Let us say, then, for the sake of argument, that we are sleeping and that such particulars as these are not true: that we open our eyes, move our heads, extend our hands. Perhaps we do not even have these hands, or any such body at all. Nevertheless, it really must be admitted that things seen in sleep are, as it were, like painted images, which could have been produced only in the likeness of true things. Therefore at least these general things (eyes, head, hands, the whole body) are not imaginary things, but are true and exist. For indeed when painters wish to represent sirens and satyrs by means of bizarre and unusual forms, they surely cannot ascribe utterly new natures to these creatures. Rather, they simply intermingle the members of various animals. And even if they concoct something so utterly novel that its likes have never been seen before (being utterly fictitious and false), certainly at the very minimum the colors from which the painters compose the thing ought to be true. And for the same reason, although even these general things (eyes, head, hands, and the like) can be imaginary, still one must necessarily admit that at least other things that are even more simple and universal are true, from which, as from true colors, all these things—be they true or false—which in our thought are images of things, are constructed.

To this class seems to belong corporeal nature in general, together with its extension; likewise the shape of extended things, their quantity or size, their number; as well as the place where they exist, the time of their duration, and other such things.

Hence perhaps we do not conclude improperly that physics, astronomy, medicine, and all the other disciplines that are dependent upon the consideration of composite things are all doubtful. But arithmetic, geometry, and other such disciplines—which treat of nothing but the simplest and most general things and which are indifferent as to whether these composite things do or do not exist—contain something certain and indubitable. For whether I be awake or asleep, two plus three makes five, and a square does not have more than four sides; nor does it seem possible that such obvious truths can fall under the suspicion of falsity.

All the same, a certain opinion of long standing has been fixed in my mind, namely that there exists a God who is able to do anything and by whom I, such as I am, have been created. How do I know that he did not bring it about that there be no earth at all, no heavens, no extended thing, no figure, no size, no place, and yet all these things should seem to me to exist precisely as they appear to do now? Moreover—as I judge that others sometimes make mistakes in matters that they believe they know most perfectly—how do I know that I am not deceived every time I add two and three or count the sides of a square or perform an even simpler operation, if such can be imagined? But perhaps God has not willed that I be thus deceived, for it is said that he is supremely good. Nonetheless, if it were repugnant to his goodness that he should have created me such that I be deceived all the time, it would seem, from this same consideration, to be foreign to him to permit me to be deceived occasionally. But we cannot make this last assertion.

Perhaps there are some who would rather deny such a powerful God, than believe that all other matters are uncertain. Let us not put these people off just yet; rather, let us grant that everything said here about God is fictitious. Now they suppose that I came to be what I am either by fate or by chance or by a continuous series of events or by some other way. But because being deceived and being mistaken seem to be imperfections, the less powerful they take the author of my being to be, the more probable it will be that I would be so imperfect as to be deceived perpetually. I have nothing to say in response to these arguments. At length I am forced to admit that there is nothing, among the things I once believed to be true, which it is not permissible to doubt—not for reasons of frivolity or a lack of forethought, but because of valid and considered arguments. Thus I must carefully withhold assent no less from these things than from the patently false, if I wish to find anything certain.

But it is not enough simply to have made a note of this; I must take care to keep it before my mind. For long-standing opinions keep coming back again and again, almost against my will; they seize upon my credulity, as if it were bound over to them by long use and the claims of intimacy. Nor will I get out of the habit of assenting to them and believing in them, so long as I take them to be exactly what they are, namely, in some respects doubtful as by now is obvious, but nevertheless highly probable, so that it is much more consonant with reason to believe them than to deny them. Hence, it seems to me, I would do well to turn my will in the opposite direction, to deceive myself and pretend for a considerable period that they are wholly false and imaginary, until finally, as if with equal weight of prejudice[5] on both sides, no bad habit should turn my judgment from the correct perception of things. For indeed I know that no

---

[5]A "prejudice" is a prejudgment, that is, an adjudication of an issue without having first reviewed the appropriate evidence.

danger or error will follow and that it is impossible for me to indulge in too much distrust, since I now am concentrating only on knowledge, not on action.

Thus I will suppose not a supremely good God, the source of truth, but rather an evil genius, as clever and deceitful as he is powerful, who has directed his entire effort to misleading me. I will regard the heavens, the air, the earth, colors, shapes, sounds, and all external things as nothing but the deceptive games of my dreams, with which he lays snares for my credulity. I will regard myself as having no hands, no eyes, no flesh, no blood, no senses, but as nevertheless falsely believing that I possess all these things. I will remain resolutely fixed in this meditation, and, even if it be out of my power to know anything true, certainly it is within my power to take care resolutely to withhold my assent to what is false, lest this deceiver, powerful and clever as he is, have an effect on me. But this undertaking is arduous, and laziness brings me back to my customary way of living. I am not unlike a prisoner who might enjoy an imaginary freedom in his sleep. When he later begins to suspect that he is sleeping, he fears being awakened and conspires slowly with these pleasant illusions. In just this way, I spontaneously fall back into my old beliefs, and dread being awakened, lest the toilsome wakefulness which follows upon a peaceful rest, have to be spent thenceforward not in the light but among the inextricable shadows of the difficulties now brought forward.

Even skunks can be foundationalists!

Used by permission of Atlantic Feature Syndicate.

A BRIEF HISTORY OF TIME

Stephen Hawking

A well-known scientist (some say it was Bertrand Russell) once gave a public lecture on astronomy. He described how the earth orbits around the sun and how the sun, in turn, orbits around the center of a vast collection of stars called our galaxy. At the end of the lecture, a little old lady at the back of the room got up and said: "What you have told us is rubbish. The world is really a flat plate supported on the back of a giant tortoise." The scientist gave a superior smile before replying, "What is the tortoise standing on?" "You're very clever, young man, very clever," said the old lady. "But it's turtles all the way down!"

STUDY QUESTIONS

1. Do you ever feel, like Descartes, that you are uncertain about everything? Why or why not?
2. How does the fact that you *think* prove that you exist?
3. Why is "I stink, therefore I am" not as powerful as "I think, therefore I am"?
4. Name five things of which you are absolutely certain.
5. Describe a time when you were absolutely certain that you were right about something and later found out that you were mistaken. How did this happen?
6. What is wrong with the ". . . it's turtles all the way down. . . ." explanation?
7. How is the "turtles hypothesis" a foundational approach to cosmology?

CONSENSUS AND THE WEB OF BELIEF

Good critical thinking does not lead to certainty in the traditional sense of infallible knowledge. What it does help us to do is to weed out errors from our own webs of belief and to participate more effectively in the shared web of belief of the larger community. We acquired many of the beliefs of this communal web as children learning to talk. Our efforts as children are encouraged when our beliefs match those of our parents and discouraged when they do not. We learn to believe that this four-legged animal is a dog and that other four-legged animal is a cat, and so on. As we get older and more social, we become members of various groups and communities that share webs or world views. You probably belong to several different communities: a college or university community, a community of family and extended family, a community defined by the geographic location of your home, a community of people who share your interest in your particular hobby or sport, and so on. Each of these communities shares a consensus about appropriate vocabularies and beliefs. To join a community is to accept the web of belief about which the members of the community have established a consensus. To become a chemist, for example, you must learn the language of chemistry and accept the beliefs that chemists have that describe their world of elements and molecules. To be an American, one shares a certain set of beliefs for which there is general consensus among Americans such as the importance of freedom of speech and how government should work.

Consensus is important in our day-to-day activities as well. Warranting our statements to other people helps to create consensus. We want other people to share our beliefs about the world. If you think the lady with the red hat (from the earlier chapter) has taken your book and she claims the book to be hers, then there is no consensus. If it turns out that the book has her name on the flyleaf, not yours, you will most likely have to alter your web of belief. The community in this case will probably agree that the book is hers, not yours.

Communities, of course, are not always correct in their beliefs. Their webs of belief may contain mistakes. You may insist against the community that your belief is the correct one. Your options at this point are three. You can leave the community and go away mad, you can start a fight, or you can try to convince the community of your point of view by open rational dialogue. Obviously critical thinkers favor the last option. The first two options cannot promote our goals of having friends and being loved, and having pleasant rather than unpleasant experiences. Future experience can often lead to correcting a web of belief, yours or the community's. If, to continue our book example, the laboratory technician does find hairs that match perfectly the hairs of Fred, your cat, between pages 100 and 101 in the book, then the community will likely change its consensus on who owns this wonderful copy of *Thinking Socratically.*

Communities that share a web of belief try to build consensus among their members. The two readings that follow show two different communities and their efforts at creating consensus. The first reading is about a plane crash and the efforts of the National Transportation Safety Board to find consensus among the eye witnesses to that crash in order to create a coherent web of belief about how the crash occurred. Besides showing the difficulty of creating a coherent web of belief about the crash, the article also shows how experience, in the form of eyewitness accounts, is not adequate to that task. As we noted above, observers do not experience the same thing because their experiences are influenced by their webs of belief.

Historians are also a community, and history is the story they collectively tell about the past. This story is arrived at by building up consensus through open rational dialogue about what has happened; however, historians do not always see the events the same way, depending on their perspective. An American historian will describe the Revolutionary War quite differently from the way a British historian does. Often the story is changed to accommodate new evidence that is uncovered. The second reading is about historians and the story they have told about Thomas Jefferson and his relationship with his slave, Sally Hemings. It is a good example of how the story that is history is always open to new evidence. It also shows how historians themselves have webs of belief that influence how they receive new evidence and the difficulty of adjusting their webs to accommodate it.

IDEAS & TRENDS; FOR AIR CRASH DETECTIVES, SEEING ISN'T BELIEVING

Matthew L. Wald

June 23, 2002 **WASHINGTON**—HUNDREDS of people watched the crash of American Airlines Flight 587 near Kennedy International Airport in New York on Nov. 12, and in the course of 93 seconds they apparently saw hundreds of different things.

According to the National Transportation Safety Board, which announced this month that it had gathered 349 eyewitness accounts through interviews or written statements, 52 percent said they saw a fire while the plane was in the air. The largest number (22 percent) said the fire was in the fuselage, but a majority cited other locations, including the left engine, the right engine, the left wing, the right wing or an unspecified engine or wing.

Nearly one of five witnesses said they saw the plane make a right turn; an equal number said it was a left turn. Nearly 60 percent said they saw something fall off the plane; of these, 13 percent said it was a wing. (In fact, it was the vertical portion of the tail.)

The investigators say there is no evidence in the wreckage or on the flight recorders of an in-flight fire or explosion. A plane breaking up in flight, as this one did, might in its last moments produce flashes of fire from engines ripping loose, but the idea that the plane caught fire is a trick of memory, they say.

None of this is surprising, said Dr. Charles R. Honts, a professor of psychology at Boise State University and the editor of the Journal of Credibility Assessment and Witness Psychology. "Eyewitness memory is reconstructive," said Dr. Honts, who is not associated with the safety board. "The biggest mistake you can make is to think about a memory like it's a videotape; there's not a permanent record there."

The problem, he said, is that witnesses instinctively try to match events with their past experiences: "How many plane crashes have you witnessed in real life? Probably none. But in the movies? A lot. In the movies, there's always smoke and there's always fire."

As a result, the safety board generally doesn't place much value on eyewitness reports if data and voice recorders are available. For many investigators, the only infallible witness is a twisted piece of metal.

Benjamin A. Berman, a former chief of major aviation investigations at the safety board, said pilots actually make the worst witnesses, because their technical knowledge can lead them too quickly to identify a mechanical problem that may not have occurred. "Children make among the best witnesses," he added, "because they don't tend to place an interpretation on what they've seen."

The safety board's skepticism of eyewitness accounts was deepened by the explosion of TWA Flight 800 off Long Island six years ago: hundreds of people saw an upward streak that they assumed was a missile, although investigators said it was the body of the plane itself, streaking upward after the forward portion had fallen off following a fuel tank explosion.

THAT disaster highlighted another pitfall for investigators, Mr. Berman and others say: F.B.I. agents asked witnesses where the missile came from, presupposing the presence of a weapon. "It wasn't good aircraft accident investigation," Mr. Berman said.

There are other well-known cases of witness error, including the crash of a Lauda Air Boeing 767 near Bangkok in May 1991. Witnesses said they heard a bomb and saw the plane fall in flames, but it turned out to be a mechanical problem.

So why do investigators bother asking witnesses at all? Dr. Bernard S. Loeb, who retired as the safety board's director of aviation safety last year, said, "In the case of 587, it's unlikely that the witnesses will provide much to help the investigation, but you never know that when you begin an investigation—where you're going to get important leads, from the recorders, from witnesses, from the structure itself."

And in any crash, he said, conflicting witness statements can still be useful. "What was very clear from the Flight 800 witnesses was that many did see something up in the sky," he said.

Even if the accounts are likely to be wrong, they are still routinely gathered and evaluated by both the board and police agencies. "Can you imagine if we didn't interview the witnesses?" said one current board official.

Mr. Berman, who left the board last year, said investigators may have released the summary of what the Flight 587 witnesses saw just to show publicly that the statements showed "scatter"—an engineering term for plotted data that does not fit a pattern. A release at this late date is unusual, but a spokesman for the board, Ted Lopatkiewicz, said it was done because it was ready. But, he added, "I don't think I'm making any news by saying that eyewitness testimony at a plane crash and probably at many traumatic events is unreliable."

Witness statements can be more valuable in crashes of small planes that don't have flight data recorders or cockpit voice recorders, Mr. Berman said.

Mr. Loeb said his experience with witnesses had led him to question the reliability of criminal convictions based on eyewitness identifications. In Illinois, he noted, a commission appointed by the governor recommended in April that the death penalty not be applied to murder convictions based on a single eyewitness identification.

Mr. Loeb said his personal experience also played into his skepticism. Recently he and his wife saw a two-vehicle collision, and unlike plane crash witnesses, they both saw it from the same angle. Within moments, they disagreed about what they had seen. Among other key details, Mr. Loeb said he could not recall whether one of the vehicles had been a truck or an S.U.V.

PRESIDENT TOM'S CABIN

Jill Lepore

. . . After [Thomas] Jefferson's death, on July 4, 1826, his slaves were sold at auction. But that auction did not include Sally Hemings's children, as Annette Gordon-Reed records in her commanding and important book, "The Hemingses of Monticello: An American Family" (Norton; $35). Jefferson freed two of Hemings's three surviving sons, Madison and Eston, in his will; the other son, Beverly, had already left Monticello. Hemings had a daughter, too, Harriet, who left Monticello in 1822, when she was twenty-one. "Harriet.

Sally's run," Jefferson wrote in his "Farm Book," where he kept track of his human property, a population that needed minding, since Jefferson was one of the largest slavehold-
ers in Virginia. Harriet didn't exactly run. "She was nearly as white as anybody, and very
beautiful," recalled one of Jefferson's overseers, who also said that Jefferson ordered him
to give fifty dollars to the girl, and paid for her ride, by stage, to Philadelphia.

It has taken a very long time for historians to regard this story seriously, or even
to begin to bother to sort out fact from fiction. Just why was the subject of Gordon-
Reed's 1997 tour de force, "Thomas Jefferson and Sally Hemings: An American
Controversy," a book that was as much a painstaking investigation of the documentary record as a devastating brief on standards of evidence in historical research. For
Gordon-Reed, a legal scholar, the real scandal wasn't what happened between
Jefferson and Hemings but how willing earlier generations of Jefferson biographers
had been to ignore the implications of evidence right in front of them, even documents
like Jefferson's "Farm Book," but, especially, testimony about things said and done
by the Hemingses themselves. Behind the Jefferson-Hemings affair, Gordon-Reed
wrote, lay yet another buried family tie: Sally Hemings was the half sister of Jefferson's
wife, Martha Wayles. Taking a lawyer's view of the case, Gordon-Reed pieced
together the evidence and weighed it. She presented a strong case in support of the
claim that Jefferson fathered Hemings's children, and freed them, or let them go when
they reached the age of twentyone, because Hemings had extracted from him, in 1789,
at the beginning of their decades-long affair, a promise that he would do exactly that.

Gordon-Reed's "Thomas Jefferson and Sally Hemings" was published the same
year as Joseph Ellis's stirring and elegiac biography "American Sphinx: The Character
of Thomas Jefferson," in which Ellis asserted—intuited, actually, since there is no
evidence for this—that Jefferson, who had got his wife pregnant six times in ten years,
had never slept with the very beautiful Sally Hemings (who reportedly resembled his
wife, a woman Jefferson adored), because "for most of his adult life," and, presumably, especially after his wife died (when Jefferson was thirty-nine), "he lacked the
capacity for the direct and physical expression of his sexual energies." The man was a
statue. "American Sphinx" won the National Book Award.

A year later, Eugene Foster, a retired University of Virginia pathologist, published in *Nature* the results of DNA tests he had undertaken, working with scientists in
Oxford, Leicester, and Leiden. Foster tested the blood of the descendants of Field
Jefferson, Thomas Jefferson's uncle; Eston Hemings, Sally's youngest son; and
Thomas Woodson, who some believe was Sally's eldest child. (The Y chromosome
passes down through males virtually unaltered, but Jefferson's only son by his wife
died in infancy, which is why Foster had to find his Jeffersonian Y elsewhere.) The
tests cast doubt on one relationship and proved another. Thomas Woodson's descendants don't have the Jefferson Y. Eston Hemings's do. This doesn't prove that Eston,
let alone Sally Hemings's other children, were fathered by Thomas Jefferson. It proves
only that Eston's father was a Jefferson. Alas, there just wasn't another Jefferson
handy, there at Monticello, and with a Y in his pocket, each time Hemings conceived.
Ellis, in later editions of his biography, graciously conceded the argument. "Prior to
the DNA evidence," he wrote, "one might have reasonably concluded that Jefferson
was living a paradox. Now it was difficult to avoid the conclusion that he was living a
lie." Dissenters persist, citing the circumstantial nature of the evidence. But today

most historians agree with the conclusion of a research committee convened by the Thomas Jefferson Foundation, at Monticello: Jefferson "most likely was the father of all six of Sally Hemings's children."

Lost in the DNA-driven consensus, however, was Gordon-Reed's point. It ought never to have taken a lab test to bolster a claim deducible from the documentary record. For a conference at Monticello and the University of Virginia in 1999, Gordon-Reed revisited the case:

> It is true that we do not and will never have the details of what went on between Jefferson and Hemings and their children. This does not mean that we have nothing to go on. Perhaps the most persistent, and ultimately damaging, feature of the original debate over whether the relationship existed at all was the tight rein placed upon the historical imagination. One was simply not to let one's mind wander too freely over the matter. Brainstorming, drawing reasonable inferences from actions, attempting to piece together a plausible view of the matter were shunted into the category of illegitimate speculation, as grave an offense as outright lying.

Deductions and inferences can be wrong. But they're not illicit; they're how history, at its best, makes sense of a senseless world.

. . .

"The Hemingses of Monticello" tells a family story, across the generations. Harriet Hemings had seven white great-grandparents; she was, in the idiom of the time, an "octoroon." She was also, because of a precedent-defying seventeenth-century Virginia statute, Thomas Jefferson's property. In 1655, a woman with an African mother and an English father successfully sued for her freedom by relying on English precedent, in which children inherit status from their father. Not long after, the House of Burgesses, eager to avoid another legal challenge, turned English law upside down, answering doubts about "whether children got by an Englishman upon a Negro woman should be slave or free" by reaching back to an archaic Roman rule, *partus sequitur ventrem* (you are what your mother was).

Generations passed. There was much begetting. In about 1735, Gordon-Reed recounts, an Englishman named Captain Hemings had sex with an enslaved "full-blooded African" whose name has not survived. She gave birth to a daughter. Hemings tried to buy the child, but her owner refused to sell, curious to see how the girl would turn out. Hemings hoped to steal her; he failed. In 1746, the girl, Elizabeth Hemings, was transferred to the plantation of an Englishman named John Wayles, when he married Martha Epps. (Hemings, who was about eleven years old, was part of the marriage settlement.) Wayles married three times; his first wife bore him a daughter, Martha, in 1748. After the death of his third wife, Wayles did not marry again. But, as Gordon-Reed relates, he did start having sex with Elizabeth Hemings, by whom he had six children, including a daughter, Sally, born in 1773. In 1772, Martha Wayles married Thomas Jefferson. After John Wayles's death, the following year, Elizabeth Hemings and all of her children went to live at Monticello. In 1782, when Sally Hemings was still a child, Martha Jefferson died. Mrs. Jefferson, on her deathbed, extracted from her altogether bereft and nearly unmoored husband a promise that he would never remarry. In 1789, when sixteen-year-old Sally Hemings was living with forty-six-year-old

Jefferson in Paris, she became pregnant. Madison Hemings said that the child "lived but a short time." Woodson's descendants claim that the boy grew up to be Thomas.

Gordon-Reed argues that Hemings made a deal with Jefferson. She knew that she could stay in Paris, where she would be free; slavery was illegal in France. She decided to return to Virginia because she missed her family. And Jefferson promised her that he would free all of her children when they reached the age of twenty-one. Maybe Hemings loved Jefferson; maybe he loved her, too. (In 1974, Fawn Brodie wrote a history supposing this to be the case, and more than one romance novel assumes the same.) Gordon-Reed knows that this question is important, since Jefferson and Hemings are more than people—they're symbols, too. But symbols get you only so far. "The romance is not saying that they may have loved one another," Gordon-Reed writes. "The romance is in thinking that it makes any difference if they did."

Jefferson, the architect of our freedom, could not reckon slavery's toll. "The whole commerce between master and slave is a perpetual exercise of the most boisterous passions, the most unremitting despotism on the one part, and degrading submissions on the other," he wrote in the early seventeen-eighties. "The man must be a prodigy who can retain his manners and morals undepraved by such circumstances." Neither could Jefferson imagine his life, or the Union, freed of slavery, without bloodshed. "I tremble for my country when I reflect that God is just; that his justice cannot sleep forever."

Moral impotence is a muffled, crippled agony. American sphinx? American Achilles.

STUDY QUESTIONS

1. Describe an event where you and your friends told quite different stories about what happened. How did you settle your differences?
2. Why do we value consensus among groups of common language users?
3. What other controversial examples from history do you know about which historians lack consensus?
4. Why do historians have difficulty accepting the story of Sally Hemings and her children?
5. What does the story of Sally Hemings and Thomas Jefferson tell you about the history (the story) of race in the United States?

Summary

Most people would claim that they know quite a lot, especially about themselves, their families, their friends, their neighborhood, and perhaps even about their country. When pressed, however, they usually begin to back off a bit, acknowledging that they certainly cannot prove all the things they would claim to know. Still, they are pretty sure that their knowledge claims are justified. That is, when they stop to consider, they realize that they could be mistaken about some of the claims they would make. Most of these claims, they would admit, are really belief statements, not knowledge statements.

We usually don't think about whether a statement is a statement of knowledge or a statement of belief. If we feel certain, then we say *know*. If we feel somewhat uncertain, then we say *believe*. This distinction in the use of these terms tells our listener something about our ability to warrant our claims, and, therefore, how much the listener should believe our claim. These common sense distinctions are important to good critical thinking. After all, what we would like is to know, not just to believe. To be able to do this, we have to have a clearer idea of the distinction between a knowledge statement and a belief statement. **Knowledge statements** are those that we can warrant. We warrant our statements by appeal neither to sense experience alone nor to rationally indubitable foundational statements. Rather we warrant our statements by locating them in our **web of belief**. That is, we show that they support and are supported by other statements we hold as warranted.

The knowledge statements with the most and/or strongest connections are near the center of our webs. Those with the fewest connections are near the margins of our web of belief. Those of our statements which are most warranted—which are so much a part of our web of belief and everyone else's that they are seldom if ever called into question—we call **factual statements**.

Our beliefs and our webs of belief are connected to the webs of belief of others. If we are the only persons in the room who believes a particular statement, then we are likely to reconsider our belief and wonder how entrenched it is for us and whether we might be wrong in holding it. This consensus or agreement with the beliefs of others is important to us. If others disagree with us, then we try to convince them of our point of view through open rational dialogue. Sometimes, we may find our own web of belief is the one that needs to be amended. It may be the case that the consensus of the group is overwhelming, open rational dialogue convinces us that we are wrong, or future events suggest that revision is warranted. That revision can be great or small depending on how entrenched in our web the offending belief(s) might be. This is all part of critical thinking.

Exercises

3–I

1. Why is it better to know something rather than just believe it?
2. List five belief statements in the center of your web of belief. If you were to take one of these out of your web of belief, what other beliefs would have to be weeded out also?
3. List five belief statements which you find yourself unable to warrant to others but which are sufficiently enmeshed in your web of belief that you continue to believe them.

3–II

1. In your own words, explain why empiricism and foundationalism cannot save us from uncertainty.
2. Can we ever be certain—in the sense of infallible? Explain.
3. Why is consensus important? What does it tell us about our own web of belief?
4. Find an example in the news about an episode for which there is no consensus. That is, there is much disagreement about what happened. Explain why this disagreement occurs in this particular incident.

Arguments and Explanations

ARGUMENTS: PREMISES AND CONCLUSIONS

We have seen that warranting our statements to ourselves and to others is a very important part of critical thinking. Since no statement is self-warranting, simply asserting a statement over and over or asserting it more loudly each time is not very useful. Nor is repeating it with slight variation. The excerpt you read from Gertrude Stein illustrates this all-too-human behavior. As we have pointed out, the best way to warrant a statement is by connecting it to other statements, hoping finally to arrive at a statement or statements which are accepted as factual statements.

> STATEMENT—a group of words which is used to assert something.

Whenever we attempt to warrant one statement by offering other statements, we are making an **argument**. An argument in this sense is a pattern of reasoning, part of an open rational dialogue. It is not an altercation or a fight. Arguments abound. We are always trying to convince each other or ourselves of different claims or points of view. Arguments can be simple, such as giving a reason for doing something (It will make me feel better), or complex as in deciding whether to accept this job or that proposal. In the larger community, politicians and journalists create arguments to support one side or another of important issues such as global warming and national defense and try to convince others to agree with them.

In an argument, the statement we wish to warrant is called the **conclusion**, while the statement or statements which do the supporting are called the **premise(s)**. Premises and conclusions are often introduced by, or contain, clue words, which help you recognize that the speaker or author intends to give an argument and also help you distinguish the statement being warranted from the supporting statements being offered.

Typical **clue words indicating premises** are *since, for, being that, because, if, on the supposition that, assuming that, follows from, seeing that, in view of the fact that, as shown by, as indicated by, may be inferred from,* and so on.

Clue words indicating conclusions are *therefore, consequently, it follows that, thus, hence, so, implies that, entails that, allows us to infer that, suggests strongly that, you see that, which shows that, which proves that, bears out the point that,* and so on.

These words are useful but not infallible guides to recognizing premises and conclusions. Sometimes the author of an argument may misuse them by mistake and sometimes even deliberately as, for instance, when he is trying to make an argument look stronger than it is. The best way to analyze an argument is to ask yourself what this person is trying to prove, show, or make a point of. The answer to this question will lead you to the conclusion. Once you have the conclusion, then ask yourself what evidence, if any, is being offered in support of that claim. The evidence or support is/ are the premises and they, together with the conclusion, constitute an argument.

Consider the following example of an argument. Suppose Tom says, "The Beatles were the greatest musical artists of all time." Given the differences that we all know exist from person to person with respect to musical taste, we would expect someone somewhere to question Tom's bold pro-Beatle announcement. Suppose that Tom made his "Beatles were the greatest" statement in front of Joan, an avid admirer of classical music in general and of Mozart's music in particular. Joan might well challenge Tom's statement by replying, "Tom, are you nuts? The Beatles greater than Mozart? You'll never convince me of that!"

Now suppose that Tom takes up Joan's challenge and tries to convince her that she ought to accept his "Beatles were the greatest" statement as factual. If you were Tom, how would you attempt to do that? One way might be to show Joan that other statements that she accepts as factual support the statement that "The Beatles were the greatest." Again, when we support statements which have not been accepted as factual by using statements which we expect will be accepted as factual, we are giving **arguments**. An argument can be more precisely defined as follows:

> ARGUMENT—Two or more statements one of which—the conclusion—is supposed to be supported by the other(s)—the premise(s).

The phrase "is supposed to be supported" indicates that not every argument is successful. That is, sometimes we assume or suppose that our premises support our conclusions when they do not. Part of being a good critical thinker is distinguishing between arguments where the premises give support for the conclusion and those where the statements made to support the conclusion are inadequate. Improving your ability to make this distinction will be the task of the next several chapters.

IMPLICIT PREMISES AND CONCLUSIONS

Arguments are all around us—in books, in newspaper editorials, in advertisements, and in our discussions with our friends. The arguments which surround us, however, are not always clear or complete. Sometimes, merely to avoid repetition or sometimes deliberately to "trick" the recipient of the argument, the premises or even the conclusion of an argument will be left out. This is called an **enthymeme**. Consider the following enthymeme which was part of a very successful advertising campaign:

> The bigger the burger, the better the burger.

> The burgers are bigger at Burger King.

These two statements, whether or not they are factual (whether or not you or anyone at all agrees with them), are premises which logically imply the following *unstated* conclusion:

> The burgers are better at Burger King.

By not stating the conclusion, the writer leads the reader to draw the conclusion for himself, perhaps leaving the impression that the reader *made up his own mind* about the goodness of Burger King's burgers. The writer of the advertisement imagines that you are driving down the highway at lunch time and, barely noticed by you, your car radio plays the Burger King jingle. A few minutes later as you approach a Burger King restaurant, you hear the implicit conclusion of the jingle/argument playing in your head ("the burgers are better at Burger King") and you turn, zombie-like, into the Burger King parking lot.

Advertisements often leave off the conclusion and let you supply it because it is so obvious: You ought to buy product X. Other arguments leave out premises, sometimes on purpose because of their obviousness, sometimes by accident. Consider the following familiar exchange which is an argument with implicit premises:

> SON: Dad, can I have the car tonight?

> DAD: No

> SON: Why not?

> DAD: Because I said so.

This argument will probably be successful even though only one premise is offered because of the implicit premises: (1) I am your father and (2) what the father says is the law. They are left unsaid because the speaker considers them just too obvious.

ARGUMENTS: STANDARD FORM

In our everyday experience, arguments appear in many patterns. Sometimes the conclusion is given first, and then the support is offered for it. Other times the conclusion appears in the midst of a series of premises. On occasion, especially in formal writing like law and geometry, the conclusion is put clearly at the end. Reading, writing, talking, listening, and even thinking would be very dull if all arguments were stated in exactly the same pattern. We like variety in our language and in our sentence order.

It is helpful, however, to have one standard form of argument when we try to analyze arguments. Then we can all be talking about the same thing at the same time. For that reason, when we analyze arguments, we put them into what is called standard form with the premises first and the conclusion last. Sometimes the premises are themselves warranted by other statements. The premises in that case are the conclusions of smaller arguments within the larger argument. In putting an argument into standard form, we try to make this structure as clear as we can.

Consider the following argument from *Through the Looking Glass* by Lewis Carroll. Here Alice is talking to Humpty Dumpty.[1]

> ... "Good-bye, till we meet again!" she [Alice] said as cheerfully as she could.
>
> "I shouldn't know you again if we *did* meet," Humpty Dumpty replied in a discontented tone, giving her one of his fingers to shake: "you're so exactly like other people."
>
> "The face is what one goes by, generally," Alice remarked in a thoughtful tone.
>
> "That's just what I complain of," said Humpty Dumpty. "Your face is the same as everybody has—the two eyes, so—" (marking their places in the air with his thumb) "nose in the middle, mouth under. It's always the same. Now if you had the two eyes on the same side of the nose, for instance—or the mouth at the top—that would be *some* help."

This delightful argument is a good one to put into standard form. First we look for the conclusion. That helps us understand the relationships among the statements. Here the conclusion is in the middle, so to speak: "I shouldn't know you again if we did meet." Then we need to ask: How does Humpty Dumpty support this claim? Why wouldn't Humpty Dumpty know Alice in the future? Because her face is the same as everyone else's! There's our premise. There's also an implicit premise here, a premise left unstated because most readers would automatically assume it, namely, that it is impossible to recognize a person whose face is the same as everyone else's. You have probably also noticed that there are some subpremises here about the placement of eyes, nose, and mouth that support the first premise that Alice has the same face as everyone else. If we put the argument into standard form, it looks something like this:

P_1 Your face is the same as everyone else's.
  Warranting Statements for P_1: W_1: Your eyes are one on each side.
                                      W_2: Your nose is in the middle.
                                      W_3: Your mouth is under [your nose].

P_2 (Implicit)   It is impossible to recognize a person whose face is the same as everyone else's.

[Therefore,]

C: I shouldn't know you again if we did meet.

Lewis Carroll's argument is interesting on other grounds besides its structure. Carroll was also a logician and mathematician whose real name was Charles Dodgson. He loved plays on words and logical twists. What word is being played with in this argument?

---

[1]Found in *The Annotated Alice,* Introduction and Notes by Martin Gardner (Bramhall House, 1960), pp. 275, 276.

To summarize: To analyze an argument, it is best to put the argument in standard form. First pick out the conclusion or the statement that is being supported. Sometimes there will be a clue word or words to help you do this. Then pick out the premises or supporting statements. These may or may not be indicated by clue words. Put the premises first and the conclusion last. If the premises are connected in some way, try to make that connection clear by the order you place the premises. If there are implicit premises or an implicit conclusion, add it to them (it) to the argument. When the argument is in standard form, it then can be evaluated as to the amount of support the premises give to the conclusion.

LOGICAL WARRANTING

There are different kinds of support which a premise or a set of premises can give to a conclusion. One kind of support is logical in nature and concerns the ways that premises are linked to the conclusion. The other kind of support concerns the factual status and the relevance of the statements being offered in support. We will consider the logical linkages first. Logical warranting occurs when there is a logical connection between the premises and the conclusion so that the factual status of the premises conveys factual status to the conclusion. There are two kinds of logical connections that can occur between the premises and the conclusion. One kind of logical connection is very strong such that if the premise statements are considered to be factual, then the conclusion statement logically linked to it would, as a result of that linking, *have* to be regarded as factual. The second kind of logical linkage is less strong. In arguments of this second kind, the linkage is such that the factual status of the premise(s) makes the factual status of the conclusion *more likely* but there is no guarantee or necessity. The first kind of logical warranting, where the conclusion must be regarded as factual if the premise(s) is regarded as factual, is called **deductive reasoning**. The second kind of logical warranting where the conclusion is only more likely is called **inductive reasoning**. These two types of logical warranting are different from **factual warranting** where the support is provided but by the supporting statement's being factual and/or relevant and not simply by any logical linkage between statements. Factual warranting will be discussed below.

DEDUCTIVE REASONING

In deductive reasoning, the goal is to give a logically **valid** argument. **In a valid argument, the conclusion is said to follow from or be implied by the premises so that if you accept the premises as factual then you must also accept the conclusion as factual.** Logicians call these arguments using deductive reasoning deductive arguments. The reason why the conclusion of a logically valid argument must be accepted as factual has nothing to do with what the premise(s) actually say or assert. The necessity to accept the conclusion is entirely logical—due to the logical structure of the argument. The premises may even be obviously nonfactual or nonsensical as in the following example, again from Lewis Carroll.

All old gorilla keepers are good-tempered people.

All good-tempered people ride bicycles.

Therefore, all old gorilla keepers ride bicycles.

We do not know whether the premises of this argument are factual or not, but the logical structure of the argument is such that the conclusion is necessarily implied by the premises, which is just to say that *if* all old gorilla keepers were good-tempered people and *if* all good-tempered people did ride bicycles *then* all gorilla keepers would ride bicycles. This logical relationship between the premises and the conclusion of a valid argument is completely independent of anyone's *actually* accepting any of them as factual. When this logical relationship is present, you have to recognize the argument as logically **valid** even if you disagree with the premises. But if you do accept the premises as factual, then you *have* to accept the conclusion as factual also.

Michele Scalza, in the story you are about to read of the same name, argues to win a bet. To win the bet and claim the prize of a free dinner, Scalza must convince his companions that a certain family—the Baronci—are the oldest and thus the most noble family in the whole world. To do this he uses a common deductive argument known as *modus ponens*. (*Modus ponens* will be discussed in detail in Chapter 6.) He argues, if the members of a certain family are all very ugly, then this indicates that the family is a very ancient one. And furthermore, if a family is a very ancient one, then it must also be a very noble one. Thus, since the Baronci family is the ugliest family in Florence, they must also be the most noble family in Florence. Scalza's winning argument buys him a dinner at the expense of his friends. That is, *if* you accept the claims in his premises about the connection of ugly with ancient, and *if* you accept as factual his claim about the ugliness of the Baronci family, then you *must* accept his conclusion that the Baronci family is the most noble family in Florence. The statements of the premises are logically linked with that of the conclusion so that if the premises are regarded as factual, one must regard the conclusion as factual as well. The premises logically warrant the conclusion—making this argument a valid argument.

INDUCTIVE REASONING

When the logical linking is such that the statement supported by the linking becomes, as a result of that linking, more likely to be factual—but not *necessarily* factual, we are **reasoning inductively**. The objective in inductive reasoning is to give a **strong** argument rather than a valid argument. **In a strong argument, if the premises are accepted as factual, then the conclusion is more likely than not to be factual.** With inductive arguments, just as with deductive arguments, the question of factual warranting is separate from the logical warranting. So in inductive reasoning, as in reasoning with necessity, you may find that the conclusion is logically warranted by the premises even though you do not accept those same premises as factual. For example, consider the following strong inductive argument:

The sun has risen in the west for over two thousand years.

Therefore, the sun will rise in the west tomorrow.

Now, the premise of this argument is clearly nonfactual, but let's pretend for a moment that the premise is factual—that it is generally accepted without question that the sun has risen in the west for over two thousand years. Then, the conclusion would also have to be regarded as more likely than not to be factual. That is, it would be reasonable to believe *on the basis of the premise offered in support* that it is more likely than not that the sun will rise in the west tomorrow. This, then, is a strong inductive argument, even though we all believe that both its premise and its conclusion are both nonfactual.

A different type of inductive reasoning with a different kind of logical warranting is used by Melchizedek in the second story you are about to read, when he tells the story of the three rings in order to save his life. This argument has a well-known form called "argument by analogy." This argument form is very common and very useful, especially when dealing with very sensitive issues—like religion or moral behavior. A well-known example of argument by analogy is "The Story of the Little Child Who Cried 'Wolf'," a story you were probably told by your parents and have heard many times.

A person arguing by analogy presents the audience with an argument about a neutral topic in exactly the same form as the argument with the sensitive topic in order to concentrate on the reasoning and to avoid the emotional content of the sensitive material. For example, in this case Melchizedek discusses rings instead of religions so that he can avoid the emotional issue of religion.

The principle which justifies this form of reasoning is that it is reasonable to assume that if two things share a number of features, they also have additional properties in common. So, if Sue and Sam are both children of Jim and Jane Smith, and Sue was allowed to drive the car at age 16, then Sam also should be allowed to drive the car at age 16.

Surely you have used this argument by analogy form yourself. Consider: "Mom, why can't I stay out all night after the prom? Mary's Mom says she can." Or, "I studied as long as Bob did. Why did he get an 'A' and I only got a 'C'?" Keep this argument form in mind since it can be used to relate a familiar, less controversial example to an unfamiliar or controversial one which is the focus of a present dispute. Thus, it can be very useful in discussions when tempers are starting to rise or when very sensitive feelings are aroused.[2]

FACTUAL WARRANTING

Besides giving a conclusion logical support, premises can support a conclusion by **factually warranting** it, which is just to say that statements that are widely accepted offer stronger support than do ones that are not widely accepted. Factual warranting can characterize both deductive reasoning and inductive reasoning. If we offer factual statements as premises in our arguments, we are factually warranting the conclusions of those arguments. It will be recalled from Chapter 2 that **factual statements** are

---

[2]An excellent example of using argument by analogy to shed light on a very sensitive topic is Judith Jarvis Thomson's article "A Defense of Abortion," *Philosophy and Public Affairs,* vol. 1, no. 1 (Fall 1971), pp. 47–66, where she draws an analogy between being pregnant and being kidnapped by the Society of Music Lovers who want to use your body for nine months to save the life of a famous unconscious violinist. Her examination of this analogy leads to a better understanding of what it means to say that someone has a "right to life." If you are interested in the issues of analogy or abortion, this article is worth reading.

statements which have themselves been warranted to the point where they are seldom questioned. A factual statement is defined as follows:

FACTUAL STATEMENT—A factual statement is a warranted statement which is seldom questioned.

In factual warranting we are using statements which have been warranted elsewhere to warrant the statements we now wish to support. We are borrowing warrant from another place and time, however close or recent that place or time was, for the present. We *must* repeatedly borrow like this. Otherwise we would be condemned to an endless chain of warranting, warranting one statement after another until the end of time. In order for factual warranting to be successful, the statement which is providing the support has to be less open to question than the statement which is being supported.

In addition, the supporting statement should be **relevant** to the supported statement. The minimum condition for relevance is that one statement is relevant to another when it contains an unequivocal use of one of the terms of that statement. For it to be possible for the premises to add support to the conclusion in an argument, each premise must be relevant to at least one other premise and at least one premise must be relevant to the conclusion. Irrelevant statements do not weaken the logical or factual warranting of the relevant premises, but they do sometimes confuse us, causing us to think that a conclusion is warranted when it is not.[3]

Factual warranting can be better understood by considering the following examples. The first two examples are deductive; the last two are inductive.

1. If the sun is rising in the east, it must be morning.
   The sun is rising in the east.
   Therefore, it must be morning.
2. If the sun is rising in the west, it must be morning.
   The sun is rising in the west.
   Therefore, it must be morning.
3. The sun has risen in the east every morning for over two thousand years.
   Therefore, the sun will rise in the east tomorrow morning.
4. The sun has risen in the west every morning for over two thousand years.
   Therefore, the sun will rise in the west tomorrow morning.

In the first example the first premise, "If the sun is rising in the east, it must be morning," is *both factual and relevant*. Both it and the conclusion are about the rising of the sun, and it is a fact that the sun rises in the east in the morning. So if the sun is now rising in the east, as the second premise asserts, then the conclusion will be factual also. It *must* be morning. In the second example the premise, "If the sun is rising in the west then it must be morning," is *relevant but not factual*. It is relevant because both it and the conclusion are about the same thing—the rising of the sun. However, since it is not widely accepted that the sun rises in the west, this premise cannot be regarded as factual.

---

[3]Some of these confusions occur so regularly that they have specific names and are often grouped under the heading "fallacies of irrelevance." These will be discussed in Chapter 9.

Although the conclusion of this argument is *logically* supported by its premises, it is not *factually* supported. In the third example, the premise is both relevant and factual and so lends support to the conclusion. In the fourth example, the premise is relevant. Both it and the conclusion are about the sun. But it is not a factual statement that the sun rises in the west, so the premise does not make the conclusion any more likely to be factual.

Notice that the above examples show that what goes on in factual warranting is not exactly the same in deductive reasoning as in inductive reasoning. In inductive reasoning, the factual warranting is closely connected to the logical linking. In deductive reasoning, it is not. A relevant statement nearly always adds to the **strength** of an argument when reasoning with probability. When the premises of such an argument are both relevant and factual, we call the argument a **cogent** argument. When reasoning with necessity, the statements in the premises must be logically linked to the statement they are supposed to be warranting in order to contribute to the **validity**. To be logically linked, they must be relevant but they need not be factual. A valid argument with factual premises is said to be a **sound** argument.

Logical warranting and factual warranting help us create good arguments and distinguish good arguments from bad arguments. We will develop both these ideas further in the chapters which follow. The two stories which are included here are examples of good arguments. The two main characters make good use of both logical and factual warranting to convince their listeners and achieve their objectives.

The stories come from *The Decameron,* which is a famous collection of stories written during the Renaissance by Giovanni Boccaccio. They are among the earliest pieces of Italian prose. In the first story, a young man, Michele Scalza, argues in order to win a bet. He uses deductive reason to convince his companions that a certain family is the most noble in the whole world. In the second story Melchizedek, the hero, argues to save his life. If he doesn't convince Saladin of the correctness of his answer, he will die. Saladin's question is a tricky one: "Which one of the world's great religions is the true one?" Melchizedek convinces Saladin that there is no answer to the question which of the world's great religions is the true religion without getting enmeshed in highly charged religious issues. The story of the three rings, which is neutral and analogous to the story of the three great religions, gives Saladin the insight to accept Melchizedek's point of view. While his argument is inductive, and the conclusion is only more likely than not to be factual, it is a strong enough argument to convince Saladin—which is Melchizedek's goal.

THE DECAMERON

Michele Scalza
Giovanni Boccaccio

Michele Scalza proves to certain young men that the Baronci are the most noble family in the whole wide world, and wins a supper.

In our city, not so very long ago, there was a young man called Michele Scalza, who was the most entertaining and agreeable fellow you could ever wish to meet, and he was always coming out with some new-fangled notion or other, so that the young men of Florence loved to have him with them when they were out on the spree together.

Now, one day, he was with some friends of his at Montughi, and they happened to start an argument over which was the most ancient and noble family in Florence. Some maintained it was the Uberti, some the Lamberti, and various other names were tossed into the discussion, more or less at random.

Scalza listened to them for a while, then he started grinning, and said:

'Get along with you, you ignorant fools, you don't know what you're talking about. The most ancient and noble family, not only in Florence but in the whole wide world, is the Baronci. All the philosophers are agreed on this point, and anyone who knows the Baronci as well as I do will say the same thing. But in case you think I'm talking about some other family of that name, I mean the Baronci who live in our own parish of Santa Maria Maggiore.'

His companions, who had been expecting him to say something quite different, poured scorn on this idea, and said:

'You must be joking. We know the Baronci just as well as you do.'

'I'm not joking,' said Scalza. 'On the contrary I'm telling you the gospel truth. And if there's anyone present who would care to wager a supper to be given to the winner and six of his chosen companions, I'll gladly take him up on it. And just to make it easier for you, I'll abide by the decision of any judge you choose to nominate.'

Whereupon one of the young men, who was called Neri Mannini, said:

'I am ready to win this supper.' And having mutually agreed to appoint Piero di Fiorentino, in whose house they were spending the day, as the judge, they went off to find him, being followed by all the others, who were eager to see Scalza lose the wager so that they could pull his leg about it.

They told Piero what the argument was all about, and Piero, who was a sensible young man, listened first to what Neri had to say, after which he turned to Scalza, saying:

'And how do you propose to prove this claim you are making?'

'Prove it?' said Scalza. 'Why, I shall prove it by so conclusive an argument that not only you yourself, but this fellow who denies it, will have to admit that I am right. As you are aware, the older the family, the more noble it is, and everyone agreed just now that this was so. Since the Baronci are older than anyone else, they are *ipso facto* more noble; and if I can prove to you that they really are older than anybody else, I shall have won my case beyond any shadow of a doubt.

'The fact of the matter is that when the Lord God created the Baronci, He was still learning the rudiments of His craft, whereas He created the rest of mankind after He had mastered it. If you don't believe me, picture the Baronci to yourselves and compare them to other people; and you will see that whereas everybody else has a well-designed and cor-rectly proportioned face, the Baronci sometimes have a face that is long and narrow, some-times wide beyond all measure, some of them have very long noses, others have short ones, and there are one or two with chins that stick out and turn up at the end, and with enormous great jaws like those of an ass; moreover, some have one eye bigger than the other, whilst others have one eye lower than the other, so that taken by and large, their faces are just like the ones that are made by children when they are first learning to draw. Hence, as I've already said, it is quite obvious that the Lord God created them when He was still learning His craft. They are therefore older than anybody else, and so they are more noble.'

When Piero, the judge, and Neri, who had wagered the supper, and all the others, recalling what the Baronci looked like, had heard Scalza's ingenious argument, they all began to laugh and to declare that Scalza was right, that he had won the supper, and that without a doubt the Baronci were the most ancient and noble family, not only in Florence, but in the whole wide world.

And that is why Panfilo, in wanting to prove the ugliness of Messer Forese, aptly maintained that he would have looked loathsome alongside a Baronci.

THE DECAMERON

Melchizedek
Giovanni Boccaccio

Melchizedek the Jew, with a story about three rings, avoids a most dangerous trap laid for him by Saladin.

Saladin, whose worth was so great that it raised him from humble beginnings to the sultanate of Egypt and brought him many victories over Saracen and Christian kings, had expended the whole of his treasure in various wars and extraordinary acts of munificence, when a certain situation arose for which he required a vast sum of money. Not being able to see any way of obtaining what he needed at such short notice, he happened to recall a rich Jew, Melchizedek by name, who ran a money-lending business in Alexandria, and would certainly, he thought, have enough for his purposes, if only he could be persuaded to part with it. But this Melchizedek was such a miserly fellow that he would never hand it over of his own free will, and the Sultan was not prepared to take it away from him by force. However, as his need became more pressing, having racked his brains to discover some way of compelling the Jew to assist him, he resolved to use force in the guise of reason. So he sent for the Jew, gave him a cordial reception, invited him to sit down beside him, and said:

'O man of excellent worth, many men have told me of your great wisdom and your superior knowledge of the ways of God. Hence I would be glad if you would tell me which of the three laws, whether the Jewish, the Saracen, or the Christian, you deem to be truly authentic.'

The Jew, who was indeed a wise man, realized all too well that Saladin was aiming to trip him up with the intention of picking a quarrel with him, and that if he were to praise any of the three more than the others, the Sultan would achieve his object. He therefore had need of a reply that would save him from falling into the trap, and having sharpened his wits, in no time at all he was ready with his answer.

'My lord,' he said, 'your question is a very good one, and in order to explain my views on the subject, I must ask you to listen to the following little story:

'Unless I am mistaken, I recall having frequently heard that there was once a great and wealthy man who, apart from the other fine jewels contained in his treasury, possessed a most precious and beautiful ring. Because of its value and beauty, he wanted to do it the honour of leaving it in perpetuity to his descendants, and so he announced that he would bequeath the ring to one of his sons, and that whichever of them should be found to have it in his keeping, this man was to be looked upon as his heir, and the others were to honour and respect him as the head of the family.

'The man to whom he left the ring, having made a similar provision regarding his own descendants, followed the example set by his predecessor. To cut a long story short, the ring was handed down through many generations till it finally came to rest in the hands of a man who had three most splendid and virtuous sons who were very obedient to their father, and he loved all three of them equally. Each of the three young men, being aware of the tradition concerning the ring, was eager to take precedence over the others, and they all did their utmost to persuade the father, who was now an old man, to leave them the ring when he died.

'The good man, who loved all three and was unable to decide which of them should inherit the ring, resolved, having promised it to each, to try and please them all. So he secretly commissioned a master-craftsman to make two more rings, which were so like the first that even the man who had made them could barely distinguish them from the original. And when he was dying, he took each of his sons aside in turn, and gave one ring to each.

'After their father's death, they all desired to succeed to his title and estate, and each man denied the claims of the others, producing his ring to prove his case. But finding that the rings were so alike that it was impossible to tell them apart, the question of which of the sons was the true and rightful heir remained in abeyance, and has never been settled.

'And I say to you, my lord, that the same applies to the three laws which God the Father granted to His three peoples, and which formed the subject of your inquiry. Each of them considers itself the legitimate heir to His estate, each believes it possesses His one true law and observes His commandments. But as with the rings, the question as to which of them is right remains in abeyance.'

Saladin perceived that the fellow had ingeniously side-stepped the trap he had set before him, and he therefore decided to make a clean breast of his needs, and see if the Jew would come to his assistance. This he did, freely admitting what he had intended to do, but for the fact that the Jew had answered him so discreetly.

Melchizedek gladly provided the sultan with the money he required. The Sultan later paid him back in full, in addition to which he showered magnificent gifts upon him, made him his lifelong friend, and maintained him at his court in a state of importance and honour.

STUDY QUESTIONS

1. How does Michele Scalza prove his case? Put his argument into standard argument form.
2. Why is Melchizedek's argument a good one?
3. Can you think of a time when you (or perhaps one of your parents) told a story to bring someone (you) around to your (their) point of view? Were you (they) successful?
4. What if someone did not believe that the Baronci family was the most noble? How would he argue with Scalza?

EXPLANATIONS

Explanations are a type of subcategory of arguments. They have premises and conclusions like other arguments, but in the typical explanation the conclusion is already accepted as warranted, and what is missing is our understanding of that warranted statement. The premises supply the understanding and answer the question *why* this statement is warranted and not some other statement. We want to know *why* because we are curious, because we want to be able to predict similar future occurrences (like the weather), or because we want to control possible future occurrences (such as plane crashes). We accept many warranted statements without explanation, however. We don't care "why" or we think the "why" is too obvious to need explaining. For example, if your neighbor's dog is named "Fido," you probably don't care why the dog's name is "Fido." Or you think you know why. Fido is a common dog name, and your neighbor is the sort of person who would choose a common name. But if your neighbor's dog is named "Chewchuck," you might wonder why and ask for an explanation. ("Because he chews it down and chucks it up.")

In the typical argument, we reason from premises to the conclusion. We want to know if statements 1, 2, and 3 are accepted, what else must or may be accepted as well. In explanations we usually begin with a statement about an event, which we accept as warranted, and then supply statements as premises which tell us why that event occurred. Explanations can take the form of either deductive or inductive arguments, so it is sometimes difficult to determine whether an argument is an explanation or not. Often you have to know the context to know whether a piece of reasoning is an argument or a member of the subcategory of arguments called explanations. It depends on what is intended by the speaker or writer of the argument and on what the speaker thinks is "missing"—**the what or the why**. In distinguishing explanations from arguments your best judgment about the context and about what is intended is your best guide. Out of context, however, some pieces of reasoning are simply ambiguous as to whether they are intended to be arguments or explanations.

Since explanations are arguments, we evaluate them in the same way we evaluate other arguments. We expect the statements in the premises to be logically linked to the conclusion statement, and we expect the statements in the premises to be both factual and relevant to the conclusion. If the premises of an explanation are statements that are themselves frequently questioned and not considered to be warranted, then they add little to our understanding of the conclusion. For example, if your car refuses to start in the morning and your friend tells you that it is not starting because you didn't tell it "good night" the night before, you will reject his explanation as nonfactual and irrelevant. The statement to be explained, "My car won't start," is not factually warranted by the premises, "You didn't say 'Good night' to it the night before" and "Cars are more likely to start in the morning if you tell them 'Good night' the night before," which is the implicit premise in the explanation.

A very common form of explanation, especially in science but also in ordinary discourse, is to explain an event by using a universal generalization—which is a statement that claims something about all like situations—and some other statements which, together with the generalization, are thought to be sufficient to cause the event being explained. Take a simple example. Suppose you put an ordinary kitchen substance in a glass of water and it dissolves. Your younger brother who is watching wants to know why the substance dissolved in the water. Your response might be, "That was salt I dropped in the water and all salt is soluble in water." If your brother accepts your statement that the substance was salt and trusts your generalization, then he accepts your explanation as having provided conditions sufficient to produce the observed event. The argument in standard form looks like this:

All salt is soluble in water.

This substance in my hand which I put in the glass of water is salt.

Therefore, this substance dissolves in the glass of water.

Your brother, of course, may be a pain, and ask, "But why is salt soluble in water?" Although your argument is sound because you have supplied sufficient conditions for the conclusion from a logical point of view, you have not supplied sufficient conditions *for your little brother*. You may then be forced back on your knowledge of the chemical composition of salt crystals and water, which may satisfy your little brother—or at least make him go away. The point is that for an explanation to be successful, it must satisfy the listener/reader. If it does not satisfy, then it fails. What this means is that, in addition to being logically and factually warranted, the success of an explanation also depends on the nature of the audience. A good explanation for a physical-chemist is not necessarily a good explanation for a little brother.[4]

Explain why Calvin is going to have trouble.

---

[4]One of the most interesting examples of what constitutes a satisfactory explanation occurred in the government's investigation of the *Challenger* disaster mentioned in Chapter 1. The physicist Richard Feynman refused to accept NASA scientists' assertions about the safety of the *Challenger* and its rocketry even when every other member of the investigation team was satisfied. Feynman's persistent questioning of NASA's explanations finally led to reexamination of the safety of the *Challenger* spaceflights and eventually to safer missions. You may want to read his humorous account of his experiences in his book, *What Do You Care What Other People Think?*

The kind of event being explained is also an important determinant of what kind of explanation will be satisfying. Human actions, for example, can be explained psychologically or physiologically. If Joe suddenly rises from his chair and starts walking toward the door of the classroom, and someone asks, "Why is Joe walking out the door?" we could respond in several ways. We could explain that the muscles of his legs contracted and relaxed in such a way that they pulled on the tendons connected to the bones in his legs in such a way that his body went out the door. We could say that Joe went out the door because class was over. Or, we could say that Joe walked out the door because doors are easier to walk out of than walls. Sometimes we may not know the causes or reasons for an event, but we usually do understand the context sufficiently to know what kind of explanation is being called for, a psychological explanation or a physiological explanation.

You can see from the above examples that for an explanation to be satisfying and successful, it has to:

1. fit in with other things known or believed,
2. suit the level of the audience, and
3. be appropriate for the context in which it is given.

For example, if you ask for an explanation of what makes the hands in your friend's watch go around the dial, it will not do for your friend to say that there's a little tiny man who lives in the watch whose job is to walk around in a circle every hour, pushing the big hand in front of him. Nor will it do for him to give a lengthy explanation of the radioactive decay of quartz in the quartz battery that powers his watch. If the watch is a self-winding, however, you may be asking about the special properties of watches—which would make a satisfactory answer in that context. A satisfactory explanation can be long or short. Four-year-olds often demand explanations that run on forever. Exasperated parents often have a very short explanation, "Because I said so," which, because of the tone of voice, is usually accepted!

An explanation is also not acceptable to anyone if it is circular. A circular explanation is one which does not increase our understanding because it is a restatement of the statement that needs to be explained. The classic example is the response to the question, "Why does opium put people to sleep?" And the circular response is "Because it has dormitive powers." The parental response, "Because I said so," is also circular and therefore unsatisfying. It only stops the query because it makes clear that no more explanation is forthcoming. The next reading exemplifies the problem of circularity in a proposed explanation. The story is about the deaths of two infants in the same day care on the same day. We do not want to spoil it by saying more about it until after you have read it.

THE DAY-CARE DEATHS: A MYSTERY

Linda Herskowitz

Lisa Hatten and Fran McClendon met each other for the first time on an October afternoon at the day-care center. They didn't know it, but the two had much in common. Each had one child, a baby daughter. Each had nearly miscarried in the fifth month of pregnancy. And each had recovered from the loss of an earlier pregnancy: Lisa had miscarried; Fran had given birth prematurely to twins—one was stillborn, the other died within hours. Both women now used day care because both needed full-time jobs. They were having trouble just getting by.

. . .

But by the next afternoon, Friday, Oct. 15, 1982, that and everything else that once seemed to matter would not. Both babies would be dead—stricken at the day-care center—with little hope that anyone would ever know why. The parents, as well as the woman who ran the day-care center, would be devastated. The deaths would remain beyond everyone's understanding and control. Even the investigators—reconciled to the fact that, at times, a single death can defy explanation—would find themselves incredibly baffled: how could *two* babies die in the same house on the same day, with no clues as to why?

Fran McClendon, 35, slim and self-possessed, had gone back to work at the Center City insurance company where she had a job before Ashley's birth. She'd learned about Sheila Rolland's day-care service by asking the state welfare department for a list of registered day-care programs nearby. Fran had just started bringing Ashley to day care that week.

The Rolland house in Wynnefield was only a five-minute drive over a bridge from the McClendons' rowhouse on North Wanamaker Street in West Philadelphia. Fran checked the place out and liked what she saw: a white, semi-detached house on Gainor Road, a broad residential street, where neighbors added personal touches like aluminum doors and flower arrangements in picture windows. Mrs. Rolland's own living room was done in mustard and gold brocade. The house was spotless.

In the finished basement, where she ran the day-care program, there was a large playroom with a tile floor, blackboard, desk chairs, a playpen with a baby chair in it, cots for napping, a toy box, a big chair for Mrs. Rolland, and a bathroom.

Fran was impressed that Mrs. Rolland taught the kids the alphabet and arithmetic and took them on day trips. And she really took to Mrs. Rolland herself. She was a round-faced, amiable, chatty, heartwarming woman of 33, the kind who really loves kids.

Fran's little Ashley, 4 months old, was the first to die.

It was about 11:30 a.m. when the call came. Fran was typing at her desk. It was Mrs. Rolland: "I think you should call the doctor and come and get Ashley. She's not going to bed and she won't eat. Listen to her breathe." Fran could hear the baby being lifted to the phone. Ashley was whimpering, as if she were about to cry.

Fran called her pediatrician and talked to the nurse, who asked a few questions and said it sounded like Ashley had a cold. She suggested a drop of Tylenol and nose spray. Then Fran called her mother, who agreed to get a cab and pick up Ashley and tend to her for the rest of the day.

Mrs. Rolland called back before Fran could even tell her. She sounded impatient. *When was Fran coming to get her baby?* Fran explained that her mother would be there within a half-hour.

By now, it was noon. Fran had a lunch date, but she wondered whether she should break it. No, Ashley's condition didn't sound serious. She'd go to lunch, and call to check on her from the restaurant.

Mary Harris, Ashley's 56-year-old grandmother, had a night job, so even though it was after noon, she was still wearing her nightgown when she heard the knocking on her door. She peered through a small window. It was Mrs. Rolland, who had called earlier to tell her to forget the cab, she'd bring Ashley right over. She was holding the baby and seemed flustered and upset. She handed Ashley over, and as Mary Harris looked down at her granddaughter, she was horrified to see the baby's eyes rolled back in her head.

"Oh, my God," she said. "Something is wrong with my baby." She sat down in the armchair near the door, trembling as she cradled the infant. Mary Harris had seen her mother-in-law pass on. She'd been through the deaths of too many people; she knew what death looked like. The baby felt feverish, but she knew Ashley was as good as dead—Ashley, the first new baby in the family in 13 years, the first girl in nearly 20.

Mrs. Rolland, shaking, dialed the rescue squad; Mary Harris called Fran—still at lunch—then ran upstairs to put on some pants. When the rescue squad pulled up, the men yelled, *"Get this baby out of here!"* They took Mary Harris with them. Mrs. Rolland followed in her car. As they ran into street construction on 52d Street, Mrs. Harris was nearly hysterical, crying to the driver to hurry up, find a way around it. Sheila Rolland was praying behind her steering wheel, "Please, God, don't let her die."

At Misericordia Hospital, they rushed Ashley to a room in the back. Mary Harris sat in the waiting area, and Sheila Rolland cried and chanted, "I didn't do it. *I* didn't do it." That irritated Mrs. Harris. "Now wait a minute," she said. "Nobody said nothin' about anybody doin' nothin'."

Then a priest came out. He thrust a piece of paper into Mrs. Harris' pocket and said he was going to read the last rites. "Don't you be giving me no papers. My baby's dead," she said angrily. She didn't want religious words. Then a doctor came out. She looked into his face and whispered, "You know my baby's dead, right?"

It was five minutes to two. "We're sorry," he said.

Darryl Crosby, a 14-year-old, well-mannered boy from the neighborhood who helped Mrs. Rolland after school by changing Pampers and watching the kids, got to her house early, about a quarter to two.

Mrs. Rolland wasn't there. Her husband, Robert, an older man who usually came home for lunch every afternoon, had been minding the kids while his wife had gone to the hospital because one of the babies was sick. Then he went downstairs to check on the workmen who were replacing the back door in the basement.

Darryl went upstairs to check on the kids. Normally they'd be napping on cots in the basement, but today they were upstairs in the rear bedroom because of the workmen. Lisa Hatten's little girl, 10-month-old Lisa, seemed to be the only one asleep. She was lying on top of the covers on one side of the bed, her head turned to one side. Three other kids were scrunched together, giggling, on the other side of the bed. Four more were horsing around on the floor.

Tom Rolland, Darryl's buddy and at 15 the oldest of the three Rolland boys, came home from school at about 2:30. The two boys, Darryl recalled later, decided to go to the Rollands' own bedroom and watch some TV.

Fran got back to her office at 2. A co-worker was waiting with a fistful of messages. "You have a family emergency," he said. "Get to Misericordia Hospital." She was certain nothing was seriously wrong, but she got there in less than 15 minutes. When she walked through the emergency entrance, someone took her to a small waiting room. Suddenly, there was her family—her mother, two sisters, her brother—and Mrs. Rolland. They looked terrible.

Then her mother said in a choking voice, flat out, "Baby, she's dead."

Fran was still for a moment, then started screaming, "I want to see her!" A nun said, "I'm not going to let you see her until you calm down." *Reprimanded*, Fran thought, like she was disrupting a class. She wanted to hit the nun.

But Fran quieted down, and the nun ushered her into a small room in the back. There was Ashley, lying on a gurney. Her clothes were off; she was wrapped in a hospital gown. She still looked like herself. Fran picked her up; her body was still warm. Suddenly she felt someone watching her and looked up. The door was opened a crack. The eyes of the nun peered through.

"Why don't you leave me alone?" Fran screamed.

"You'll be all right," the nun said. "I have to watch you."

She had no privacy. Fran put Ashley down and stalked past the nun.

A doctor was outside. "We did everything we could," he said. "I'm sorry." She waited for something more, but he was silent. She felt a scream rising in her throat. Then he said, "We think it's a SIDS death." She knew that meant Sudden Infant Death Syndrome, something inexplicable, even to doctors.

"Are you sure?" Fran asked.

"Well, we have to do some tests," he said.

Fran's head was swimming. "If I had gotten here in time, would she have lived?"

The doctor didn't reply. His face was without expression. First the nun, now the doctor.

Fran faced Mrs. Rolland, who chanted pleadingly, almost hysterically, "Please don't blame me, please don't blame me."

What had happened?

"I don't know. I tried. Ashley started having problems breathing. I tried to call emergency, but I was so upset I dialed the number and couldn't make them understand what was wrong. So I grabbed her, got in my car, grabbed my son, and ran her over to your mother's house."

Fran was numb, dazed. She hugged Mrs. Rolland. "I'm sorry," she said. "I know you did everything you could."

She thought of calling her husband, John, at work, but she was so shaken that she couldn't remember his telephone number. Her mother was tugging at her, trying to get her out of the hospital. Mrs. Harris was saying, "We'll call him when we get home."

Fran let herself be led outside to a car.

The men were still working on the back door when they heard Mrs. Rolland's car pull into the driveway. Robert Rolland's car was just pulling away from the curb. It was about 3 o'clock. She trudged through the back door, into the basement, leaned heavily against the wall and said to the workmen, "She's gone."

Then she climbed the back stairs to the kitchen. The boys, still watching television, had heard her come in. She called up to them, "Hurry up, everybody, get the kids down here." Darryl wondered what was wrong. Tom helped him lead the toddling children downstairs, then Darryl went back up for the sleeping Lisa. Leaning over the bed, he noticed that one of her shoes was on the floor. When he bent over to pick it up, he saw dried blood on her face. He carried her downstairs and said to Mrs. Rolland, "What's wrong with this child?"

Sheila Rolland took her, then in a strangled voice, she said, "Oh, my God, she's dead."

Still holding the baby, she dampened a towel in the kitchen, wiped the blood away, then returned to the living room, laying the baby in her lap as she sat down on the sofa. She put her mouth over the baby's nose and mouth, trying to breathe life into it. Then she lifted her head and started screaming.

The workmen downstairs heard the screams, then the steps of someone running to the top of the basement staircase. A teenaged boy yelled down to them, "My mother needs you." As they came upstairs, Darryl heard one of the workmen say to the other, "Yo, Bob, another one's dead."

Darryl thought to himself, *another one?*

At 3:30, Lisa Hatten was practicing on a word processor at the Center for Innovative Training, a secretarial school near 13th and Arch. She was serious about job training and eager to find work because her relationship with Sahib Easley, the father of her child, was rocky after five years. If they went separate ways, she wanted to be able to support herself and the baby.

Lisa heard her name being called on the loudspeaker, *"EMERGENCY CALL."*

Her first thought was *my baby*.

Lisa moved and spoke in a deliberate, thoughtful manner that made her appear older than 23. Even with growing fear and apprehension, she maintained this dignity and reserve as she walked to the school's main office and picked up the phone.

On the other end, Sheila Rolland was crying hysterically, yelling, "Lisa's dead. Lisa's dead."

"What are you talking about? What's wrong with my baby? Where's she at?" Lisa said, her voice rising above its usual deep murmur.

"She's dead, she's dead," Mrs. Rolland said in a nervous staccato. "Another baby died here today. I took the baby to the hospital and when I came back, I checked on her and the baby wouldn't wake up. I was walking around, trying to get her to wake up and she wouldn't wake up."

Lisa was now shaking, overcome by the unreality of what she'd heard. She handed the phone to her friend Susie, the baby's godmother, who worked at the school. But before Susie could finish asking what hospital the baby had been taken to, Mrs. Rolland hung up. Lisa sat in the school office, crying, "This lady keeps telling me my baby is dead."

Susie dialed the Rolland number repeatedly, but it was busy. Finally, she got through, and someone said the baby had been taken to Misericordia. Lisa called her mother, then the grain shipping company where Sahib worked. She left him a message to call the school, and ran out with Susie.

While Susie drove, Lisa sat silently in the car, repeating to herself, *nothing's wrong with my baby. They got the wrong parent. They called the wrong one. This isn't happening.*

They ran into Misericordia's emergency entrance, but were told the baby had been taken to Osteopathic Hospital. They rushed over, and a young doctor ushered them into a small conference room. As they walked in, Lisa saw her mother and sister sitting there, sobbing.

Now she knew something terrible *had* happened. The doctor was talking softly to her, inviting her to sit down. She asked to see the baby, wanting them to say she was all right.

Her mother said, "They did all they could do."

"Everything we did failed," the doctor said softly. The baby had been declared dead at 4:59 p.m.

She sat numbly while the doctor asked questions. All she grasped was this: Had she known that another baby in that house had died that day also?

Her first thoughts were, *something went on that shouldn't have. Something happened. Two babies dying in the same house the same day. It's strange, very strange. She remembered Mrs. Rolland saying something about another baby, but she hadn't comprehended that two babies had died. She thought Mrs. Rolland was talking only about Lisa.*

No, she said, she didn't know anything about that.

. . .

At 10:30 Friday night, the phone rang in the Fairmount home of Dr. Robert Sharrar, the city's epidemiologist. On the other end was his boss, Dr. Stuart Shapiro, Philadelphia's health commissioner, who told him about the deaths of the two babies. Shapiro wanted to make certain the other kids at the day-care center were all right, that they had not been exposed to something contagious.

Sharrar called Marvin Aronson, the city's chief medical examiner. Aronson said homicide detectives had already made sure that the other kids—there were 10 of them, including three of Mrs. Rolland's own—were examined at hospitals. They all checked out fine.

When Sharrar called Shapiro back, the commissioner told him to attend the autopsies the next morning. That was unusual. Normally, if homicide detectives are looking into a death, the health department leaves the case to the medical examiner. But Shapiro felt that this time, epidemiologists also should be involved.

After he hung up, Sharrar thought about it. Two babies in the same house on the same day. What could it have been?

Bacterial meningitis was the first thing that came to mind. But, he debated with himself, that didn't usually kill within hours. And usually there were more symptoms: fever, stiff neck, sometimes skin rash. And even as lethal as it could be, it wouldn't kill two kids that fast.

Another possibility was homicide—perhaps the children had been abused. But Aronson had told him on the phone that he saw no outward evidence of trauma.

Other possibilities were legion: a malfunctioning heater could have poisoned the kids with carbon monoxide; they could have had a virus or a toxin . . . but so fast?

. . .

Sharrar got to the medical examiner's building by 9 a.m. He saw the babies lying on the table as soon as he walked into the room. They looked like healthy, well-kept little girls.

Sharrar watched Dr. Robert Segal, an assistant medical examiner, make a half-moon-shaped incision beneath the throat of each body. He peeled back the skin, opened the skull, and took out the brains. They looked perfectly normal. No layer of filmy haze—the sign that white cells had fought against the inflammation of meningitis, which was really what Sharrar had suspected. Nor was the cerebrospinal fluid cloudy. It was clear, showing no signs of infection. So was the middle ear, where infection can spread to the lining of the brain cavity.

They removed the tongue and pharynx for examination, because if they were only slightly inflamed, they could block the throat and cause death. They were normal. They looked at the trachea for signs of infection. One child's trachea was a little congested, and had little streaks of red through it, but that wouldn't cause death. Besides, it was the baby who was said to have had a slight cough that day, and the streaks were consistent with that.

They even got down to checking basic things, like making sure the heart vessels led to the right places. It took about three hours to examine both bodies. Sharrar then took tissue specimens to his office building, where he put them in a special incubator to see if any bacteria or virus would grow.

The next morning, Sunday, Sharrar met the city's lab director to interpret the culture plates. The cerebrospinal fluid showed nothing. The trachea grew some organisms, but only what would be expected. In short, nothing.

Over the next few days, the most plausible explanations were being knocked off, one by one.

When Aronson, the chief medical examiner, first heard about the deaths, he thought the weather had turned suddenly cool and that the day-care center had "turned on the goddamn heater and they got carbon monoxide poisoning." That was disproved when the medical examiner's office sent two investigators to the scene and found it wasn't so.

Neither baby had suffered physical injury. Aronson was convinced that no kind of negligence had contributed to their deaths. And suicide was obviously out. As were barbiturates, opiates, any identifiable poison, or heavy metals. There were no bad reactions to vaccinations, because neither child had been recently vaccinated. The tissues revealed no presence of the types of botulism or viral infections that could kill a baby quickly. The paint and plastering was found free of toxic substances.

Aronson was beginning to consider the impossible—that each baby had been the victim of Sudden Infant Death syndrome, and had just happened to be in the same place at the same time.

SIDS has been around since biblical times, but only recently has it been studied. In the typical case, an apparently healthy baby, usually three weeks to seven months old, is put to bed without the slightest suspicion that anything is wrong. At most, there may be signs of a slight cold. Some time later, the infant is found dead. No one has heard the baby make a sound, and there is no evidence of a struggle. An autopsy reveals, at most, minor inflammation of the upper respiratory tract, but nothing that would kill. Often, the autopsy reveals no evidence of illness.

Individually, Lisa and Ashley were textbook examples of SIDS. But the mathematical odds of two babies being stricken in the same place on the same day were just too unbelievable—one in a billion, maybe one in a trillion, Aronson thought.

He decided it was time to ask for outside help. He conferred with Shapiro, and they agreed to call the Centers for Disease Control (CDC), headquartered in Atlanta. The federal agency had the resources and expertise to perform advanced bacteriological studies.

Hell, Aronson thought, we pay taxes for it, we might as well use it.

Stephen Bowen, the CDC epidemiologist assigned to the New Jersey Health Department, has the look of the outdoors about him. He was, in fact, out in a field in Monmouth County, N.J., collecting ticks suspected of carrying a bacteria that causes arthritis, when his beeper went off. It was Thursday afternoon, Oct. 21, nearly a week after the babies had died.

His boss in Atlanta, the man in charge of about 40 agents assigned to health departments around the country, was calling him to tell him he was on the case. Bowen was pleased; he liked unusual cases.

The next morning he went to see Sharrar, whom he'd known for years. They reviewed the investigation. Practically everything plausible had been ruled out. Except SIDS. The younger baby was well within the common age range, but the 10-month-old was a little old for it. The autopsy findings, they agreed, didn't lean strongly toward or against a SIDS diagnosis.

. . .

It didn't take long before Bowen realized there just weren't many untouched bases. It was becoming increasingly likely that they were heading toward a conclusion that went against the basic tenet of epidemiology: perhaps this *was* that one-in-a-trillion case. If enough cases of anything occur, sooner or later more than one is going to happen in the same place at the same time. It was just a statistical truth. Besides, they had no other explanation.

He knew this was the worst thing to tell the families. They wouldn't accept it. They'd be torn between wanting to blame somebody and feeling guilty that they hadn't done something differently. But there was nothing to say except that these things happen. It's no one's fault.

He concluded his report and sent it off to Atlanta, where it was added to the bulging epidemic assistance file. As often as epidemiologists found the answer, they did not. It would always be that way; new mysteries would come along to replace the solved ones.

Bowen returned to collecting ticks.

Epilogue

. . .

On Dec. 14, 1982, Dr. Robert Segal signed the death certificates of Lisa Easley and Ashley McClendon. Segal and Aronson agreed that the deaths of these two babies should not get lost among the thousands of cases of SIDS. They listed the cause of death as "UNDETERMINED." Maybe other babies had died under similar circumstances somewhere else. Maybe it would happen again. Maybe someday someone would figure out why.

STUDY QUESTIONS

1. What is SIDS? Is SIDS a good explanation of the deaths in the "Day-Care Deaths" story? Why or why not?
2. How is the investigation in the "Day-Care Deaths" like playing the parlor game "Clue"?

Summary

Arguments are everywhere. We are always trying to convince someone of something: to vote for a particular candidate, to buy a certain product, to give permission to stay out all night after the prom, to accept that we didn't mean it when we insulted them. Studying the structure of arguments can help us become better reasoners and more convincing in presenting our point of view to others.

Arguments consist of premises and conclusions and often have clue words which tell us that a statement is intended to be a premise or intended to be a conclusion. Other times the clue words are implied but not stated, and sometimes even premises or the conclusion might not be explicitly stated. That is why it is a good idea to organize an argument into standard form, putting the premises first and the conclusion last, supplying any implicit claims as you do. Then you are in a better position to evaluate the argument.

Arguments can be deductive or inductive, depending on whether the speaker intends the conclusion to follow necessarily from the premises or to be only strongly supported by the premises. We will be learning a lot more about these logical connections of deduction and induction in the chapters that follow. The two stories from *The Decameron* by Boccaccio show how we use both of these types of arguments in our everyday lives. We hope you will not have to argue for your life like Melchizedek, but lawyers, diplomats, and even scientists may use arguments in life-threatening situations!

Explanations are another form of argument that help us live happier and healthier lives. Knowing why a particular event happened can help us repeat or not repeat the same actions. For an explanation to be helpful or useful to us, however, it cannot be circular. Knowing that the two infants in the day-care died of SIDS does not help us avoid future deaths. "The child's death is a mystery." "The child died of SIDS." They say the same thing. Two children dying of SIDS on the same day, in the same day-care center is more than a mystery. It's bizarre. It does not fit in with other things we believe about the likelihood of such an event's taking place. That is why it is so unsatisfying even if it is conversation ending.

Exercises

4–I

1. Bring in five examples of arguments from newspapers, magazines, or books. Try to find a variety of different kinds of arguments, some deductive, some inductive.
2. Explanations can take forms similar to those of arguments. One inductive argument form we talked about is the argument by analogy. Can you think any examples of explanations in that form, that is, an explanation that uses an analogy to aid our understanding?

3. Rewrite the following arguments, putting the premises first and the conclusion last. If there is an implicit premise, add it and circle it. If there is an implicit conclusion, add it and circle it.

   a) Also, what is simple cannot be separated from itself. The soul is simple; therefore, it cannot be separated from itself.

   b) Pure Schwalmbach's Baby Powder helps you feel good about yourself by keeping you feeling soft and smelling clean. It helps you come across to other people, too, because it helps bring out your best. Your skin looks soft and feels silky. And you smell so clean and natural. Now that you're older, haven't you got your own reasons for using Schwalmbach's Baby Powder?

   c) "How do you feel about the metric system?" he asked.
   "I'm opposed to it," I said. "Inalterably opposed to it."
   "But why?"
   "Because," I said, "I'm sick and tired of people fooling around with my habits. Why should I, at my advanced stage of life, have to learn to measure all over again in some strange, new system?"

   d) Why, then, did it all end in the Great Depression of the 1930s? The answer is that changes that imparted thrust to capitalism at the end of the nineteenth century slowly lost their vitality and relevance during the first quarter of the twentieth century. The trusts and monopolies, for instance, temporarily lessened but could not eliminate competition so that, as time went on, the great giants watched the unruly forces of the market once again invade their precincts.

   e) It is peculiar that we put such great emphasis on debating. As Richard Nixon found out, the mechanism whereby the candidates are asked by a panel of questioners to respond in turn to softball inquiries doesn't amount to debating at all. Candidates can simply memorize harmless answers, and if something unexpected comes up, they can politely beg off and give a speech.

   f) He'll drive recklessly only if he's upset—and he's not upset.

   g) Why are there not enough data? One reason is that the academics and international functionaries have too seldom gone into the field to collect them. The voluntary agencies in direct contact with local populations have made the ethical choice to devote their limited energies to relieving suffering, not collecting data.

   h) Economically, women are substantially worse off than men. They do not receive any pay for the work that is done in the home. As members of the labor force, their wages are significantly lower than those paid to men, even when they are engaged in similar work and have similar education backgrounds.

   i) Previously, the Pope had said that women may not be ordained because Christ, faced with the possibility of choosing women to be priests, did not do so, and the practice of the church today must model that of its founder.

   j) He's guilty. He's confessed.

   k) McDonald's advertisement: Our hot fudge sundaes are "just what your desire requires."

   l) The fetus does not have rights. Individual rights begin at birth with the creation of a new separate human being. Rights are a concept applicable to individuals, actual human beings, not merely a potential one.

4. Determine whether the following arguments are deductive or inductive. Be careful to pick out the conclusion before deciding.

   a) John held his cards loosely between his thumb and two fingers. That made it easy to arrange them in various combinations.

   b) John held his chopsticks between his thumb and forefinger. That left three fingers for holding the chopsticks steady.

   c) When John takes his girlfriend Hilda to the casino, he spends most of his time talking with his poker buddies. Hilda does not like to go with him.

d) Poker is not everyone's cup of tea. It takes patience and the ability to control one's expressions.

e) If John wins more than everyone else at the table, that will attract suspicion to him. Since he is winning more than others, he is attracting suspicion.

f) John says Table #5 is paying off. I played Table #5 and lost. I think John is lying.

g) Every Saturday John goes to the casino. John is on his way to the casino, since today is Saturday.

h) Hilda told John, "It's poker or me." John is not about to give up his poker, so Hilda is out of luck.

5. Consider the following arguments and decide whether you think the author of the argument intends it to be deductive reasoning or inductive reasoning.

a) Janet must have gone south for her vacation. She has a beautiful tan.

b) Although I couldn't have an abortion myself, I support that right for other women. The quality of life is important, and what kind of life do many unwanted children end up having?

c) Bible scholars found that most of Mark is reproduced in Matthew or Luke. They also found that where one departs from the order of events in Mark, the other usually retains the order in Mark. Therefore, they concluded that Matthew and Luke each used Mark as a source when composing his own gospel.

d) If John had asked me to the dance, then I would have gone. Since you didn't see me there, you know he didn't ask me.

e) The murder had to have been done by Mrs. White, Miss Scarlet, or Colonel Mustard. It wasn't Mrs. White or Colonel Mustard, so Miss Scarlet had to be the murderer.

f) Forty-five percent of the people surveyed are not happy with the job the president is doing. Thus, 45 percent of the American public is down on the president.

4–II

1. Distinguish logical warranting from factual warranting.

2. Explain why, in our daily lives, reasoning with probability is more common than reasoning with necessity.

3. Suppose you just bought a brand new Excalibur sports car. Today you go out to start it, and it does not start. You call the dealership, and their mechanic comes over and checks out the car. He tells you, "There's nothing wrong with the car. It's perfect. It just won't start. The warranty covers every mechanical and electrical defect but there are none. Some of the Excaliburs are like that. So there is nothing we can do for you. It just doesn't start." How would you react to this explanation?

4. Why is reasoning using analogies a very common practice in religious argument and discussion?

5. What problem do you see in the explanation and consequent advice given by a local computer columnist?

Q: All of a sudden, Windows Explorer does not provide the capability of creating a new folder on any drives or inside any of my folders. Any thoughts?

A: . . . there is an outside chance that you have created the maximum number of folders allowed in the C, or root, directory. If you think that that is the case, try reorganizing your data to nest folders under common topics. Example: If you have a Personal Letters folder, a Business Letters folder, and a My Club Letters folder, create a new folder and name it Letters. Then turn the other three folders into subfolders under Letters. All you need to do is drag and drop them into their new home.

II

Deductive Reasoning

Part I introduced you to some new concepts that we think are important to master to become a good critical thinker. These concepts start with open rational dialogue and the importance of language to thinking. Then we introduced the idea of warranting our statements by open rational dialogue and connecting them to other statements we believe that are already part of our web of belief. We warrant these statements to ourselves and also to others. The statements we find to be well-warranted we call factual statements. We test our webs of belief with the webs of beliefs of others, particularly the people in our communities. Part of what makes a community is its shared belief system. In general, we work toward consensus. In order to achieve a consensus, we warrant our claims to others. We might do this by repeating them à la Gertrude Stein, by shouting them, or by threats and intimidation. A better way to work toward a consensus is to warrant our beliefs with other statements in the form of an argument that consists of a set of supporting statements—the premises—and the statement being warranted or supported—the conclusion. We saw in the last chapter that there are two different kinds of arguments: those that necessarily imply the conclusion called deductive arguments and those that make their conclusion more probable but which do not guarantee it, called inductive arguments.

In the next two sections, we will work on developing the skills of recognizing good deductive and inductive arguments and sorting out and eliminating the bad forms of these two ways of reasoning. As in the development of any skills, it will take practice on your part to master them. The homework sections in this part are more drill-like. To be successful, you must do the homework with diligence. You cannot become a good critical thinker without effort, just as you cannot become a good basketball player without effort. Michael Jordan, perhaps the greatest basketball player of all time, was not a natural at basketball. He was cut from his high school basketball team. But that made him work all the harder to learn the skills he needed to be great.

5

Deductive Links

REASONING WITH NECESSITY

Generally we are happier when other people agree with the statements we make than when they disagree. When we think our audience might not agree with one of our statements or claims, we often try to support that claim by giving an argument. We could use arguments that involve either deductive reasoning (reasoning with necessity) or inductive reasoning (reasoning with probability) to support our claim. You might think that deductive reasoning (reasoning with necessity) is always preferable to reasoning with probability since the link between the premises and the conclusion of such an argument is a necessary one. Deductive reasoning, however, has an important limitation. While the link between the premises and the conclusion of a valid deductive argument is a necessary one, if the premises of the argument are not accepted as factual, the audience does not have to accept the conclusion as factual—despite its being linked with necessity to the premises—and therefore they may not be convinced. So while the linkage in a deductive argument is as logically strong as it can be, your argument may still not be convincing. This is why it is important to keep the dialogue open and ongoing. You may have to provide support for your premises as well.

Deductive reasoning is the basis of most mathematics. You are probably familiar with traditional Euclidian geometry, which is an excellent example of reasoning with necessity. In plane geometry, we begin by accepting certain statements as factual (axioms or definitions), and then determine through reasoning with necessity the postulates and theorems that follow logically from those accepted statements. The most prevalent contemporary example of deductive reasoning is the computer. Computers "reason with necessity" as they carry out the commands we give them. They calculate, they sort, and they combine. Every search engine uses the logical operators of deductive reasoning to combine words into patterns that are then sought throughout the Web. Computers are not nearly as well suited to reasoning with probability. For this reason, the artificial intelligence experts who have tried to make computers mimic the human mind, which reasons inductively much more frequently than deductively, have found this to be a much harder task than they first thought it would be.

The logical linking that occurs in deductive reasoning is called **logical consequence**, and when the conclusion is a logical consequence of the premises, we say that the argument has the property of **validity**. When arguments are valid, the relationship between the premises and the conclusion is such that the premises **guarantee** the conclusion. That is, *if* the premises are factual, the conclusion is factual. It is not necessary, however, that (all) the premises are factual for the argument to be valid. When an argument is valid, we can also say that the premises *logically imply* the conclusion. This strong relationship between premises and conclusions characterizes our reasoning in other areas besides mathematics. If you have ever read a legal contract or some other piece of legal reasoning, much of the reasoning will be in the form of valid deductive arguments. Political arguments are often pieces of deductive reasoning ("If you elect my opponent, then. . . ."). And we use deductive reasoning when we make decisions in our lives, in everything from playing board games like Clue to determining which candidate to vote for office ("If I vote for candidate X, then. . . .") Valid arguments make "good sense" to us because they are so logical! At the same time, they sometimes give us trouble because they can be used fallaciously, and sometimes we miss the mistake in the reasoning. Reasoning with necessity, however, is like arithmetic. When we use it, it is either right or wrong. So, it pays to study it in some detail.

The reading in this chapter is a piece of legal reasoning, an excerpt from the dissenting opinion of Justice Thurgood Marshall in the 1976 case, *Gregg v. Georgia*. In 1972, the Supreme Court held in *Furman v. Georgia* that the death penalty was unconstitutional because it was being applied in a capricious and discriminatory manner. Between 1972 and 1976 the state of Georgia established rules to guard against the discriminatory imposition of this sentence, so the Court was asked to reconsider the death penalty. The Court's decision was 7–2 that the death penalty is not inherently cruel and unusual punishment and is, therefore, not prohibited by the Constitution. Justices Marshall and Brennan dissented. The significance of the issue in this reading makes clear how important reasoning with necessity is in helping us to consider and decide important issues through warranting our claims with arguments.

DISSENTING OPINION IN *GREGG V. GEORGIA*

Thurgood Marshall

The two purposes that sustain the death penalty as non-excessive in the Court's view are general deterrence and retribution. In *Furman*, I canvassed the relevant data on the deterrent effect of capital punishment. The state of knowledge at that point, after

Excerpt, Thurgood Marshall, *Dissent in Gregg vs. Georgia*, 428 U.S. 153.

literally centuries of debate, was summarized as follows by a United Nations Committee:

> "It is generally agreed between the retentionists and abolitionists, whatever their opinions about the validity of comparative studies of deterrence, that the data which now exist show no correlation between the existence of capital punishment and lower rates of capital crime."

The available evidence, I concluded in *Furman*, was convincing that "capital punishment is not necessary as a deterrent to crime in our society." . . .

. . . The evidence reviewed in *Furman* remains convincing, in my view, that "capital punishment is not necessary as a deterrent to crime in our society." The justification for the death penalty must be found elsewhere.

The other principal purpose said to be served by the death penalty is retribution. The notion that retribution can serve as a moral justification for the sanction of death finds credence in the opinion of my Brothers STEWART, POWELL, and STEVENS. . . . It is this notion that I find to be the most disturbing aspect of today's unfortunate [decision].

The concept of retribution is a multifaceted one, and any discussion of its role in the criminal law must be undertaken with caution. On one level, it can be said that the notion of retribution or reprobation is the basis of our insistence that only those who have broken the law be punished, and in this sense the notion is quite obviously central to a just system of criminal sanctions. But our recognition that retribution plays a crucial role in determining who may be punished by no means requires approval of retribution as a general justification for punishment. It is the question whether retribution can provide a moral justification for punishment—in particular, capital punishment—that we must consider.

My Brothers STEWART, POWELL, and STEVENS offer the following explanation of the retributive justification for capital punishment:

> The instinct for retribution is part of the nature of man, and channeling that instinct in the administration of criminal justice serves an important purpose in promoting the stability of a society governed by law. When people begin to believe that organized society is unwilling or unable to impose upon criminal offenders the punishment they "deserve," then there are sown the seeds of anarchy—of self-help, vigilante justice, and lynch law.

This statement is wholly inadequate to justify the death penalty. As my Brother BRENNAN stated in *Furman*, "[t]here is no evidence whatever that utilization of imprisonment rather than death encourages private blood feuds and other disorders." It simply defies belief to suggest that the death penalty is necessary to prevent the American people from taking the law into their own hands.

In a related vein, it may be suggested that the expression of moral outrage through the imposition of the death penalty serves to reinforce basic moral values—that it marks some crimes as particularly offensive and therefore to be avoided. The argument is akin to a deterrence argument, but differs in that it contemplates the individual's shrinking from antisocial conduct, not because he fears punishment, but because he has been told in the strongest possible way that the conduct is wrong. This contention, like the previous one, provides no support for the death penalty. It is inconceivable that any individual concerned about conforming his conduct to what society says is "right" would fail to realize that murder is "wrong" if the penalty were simply life imprisonment.

The foregoing contentions—that society's expression of moral outrage through the imposition of the death penalty pre-empts the citizenry from taking the law into its own hands and reinforces moral values—are not retributive in the purest sense. They are essentially utilitarian in that they portray the death penalty as valuable because of its beneficial results. These justifications for the death penalty are inadequate because the penalty is, quite clearly I think, not necessary to the accomplishment of those results.

There remains for consideration, however, what might be termed the purely retributive justification for the death penalty—that the death penalty is appropriate, not because of its beneficial effect on society, but because the taking of the murderer's life is itself morally good. Some of the language of the opinion of my Brothers STEWART, POWELL, and STEVENS . . . appears positively to embrace this notion of retribution for its own sake as a justification for capital punishment. They state:

> [T]he decision that capital punishment may be the appropriate sanction in extreme cases is an expression of the community's belief that certain crimes are themselves so grievous an affront to humanity that the only adequate response may be the penalty of death.

They then quote with approval from Lord Justice Denning's remarks before the British Royal Commission on Capital Punishment:

> The truth is that some crimes are so outrageous that society insists on adequate punishment, because the wrong-doer deserves it, irrespective of whether it is a deterrent or not.

Of course, it may be that these statements are intended as no more than observations as to the popular demands that it is thought must be responded to in order to prevent anarchy. But the implication of the statements appears to me to be quite different— namely, that society's judgment that the murderer "deserves" death must be respected not simply because the preservation of order requires it, but because it is appropriate that society make the judgment and carry it out. It is this latter notion, in particular, that I consider to be fundamentally at odds with the Eighth Amendment. The mere fact that the community demands the murderer's life in return for the evil he has done cannot sustain the death penalty, for as JUSTICES STEWART, POWELL, and STEVENS remind us, "the Eighth Amendment demands more than that a challenged punishment be acceptable to contemporary society." To be sustained under the Eighth Amendment, the death penalty must "compor[t] with the basic concept of human dignity at the core of the Amendment;" the objective in imposing it must be "[consistent] with our respect for the dignity of [other] men." Under these standards, the taking of life "because the wrongdoer deserves it" surely must fail, for such a punishment has as its very basis the total denial of the wrongdoer's dignity and worth.

The death penalty, unnecessary to promote the goal of deterrence or to further any legitimate notion of retribution, is an excessive penalty forbidden by the Eighth and Fourteenth Amendments. I respectfully dissent from the Court's judgment upholding the [sentence] of death imposed upon the [petitioner in this case].

STUDY QUESTIONS

1. You may disagree with Marshall's argument. If so, construct a deductive argument of your own to support your conclusion. If you agree with it, what do you find compelling about it?
2. What do you think is most questionable in Marshall's argument? Why do you think that a majority of the justices did not agree with Marshall?

ANALYZING A DEDUCTIVE ARGUMENT

Sometimes, it is hard to see the deductive arguments in a larger body of text. They are surrounded by supporting ideas or even extraneous ideas. So it is helpful to put the argument into **standard form**. We have set out what we see as the main outline of Justice Marshall's argument and put it into standard argument form, and it turns out to be an often-used argument form that actually has a name. Study this argument and its form to see how the premises are **logically** linked to the conclusion.

> *Premise One:* If the death penalty is non-excessive (not cruel and unusual), then it must result in either deterrence (i.e., must make it less likely that others will commit the crime punished by death) or it must serve the purpose of retribution (i.e., must satisfy society's demand that offenders get the punishment they deserve) [from paragraph #1].
>
> *Premise Two:* The evidence reviewed in *Furman* is convincing that the death penalty is not necessary as a deterrent to crime in our society [from paragraphs #2 and #3].
>
> *Premise Three:* There is no constitutionally legitimate valid form of retribution that requires the death penalty [from paragraphs #3 through #6].
>
> *Conclusion:* Since the death penalty is unnecessary to promote the goal of deterrence or to further any legitimate notion of retribution, the death penalty is an excessive penalty [logically warranted by the combination of premises one through three].

When we consider Marshall's argument as a deductive argument, the argument is perfectly constructed. That is, it is constructed in such a way that its conclusion follows necessarily from its premises. The form of this deductive argument is actually one that is used quite frequently. It is called a **destructive dilemma**. In a destructive dilemma (an argument form often deployed in formal debating), you claim that either one thing or another is a necessary consequence of the point you wish to refute. You then show that neither of the consequences is plausible or desirable and by so doing you refute the point you wished to refute. That is, since neither consequence of the initial assumption is plausible or desirable, one is not justified in assuming it or supporting it. In the above decision, Marshall argues that in order for the death penalty to be legitimate it must have either deterrence or retribution as its necessary consequence. He then argues that since the death penalty results in neither, it is illegitimate. Even if you disagree with Marshall's conclusion, there is no fault in his reasoning. If you think that Marshall is mistaken in his belief that the death penalty ought to be considered an illegitimate punishment, then you will have to attack the alleged factual status of his premises, for the logic of the argument is beyond reproach.

VALIDITY AND LOGICAL IMPLICATION

The objective in deductive reasoning (reasoning with necessity), it will be recalled, is to give a **valid** argument. A logically valid argument is one where if the premises are regarded as factual then the conclusion must also be regarded as factual because of the logical linking present. Another way of saying this is to say that the premises **logically imply** the conclusion, or we could say that the conclusion is a **logical consequence** of the premises.

To return to our "Beatles were the greatest" example above, let us suppose that Tom intends to reason with necessity and wants to present a **valid** argument. What Tom needs is an argument with premises, which Joan accepts as factual and which necessarily supports his conclusion that the Beatles were the greatest musical artists of all time. What might such premises be? Tom might try, for example, the following argument:

> *PREMISE ONE*   If a musical artist (or group) had the largest amount of commercial success (air play, record sales, earnings, etc.), then he/she/they were the greatest musical artist(s) of all time.
>
> *PREMISE TWO*   The Beatles have had the largest amount of commercial success.
>
> *CONCLUSION*   Therefore, the Beatles were the greatest musical artists of all time.

Now if Joan regards Tom's premises as factual, then logically she must regard his conclusion as factual also, because that conclusion is logically warranted by those premises. In this case, Tom's conclusion is **logically implied** by his premises, which means that *if* his premises are factual then his conclusion *must* be factual also. The notion of **logical implication** may seem at first to be mysterious. "How," it might be asked, "can one statement cause another statement to be factual?" The answer to this question is that logical implication relies on the meanings of ordinary connecting words used in specific patterns to link statements together logically so that their factual nature is also linked. To see this, consider the next example that Tom might offer to Joan:

> *PREMISE ONE*   **Either** the Beatles **or** Mozart are/is the greatest musical artist(s) of all time.
>
> *PREMISE TWO*   Since Mozart was not commercially successful, he is not the greatest musical artist of all time.
>
> *CONCLUSION*   Therefore, the Beatles are the greatest musical artists of all time.

We can see that if we regard Tom's premises as factual, we must regard Tom's conclusion as factual also. The premises logically imply the conclusion. It is also clear that Tom's argument relies on the meaning of the ordinary English words "either" and "or" used in a certain pattern. When we say "either A or B" and then say "and not A," this logically implies "B." There is really nothing very mysterious about this. Suppose I tell

Aristotle called this logical difficulty the Law of the Excluded Middle.

you that I will be either in my office or in Room 2 at 4 PM on Tuesday, and later I tell you that I will not be in my office at all on Tuesday. My statements about my whereabouts on Tuesday together logically imply that at 4 PM on Tuesday I will be in Room 2 and you would know that this is where you can find me. This is just the way the words I uttered, "either" and "or," work when they occur in the patterns I used. The traditional name of arguments in this pattern is disjunctive argument. In the first argument, the logical words are "if" and "then." These little words do the work and make the argument valid.

All languages contain words that are logically significant when used in certain recognized patterns. We use these logically significant words and patterns when we want to establish very strong links between statements, logical implication being the strongest possible link. Obviously, the person who has mastered the use of these logical links has a big advantage when it comes to expressing her ideas clearly and forcefully.

Notice again that the question of **logical warranting** is separate from the question of **factual warranting**. This means Tom's conclusion is logically warranted by his premises even if we do not accept his premises as factual. If we reject any of Tom's premises as nonfactual, however, we need not accept his conclusion as factual, even if it is logically implied by his premises.

Now let us return to Joan and Tom. Suppose that Joan rejects Tom's conclusion because she doesn't accept one of the premises that supports it, say premise one, which claims a direct connection between commercial success and musical greatness. Perhaps on Joan's view, musical greatness depends on how long a time an artist has been a major influence on other musicians. If Joan were to offer a logical counterargument, it might be the following:

PREMISE ONE   If an artist(s) has/have been a major influence on other musicians for the longest period of time, then that artist(s) is/are the greatest musical artist(s) of all time.

PREMISE TWO   Mozart has been a major influence on other musicians for the longest period of time.

CONCLUSION   Therefore, Mozart is the greatest musical artist of all time.

Just as Joan should accept Tom's conclusion *if* she accepts his premises, so now Tom should accept Joan's conclusion *if* he accepts her premises. This is because Joan has also come up with an argument the conclusion of which is logically implied by its premises. So if Joan's premises are factual, then her conclusion is also factual.

Like Tom's first argument, Joan's argument is an example of a conditional argument. Conditional arguments always contain at least one conditional statement, an *if . . . then* statement. Conditional statements are our main language tool for describing and establishing conditional relationships. Conditional relationships exist whenever one thing is either necessary (required) or sufficient (enough) for another. In Joan's argument the conditional premise, "If an artist(s) has been a major influence on other musicians for the longest period of time, then that artist(s) is the greatest musical artist(s) of all time," says that being a major influence on other musicians for the longest period of time is a sufficient condition (is enough) for being the greatest musical artist of all time. So if we accept this statement as factual and if we also accept as factual that Mozart has been a major influence on other musicians for the longest period of time, then we would also have to accept as factual Joan's conclusion that Mozart was the greatest musical artist of all time.

Joan, like Tom, has presented us with a logical implication and a valid argument to support her belief that Mozart is the greatest musical artist of all time. Since *both* Tom's and Joan's conclusions are logically implied by their premises, *both* would have to be regarded as factual if their premises are factual. We can see that it is unlikely that Joan and Tom are going to resolve their difference of opinion about music—unless they first come to some agreement about the various factual claims made in the premises of their arguments.

One way they might try to come to an agreement about the facts is to offer further arguments, either necessary or probable, in support of the factual claims in their premises. "But," it might be objected, "if the arguments which are supposed to establish or warrant our factual claims themselves depend on further factual claims, won't we need to warrant those factual claims with even more arguments which will require further factual claims, which will require more arguments, which will require further factual claims, and so on and so forth forever and ever?" In reality, our attempts to establish statements as factual usually end when we arrive at statements which, for whatever reason, are not called into question. In the music dispute between Tom and Joan, a stalemate can likely be averted only if they can first agree that some statement in one of their arguments is warranted and should be considered factual.

The notions of valid argument, logical implication, and arguing with necessity can be further understood by considering this example about Tony. Suppose Tony is a tiger. Which of the following statements are logically implied by that supposition (premise)?

1. Tony does not like carrots.
2. It is not the case that Tony is not a tiger.
3. Tony is either a tiger or a mouse.

Although you might think that "Tony does not like carrots" follows from the claim that Tony is a tiger, it is not **logically implied** by it. For us to regard "Tony does not like carrots" as logically implied we would need an additional factual statement, "Tigers do not like carrots," which we do not have. Statement #2 is logically implied by "Tony is a tiger" because it is the denial of "Tony is a tiger," which is just to say that Tony *is* a tiger. It may surprise you, but statement #3 is also logically implied by

"Tony is a tiger" because, although we know Tony is not a mouse, all that is required for statement #3 to be factual is that either Tony be a tiger or Tony be a mouse. Both are not required. And since Tony is a tiger is a factual statement (our original supposition), "Tony is either a tiger or a mouse" must be factual.

Validity is sometimes a hard concept to grasp because it cannot be defined in a way that does not presuppose some logical insight, but once you have it you somehow know that you do. Sometimes, it can be seen more easily by looking at arguments that occur in the form of **syllogisms**. This is one of the oldest deductive argument forms and was studied by Aristotle in ancient Greece. Syllogisms are about the connections between sets of things with certain properties, and they generally have two premises and a conclusion. Syllogisms are discussed again in Chapter 6. They can be very useful in helping us to understand validity and logical consequence. Consider the following two syllogisms:

1. *All women are nuns.*
   Lady Gaga is a woman.
   Therefore, Lady Gaga is a nun.
2. *All nuns are women.*
   Sr. Teresa is a nun.
   Therefore, Sr. Teresa is a woman.

Do the premises of the first argument guarantee its conclusion? That is, if the premises are considered factual, must one then consider the conclusion factual? Clearly if all women are nuns and Lady Gaga is a woman, then she *must* be a nun. The argument is valid even if we do not accept the conclusion as factual (or true). The reason the argument can be valid but not have a true conclusion is that one of the premises is surely not true. [In logic, it is more common to speak of "true" and "false" as opposed to "factual" and "non-factual." That is, in logic there are only two options that can be assigned to a statement, true and false. In our own lives we are not always so certain about what is factual (true) and non-factual (false). For convenience in this section, we will adopt the vocabulary common to deductive logic.] In the second argument, it is clear that the conclusion follows from the premises—but knowing the truth of the conclusion is not what determines the argument's validity. The two arguments have exactly the same form. If #1 is valid, so is #2 and vice versa.

Consider another argument in the same form as the two above:

All widgets are gidgets

All gidgets are smidgets

Therefore, all widgets are smidgets.

If you think this argument is nonsense, it certainly is—but it is also valid. To see this, notice that it is in exactly the same form as the two arguments above. This silly argument makes it even more clear that validity is not the same as truth. A valid argument may have premises that are true or false, and it may have a true or false conclusion. What a valid argument *cannot* have is true premises and a false conclusion. What this means is that if an argument is valid and the conclusion false, then at least one of the premises is false.

Summary

In this chapter, we have discussed the basics of deductive reasoning or reasoning with necessity. Our language, whether spoken, written, or read, contains logically significant words—words like *if, then, either, or, not,* and *all.* Using these words and others like them, we can construct arguments that attempt to forge a logically necessary link between premises and conclusion. When the outcome is successful, we have a **valid deductive argument**—one where if you accept the premises, you must also accept the conclusion. We have also found that the logical validity of an argument is completely independent of the factual status of its premises. In other words, if someone has just presented you with an argument you recognize as logically valid but you don't like or accept the conclusion, then you need either to find a factual error in one of the premises (prove one of the premises false) or to change your mind and learn to like or accept the conclusion!

Exercises

5–I

1. Who, in your opinion, is the greatest musical artist of all time? Write a *deductive* argument to support your claim in which the premises logically imply the conclusion.
2. Suppose someone questions the premises you used in your deductive argument in exercise one. Now write an argument(s) to support those premises. Tell whether your new arguments are necessary or probable.
3. Suppose, as probably happened, that the other Supreme Court Justices questioned Justice Marshall's second premise, in *Dissenting Opinion in Gregg v. Georgia,* about the deterrent effect of the death penalty and his claim that no human being deserves to be put to death. How would you help Justice Marshall defend his premise? Write at least two arguments that use logical implication to support premise two.
4. Tell whether the following arguments are valid or invalid:

   a. Some women are nuns.

   Sr. Teresa is a woman.

   Therefore, Sr. Teresa is a nun.

   b. Some women are nuns.

   Lady Gaga is a woman.

   Therefore, Lady Gaga is a nun.

   c. All cats have four legs.

   All dogs have four legs.

   Therefore, all cats are dogs.

   d. All cats have four legs.

   All four-legged animals are dogs.

   Therefore, all cats are dogs.

5. Explain how truth and validity are related in each of the arguments in #4.

5–II

1. We saw that from "Tony is a tiger" it logically follows that Tony is either a tiger or a mouse. How many possible conclusions, then, are logically implied by "Tony is a tiger" (or any other claim)?
2. What limitations do you see to reasoning with necessity?

6

Deductive Argument Forms

LOGIC

Deductive argument forms, which we use when we reason with necessity, are part of our natural reasoning processes. We use these patterns in our everyday reasoning without even thinking about them. They are an important aspect of good critical thinking—but they are only a small part of it. Most of our everyday reasoning is reasoning with probability or inductive reasoning rather than reasoning with necessity. When we do reason deductively or with necessity, it is often intermixed with inductive reasoning. Mathematics and computer programming, as mentioned above, are examples of reasoning which more exclusively involve deduction rather than induction. But, although deductive reasoning occurs less frequently than inductive reasoning in our everyday reasoning, its importance to detailed, lengthy argument in such areas as law can make our deductive mistakes costly ones. So, it is helpful to learn some common valid deductive argument forms to avoid making mistakes and to avoid being misled by the mistakes of others.

Formal deductive reasoning can be called logic, formal logic, or deductive logic. *Logic* comes from the Greek word *logos*, the most basic meaning of which is "word." Logic refers to the use of patterns of words, namely, patterns of words that are considered to be valid arguments—where the links between the premises and the conclusions are necessary. If symbols like "x" and "y" or "P" and "Q" are used instead of words, then the patterns are referred to as symbolic logic. Symbols are helpful because they allow us to avoid the confusions of language that we talked about in Chapter 2. We will use some simple symbols in this chapter to avoid these confusions and to make the patterns of the valid arguments clearer and easier to recall. You may be surprised that the logical words of our language are actually the little words, words like *and*, *or*, *if . . . then*, *all*, and *some*. These little words do most of the work in our reasoning with necessity.

SOME COMMON VALID ARGUMENTS FORMS

There is a group of simple forms or patterns that we all—as rational people—agree are patterns of valid arguments. Formal reasoning consists of following these argument patterns which have long been accepted by philosophers and logicians as valid, so that if the premises are considered factual the conclusion must also be considered factual. As we noted above, logicians usually use the terms *true* and *false* rather than *factual* and *not factual*. We will use "true" and "false" as well as "factual" and "not factual" in this chapter, partly for convenience and partly because in symbolic logic "true" and "false" are merely assigned values and generally do not refer to actual beliefs about the world. There are two fundamental assumptions in formal reasoning. The first is that any argument we might encounter that has the same pattern as one of the accepted valid argument patterns is also valid. And the second is that valid argument patterns may be combined into larger arguments which are then also valid.

There are several systems of formal reasoning and they vary in the way they symbolize valid argument patterns and they also vary somewhat in the number of valid argument patterns they contain. Consequently, all logic textbooks are not alike. Some logic textbooks can even contain more than one system of formal reasoning. All of these systems of formal reasoning, however, try to capture the same fundamental patterns we use when we reason with necessity in our ordinary rational discourse and try to make them clearer by making them more explicit.

We are going to look at the definitions or forms of 12 common formal reasoning patterns. Seven are valid but five are invalid and are often mistakenly used by people who think they are using a valid form. All of them should be somewhat familiar to you. It is helpful to know and to recognize these valid and invalid patterns so that you can check your own or someone else's reasoning when you are in doubt about the validity of an argument. For example, you may find that you accept the premises of an argument as factual statements, the linkage between the premises and the conclusion seem to be necessary, yet you find yourself unable to accept the conclusion as a factual statement. Since **a valid argument cannot have all factual premises and a non-factual conclusion**, in such a case either one or more of the premises is not a factual statement (or true) or the linkage between the premises and the conclusion is not a necessary one or both. Knowing the forms of valid and invalid arguments will enable you to check the presence or absence of that link. In the following paragraphs, we will examine three groups of deductive argument patterns—conditionals, disjunctions, and categoricals—and we will use symbols instead of words to express the deductive patterns more clearly.

Patterns of Conditional Arguments

One group of argument patterns involves conditional statements, statements in English that express or establish conditional relations between things. One conditional relation is that of being a sufficient condition. To say "If P, then Q" is to say that P is a **sufficient condition** for Q, which is to say that having P is adequate for having Q also. To put it still another way, if P is a sufficient condition for Q, if you have P, then you have Q. That is what being a sufficient condition means: Every time we have P, we have Q.

The valid argument pattern which depends on this relation of sufficient condition is called **modus ponens**. This name may be unfamiliar to you, but it is a very familiar pattern. Modus ponens is defined:

If P, then Q.

P

Therefore, Q

"P" and "Q" each stand for a description of an event or set of circumstances. It does not matter what these circumstances are. As long as P is sufficient for Q, if you have P, then you have Q. For example, suppose Mary says, "If Paul invites me to the dance, then I'll go." Furthermore, suppose that Paul does invite Mary to the dance. You would expect, then, to see Mary at the dance. Paul's invitation is a sufficient condition for Mary's going, and he has invited her. This pattern is perfectly clear to us. We use it all the time. All arguments in this pattern are valid arguments: If P then Q, P, therefore Q. That is what being a **sufficient condition** means.

The other important conditional relation is a **necessary condition**. To say that Q is a necessary condition for P is to say that you cannot have P without Q. Two ways of expressing this relation in English are "P only if Q" and "Not P unless Q." Both of these English sentences say that Q is a necessary condition for P. Without Q, there can be no P. Q is necessary for P. It is important to realize that every time we establish one of these two conditional relations, necessary or sufficient, we actually establish both of them. That is, **if P is a sufficient condition for Q, then Q is a necessary condition for P**. You can see this clearly by looking at the Paul and Mary example again. If Paul's inviting Mary to the dance is a sufficient condition for Mary's going to the dance, then when he asks her, she will say "Yes." So P cannot happen without Q's happening. Mary's going to the dance is, therefore, a necessary condition for Paul's asking her. If Mary does not go with Paul, we can assume that Paul did not ask her. This gives us our second valid argument pattern called **modus tollens.** The definition of modus tollens is:

If P, then Q

Not Q

Therefore, not P

That is, if P is a sufficient condition for Q, Q is a necessary condition for P. So if we do not have Q, we cannot have P because a necessary condition for having P, which is to say Q, is missing.

We have seen that if P is a sufficient condition for Q then Q must be a necessary condition for P. This means that there are several ways we can express this conditional relationship in English:

If P, then Q

P implies Q

P only if Q

Not P unless Q

All of these English sentences express the assertion "P is a sufficient condition for Q" and the assertion that "Q is a necessary condition of P." The best way to master the definitions of modus ponens, modus tollens, and the various expressions in English of the relationships of necessary and sufficient conditions (and the other definitions of valid arguments which follow) is to think through the meanings of these English sentences until it is clear to you that they all express the same logical relationship. Then memorize them, being careful to get the Ps and the Qs in the right places, so you do not have to reason them through each time you encounter them. (Logicians like to say this is where the expression "Mind your Ps and Qs" comes from!) In general, memorization is the opposite of good critical thinking, but here memorization is a convenient short-hand. It makes the reasoning go faster and helps to avoid mistakes—just like memorizing a mathematical formula does.

Suppose, again, that Mary says, "If Paul asks me, I will go to the dance." And suppose we know that Mary did go to the dance. Can we conclude that she went with Paul? This version of the story of Mary, Paul, and the dance would have the following *invalid* form:

> If P then Q
>
> Q
>
> Therefore, P

This form is invalid because although we know that Q is a **necessary** condition for P, so if Mary wasn't at the dance we could conclude that Paul did not ask her, it is not a **sufficient** condition for P. Thus from the fact that we observe Mary at the dance, we cannot conclude that Paul asked her. For all we know, she may have gone with Archibald or Marlon. So, the conditional statement "If P then Q" plus the presence of "Q," do not imply "P." Similarly, all arguments in this same argument form are invalid and are known as the **Fallacy of Affirming the Consequent** (FAC).

Suppose we know that Paul did not ask Mary to the dance. Can we now conclude that Mary is not at the dance? The form of this argument is the following *invalid* form:

> If P then Q
>
> Not P
>
> Therefore, not Q

This form is invalid because although we know that P is a **sufficient** condition for Q (if Paul asks Mary, she will go), we do not know whether P is a **necessary** condition for Q. So we know nothing about what happens if Paul doesn't ask Mary. Mary could go with someone else. All instances of this argument form are invalid and are known as the **Fallacy of Denying the Antecedent** (FDA).

Let's look at some more examples of reasoning which involve sufficient and necessary conditions to practice using these valid argument patterns.

> Example 1 If the Eagles win the Superbowl, then the Cardinals don't.
>
> The Cardinals do win the Superbowl.
>
> What about the Eagles?

Example 2   If the Eagles win the Superbowl, then the Cardinals don't.
The Cardinals don't win the Superbowl.

What about the Eagles?

Example 3   If the Eagles win the Superbowl, then the Cardinals don't.
The Eagles don't win the Superbowl.

What about the Cardinals?

Example 4   If the Eagles win the Superbowl, then the Cardinals don't.
The Eagles do win the Superbowl.

What about the Cardinals?

The answer to the question at the end of each example is easy to determine if we pay attention to the valid argument forms modus ponens and modus tollens, which are the primary patterns of conditional arguments—arguments that contain "if . . . then . . ." statements. If you look carefully at example #1, you will notice that the second premise is a denial of the Q statement in the conditional statement, or, as logicians say, the **consequent** of the conditional. (If "Q" is "the Cardinals do not win the Superbowl," then "Not Q" is "the Cardinals do win the Superbowl.") The two premises, then, are in the form of **modus tollens** and, consequently, we know that P cannot occur. The Eagles do not win the Superbowl. It is helpful to put the argument into more symbolic form, using "Ps" and "Qs" instead of words, to see that it is the valid argument form, modus tollens:

If P then Q

Not Q

Therefore, not P

The second example looks similar but be careful. It is not the same. In the second example, the second premise is simply Q. "If P, then Q" and "Q" is *not* one of our valid argument patterns. Consequently, we cannot say anything about whether the Eagles win the Superbowl. Maybe they do, maybe they don't. Maybe the 49ers win or the Redskins. There is no **necessary** link between the two premises and the fate of the Eagles. This form of invalid conditional argument is the FAC. The general form of this invalid argument is:

If P then Q

Q

Therefore, P

The third example looks something like modus ponens but is clearly not modus ponens because the second premise asserts "Not P" instead of "P." (Logicians call "P" the **antecedent**.) From this argument, we cannot know the fate of the Cardinals. The Eagles' winning is a sufficient condition for the Cardinals' not winning but it is not a necessary condition. The Cardinals may win the Superbowl or they may not. The premises do not give us sufficient information to conclude anything about the fate of the Cardinals. There is no necessary link between the two premises of this argument and its conclusion. So the third example has, like the second, a fallacious form. In this case, the form is the FDA. The general form of this invalid argument is:

If P then Q

Not P

Therefore, not Q

The fourth example is obviously in the pattern of **modus ponens**. The Eagles' winning is sufficient for the Cardinals' not winning and the Eagles do win, so the Cardinals do not. The general form of this valid argument is:

If P then Q

P

Therefore, Q

The pattern of modus ponens seems so much a part of our common everyday reasoning that we do not think about it when we are using it. But every now and then, we are not sure about our own or another person's reasoning. By knowing which of these patterns are valid and which are not, we can check our reasoning and make sure that we are reasoning correctly.

Another very common pattern of formal reasoning using conditionals is the **pure hypothetical argument** (sometimes referred to as hypothetical syllogism). For example, suppose Mary says, "If Paul asks me to the dance, then I'll go with him. If I go with Paul, then I won't go with Ron. So if Paul asks me, then I won't go with Ron." In the pure hypothetical argument, all the premises are hypothetical or conditional statements, and so is the conclusion. We define pure hypothetical argument as having the pattern:

If P, then Q

If Q, then R.

Therefore, if P, then R.

Pure hypothetical arguments can have a longer chain of premises than two and will be valid as long as this pattern is continued. You probably have heard this pattern being used by politicians, for example, "If my opponent is elected, then . . .," etc. until some horrible consequent is claimed to follow.

Disjunctive Argument Forms

The **disjunctive argument** is another common valid argument pattern. We often use it, especially when we are trying to make a decision. Mary says to herself, for instance, "I don't know with whom to go to the dance, Paul or Ron. They have both asked me. Which will it be? I don't think I really want to go with Ron. So, I guess I'll go with Paul." The general form of the valid disjunctive argument is

P or Q.

Not Q.

Therefore, P.

Is Calvin Lying?

Calvin and Hobbes © 1994 Waterson. Reprinted with permission of UNIVERSAL PRESS SYNDICATE. All rights reserved.

There is a similar but usually invalid form of disjunctive argument, which has the following general form:

P or Q

P

Therefore, not Q

The above form of the disjunctive argument is often invalid because it assumes that P and Q cannot both be true. However, the ordinary use of *either/or* is equivalent in meaning to "one or the other and possibly both." For example, you would not think that I lied to you in saying "If you try to call me on Tuesday, I'll either be in Newark or in Trenton" if you later found out that I visited both places on the day in question. So, if you somehow learned that I had been seen in Trenton on Tuesday, you couldn't logically conclude that I was not also in Newark on the same day. Like the pure hypothetical argument, the disjunctive argument can be longer and give the appearance of being more complicated, but the definition of the logical linkage is still the same.

A familiar example of the disjunctive argument is the detective trying to solve a murder. If he has five murder suspects, then he will try to eliminate possible suspects until he has only one who is presumed to be the murderer. If you ever played the game Clue, you did this yourself: If the murder was done by either A or B or C or D or E (Colonel Plum, Miss Scarlet, Mr. Green, etc.), and it wasn't A or B or C or D, then it has to have been done by E. The necessary link between the premises of the disjunctive argument and its conclusion is quite obvious to us. Where we sometimes make mistakes in our disjunctive reasoning is when we think we have considered all the possibilities and we have not. With Clue we know how many possible suspects there are but the professional detective does not.

Categorical Argument Forms

The final formal reasoning patterns that we will define here are as familiar as those we have already looked at. They are called **categorical arguments**. The most well-known categorical argument is probably "All men are mortal, Socrates is a man, therefore, Socrates is mortal," which everyone has heard of and which everyone knows is a valid argument. The general form of this categorical argument is the following:

All As are Bs.

All Bs are Cs.

Therefore, all As are Cs.

The argument about Socrates can be seen to be a categorical argument if we think of "Socrates" as standing for the class or group of all things identical with Socrates, which is how logicians have traditionally thought of it.

The necessary linkage between the premises and the conclusion of this argument is easily seen. In many other categorical arguments, the logical links between the premises are not so easily seen, and so various techniques have been developed to help determine the validity of categorical arguments. One such technique is that of using pictures or diagrams called Venn Diagrams after the mathematician who first introduced them. In this technique, one begins by drawing three overlapping circles (see Figure 6–1) labeled A, B, and C—one for each of the terms (A, B, and C) contained in the three premises of a standard three-statement categorical argument. The next step is to draw the premises of the argument onto the three circle diagram. This may sound difficult, but it is actually quite simple. For example the statement "All As are Bs" implies that "there are no As that are not Bs," so we draw this by crossing out with lines the area of the "A" circle that doesn't overlap the "B" circle, showing that this part of the A circle is empty (see Figure 6–2).

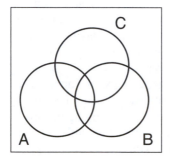

FIGURE 6–1

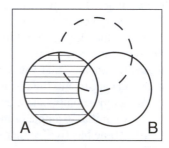

FIGURE 6–2

Similarly, to draw "All Bs are Cs," we cross out that part of the "B" circle that doesn't overlap the "C" circle, showing that this part of the diagram is also empty (see Figure 6–3). The final step is to see if the conclusion of the categorical argument, "All As are Cs," can be read from the diagram. If the conclusion of the categorical argument can be read from the diagram onto which the premises have been previously drawn, the argument is valid (showing that the conclusion follows necessarily from the premises). When we look at the argument we have diagramed (see Figure 6–4), we see that we can read the conclusion—"All As are Cs"—from the diagram. We can read "All As are Cs" because, when we look at Figure 6–4, we see that the "A" circle is crossed out except for the part within the "C" circle. So we can conclude that there are no As that are not Cs, or in other words, "All As are Cs." Since we can read the conclusion of the categorical argument from our Venn diagram, we have shown that the argument is a valid one.

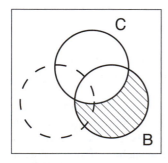

FIGURE 6–3

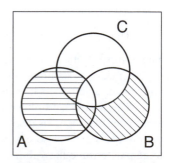

FIGURE 6–4

There are many categorical arguments, some of them valid, some invalid. It is worthwhile to look at a couple of very common invalid or fallacious categorical arguments. The two following invalid categorical arguments are very frequently encountered:

All As are Bs	All As are Bs
All As are Cs	All Cs are Bs
Therefore, all Bs are Cs	Therefore, all As are Cs

In Figure 6–5 through Figure 6–10, these arguments are diagramed using Venn diagrams, and both can readily be seen to be invalid since the conclusion of neither argument can be read from the completed diagrams (see Figure 6–7 and Figure 6–10).

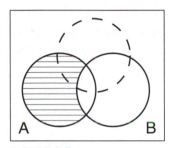

FIGURE 6–5

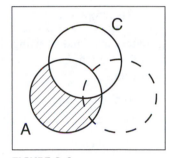

FIGURE 6–6

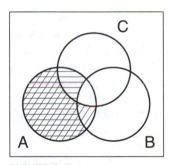

FIGURE 6–7

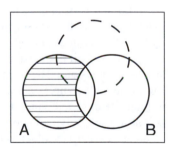

FIGURE 6–8

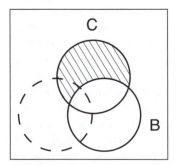

FIGURE 6–9

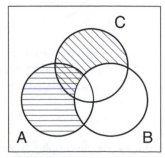

FIGURE 6–10

The simple valid arguments we have defined and examined above are part of our everyday reasoning. We use them frequently. They give us more power in reasoning than may be apparent from their simplicity because they can be combined to create more complicated valid arguments. For example, we can combine modus ponens and disjunctive argument to form a more complicated pattern which actually has a name of its own, **constructive dilemma**. Here is the definition of constructive dilemma. Look at it closely to see that it is a combination of the two arguments we have already introduced:

A or B

If A, then C

If B, then D

Therefore, C or D

Debaters are fond of using this valid argument to set the stage for leading you out of the dilemma they have created for you! We could also have a **destructive dilemma**:

Not A or not B

If C, then A

If D, then B

Therefore, not C or not D

Formal reasoning or logic is a basic component of good critical reasoning. In many ways, it is the easiest component because the conclusions either follow necessarily from the premises or they do not. We only have to follow the forms or patterns carefully, and we will not make reasoning mistakes about the links between the premises and the conclusions. The forms of the valid arguments are not very complex, but we can make very complex arguments by combining them or by stringing them together in long chains of reasoning. Formal reasoning is fun and useful, and sometimes it can be put to use resolving major issues which many human beings have pondered—like whether God exists—which is the topic of the reading in this chapter.

This selection is a version of a very famous argument by St. Anselm who is trying to convince others to accept as factual the belief that God exits. The argument is so famous that it has a name, Anselm's Ontological Argument. *Ontological* comes from the Greek word *ontos,* which means *to be* or *to exist*. This is an argument about the being or existence of God. It is different from most other arguments about God's being or existence (or the existence of any other being) because it does not use any premises which are about experience. It uses premises which are about the meanings of words, in particular, the word *God*. What Anselm is saying, in effect, is if you accept his definition of God, then you must also accept his conclusion that God necessarily exists because of the necessary links between the premises and the conclusion. (This particular version of Anselm's argument comes from a discussion of the argument by the philosopher Norman Malcolm.) The argument is very short, but you will probably want to read it several times.

ANSELM'S ONTOLOGICAL ARGUMENT

Norman Malcolm

1. Let me summarize the proof. If God, a being greater than which cannot be conceived, does not exist then He cannot *come* into existence. For if He did He would either have been *caused* to come into existence or have *happened* to come into existence, and in either case He would be a limited being, which by our conception of Him He is not. Since He cannot come into existence, if He does not exist His existence is impossible. If He does exist He cannot come into existence (for the reasons given), nor can He cease to exist, for nothing could cause Him to cease to exist nor could it just happen that He ceased to exist. So if God exists His existence is necessary. Thus God's existence is either impossible or necessary. It can be the former only if the concept of such a thing is self-contradictory or in some way logically absurd. Assuming that this is not so, it follows that He necessarily exists.

STUDY QUESTIONS

1. What is the first premise of Anselm's argument? How does Anselm justify this premise?
2. What is the conclusion?
3. Do you think Anselm's argument is successful? Why or why not?
4. Do you see any patterns of reasoning which are described above in Anselm's argument?

ANSELM'S ONTOLOGICAL ARGUMENT

Anselm's ontological argument is the most famous argument that tries to prove God's existence only from the definition of God, without reference to experience. There are other arguments which also try to do this, but none has generated as much interest as Anselm's. The philosophical questions it raises have intrigued philosophers since Anselm first formulated it in the eleventh century. The version of it that you read, for example, comes from an article on the argument by the twentieth-century philosopher Norman Malcolm. Our focus here is only on the logical structure of the argument, but you may want to think about the force of the argument in general and whether one can prove the existence of God—or any other thing—simply by reasoning about its definition.

To look at the logical structure, we will set out the reasoning explicitly, from the first premise through to the conclusion. Keep in mind as you read this that you are reading our version of Malcolm's version of Anselm's argument. You may see other

Excerpt from Norman Mahler, "Anselm's Ontological Arguments," *Philosophical Review,* 69 (1960), 49–50.

accounts of Anselm's argument that are somewhat different in structure. All of these accounts, however, are trying to clarify a very interesting but challenging argument about a question which many people ask: whether there is good reason to believe that God exists.

The Argument:

1. If God, a being so great that no greater being can be thought, does not exist, he cannot come into existence.

   > Argument for premise (1): If he did come into existence, he would be caused, or he would just have happened (by chance), and then he would be limited. But God, by definition, is not limited. [If God were caused, then He would be dependent on that which caused Him. If He happened by chance, then He would be just an accident, a bit of luck.]

2. Therefore, if God does not exist, his existence is impossible. (Since he cannot come into existence or have ceased.)
3. And if God exists, his existence is necessary.
4. God either does or does not exist.
5. Therefore, God's existence is either impossible or necessary.
6. God's existence is not impossible since the concept of God is not inconsistent.
7. Therefore, God's existence is necessary.

Now we will look at the structure still more explicitly, looking for the valid argument patterns we have defined above. The purpose of the first premise is to rule out the possibility that God's existence is contingent, like the existence of other things in the world. That is, most things in the world do not have to exist or happen. They could have not existed, or they could have not happened. They exist or happen because the right set of causal circumstances came together, but it is possible those circumstances could have not occurred. Your existence, for example, is contingent. If your parents had never met, then you would not exist. To be contingent is to be dependent on those causal circumstances coming together.

Anselm assumes but does not explicitly state, as can be seen from the rest of his argument, that existence is either necessary, impossible, or contingent, because he goes on to reason that if God's existence is not contingent, then it must be either necessary or impossible. We can symbolize this implicit argument:

Either N or I or C.

Not C.

Therefore, N or I.

This is clearly an example of **disjunctive argument**. Now we will look more closely at his argument for "Not C." If God's existence is contingent, then God would be dependent on the right causal circumstances coming together. But then God would be limited, and God would not be that "being greater than which cannot be conceived" because we could then conceive of a being like God but without this dependence and limitation. But God is God. That is, we assume that God is that being greater than which cannot be conceived. Let's look at a simplified version of the structure of this argument in support of premise (1):

If C, then not G. (If God's existence is contingent, then God is not God.)

G [Not G] (But God is God, that being greater than which cannot be conceived.)

Therefore, not C. (God's existence is not contingent.)

You can now see this argument is an example of **modus tollens**.

Let's look at the structure of the argument as a whole:

1. If G and not E (E = God exists), then not C.
   - [(1a)   If C, then not G.
   - (1b)   G
   - (1c)   Therefore, not C.
   - (1d)   Either N or I or C.
   - (1e)   Not C.
   - (1f)   Therefore, either N or I.]
2. If not E, then I. (If God does not exist, then his existence is impossible.)
3. If E, then N. (If God does exist, then his existence is necessary.)
4. Either E or not E. (God exists or he does not exist. There are no other alternatives.)
5. Therefore, either I or N. (God's existence is either impossible or necessary.)
6. Not I. (God's existence is not impossible, since the concept is consistent and not self-contradictory.)
7. Therefore, N. (God's existence is necessary.)

By symbolizing the argument in this way, we can see that premises (2)–(5) form a **constructive dilemma**. Lines (5)–(7) are a **disjunctive argument**. Notice that one line of argument (in this case line 5) can be a conclusion of one valid argument and a premise of another. That way we can create long, significant pieces of formal reasoning. By combining these arguments into one longer argument, Anselm has argued that *if* we assume that God is a being so great that no greater being can be thought of [premise (1)] and that this concept or definition of God is not inconsistent [premise (6)], God exists and He exists necessarily.

We can see from this example that simple valid arguments can be used to prove very interesting conclusions. That is, if the premises are regarded as factual (i.e., we accept the assumptions or initial premises) and the links between each set of premises and their respective conclusions are necessary, then the final conclusion should also be regarded as factual.

Summary

We do not use formal reasoning so explicitly very often in our everyday lives. When we do use it, we usually use it without even thinking about it. We use modus ponens and disjunctive argument, and even constructive dilemma. It is helpful to learn these valid arguments and practice them so that when we are not sure of our reasoning or of someone else's reasoning, we can check it by explicitly formalizing it to make sure that it uses only valid arguments. This is particularly useful when we accept the assumptions or premises as factual, but we do not think the conclusion which is claimed to follow from them is factual. Then we want to look closely at the links between the premises and the conclusions to see if they are necessary as claimed. This is why Anselm's argument has generated so much attention. Many people find it not hard to accept his assumptions or his reasoning but then balk at accepting his conclusion. As a consequence, his argument has been the subject of much discussion and analysis through many centuries.

I. REVIEW OF COMMON VALID ARGUMENTS

Modus Ponens

If P, then Q

P

Therefore, Q

Modus Tollens

If P, then Q

Not Q

Therefore, not P

Logically equivalent English expressions of "If P, then Q":

P implies Q

P only if Q

Not P unless Q

Pure Hypothetical Argument

If P, then Q

If Q, then R

Therefore, if P, then R

Disjunctive Argument

P or Q

Not Q

Therefore, P

Constructive Dilemma

A or B

If A, then C

If B, then D

Therefore, C or D

Destructive Dilemma

Not A or not B

If C, then A

If D, then B

Therefore, not C or not D

Categorical Argument

All As are Bs

All Bs are Cs

Therefore, all As are Cs

II. REVIEW OF COMMON FALLACIOUS ARGUMENTS

Denying the Antecedent

If A then B

Not A

Therefore, not B

Affirming the Consequent

If A then B

B

Therefore, A

Fallacious Disjunction

Either A or B

A

Therefore, not B

Fallacious Categoricals

All As are Bs	All As are Bs
All As are Cs	All Cs are Bs
Therefore, all Bs are Cs	Therefore, all As are Cs

Exercises

6–I

1. Determine the validity of each of the following arguments. (Hint: It is best to put the argument into symbols (P and Q) first and then determine the validity.) If it is valid, name its argument form. If it is invalid, name the fallacy.

   A. If you feel great, then you look great.

   You look terrible.

   Therefore, you don't feel great.

   B. If you feel terrible, then you look terrible.

   You look terrible,

   Therefore, you feel terrible.

   C. If you feel terrible, then you do not look great.

   You do not feel terrible.

   Therefore, you do not look great.

   D. If you feel terrible, then you do not look great,

   You look great.

   Therefore, you do not feel terrible.

   E. If you feel terrible, then you do not look great.

   You do not look great.

   Therefore, you feel terrible.

   F. You do not look great.

   If you feel terrible, then you look great.

   Therefore, you do not feel terrible.

   G. You look great.

   If you feel terrible, then you do not look great.

   Therefore, you do not feel terrible.

   H. You must not feel good.

   If you felt good, you would look better.

   You look terrible.

   I. For my next car, I want either a Corvette or a Maserati.

   I don't think I want a Maserati.

   Therefore, I think I'll buy a Corvette.

J. For my next car, I want either a Corvette, a Maserati, or a Jaguar.
    I don't want a Jaguar.

    Therefore, I want a Maserati.

K. All students who study hard pass their courses.
    Roland studies hard,

    Therefore, Roland will pass his courses.

L. All students who study hard pass their courses.
    Roland passed his courses.

    Therefore, Roland studied hard.

M. All students want to pass their courses.

    Some students who want to pass their courses study hard.

    Therefore, all students study hard.

N. All four-legged creatures are dogs.
    Fido is a dog.

    Therefore, Fido is a four-legged creature.

O. All dogs are four-legged creatures.
    All dogs are canines.

    Therefore, all four-legged creatures are canines.

P. All philosophy teachers are gurus.
    Ludwig is a philosophy teacher.

    Therefore, Ludwig is a guru.

Q   All philosophy teachers are gurus.
    All gurus are wise.

    Therefore, all philosophy teachers are wise.

2. Which of the following arguments are valid? Where valid, name the valid argument form. Name the fallacies in those which are fallacious.

A. He'll drive recklessly only if he's upset.

    He's not upset.

    Therefore, he won't drive recklessly.

B. If he's upset, he'll drive recklessly.

    He's not upset.

    Therefore, he won't drive recklessly.

C. He'll drive recklessly if he's upset.

    He is driving recklessly.

    Therefore, he is upset.

D. He won't drive recklessly, unless he's upset.

    He is driving recklessly.

    Therefore, he is upset.

E. If he's upset, he'll drive recklessly.

    He is not driving recklessly.

    Therefore, he's not upset.

F. If he's upset, he'll drive recklessly.

    He is driving recklessly.

    Therefore, he is upset.

6–II

1. (1) If Jones is having tea, then if he is eating crumpets, he is not in London.
   (2) If Jones is not in Africa, he is not in Tanzania.
   (3) If he is not in Tanzania, he does not smell the odor of spices.
   (4) If he does not smell the odor of spices, he is in London.
   (5) Jones is having tea.
   (6) He is not in Africa.

   Is Jones eating crumpets? What valid argument forms did you use to help you determine the right answer?

2. PAUL: "What are you going to do tonight?"
   JOE: "I don't know. There's a good movie at the Cinema 3. But I have a paper due tomorrow. I also heard there's a fraternity party. What are you going to do?"
   PAUL: "I heard no one is going to the party. They've got a lousy DJ coming. And my brother saw that movie. He hated it."
   JOE: "I guess I'll study, then—and wait for something to happen."

   What valid argument is Joe using in determining what to do?

3. Many everyday situations involve multiple sufficient or necessary conditions.
   a) Suppose your television broke and you are shopping for a new television. List as many sufficient conditions that you can think of that would enable you to leave the store with a new television.
   b) Suppose you are obtaining a driver's license. What are the necessary conditions for obtaining a driver's license?

4. Use Venn diagrams to prove the validity or invalidity of the arguments in Exercise 6–I that are categorical. Do the results match up with your earlier determination of validity? Your reasoning and your proof of your reasoning should match.

6–III

1. Describe three recent instances when you used a valid argument to make a decision, persuade someone, prove a point, and so on.

2. Why do we not need to know anything about football and the organization of professional teams into leagues to be able to answer or not answer the questions about the Eagles and the Cardinals in this chapter?

3. What are the assumptions Anselm uses to construct his ontological argument? Do you find any of these unacceptable?

III

Inductive Reasoning

This section introduces you to some of the most important concepts of critical thinking. As we said above, much of the day-to-day critical thinking we do uses our powers of inductive reasoning. We do not always deliberately use them, of course. We frequently employ them automatically. We used them even as little children. For example, we knew that if Mom raised her voice, she was probably mad and we ought to stop whatever was annoying her or if grandma was coming for dinner she was likely to bring a treat, and so on. We knew these things because we looked to past experience and used it to anticipate the future. This is reasoning inductively. Without inductive reasoning we wouldn't be able to know what to expect from one day to the next or even from one minute to the next. As we grow and learn from experience, we collect a large storehouse of information, which forms our background knowledge, and we use this background knowledge to draw inductive conclusions about the future that enable us to anticipate, predict, and often control our futures.

In Part II we discussed some of the important concepts of deductive reasoning, and we set out some of the most basic patterns of deduction that yield valid arguments. In this part we will do the same for inductive reasoning. In Chapter 7, we will set out some of the concepts of inductive reasoning. In the other chapters of Part III, we will look at some basic patterns of inductive reasoning, both good ones and poor ones. Inductive reasoning is different from deductive reasoning in that the conclusions do not follow with necessity from the premises. The connections between the premises and the conclusions are weaker in induction. We are looking at probable or likely conclusions, not guaranteed conclusions. This means that how strong we see the connection to be between the premises and conclusion will depend more on our background knowledge than it does in deductive reasoning, and this means that we will not all judge the links between the premises and the conclusions in inductive arguments the same way. There is more room for disagreement—and more room to make mistakes in our expectations for the future. Becoming a better inductive thinker can help us avoid those mistakes and live happier lives.

Supporting Our Claims

EVIDENCE: TRACES AND PATTERNS

There are many beliefs of which we are absolutely certain. It would take a lot of work for someone to convince us to give up one of these beliefs. These beliefs range from common ordinary everyday kinds of beliefs, such as "My name is Hildegaard Higgenbottom," to more complicated kinds of beliefs, such as "The United States is the most powerful country in the world." We realize when pressed, of course, that we cannot be *absolutely* certain about these beliefs. There is always a chance that we might be mistaken. (A famous puzzle about this kind of certainty was raised by the philosopher Bertrand Russell who pointed out that we cannot prove that the world was not created yesterday— complete and just as it is, with all its books, fossil evidence, memories, and other records of the past!)

For instance, you now believe that when you are finished reading this book, you will put it down, stand up, and walk across the room. You believe that the floor will feel firm under your feet, that your legs will move as they have in the past. In fact, you won't even think about it. You will just do it. Although you are quite justified in this belief, there is always the possibility that something will be amiss—that the floor will collapse under your feet, for example, or that your knee will suddenly give out and send you sprawling on the floor. But these possibilities are not sufficient to cause you any worry. You do not get up slowly, tentatively putting one foot before the other, testing the floor or your knee. In fact, people would think you very neurotic if you did! Ordinary reasoning tells you not to worry. Experience leads us to expect certain **patterns**, and we act in accordance with those patterns. When you brush your teeth in the morning, you do so expecting not to get cavities, to have better smelling breath, not to have fuzzy teeth, to have a peppermint (or some other flavor) taste in your mouth, and so on. If you use the same brand of toothpaste today as you did yesterday, you expect to have the same taste in your mouth as yesterday morning. It is highly probable that you will.

Ordinary reasoning of this sort is reasoning with probability. Philosophers call this type of reasoning **inductive reasoning**. You believe it is highly improbable that the floor will collapse under your feet since it looks to be made of wood, was firm a few minutes ago, and has not suffered any obvious damage in the meantime. Consequently, you act with assurance when you finish your reading, despite the remote chance that your expectations could be wrong.

But remember the time someone pulled that chair out from under you just as you sat down? Or the time you were going down the stairs in the dark and thought you were at the bottom and almost fell down that last step? The point is sometimes we mistake the probabilities and our ordinary reasoning lets us down—literally. And sometimes the unexpected is just plain unforeseeable, even though we have reasoned well—as when your friend decides to become a practical joker with the chair. In this section, we will begin to examine inductive reasoning in order to improve the skills we all already have. Although these skills generally get us safely through the day without anxiety, we do make some mistakes and sometimes mistakes can be quite serious. (Remember the *Challenger*.) Also, sometimes we are uncertain. We are not sure whether to buy a Buick or a Ford, or whether the price of gas will go down or up in the future, or whether the crisis in the Middle East can be solved by diplomacy alone. When we make decisions about the future, we are relying on inductive reasoning, using probability. Even scientists use inductive reasoning. You may think of science as giving us laws about what must be the case. We will see, however, that science uses the same kind of reasoning with probability that we all use every day.

When someone asks us why we believe a certain claim to be true or why we have made the assertion we have just made, she is usually asking us for **evidence** for that claim or assertion. She wants to know whether the claim is credible, that is, worth believing herself. "I just think so" or "That's what my mother taught me" does not (except in rare cases) make a statement credible. The questioner wants to know why she should believe the claim, not our psychological history.

Evidence, however, is not a simple matter. What constitutes evidence for one person may not be evidence for another. Newspapers often have stories of trials where the parties do not agree about the nature of the evidence. They may disagree about what happened, or they may agree about what happened but disagree about what it shows as evidence. Consider a soft-drink bottle found on the beach. To a contemporary American, the bottle appears as someone's trash, left over from a beach party, or washed ashore from a boat. To a person unfamiliar with glass bottles, the soft-drink bottle may appear to be a treasure, washed ashore or unearthed by the tide. (The film *The Gods Must Be Crazy* presents an amusing example of this situation.)

Evidence can be strong or weak. Sometimes, we have very little doubt that our belief is correct; in fact, we are apt to say that we are certain—even though we know that nothing (except death and taxes) is certain. Sometimes, however, we believe a statement only because it has more warrant than any of the alternatives we can think of. We say that it is plausible or likely and, therefore, we are justified in believing it—given the evidence at hand.

We are continually engaged in gathering evidence for our beliefs, yet we never articulate "rules" of evidence to ourselves. Despite this, we do surprisingly well. The ordinary skills that we all have, however, can be improved by thinking about the nature of evidence. To start: Evidence is based on **traces**. Traces are marks on the world that indicate something has happened. Traces are everywhere. Those footsteps in the sand. These fingerprints on the wall. The candy wrapper blowing by in the wind. The list is endless. Traces indicate that something has happened, but what? Most traces go unnoticed by us. As we pointed out in the second chapter, we tend to see what we are prepared to see. If we are not looking for evidence or clues, we ignore the traces. Sherlock Holmes, the famous fictional detective, was very good at noticing traces. Is this because he was just more observant? Yes and no.

A detective, like Holmes, sets out to gather evidence. To do this, she looks for marks or disturbances. These marks or disturbances are a trace of something's having happened or that something is happening. The detective notices these traces because they fit into a pattern that is familiar. The pattern is familiar because it is part of the detective's background knowledge. For example, the detective may notice the way the victim of a murder is lying on the floor. This trace might not even be noticed by someone untrained in detective work, but to the detective it is part of a familiar pattern that may indicate how the victim was killed. You have probably watched crime dramas on television and noticed how the members of the crime lab team are very good at picking up traces and organizing them into patterns that give a picture of what has happened. Their background knowledge enables them to see traces that others would miss. By contrast, remember what happened to Stephen Jay Gould when he went looking for hominid traces (Chapter 2). Even though he was looking for bone fragments, what he saw was lumps of sediment and snail fossils. This is because his background knowledge included much about snail fossil patterns and little if anything about hominid fossils. Richard Leakey and his wife, however, are experienced hominid fossil finders and consequently find more hominid fossils than other people do. Less successful fossil finders refer to this as "Leakey's luck," but it is the Leakeys' accumulated background knowledge that makes them so successful. **Background knowledge is the key to spotting traces and seeing them *as* evidence and, therefore, it is the key for successful inductive reasoning.**

Let's see what this means by considering another example. Suppose you were traveling through the woods with a guide who is a noted woodsperson and tracker. Along the trail there are many traces left by the animals which normally inhabit those woods. You see few of them, but the guide sees traces everywhere. A broken twig. A footprint in the mud. A scent in the air. A rustle of the leaves. He then announces that you are about to come upon a herd of deer, which you soon do. The guide has observed things you have not because he sees **traces** where you have not. He sees traces because he sees **patterns**. That is, he notices the broken twig because he knows that broken twigs go together with certain animal behaviors. He knows that pattern from his background knowledge of animal habits. The guide sees something to be a trace because he sees it as a sign of something else.

One more example that you may find familiar is the former basketball player and coach, Larry Bird. Bird is considered to be one of the best players of recent history.

A smart cat consults her background knowledge to find a way to get the ball off the table!
The New Yorker, Jack Ziegler SKU: 121311

Bird was not particularly fast, nor did he jump particularly high. But Bird had an uncanny ability to know where the court was open and thereby to set up the winning play. He saw things that other players didn't see. This is because he saw the opponent's behavior as a trace of a particular mode of attack or defense and then played off that pattern. He saw patterns where other players did not! In basketball, at least, Bird had excellent skills in reasoning with probability.

The guide's background knowledge about the ways of animals, the kind of animals which might be found in that particular woods, the nature of the pattern in the mud, all contribute to drawing the best conclusion about what lies ahead. Same for Larry Bird. His knowledge of passing patterns, of body language, and of a particular player's talent contributes to his gamesmanship. And the CSI teams' wide range of background information enables them to see patterns of traces that are familiar to them, when they are not apparent to us. The crime team then creates a **story** that weaves the traces into an even larger **pattern** so that the traces become **evidence** for something that happened in that story.

To put the matter another way, a detective's solution is really the conclusion of a long inductive argument which explains the traces, or what happened. A detective's background information is her most important asset in making this argument. *A trace is evidence for what has gone before because of the story she tells.* We would be very angry at a mystery writer if her detective at the end of the story just gave us the name of the culprit without the evidence which explains how and why. The evidential character of the traces comes about as a consequence of the role it plays in her report and is not independent of that report.

Evidence, then, is just a collection of relevant traces—made relevant by background knowledge and the story told which organizes the traces into an ordered whole. As we tell this story, we must be careful not to overlook other traces and other possible stories. Like any good detective, we must continually look for additional traces that support our story and confirm the absence of traces that would refute our story.

The following two readings illustrate these concepts of traces, patterns, background knowledge, story, and evidence. The first one is about a murder investigation and the arrest of a prime suspect. As you read this article about the arrest, think about the traces and how your own background knowledge of patterns of human behavior may or may not suggest a story that weaves these traces into evidence about what happened. Also, think about what is still missing from this story. The second reading is also about a crime. It is a particularly good reading for understanding the relationship between traces and evidence, because it makes clear the importance of patterns and how background knowledge influences the story that gets told that turns the traces into evidence that a crime has been committed. The local police, in this case, see one set of traces and tell one story about what happened. Later, an expert on fire patterns sees the traces quite differently, leading the reader to believe that an innocent man may have been convicted and executed in this case.

REPORT ON YALE MURDER OUTLINES SUSPICIONS

James Barron and Alison Leigh Cowan
November 14, 2009

Raymond Clark III walked into Room G-13 in the basement of a Yale research center in New Haven and saw it sitting on a metal cart: a box of disposable wipes, splattered with blood.

But there was a Yale police officer in the room. So as he turned toward her, he slid the box from one side of the cart to the other, turning the carton until the blood faced the other way, in what "appeared to be a deliberate attempt by Clark to block her view of the box in question," according to an affidavit for an arrest warrant that was unsealed on Friday. Then he leaned against the cart and made small talk.

But the officer, Sabrina Wood, alerted by a Yale student, had already seen the box.

Mr. Clark, 24, a technician at the lab, was arrested a week later, on Sept. 17, and charged with strangling Annie Le, a graduate student in pharmacology who also spent time in the lab, conducting medical experiments on animals. Ms. Le, also 24, was killed five days before her wedding.

The affidavit laid out evidence the police had collected, including a bloody sock with the DNA of both Ms. Le and Mr. Clark on it; a pair of bloody boots marked "Ray-C" that were missing their laces; and a green pen that was found with Ms. Le's body when the authorities eventually discovered it hidden behind a wall. On the day she disappeared, the affidavit said, Mr. Clark initialed his worksheets in green ink in the morning, but black ink later in the day.

The affidavit also described a suspect who seemed to be trying a little too hard to hide in plain sight. It presented Mr. Clark as a frenzied employee, busying himself—and arousing investigators' suspicions even before they zeroed in on him—by scrubbing the floor under a sink in the very room where Ms. Le was last seen. The officers were surprised when Mr. Clark took out cleaning supplies and went to work on the floor because, the affidavit said, "it did not appear to need cleaning."

Mr. Clark changed his clothes at least three times the day Ms. Le was strangled, according to the affidavit. It also said Mr. Clark was recorded using his employee identification card at least 55 times that day, far more than usual, to gain access to various rooms in the basement.

Despite all the details about what investigators found in the lab, the affidavit did not explain why Mr. Clark would have strangled Ms. Le: it contained no discussion of a possible motive. Nor did it explain how Mr. Clark could have killed her, moved her body to a different room, hidden it behind a wall and cleaned up—all without anyone noticing. The affidavit said the investigators had concluded that there had been blood on a wall in the lab, but that it had been washed off.

On Friday, Officer Joe Avery, a spokesman for the New Haven police, said the department would not answer questions about the affidavit. "The affidavit speaks for itself," he said.

Joseph Lopez, a lawyer for Mr. Clark, declined to comment on the affidavit. "We go forward on the case," he said. A spokesman for Ms. Le's family did not respond to an e-mail message seeking their reaction to the details in the affidavit.

Ms. Le's disappearance on Sept. 8 soon preoccupied Yale's storied Gothic campus and the modernistic research buildings in the neighborhood near Yale-New Haven Hospital, a short walk away. For some, the case brought back memories of a haunting, unsolved case from 11 years ago: the fatal stabbing of Suzanne Jovin, a Yale senior whose body was found not far from the campus.

By contrast, the authorities did not know at first whether Ms. Le had been harmed or had simply walked away, perhaps in a case of pre-wedding jitters. The first clue came on Sept. 10, when another graduate student in the lab saw the box of WypAlls and alerted the police. Officer Wood was waiting for the F.B.I. to arrive when Mr. Clark showed up, and his moving the box and scrubbing the floor quickly aroused suspicion.

Investigators spoke with Mr. Clark that day; he said he had last seen Ms. Le leaving Room G-13 around lunchtime, holding her notebook and two bags of mouse food. Mr. Clark had scratches on his face and left arm, which he said had come from one of his cats at home.

A blood-stained lab coat was found in a recycling box; investigators matched DNA from toiletries they had taken from Ms. Le's home to the lab coat and the blood on the box, according to the affidavit. But it was not until Sept. 13 that Ms. Le's body was found, after investigators detected an odor. With the body was the green pen, which had Ms. Le's DNA on the shaft and Mr. Clark's inside the cap, according to the affidavit.

The 13-page document had been sealed at the request of prosecutors and defense lawyers but was released on Friday after a judge granted a motion by several newspapers, including The New York Times, that it be made public. Small sections were redacted, including a description of Ms. Le's body when it was found.

Still, evidence described by the affidavit suggested that there might have been a struggle, with signs of blood on the wall in addition to the scratches on Mr. Clark. Based on his card swipes, the affidavit indicated, Mr. Clark could have been alone with Ms. Le—or her body—for 46 minutes.

After Mr. Clark's arrest, Chief James Lewis of the New Haven police attributed Ms. Le's killing to "workplace violence," without providing any details. The affidavit did not indicate that Mr. Clark gave any statements, and the police have said they may never know the motive.

TRIAL BY FIRE

DID TEXAS EXECUTE AN INNOCENT MAN?

David Grann

The fire moved quickly through the house, a one-story wood-frame structure in a working-class neighborhood of Corsicana, in northeast Texas. Flames spread along the walls, bursting through doorways, blistering paint and tiles and furniture. Smoke pressed against the ceiling, then banked downward, seeping into each room and through crevices in the windows, staining the morning sky.

Buffie Barbee, who was eleven years old and lived two houses down, was playing in her back yard when she smelled the smoke. She ran inside and told her mother, Diane, and they hurried up the street; that's when they saw the smoldering house and Cameron Todd Willingham standing on the front porch, wearing only a pair of jeans, his chest blackened with soot, his hair and eyelids singed. He was screaming, "My babies are burning up!" His children—Karmon and Kameron, who were one-year-old twin girls, and two-year-old Amber—were trapped inside.

Willingham told the Barbees to call the Fire Department, and while Diane raced down the street to get help he found a stick and broke the children's bedroom window. Fire lashed through the hole. He broke another window; flames burst through it, too, and he retreated into the yard, kneeling in front of the house. A neighbor later told police that Willingham intermittently cried, "My babies!" then fell silent, as if he had "blocked the fire out of his mind."

Diane Barbee, returning to the scene, could feel intense heat radiating off the house. Moments later, the five windows of the children's room exploded and flames "blew out," as Barbee put it. Within minutes, the first firemen had arrived, and Willingham approached them, shouting that his children were in their bedroom, where the flames were thickest. A fireman sent word over his radio for rescue teams to "step on it."

More men showed up, uncoiling hoses and aiming water at the blaze. One fireman, who had an air tank strapped to his back and a mask covering his face, slipped through a window but was hit by water from a hose and had to retreat. He then charged through the front door, into a swirl of smoke and fire. Heading down the main corridor, he reached the kitchen, where he saw a refrigerator blocking the back door.

Todd Willingham, looking on, appeared to grow more hysterical, and a police chaplain named George Monaghan led him to the back of a fire truck and tried to calm him down. Willingham explained that his wife, Stacy, had gone out earlier that morning, and that he had been jolted from sleep by Amber screaming, "Daddy! Daddy!"

"My little girl was trying to wake me up and tell me about the fire," he said, adding, "I couldn't get my babies out."

While he was talking, a fireman emerged from the house, cradling Amber. As she was given C.P.R., Willingham, who was twenty-three years old and powerfully built, ran to see her, then suddenly headed toward the babies' room. Monaghan and another man restrained him. "We had to wrestle with him and then handcuff him, for his and our protection," Monaghan later told police. "I received a black eye." One of the first firemen at the scene told investigators that, at an earlier point, he had also held Willingham back. "Based on what I saw on how the fire was burning, it would have been crazy for anyone to try and go into the house," he said.

Willingham was taken to a hospital, where he was told that Amber—who had actually been found in the master bedroom—had died of smoke inhalation. Kameron and Karmon had been lying on the floor of the children's bedroom, their bodies severely burned. According to the medical examiner, they, too, died from smoke inhalation.

News of the tragedy, which took place on December 23, 1991, spread through Corsicana. A small city fifty-five miles northeast of Waco, it had once been the center of Texas's first oil boom, but many of the wells had since dried up, and more than a quarter of the city's twenty thousand inhabitants had fallen into poverty. Several stores along the main street were shuttered, giving the place the feel of an abandoned outpost.

Willingham and his wife, who was twenty-two years old, had virtually no money. Stacy worked in her brother's bar, called Some Other Place, and Willingham, an unemployed auto mechanic, had been caring for the kids. The community took up a collection to help the Willinghams pay for funeral arrangements.

Fire investigators, meanwhile, tried to determine the cause of the blaze. (Willingham gave authorities permission to search the house: "I know we might not ever know all the answers, but I'd just like to know why my babies were taken from me.") Douglas Fogg, who was then the assistant fire chief in Corsicana, conducted the initial inspection. He was tall, with a crew cut, and his voice was raspy from years of inhaling smoke from fires and cigarettes. He had grown up in Corsicana and, after graduating from high school, in 1963, he had joined the Navy, serving as a medic in Vietnam, where he was wounded on four occasions. He was awarded a Purple Heart each time. After he returned from Vietnam, he became a firefighter, and by the time of the Willingham blaze he had been battling fire—or what he calls "the beast"—for more than twenty years, and had become a certified arson investigator. "You learn that fire talks to you," he told me.

He was soon joined on the case by one of the state's leading arson sleuths, a deputy fire marshal named Manuel Vasquez, who has since died. Short, with a paunch, Vasquez had investigated more than twelve hundred fires. Arson investigators have always been considered a special breed of detective. In the 1991 movie "Backdraft," a heroic arson investigator says of fire, "It breathes, it eats, and it hates. The only way to beat it is to think like it. To know that this flame will spread this way across the door and up across the ceiling." Vasquez, who had previously worked in Army intelligence, had several maxims of his own. One was "Fire does not destroy evidence—it creates it." Another was "The fire tells the story. I am just the interpreter." He cultivated a Sherlock Holmes-like aura of invincibility. Once, he was asked under oath whether he had ever been mistaken in a case. "If I have, sir, I don't know," he responded. "It's never been pointed out."

Vasquez and Fogg visited the Willinghams' house four days after the blaze. Following protocol, they moved from the least burned areas toward the most damaged ones. "It is a systematic method," Vasquez later testified, adding, "I'm just collecting information. . . . I have not made any determination. I don't have any preconceived idea."

The men slowly toured the perimeter of the house, taking notes and photographs, like archeologists mapping out a ruin. Upon opening the back door, Vasquez observed that there was just enough space to squeeze past the refrigerator blocking the exit. The air smelled of burned rubber and melted wires; a damp ash covered the ground, sticking to their boots. In the kitchen, Vasquez and Fogg discerned only smoke and heat damage—a sign that the fire had not originated there—and so they pushed deeper into the nine-hundred-and-seventy-five-square-foot building. A central corridor led past a utility room and the master bedroom, then past a small living room, on the left, and the children's bedroom, on the right, ending at the front door, which opened onto the porch. Vasquez tried to take in everything, a process that he compared to entering one's mother-in-law's house for the first time: "I have the same curiosity."

In the utility room, he noticed on the wall pictures of skulls and what he later described as an image of "the Grim Reaper." Then he turned into the master bedroom, where Amber's body had been found. Most of the damage there was also from smoke and heat, suggesting that the fire had started farther down the hallway, and he headed that way, stepping over debris and ducking under insulation and wiring that hung down from the exposed ceiling.

As he and Fogg removed some of the clutter, they noticed deep charring along the base of the walls. Because gases become buoyant when heated, flames ordinarily burn upward. But Vasquez and Fogg observed that the fire had burned extremely low down, and that there were peculiar char patterns on the floor, shaped like puddles.

Vasquez's mood darkened. He followed the "burn trailer"—the path etched by the fire—which led from the hallway into the children's bedroom. Sunlight filtering through the broken windows illuminated more of the irregularly shaped char patterns. A flammable or combustible liquid doused on a floor will cause a fire to concentrate in these kinds of pockets, which is why investigators refer to them as "pour patterns" or "puddle configurations."

The fire had burned through layers of carpeting and tile and plywood flooring. Moreover, the metal springs under the children's beds had turned white—a sign that intense heat had radiated beneath them. Seeing that the floor had some of the deepest burns, Vasquez deduced that it had been hotter than the ceiling, which, given that heat rises, was, in his words, "not normal."

Fogg examined a piece of glass from one of the broken windows. It contained a spiderweb-like pattern—what fire investigators call "crazed glass." Forensic textbooks had long described the effect as a key indicator that a fire had burned "fast and hot," meaning that it had been fuelled by a liquid accelerant, causing the glass to fracture.

The men looked again at what appeared to be a distinct burn trailer through the house: it went from the children's bedroom into the corridor, then turned sharply to the right and proceeded out the front door. To the investigators' surprise, even the wood under the door's aluminum threshold was charred. On the concrete floor of the porch, just outside the front door, Vasquez and Fogg noticed another unusual thing: brown stains, which, they reported, were consistent with the presence of an accelerant.

The men scanned the walls for soot marks that resembled a "V." When an object catches on fire, it creates such a pattern, as heat and smoke radiate outward; the bottom of the "V" can therefore point to where a fire began. In the Willingham house, there was a distinct "V" in the main corridor. Examining it and other burn patterns, Vasquez identified three places where fire had originated: in the hallway, in the children's bedroom, and at the front door. Vasquez later testified that multiple origins pointed to one conclusion: the fire was "intentionally set by human hands."

By now, both investigators had a clear vision of what had happened. Someone had poured liquid accelerant throughout the children's room, even under their beds, then poured some more along the adjoining hallway and out the front door, creating a "fire barrier" that prevented anyone from escaping; similarly, a prosecutor later suggested, the refrigerator in the kitchen had been moved to block the back-door exit. The house, in short, had been deliberately transformed into a death trap.

The investigators collected samples of burned materials from the house and sent them to a laboratory that could detect the presence of a liquid accelerant. The lab's chemist reported that one of the samples contained evidence of "mineral spirits," a substance that is often found in charcoal-lighter fluid. The sample had been taken by the threshold of the front door.

The fire was now considered a triple homicide, and Todd Willingham—the only person, besides the victims, known to have been in the house at the time of the blaze—became the prime suspect.

Police and fire investigators canvassed the neighborhood, interviewing witnesses. Several, like Father Monaghan, initially portrayed Willingham as devastated by the fire. Yet, over time, an increasing number of witnesses offered damning statements. Diane Barbee said that she had not seen Willingham try to enter the house until after the authorities arrived, as if he were putting on a show. And when the children's room exploded with flames, she added, he seemed more preoccupied with his car, which he moved down the driveway. Another neighbor reported that when Willingham cried out for his babies he "did not appear to be excited or concerned." Even Father Monaghan wrote in a statement that, upon further reflection, "things were not as they seemed. I had the feeling that [Willingham] was in complete control."

The police began to piece together a disturbing profile of Willingham. Born in Ardmore, Oklahoma, in 1968, he had been abandoned by his mother when he was a baby. His father, Gene, who had divorced his mother, eventually raised him with his stepmother, Eugenia. Gene, a former U.S. marine, worked in a salvage yard, and the family lived in a cramped house; at night, they could hear freight trains rattling past on a nearby track. Willingham, who had what the family called the "classic Willingham look"—a handsome face, thick black hair, and dark eyes—struggled in school, and as a teen-ager began to sniff paint. When he was seventeen, Oklahoma's Department of Human Services evaluated him, and reported, "He likes 'girls,' music, fast cars, sharp trucks, swimming, and hunting, in that order." Willingham dropped out of high school, and over time was arrested for, among other things, driving under the influence, stealing a bicycle, and shoplifting.

In 1988, he met Stacy, a senior in high school, who also came from a troubled background: when she was four years old, her stepfather had strangled her mother to death during a fight. Stacy and Willingham had a turbulent relationship. Willingham, who was unfaithful, drank too much Jack Daniel's, and sometimes hit Stacy—even when she was pregnant. A neighbor said that he once heard Willingham yell at her, "Get up, bitch, and I'll hit you again."

On December 31st, the authorities brought Willingham in for questioning. Fogg and Vasquez were present for the interrogation, along with Jimmie Hensley, a police officer who was working his first arson case. Willingham said that Stacy had left the house around 9 a.m. to pick up a Christmas present for the kids, at the Salvation Army. "After she got out of the driveway, I heard the twins cry, so I got up and gave them a bottle," he said. The children's room had a safety gate across the doorway, which Amber could climb over but not the twins, and he and Stacy often let the twins nap on the floor after they drank their bottles. Amber was still in bed, Willingham said, so he went back into his room to sleep. "The next thing I remember is hearing 'Daddy, Daddy,'" he recalled. "The house was already full of smoke." He said that he got up, felt around the floor for a pair of pants, and put them on. He could no longer hear his daughter's voice ("I heard that last 'Daddy, Daddy' and never heard her again"), and he hollered, "Oh God—Amber, get out of the house! Get out of the house!'"

        . . .

During the interrogation, Vasquez let Fogg take the lead. Finally, Vasquez turned to Willingham and asked a seemingly random question: had he put on shoes before he fled the house?

"No, sir," Willingham replied.

A map of the house was on a table between the men, and Vasquez pointed to it. "You walked out this way?" he said.

Willingham said yes.

Vasquez was now convinced that Willingham had killed his children. If the floor had been soaked with a liquid accelerant and the fire had burned low, as the evidence suggested, Willingham could not have run out of the house the way he had described without badly burning his feet. A medical report indicated that his feet had been unscathed.

Willingham insisted that, when he left the house, the fire was still around the top of the walls and not on the floor. "I didn't have to jump through any flames," he said. Vasquez believed that this was impossible, and that Willingham had lit the fire as he was retreating—first, torching the children's room, then the hallway, and then, from the porch, the front door. Vasquez later said of Willingham, "He told me a story of pure fabrication. . . . He just talked and he talked and all he did was lie."

Still, there was no clear motive. The children had life-insurance policies, but they amounted to only fifteen thousand dollars, and Stacy's grandfather, who had paid for them, was listed as the primary beneficiary. Stacy told investigators that even though Willingham hit her he had never abused the children—"Our kids were spoiled rotten," she said—and she did not believe that Willingham could have killed them.

Ultimately, the authorities concluded that Willingham was a man without a conscience whose serial crimes had climaxed, almost inexorably, in murder. John Jackson, who was then the assistant district attorney in Corsicana, was assigned to prosecute Willingham's case. He later told the Dallas *Morning News* that he considered Willingham to be "an utterly sociopathic individual" who deemed his children "an impediment to his lifestyle." Or, as the local district attorney, Pat Batchelor, put it, "The children were interfering with his beer drinking and dart throwing."

. . .

Willingham was charged with murder. Because there were multiple victims, he was eligible for the death penalty, under Texas law. . . . Willingham couldn't afford to hire lawyers, and was assigned two by the state: David Martin, a former state trooper, and Robert Dunn, a local defense attorney who represented everyone from alleged murderers to spouses in divorce cases—a "Jack-of-all-trades," as he calls himself. ("In a small town, you can't say 'I'm a so-and-so lawyer,' because you'll starve to death," he told me.)

Not long after Willingham's arrest, authorities received a message from a prison inmate named Johnny Webb, who was in the same jail as Willingham. Webb alleged that Willingham had confessed to him that he took "some kind of lighter fluid, squirting [it] around the walls and the floor, and set a fire." The case against Willingham was considered airtight.

. . . shortly before jury selection, Jackson approached Willingham's attorneys with an extraordinary offer: if their client pleaded guilty, the state would give him a life sentence. "I was really happy when I thought we might have a deal to avoid the death penalty," Jackson recalls.

Willingham's lawyers were equally pleased. They had little doubt that he had committed the murders and that, if the case went before a jury, he would be found guilty, and, subsequently, executed. "Everyone thinks defense lawyers must believe their clients are innocent, but that's seldom true," Martin told me. "Most of the time, they're guilty as sin." He added of Willingham, "All the evidence showed that he was one hundred per cent guilty. He poured accelerant all over the house and put lighter fluid under the kids' beds." It was, he said, "a classic arson case": there were "puddle patterns all over the place—no disputing those."

Martin and Dunn advised Willingham that he should accept the offer, but he refused. The lawyers asked his father and stepmother to speak to him. According to Eugenia, Martin showed them photographs of the burned children and said, "Look what your son did. You got to talk him into pleading, or he's going to be executed."

His parents went to see their son in jail. Though his father did not believe that he should plead guilty if he were innocent, his stepmother beseeched him to take the deal. "I just wanted to keep my boy alive," she told me.

Willingham was implacable. "I ain't gonna plead to something I didn't do, especially killing my own kids," he said. It was his final decision. Martin says, "I thought it was nuts at the time—and I think it's nuts now."

. . .

During his closing arguments, Jackson said that the puddle configurations and pour patterns were Willingham's inadvertent "confession," burned into the floor. Showing a Bible that had been salvaged from the fire, Jackson paraphrased the words of Jesus from the Gospel of Matthew: "Whomsoever shall harm one of my children, it's better for a millstone to be hung around his neck and for him to be cast in the sea."

The jury was out for barely an hour before returning with a unanimous guilty verdict. As Vasquez put it, "The fire does not lie."

II

When Elizabeth Gilbert approached the prison guard, on a spring day in 1999, and said Cameron Todd Willingham's name, she was uncertain about what she was doing. A forty-seven-year-old French teacher and playwright from Houston, Gilbert was divorced with two children. She had never visited a prison before. Several weeks earlier, a friend, who worked at an organization that opposed the death penalty, had encouraged her to volunteer as a pen pal for an inmate on death row, and Gilbert had offered her name and address. Not long after, a short letter, written with unsteady penmanship, arrived from Willingham. "If you wish to write back, I would be honored to correspond with you," he said. He also asked if she might visit him. Perhaps out of a writer's curiosity, or perhaps because she didn't feel quite herself (she had just been upset by news that her ex-husband was dying of cancer), she agreed. Now she was standing in front of the decrepit penitentiary in Huntsville, Texas—a place that inmates referred to as "the death pit."

She filed past a razor-wire fence, a series of floodlights, and a checkpoint, where she was patted down, until she entered a small chamber. Only a few feet in front of her was a man convicted of multiple infanticide. He was wearing a white jumpsuit with "DR"—for death row—printed on the back, in large black letters. He had a tattoo of a serpent and a skull on his left biceps. He stood nearly six feet tall and was muscular, though his legs had atrophied after years of confinement.

. . .

Their visit lasted for two hours, and afterward they continued to correspond. She was struck by his letters, which seemed introspective, and were not at all what she had expected. "I am a very honest person with my feelings," he wrote her. "I will not bullshit you on how I feel or what I think." He said that he used to be stoic, like his father. But, he added, "losing my three daughters . . . my home, wife and my life, you tend to wake up a little. I have learned to open myself."

She agreed to visit him again, and when she returned, several weeks later, he was visibly moved. "Here I am this person who nobody on the outside is ever going to know as a human, who has lost so much, but still trying to hold on," he wrote her afterward. "But you came back! I don't think you will ever know of what importance that visit was in my existence."

They kept exchanging letters, and she began asking him about the fire. He insisted that he was innocent and that, if someone had poured accelerant through the house and lit it, then the killer remained free. Gilbert wasn't naïve—she assumed that he was guilty. She did not mind giving him solace, but she was not there to absolve him.

. . .

Gilbert took the files and sat down at a small table. As she examined the eyewitness accounts, she noticed several contradictions. Diane Barbee had reported that, before the authorities arrived at the fire, Willingham never tried to get back into the house—yet she had been absent for some time while calling the Fire Department. Meanwhile, her daughter Buffie had reported witnessing Willingham on the porch breaking a window, in an apparent effort to reach his children. And the firemen and police on the scene had described Willingham frantically trying to get into the house.

The witnesses' testimony also grew more damning after authorities had concluded, in the beginning of January, 1992, that Willingham was likely guilty of murder. In Diane Barbee's initial statement to authorities, she had portrayed Willingham as "hysterical," and described the front of the house exploding. But on January 4th, after arson investigators began suspecting Willingham of murder, Barbee suggested that he could have gone back inside to rescue his children, for at the outset she had seen only "smoke coming from out of the front of the house"—smoke that was not "real thick."

An even starker shift occurred with Father Monaghan's testimony. In his first statement, he had depicted Willingham as a devastated father who had to be repeatedly restrained from risking his life. Yet, as investigators were preparing to arrest Willingham, he concluded that Willingham had been *too* emotional ("He seemed to have the type of distress that a woman who had given birth would have upon seeing her children die"); and he expressed a "gut feeling" that Willingham had "something to do with the setting of the fire."

Dozens of studies have shown that witnesses' memories of events often change when they are supplied with new contextual information. Itiel Dror, a cognitive psychologist who has done extensive research on eyewitness and expert testimony in criminal investigations, told me, "The mind is not a passive machine. Once you believe in something—once you expect something—it changes the way you perceive information and the way your memory recalls it."

After Gilbert's visit to the courthouse, she kept wondering about Willingham's motive, and she pressed him on the matter. In response, he wrote, of the death of his children, "I do not talk about it much anymore and it is still a very powerfully emotional pain inside my being." He admitted that he had been a "sorry-ass husband" who had hit Stacy—something he deeply regretted. But he said that he had loved his children and would never have hurt them. Fatherhood, he said, had changed him; he stopped being a hoodlum and "settled down" and "became a man." Nearly three months before the fire, he and Stacy, who had never married, wed at a small ceremony in his home town of Ardmore. He said that the prosecution had seized upon incidents from his past and from the day of the fire to create a portrait of a "demon," as Jackson, the prosecutor, referred to him. For instance, Willingham said, he had moved the car during the fire simply because he didn't want it to explode by the house, further threatening the children.

Gilbert was unsure what to make of his story, and she began to approach people who were involved in the case, asking them questions. "My friends thought I was crazy," Gilbert recalls. "I'd never done anything like this in my life."

. . .

Over the next few weeks, Gilbert continued to track down sources. Many of them, including the Barbees, remained convinced that Willingham was guilty, but several of his friends and relatives had doubts. So did some people in law enforcement. Willingham's former probation officer in Oklahoma, Polly Goodin, recently told me that Willingham had never demonstrated bizarre or sociopathic behavior. "He was probably one of my favorite kids," she said. Even a former judge named Bebe Bridges—who had often stood, as she put it, on the "opposite side" of Willingham in the legal system, and who had sent him to jail for stealing—told me that she could not imagine him killing his children. "He was polite, and he seemed to care," she said. "His convictions had been for dumb-kid stuff. Even the things stolen weren't significant." Several months before the fire, Willingham tracked Goodin down at her office, and proudly showed her photographs of Stacy and the kids. "He wanted Bebe and me to know he'd been doing good," Goodin recalled.

Eventually, Gilbert returned to Corsicana to interview Stacy, who had agreed to meet at the bed-and-breakfast where Gilbert was staying. Stacy was slightly plump, with pale, round cheeks and feathered dark-blond hair; her bangs were held in place by gel, and her face was heavily made up. According to a tape recording of the conversation, Stacy said that nothing unusual had happened in the days before the fire. She and Willingham had not fought, and were preparing for the holiday. Though Vasquez, the arson expert, had recalled finding the space heater off, Stacy was sure that, at least on the day of the incident—a cool winter morning—it had been on. "I remember turning it down," she recalled. "I always thought, Gosh, could Amber have put something in there?" Stacy added that, more than once, she had caught Amber "putting things too close to it."

Willingham had often not treated her well, she recalled, and after his incarceration she had left him for a man who did. But she didn't think that her former husband should be on death row. "I don't think he did it," she said, crying.

Though only the babysitter had appeared as a witness for the defense during the main trial, several family members, including Stacy, testified during the penalty phase, asking the jury to spare Willingham's life. When Stacy was on the stand, Jackson grilled her about the "significance" of Willingham's "very large tattoo of a skull, encircled by some kind of a serpent."

"It's just a tattoo," Stacy responded.

"He just likes skulls and snakes. Is that what you're saying?"

"No. He just had—he got a tattoo on him."

The prosecution cited such evidence in asserting that Willingham fit the profile of a sociopath, and brought forth two medical experts to confirm the theory. Neither had met Willingham. One of them was Tim Gregory, a psychologist with a master's degree in marriage and family issues, who had previously gone goose hunting with Jackson, and had not published any research in the field of sociopathic behavior. His practice was devoted to family counselling.

At one point, Jackson showed Gregory Exhibit No. 60—a photograph of an Iron Maiden poster that had hung in Willingham's house—and asked the psychologist to interpret it. "This one is a picture of a skull, with a fist being punched through the skull," Gregory said; the image displayed "violence" and "death." Gregory looked at photographs of other music posters owned by Willingham. "There's a hooded skull, with wings and a hatchet," Gregory continued. "And all of these are in fire, depicting—it reminds me of something like Hell. And there's a picture—a Led Zeppelin picture of a falling angel. . . . I see there's an association many times with cultive-type of activities. A focus on death, dying. Many times individuals that have a lot of this type of art have interest in satanic-type activities."

The other medical expert was James P. Grigson, a forensic psychiatrist. He testified so often for the prosecution in capital-punishment cases that he had become known as Dr. Death. (A Texas appellate judge once wrote that when Grigson appeared on the stand the defendant might as well "commence writing out his last will and testament.") Grigson suggested that Willingham was an "extremely severe sociopath," and that "no pill" or treatment could help him. Grigson had previously used nearly the same words in helping to secure a death sentence against Randall Dale Adams, who had been convicted of murdering a police officer, in 1977. After Adams, who had no prior criminal record, spent a dozen years on death row—and once came within seventy-two hours of being executed—new evidence emerged that absolved him, and he was released. In 1995, three years after Willingham's trial, Grigson was expelled from the American Psychiatric Association for violating ethics. The association stated that Grigson had repeatedly arrived at a "psychiatric diagnosis without first having examined the individuals in question, and for indicating, while testifying in court as an expert witness, that he could predict with 100-per-cent certainty that the individuals would engage in future violent acts."

After speaking to Stacy, Gilbert had one more person she wanted to interview: the jailhouse informant Johnny Webb, who was incarcerated in Iowa Park, Texas. She wrote to Webb, who said that she could see him, and they met in the prison visiting room. A man in his late twenties, he had pallid skin and a closely shaved head; his eyes were jumpy, and his entire body seemed to tremble. A reporter who once met him described him to me as "nervous as a cat around rocking chairs." Webb had begun taking drugs when he was nine years old, and had been convicted of, among other things, car theft, selling marijuana, forgery, and robbery.

. . .

Jailhouse informants, many of whom are seeking reduced time or special privileges, are notoriously unreliable. According to a 2004 study by the Center on Wrongful Convictions, at Northwestern University Law School, lying police and jailhouse informants are the leading cause of wrongful convictions in capital cases in the United States. At the time that Webb came forward against Willingham, he was facing charges of robbery and forgery. During Willingham's trial, another inmate planned to testify that he had overheard Webb saying to another prisoner that he was hoping to "get time cut," but the testimony was ruled inadmissible, because it was hearsay. Webb, who pleaded guilty to the robbery and forgery charges, received a sentence of fifteen years. Jackson, the prosecutor, told me that he generally considered Webb "an unreliable kind of guy," but added, "I saw no real motive for him to make a statement like this if it wasn't true. We didn't cut him any slack." In 1997, five years after Willingham's trial, Jackson urged the Texas Board of Pardons and Paroles to grant Webb parole. "I asked them to cut him loose early," Jackson told me. The reason, Jackson said, was that Webb had been targeted by the Aryan Brotherhood. The board granted Webb parole, but within months of his release he was caught with cocaine and returned to prison.

. . .

Aside from the scientific evidence of arson, the case against Willingham did not stand up to scrutiny. Jackson, the prosecutor, said of Webb's testimony, "You can take it or leave it." Even the refrigerator's placement by the back door of the house turned out to be innocuous; there were two refrigerators in the cramped kitchen, and one of them was by the back door. Jimmie Hensley, the police detective, and Douglas Fogg, the assistant fire chief, both of whom investigated the fire, told me recently that they had never believed that the fridge was part of the arson plot. "It didn't have nothing to do with the fire," Fogg said.

After months of investigating the case, Gilbert found that her faith in the prosecution was shaken. As she told me, "What if Todd really was innocent?"

IV

One day in January, 2004, Dr. Gerald Hurst, an acclaimed scientist and fire investigator, received a file describing all the evidence of arson gathered in Willingham's case. Gilbert had come across Hurst's name and, along with one of Willingham's relatives, had contacted him, seeking his help. After their pleas, Hurst had agreed to look at the case pro bono, and Reaves, Willingham's lawyer, had sent him the relevant documents, in the hope that there were grounds for clemency.

Hurst opened the file in the basement of his house in Austin, which served as a laboratory and an office, and was cluttered with microscopes and diagrams of half-finished experiments. Hurst was nearly six and half feet tall, though his stooped shoulders made him seem considerably shorter, and he had a gaunt face that was partly shrouded by long gray hair. He was wearing his customary outfit: black shoes, black socks, a black T-shirt, and loose-fitting black pants supported by black suspenders. In his mouth was a wad of chewing tobacco.

A child prodigy who was raised by a sharecropper during the Great Depression, Hurst used to prowl junk yards, collecting magnets and copper wires in order to build radios and other contraptions. In the early sixties, he received a Ph.D. in chemistry from Cambridge University, where he started to experiment with fluorine and other explosive chemicals, and once detonated his lab. Later, he worked as the chief scientist on secret weapons programs for several American companies, designing rockets and deadly fire bombs—or what he calls "god-awful things." He helped patent what has been described, with only slight exaggeration, as "the world's most powerful non-nuclear explosive": an Astrolite bomb. He experimented with toxins so lethal that a fraction of a drop would rot human flesh, and in his laboratory he often had to wear a pressurized moon suit; despite such precautions, exposure to chemicals likely caused his liver to fail, and in 1994 he required a transplant. Working on what he calls "the dark side of arson," he retrofitted napalm bombs with Astrolite, and developed ways for covert operatives in Vietnam to create bombs from local materials, such as chicken manure and sugar. He also perfected a method for making an exploding T-shirt by nitrating its fibres.

His conscience eventually began pricking him. "One day, you wonder, What the hell am I doing?" he recalls. He left the defense industry, and went on to invent the Mylar balloon, an improved version of Liquid Paper, and Kinepak, a kind of explosive that reduces the risk of accidental detonation. Because of his extraordinary knowledge of fire and explosives, companies in civil litigation frequently sought his help in determining the cause of a blaze. By the nineties, Hurst had begun devoting significant time to criminal-arson cases, and, as he was exposed to the methods of local and state fire investigators, he was shocked by what he saw.

Many arson investigators, it turned out, had only a high-school education. In most states, in order to be certified, investigators had to take a forty-hour course on fire investigation, and pass a written exam. Often, the bulk of an investigator's training came on the job, learning from "old-timers" in the field, who passed down a body of wisdom about the telltale signs of arson, even though a study in 1977 warned that there was nothing in "the scientific literature to substantiate their validity."

In 1992, the National Fire Protection Association, which promotes fire prevention and safety, published its first scientifically based guidelines to arson investigation. Still, many arson investigators believed that what they did was more an art than a science—a blend of experience and intuition. In 1997, the International Association of Arson Investigators filed a legal brief arguing that arson sleuths should not be bound by a 1993 Supreme Court decision requiring experts who testified at trials to adhere to the scientific method. What arson sleuths did, the brief claimed, was "less scientific." By 2000, after the courts had rejected such claims, arson investigators increasingly recognized the scientific method, but there remained great variance in the field, with many practitioners still relying on the unverified techniques that had been used for generations. "People investigated fire largely with a flat-earth approach," Hurst told me. "It looks like arson—therefore, it's arson." He went on, "My view is you have to have a scientific basis. Otherwise, it's no different than witch-hunting."

In 1998, Hurst investigated the case of a woman from North Carolina named Terri Hinson, who was charged with setting a fire that killed her seventeen-month-old son, and faced the death penalty. Hurst ran a series of experiments re-creating the conditions of the fire, which suggested that it had not been arson, as the investigators had claimed; rather, it had started accidentally, from a faulty electrical wire in the attic. Because of this research, Hinson was freed. John Lentini, a fire expert and the author of a leading scientific textbook on arson, describes Hurst as "brilliant." A Texas prosecutor once told the Chicago *Tribune,* of Hurst, "If he says it was an arson fire, then it was. If he says it wasn't, then it wasn't."

Hurst's patents yielded considerable royalties, and he could afford to work pro bono on an arson case for months, even years. But he received the files on Willingham's case only a few weeks before Willingham was scheduled to be executed. As Hurst looked through the case records, a statement by Manuel Vasquez, the state deputy fire marshal, jumped out at him. Vasquez had testified that, of the roughly twelve hundred to fifteen hundred fires he had investigated, "most all of them" were arson. This was an oddly high estimate; the Texas State Fire Marshals Office typically found arson in only fifty per cent of its cases.

Hurst was also struck by Vasquez's claim that the Willingham blaze had "burned fast and hot" because of a liquid accelerant. The notion that a flammable or combustible liquid caused flames to reach higher temperatures had been repeated in court by arson sleuths for decades. Yet the theory was nonsense: experiments have proved that wood and gasoline-fuelled fires burn at essentially the same temperature.

Vasquez and Fogg had cited as proof of arson the fact that the front door's aluminum threshold had melted. "The only thing that can cause that to react is an accelerant," Vasquez said. Hurst was incredulous. A natural-wood fire can reach temperatures as high as two thousand degrees Fahrenheit—far hotter than the melting point for aluminum alloys, which ranges from a thousand to twelve hundred degrees. And, like many other investigators, Vasquez and Fogg mistakenly assumed that wood charring beneath the aluminum threshold was evidence that, as Vasquez put it, "a liquid accelerant flowed underneath and burned." Hurst had conducted myriad experiments showing that such charring was caused simply by the aluminum conducting so much heat. In fact, when liquid accelerant is poured under a threshold a fire will extinguish, because of a lack of oxygen. (Other scientists had reached the same conclusion.) "Liquid accelerants can no more burn under an aluminum threshold than can grease burn in a skillet even with a loose-fitting lid," Hurst declared in his report on the Willingham case.

Hurst then examined Fogg and Vasquez's claim that the "brown stains" on Willingham's front porch were evidence of "liquid accelerant," which had not had time to soak into the concrete. Hurst had previously performed a test in his garage, in which he poured charcoal-lighter fluid on the concrete floor, and lit it. When the fire went out, there were no brown stains, only smudges of soot. Hurst had run the same experiment many times, with different kinds of liquid accelerants, and the result was always the same. Brown stains were common in fires; they were usually composed of rust or gunk from charred debris that had mixed with water from fire hoses.

Another crucial piece of evidence implicating Willingham was the "crazed glass" that Vasquez had attributed to the rapid heating from a fire fuelled with liquid accelerant. Yet, in November of 1991, a team of fire investigators had inspected fifty houses in the hills of Oakland, California, which had been ravaged by brush fires. In a dozen houses, the investigators discovered crazed glass, even though a liquid accelerant had not been used. Most of these houses were on the outskirts of the blaze, where firefighters had shot streams of water; as the investigators later wrote in a published study, they theorized that the fracturing had been induced by rapid cooling, rather than by sudden heating—thermal shock had caused the glass to contract so quickly that it settled disjointedly. The investigators then tested this hypothesis in a laboratory. When they heated glass, nothing happened. But each time they applied water to the heated glass the intricate patterns appeared. Hurst had seen the same phenomenon when he had blowtorched and cooled glass during his research at Cambridge. In his report, Hurst wrote that Vasquez and Fogg's notion of crazed glass was no more than an "old wives' tale."

Hurst then confronted some of the most devastating arson evidence against Willingham: the burn trailer, the pour patterns and puddle configurations, the V-shape and other burn marks indicating that the fire had multiple points of origin, the burning underneath the children's beds. There was also the positive test for mineral spirits by the front door, and Willingham's seemingly implausible story that he had run out of the house without burning his bare feet.

As Hurst read through more of the files, he noticed that Willingham and his neighbors had described the windows in the front of the house suddenly exploding and flames roaring forth. It was then that Hurst thought of the legendary Lime Street Fire, one of the most pivotal in the history of arson investigation.

On the evening of October 15, 1990, a thirty-five-year-old man named Gerald Wayne Lewis was found standing in front of his house on Lime Street, in Jacksonville,

Florida, holding his three-year-old son. His two-story wood-frame home was engulfed in flames. By the time the fire had been extinguished, six people were dead, including Lewis's wife. Lewis said that he had rescued his son but was unable to get to the others, who were upstairs.

When fire investigators examined the scene, they found the classic signs of arson: low burns along the walls and floors, pour patterns and puddle configurations, and a burn trailer running from the living room into the hallway. Lewis claimed that the fire had started accidentally, on a couch in the living room—his son had been playing with matches. But a V-shaped pattern by one of the doors suggested that the fire had originated elsewhere. Some witnesses told authorities that Lewis seemed too calm during the fire and had never tried to get help. According to the Los Angeles *Times*, Lewis had previously been arrested for abusing his wife, who had taken out a restraining order against him. After a chemist said that he had detected the presence of gasoline on Lewis's clothing and shoes, a report by the sheriff's office concluded, "The fire was started as a result of a petroleum product being poured on the front porch, foyer, living room, stairwell and second floor bedroom." Lewis was arrested and charged with six counts of murder. He faced the death penalty.

Subsequent tests, however, revealed that the laboratory identification of gasoline was wrong. Moreover, a local news television camera had captured Lewis in a clearly agitated state at the scene of the fire, and investigators discovered that at one point he had jumped in front of a moving car, asking the driver to call the Fire Department.

Seeking to bolster their theory of the crime, prosecutors turned to John Lentini, the fire expert, and John DeHaan, another leading investigator and textbook author. Despite some of the weaknesses of the case, Lentini told me that, given the classic burn patterns and puddle configurations in the house, he was sure that Lewis had set the fire: "I was prepared to testify and send this guy to Old Sparky"—the electric chair.

To discover the truth, the investigators, with the backing of the prosecution, decided to conduct an elaborate experiment and re-create the fire scene. Local officials gave the investigators permission to use a condemned house next to Lewis's home, which was about to be torn down. The two houses were virtually identical, and the investigators refurbished the condemned one with the same kind of carpeting, curtains, and furniture that had been in Lewis's home. The scientists also wired the building with heat and gas sensors that could withstand fire. The cost of the experiment came to twenty thousand dollars. Without using liquid accelerant, Lentini and DeHaan set the couch in the living room on fire, expecting that the experiment would demonstrate that Lewis's version of events was implausible.

The investigators watched as the fire quickly consumed the couch, sending upward a plume of smoke that hit the ceiling and spread outward, creating a thick layer of hot gases overhead—an efficient radiator of heat. Within three minutes, this cloud, absorbing more gases from the fire below, was banking down the walls and filling the living room. As the cloud approached the floor, its temperature rose, in some areas, to more than eleven hundred degrees Fahrenheit. Suddenly, the entire room exploded in flames, as the radiant heat ignited every piece of furniture, every curtain, every possible fuel source, even the carpeting. The windows shattered.

The fire had reached what is called "flashover"—the point at which radiant heat causes a fire in a room to become a room on fire. Arson investigators knew about the concept of flashover, but it was widely believed to take much longer to occur, especially without a liquid accelerant. From a single fuel source—a couch—the room had reached flashover in four and a half minutes.

Because all the furniture in the living room had ignited, the blaze went from a fuel-controlled fire to a ventilation-controlled fire—or what scientists call "post-flashover." During post-flashover, the path of the fire depends on new sources of oxygen, from an open door or window. One of the fire investigators, who had been standing by an open door in the living room, escaped moments before the oxygen-starved fire roared out of the room into the hallway—a fireball that caused the corridor to go quickly into flashover as well, propelling the fire out the front door and onto the porch.

After the fire was extinguished, the investigators inspected the hallway and living room. On the floor were irregularly shaped burn patterns that perfectly resembled pour patterns and puddle configurations. It turned out that these classic signs of arson can also appear on their own, after flashover. With the naked eye, it is impossible to distinguish between the pour patterns and puddle configurations caused by an accelerant and those caused naturally by post-flashover. The only reliable way to tell the difference is to take samples from the burn patterns and test them in a laboratory for the presence of flammable or combustible liquids.

During the Lime Street experiment, other things happened that were supposed to occur only in a fire fuelled by liquid accelerant: charring along the base of the walls and doorways, and burning under furniture. There was also a V-shaped pattern by the living-room doorway, far from where the fire had started on the couch. In a small fire, a V-shaped burn mark may pinpoint where a fire began, but during post-flashover these patterns can occur repeatedly, when various objects ignite.

One of the investigators muttered that they had just helped prove the defense's case. Given the reasonable doubt raised by the experiment, the charges against Lewis were soon dropped. The Lime Street experiment had demolished prevailing notions about fire behavior. Subsequent tests by scientists showed that, during post-flashover, burning under beds and furniture was common, entire doors were consumed, and aluminum thresholds melted.

John Lentini says of the Lime Street Fire, "This was my epiphany. I almost sent a man to die based on theories that were a load of crap."

Hurst next examined a floor plan of Willingham's house that Vasquez had drawn, which delineated all the purported pour patterns and puddle configurations. Because the windows had blown out of the children's room, Hurst knew that the fire had reached flashover. With his finger, Hurst traced along Vasquez's diagram the burn trailer that had gone from the children's room, turned right in the hallway, and headed out the front door. John Jackson, the prosecutor, had told me that the path was so "bizarre" that it had to have been caused by a liquid accelerant. But Hurst concluded that it was a natural product of the dynamics of fire during post-flashover. Willingham had fled out the front door, and the fire simply followed the ventilation path, toward the opening. Similarly, when Willingham had broken the windows in the children's room, flames had shot outward.

Hurst recalled that Vasquez and Fogg had considered it impossible for Willingham to have run down the burning hallway without scorching his bare feet. But if the pour patterns and puddle configurations were a result of a flashover, Hurst reasoned, then they were consonant with Willingham's explanation of events. When Willingham exited his bedroom, the hallway was not yet on fire; the flames were contained within the children's bedroom, where, along the ceiling, he saw the "bright lights." Just as the investigator safely stood by the door in the Lime Street experiment seconds before flashover, Willingham could have stood close to the children's room without being harmed. (Prior to the Lime Street case, fire investigators had generally assumed that carbon monoxide diffuses quickly through a house during a fire. In fact, up until flashover, levels of carbon monoxide can be remarkably low beneath and outside the thermal cloud.) By the time the Corsicana fire achieved flashover, Willingham had already fled outside and was in the front yard.

Vasquez had made a videotape of the fire scene, and Hurst looked at the footage of the burn trailer. Even after repeated viewings, he could not detect three points of origin, as Vasquez had. (Fogg recently told me that he also saw a continuous trailer and disagreed with Vasquez, but added that nobody from the prosecution or the defense ever asked him on the stand about his opinion on the subject.)

After Hurst had reviewed Fogg and Vasquez's list of more than twenty arson indicators, he believed that only one had any potential validity: the positive test for mineral spirits by the threshold of the front door. But why had the fire investigators obtained a positive reading only in that location? According to Fogg and Vasquez's theory of the crime, Willingham had poured accelerant throughout the children's bedroom and down the hallway. Officials had tested extensively in these areas—including where all the pour patterns and puddle configurations were—and turned up nothing. Jackson told me that he "never did understand why they weren't able to recover" positive tests in these parts.

Hurst found it hard to imagine Willingham pouring accelerant on the front porch, where neighbors could have seen him. Scanning the files for clues, Hurst noticed a photograph of the porch taken before the fire, which had been entered into evidence. Sitting on the tiny porch was a charcoal grill. The porch was where the family barbecued. Court testimony from witnesses confirmed that there had been a grill, along with a container of lighter fluid, and that both had burned when the fire roared onto the porch during post-flashover. By the time Vasquez inspected the house, the grill had been removed from the porch, during cleanup. Though he cited the container of lighter fluid in his report, he made no mention of the grill. At the trial, he insisted that he had never been told of the grill's earlier placement. Other authorities were aware of the grill but did not see its relevance. Hurst, however, was convinced that he had solved the mystery: when firefighters had blasted the porch with water, they had likely spread charcoal-lighter fluid from the melted container.

Without having visited the fire scene, Hurst says, it was impossible to pinpoint the cause of the blaze. But, based on the evidence, he had little doubt that it was an accidental fire—one caused most likely by the space heater or faulty electrical wiring. It explained why there had never been a motive for the crime. Hurst concluded that there was no evidence of arson, and that a man who had already lost his three children and spent twelve years in jail was about to be executed based on "junk science." Hurst wrote his report in such a rush that he didn't pause to fix the typos.

V

"I am a realist and I will not live a fantasy," Willingham once told Gilbert about the prospect of proving his innocence. But in February, 2004, he began to have hope. Hurst's findings had helped to exonerate more than ten people. Hurst even reviewed the scientific evidence against Willingham's friend Ernest Willis, who had been on death row for the strikingly similar arson charge. Hurst says, "It was like I was looking at the same case. Just change the names." In his report on the Willis case, Hurst concluded that not "a single item of physical evidence . . . supports a finding of arson." A second fire expert hired by Ori White, the new district attorney in Willis's district, concurred. After seventeen years on death row, Willis was set free. "I don't turn killers loose," White said at the time. "If Willis was guilty, I'd be retrying him right now. And I'd use Hurst as my witness. He's a brilliant scientist." White noted how close the system had come to murdering an innocent man. "He did not get executed, and I thank God for that," he said.

On February 13th, four days before Willingham was scheduled to be executed, he got a call from Reaves, his attorney. Reaves told him that the fifteen members of the Board of Pardons and Paroles, which reviews an application for clemency and had been sent Hurst's report, had made their decision.

"What is it?" Willingham asked.

"I'm sorry," Reaves said. "They denied your petition."

The vote was unanimous. Reaves could not offer an explanation: the board deliberates in secret, and its members are not bound by any specific criteria. The board members did not even have to review Willingham's materials, and usually don't debate a case in person; rather, they cast their votes by fax—a process that has become known as "death by fax." Between 1976 and 2004, when Willingham filed his petition, the State of Texas had approved only one application for clemency from a prisoner on death row. A Texas appellate judge has called the clemency system "a legal fiction." Reaves said of the board members, "They never asked me to attend a hearing or answer any questions."

The Innocence Project obtained, through the Freedom of Information Act, all the records from the governor's office and the board pertaining to Hurst's report. "The documents show that they received the report, but neither office has any record of anyone acknowledging it, taking note of its significance, responding to it, or calling any attention to it within the government," Barry Scheck said. "The only reasonable conclusion is that the governor's office and the Board of Pardons and Paroles ignored scientific evidence."

LaFayette Collins, who was a member of the board at the time, told me of the process, "You don't vote guilt or innocence. You don't retry the trial. You just make sure everything is in order and there are no glaring errors." He noted that although the rules allowed for a hearing to consider important new evidence, "in my time there had never been one called." When I asked him why Hurst's report didn't constitute evidence of "glaring errors," he said, "We get all kinds of reports, but we don't have the mechanisms to vet them." Alvin Shaw, another board member at the time, said that the case didn't "ring a bell," adding, angrily, "Why would I want to talk about it?" Hurst calls the board's actions "unconscionable."

Though Reaves told Willingham that there was still a chance that Governor Perry might grant a thirty-day stay, Willingham began to prepare his last will and testament. He had earlier written Stacy a letter apologizing for not being a better husband and thanking her for everything she had given him, especially their three daughters. "I still know Amber's voice, her smile, her cool Dude saying and how she said: I wanna hold you! Still feel the touch of Karmon and Kameron's hands on my face." He said that he hoped that "some day, somehow the truth will be known and my name cleared."

He asked Stacy if his tombstone could be erected next to their children's graves. Stacy, who had for so long expressed belief in Willingham's innocence, had recently taken her first look at the original court records and arson findings. Unaware of Hurst's report, she had determined that Willingham was guilty. She denied him his wish, later telling a reporter, "He took my kids away from me."

Gilbert felt as if she had failed Willingham. Even before his pleas for clemency were denied, she told him that all she could give him was her friendship. He told her that it was enough "to be a part of your life in some small way so that in my passing I can know I was at last able to have felt the heart of another who might remember me when I'm gone." He added, "There is nothing to forgive you for." He told her that he would need her to be present at his execution, to help him cope with "my fears, thoughts, and feelings."

. . .

Willingham had requested a final meal, and at 4 p.m. on the seventeenth he was served it: three barbecued pork ribs, two orders of onion rings, fried okra, three beef enchiladas with cheese, and two slices of lemon cream pie. He received word that Governor Perry had refused to grant him a stay. (A spokesperson for Perry says, "The Governor made his decision based on the facts of the case.") Willingham's mother and father began to cry. "Don't be sad, Momma," Willingham said. "In fifty-five minutes, I'm a free man. I'm going home to see my kids." Earlier, he had confessed to his parents that there was one thing about the day of the fire he had lied about. He said that he had never actually crawled into the children's room. "I just didn't want people to think I was a coward," he said. Hurst told me, "People who have never been in a fire don't understand why those who survive often can't rescue the victims. They have no concept of what a fire is like."

. . .

After his death, his parents were allowed to touch his face for the first time in more than a decade. Later, at Willingham's request, they cremated his body and secretly spread some of his ashes over his children's graves. He had told his parents, "Please don't ever stop fighting to vindicate me."

In December, 2004, questions about the scientific evidence in the Willingham case began to surface. Maurice Possley and Steve Mills, of the Chicago *Tribune*, had published an investigative series on flaws in forensic science; upon learning of Hurst's report, Possley and Mills asked three fire experts, including John Lentini, to examine the original investigation. The experts concurred with Hurst's report. Nearly two years later, the Innocence Project commissioned Lentini and three other top fire investigators to conduct an independent review of the arson evidence in the Willingham case. The panel concluded that "each and every one" of the indicators of arson had been "scientifically proven to be invalid."

. . .

Just before Willingham received the lethal injection, he was asked if he had any last words. He said, "The only statement I want to make is that I am an innocent man convicted of a crime I did not commit. I have been persecuted for twelve years for something I did not do. From God's dust I came and to dust I will return, so the Earth shall become my throne."

STUDY QUESTIONS

1. What are the traces in the case of the Yale killing?
2. What story would you tell to turn those traces into evidence?
3. What is missing in the newspaper account that is important to telling a story?
4. Do you think Todd Willingham committed arson? Why or why not? Be specific.
5. Why do Vasquez and Fogg tell a different story from Hurst?

CONFIRMATION AND PROOF: WEBS OF BELIEF

You can see from the two readings that the reasoning of a criminal prosecutor is not much different from that of a detective like Sherlock Holmes or from that of a crime lab investigator.

The prosecutor charges someone with a crime and then sets out to prove to the jury that this is the right choice by weaving a story around the evidence that has been gathered. The prosecutor's job is to make the pieces fit together in a way that is believable to the jury. She does this by bringing witnesses who testify to the existence of certain traces which, if the jury accepts them, become evidence for the prosecutor's story. Each bit of evidence that fits into the story makes the story more credible. Notice that no piece of evidence "proves" the story. Eyewitness accounts are often wrong, and even confessions of guilt are sometimes lies (designed, for example, to protect a loved one or to bargain for an easier sentence). Rather, each piece adds to the total picture that the prosecutor presents. Each piece helps to **confirm** or **disconfirm** the picture or story. The jury decides to accept or reject that picture.

You are familiar enough with the behavior of juries to know that, although all members of the jury have heard the same story, they sometimes do not all agree about the verdict. This is because the story that they hear must not only fit the traces together well but it must also fit in with the background knowledge of each juror. That is, it must fit the patterns with which she is familiar. Since they each have different stores of background knowledge, they will each have different reactions to the prosecutor's (or the defense attorney's) story. We can see, then, why some juries are prejudiced for or against particular defendants, even though they might not be openly hostile or even bigoted. No two of us have the same set of background knowledge, so the fit will vary. That is why it is thought important in the United States for a person to be tried by a jury of her peers.

All of this boils down to what one might call the **limits of evidence**. Evidence can confirm a hypothesis or a story but it cannot *prove* it. A story can be highly confirmed or only more than likely, but it cannot be proven like a proof in mathematics or logical reasoning.

A hypothesis (or story) which rests on inductive reasoning, which is only probable, can be credible even "beyond a shadow of a doubt" without such proof, however. You believe now—without a shadow of a doubt—that you will wake up tomorrow (sometime, anyway), even though the evidence only confirms and does not prove this belief. This simple belief is actually part of a very complex story supported by a large storehouse of background knowledge. Other beliefs are not so credible, and we have to make decisions and judgments based on less evidence than we would like. Whether the strawberry ice cream cone will taste better than the vanilla one is not so important to us over time, so we may not demand much in the way of evidence for making a decision. (But, then again, you may ask for a lick.) But we hope in our courts—and many other "high places"—that decisions are based on a pattern of evidence that fits in with the broadest collection of background knowledge.

When we reason inductively, then, we **confirm** conclusions; we do not **prove** them. What we are looking for when we seek to confirm them is a good fit, a good fit among the traces we have selected as evidence and a good fit of the story as a whole with the background knowledge we bring to it. The story must make sense to us, and it must make sense as a piece of the world around us. Our background knowledge is what enables us to judge whether or not that is so. What this means is that we must always be open to that world. We need to be curious. We need to learn as much as we can about it. Pity the poor student who says, "I don't know why I have to take chemistry. I'll never have to use chemistry." You can rest assured Holmes never said a thing like that!

Background knowledge is connected with the **web of belief** discussed in Chapter 3. Our background knowledge is not just a disconnected collection of information. Different aspects of it link together with other aspects to form a web. This web of belief is like the World Wide Web, which is so familiar to users of the Internet. Like the Web, the connections between pieces of background knowledge are what make them usable. One bit of knowledge takes us to a different piece, which takes us to a different piece, and so on. Some pieces of knowledge are very central to our webs of belief. They are extremely well-connected—like high-level host computers in the Web that route Web connections all over the world. Both make key links to other sets of beliefs. Other pieces of knowledge are quite peripheral—more like personal home pages that few people visit. For example, if a high-level host computer on the World Wide Web goes down, lots of people will know and complain about it. But if your personal home page goes down, not many people will notice. Similarly, if you have to adjust significant sections of your web of belief, it can be very disorienting and aggravating, while some pieces of one's web of belief are quite dispensable.

We can use this analogy to understand better how confirmation works. How well a hypothesis is confirmed is determined by how well it fits in with one's web of belief. The more links it has to that web, the more those links are a central part of that web, and the more links there are in the web itself, the more **confirmed** a hypothesis will be for that individual. If a hypothesis does not connect to a person's web or is in conflict with many of the other beliefs in her web, the less likely she will be to accept the hypothesis as confirmed. Sometimes, the story supporting the hypothesis in question is so strong that an individual accepts it despite its bad fit with other things in her web. Then she may be forced to give up some beliefs in her web of belief to accommodate the new belief.

The third reading in this chapter is also about a crime, a murder and trial that happened in the early 1980s. Two books and a made-for-television movie have dramatized this case, so you may already be familiar with it. The case still mystifies the police who continue to look for the bodies of the missing children. Put yourself in the place of a jury member. Would you vote to convict William Bradfield of conspiracy to commit murder?

THE WILLIAM BRADFIELD CASE

MURDER ON THE MAIN LINE

Mike Mallowe

Soon it will be two years since Susan Reinert's death.

Her children are still missing.

Her estate is still unsettled.

Whoever killed her is still at large.

The mystery of her life and the tragedy of her death remain unexplained.

There is no statute of limitations on murder, but there is a limit to patience.

The people who loved Susan Reinert and her children, the friends and relatives who cared deeply about her, the fellow professionals who taught with her at Upper Merion High School, and the neighbors who befriended her on Woodcrest Avenue in Ardmore—these are the people who are running out of hope.

Soon it will be two years since the stubborn riddle of Susan Reinert's death began and still the enigma persists.

Who killed her and why? And where are the children?

At some point later this month, Assistant U.S. Attorney Peter Schenck, the intense, young prosecutor in charge of the continuing investigation into Susan Reinert's murder and the disappearance and presumed kidnap-murder of her two young children, will be forced to stand before a grim, black-robed judge in the Federal Building at 6th and Market Streets and put up or shut up.

Schenck is preoccupied with that appearance already. He sounds testy when he discusses it; worried, afraid to say anything that might jeopardize the thin leads the government has been pursuing. When asked about the progress of the Reinert investigation, Schenck will reply sharply only, "It is not a closed shop. We are working on it and we hope to solve the thing."

Schenck's choice won't be an easy one this month when he stands before the bar.

He will either announce that the government of the United States is prepared to seek indictments against one or more individuals in the murder of Susan Reinert and the disappearance of her children; or he will find himself pressured into arguing in his most lawyerly fashion for one more continuance, one last shot at closing the 21-month-old investigation—an investigation that most of the men who have worked on, who have become obsessed with, become consumed by, would agree should have been concluded long ago.

It was the kind of murder that *should* have been wrapped up in a couple of weeks.

The police found her body stuffed into the tire well of a red Plymouth hatchback. At that point she was simply an unidentified female Caucasian in her mid-30s. She was naked and there were deep bruises on her face and arms.

She'd been bound in the fetal position, according to the coroner's report, and traces of a denim-like substance, probably fabric, had been imbedded into coarse thigh wounds. The indications of a struggle were clear.

At first, they thought she'd been raped; but the medical experts soon discounted that theory. She was very small, petite in fact, with short, brown hair and it wouldn't have been difficult to overpower her.

Her right eye was blackened and the tissues around it were visibly raised and fissured. It was impossible to determine the time of death just then, but an autopsy would later reveal that she could have been dead for as long as 24 hours before her body was discovered.

The most striking abrasion on the corpse was a long, thin line of shallow puncture marks that ran along the woman's back and buttocks. They looked like they could have been made by spurs, and this gave rise to speculation that she had been the victim of some sort of ritual killing. But that idea was soon discarded, as well, in favor of the less lurid but more likely explanation that at some point she had been bound, perhaps by a bicycle chain, and dragged for some distance.

In the beginning they would also assume that the victim had been suffocated, and her death would be listed as "homicide by asphyxiation."

That was all they had to go on when the body was discovered and the investigation opened. But back then, it seemed like more than enough—a nuts-and-bolts murder, they kept telling themselves.

. . .

It was still dark when the cops first approached the car. The call had come in at 5 a.m. on a Monday and they responded almost immediately. The parking lot was nearly empty and the little Plymouth Horizon was off by itself.

The heat that singes central Pennsylvania in midsummer was still bottled up behind the mountains, and the predawn darkness made it seem cooler than it really was.

The night dispatcher in the old courthouse in Harrisburg, the state capital, had taken the call and quickly turned it over to his supervisor, Kevin Molloy. After dark, every police call in Dauphin County, Pennsylvania, had to be routed through their switchboard, along with civil defense emergencies and act-of-God disasters, and technically speaking, the dispatcher and Molloy constituted Dauphin County's entire

Office of Emergency Preparedness and Communications, as well as the nighttime police radio network.

No one, including the civil defense officers themselves, had ever taken any of that very seriously until three months before when, on the blustery evening of March 28th, 1979, the massive nuclear reactor at Three Mile Island, just outside Harrisburg, had begun heading toward a meltdown. Since then, the night dispatcher has been taking his job very seriously.

A man who seemed to speak with a slight accent phoned the police to say, "There's a sick woman in a car out at the Host motel." He claimed to be calling from a phone booth on U.S. Route 22, about five miles north of Harrisburg. That was the last the police would ever hear from the anonymous caller.

The Host Inn was in rural Swatara Township, about three miles from the Pennsylvania Turnpike, and it was to Swatara's police department that the courthouse call was routed. Actually, the township cops had noticed the red Plymouth, parked all by itself, more than four hours earlier, first spotting it just after midnight, but no one had seen any reason to investigate. Now, there was a reason.

The Host Inn was a colorful, comfortable, family-oriented place that catered to sedate business meetings and seminars, as well as to the turnpike politicians from Philadelphia and southeastern Pennsylvania who had overnight business near the capital.

The inn had never caused the local cops any trouble, and the report of a sick woman in the parking lot seemed routine enough. They approached the car as an ordinary assist-motorist call.

But there *was* something unusual. The car's hatchback had been left conspicuously open, almost inviting notice in the deserted parking lot. When they looked inside, they saw the tiny, broken body jammed into the tire well.

Three Mile Island's nuclear problems notwithstanding, homicide was a little out of the township cops' normal range of activity. Their customary procedure, in rare cases like this, was to contact the Pennsylvania State Police Barracks out of Troop H, near Harrisburg, and let it handle things.

That's exactly what they did. But somewhere between the initial discovery of the body and the commencement of the homicide probe, mistakes—costly, frustrating mistakes, with ultimately irrevocable consequences—would be made that would still haunt law enforcement nearly two years later.

But back then, back during the early morning hours of June 25th, 1979 in the fresh coolness of the Pennsylvania dawn, the battered body in the Host Inn parking lot would still look like a nuts-and-bolts case.

In big cities, like Philadelphia or Pittsburgh, the body in the parking lot would have been assigned routinely to whichever detective was on duty, or "up" in the homicide squad. In Philadelphia, at homicide headquarters downtown, the detective would actually pluck the case from a "spinning wheel" file that seems to be in perpetual motion, since, in a good year, close to 400 Philadelphians could be counted on to assassinate each other in a bewildering variety of ways.

But even before the big-city homicide cop got the case, he could be reasonably certain that the crime scene and any physical evidence was preserved, that any witnesses were on call, and that the expert pathologists in the crime lab were busily at work identifying and tagging the grisly artifacts of medical jurisprudence.

That's the way it's done where homicide is as common as a domestic disturbance. But out in gorgeous, summer-green Dauphin County, an unidentified white female's naked corpse is something of an event.

While the state troopers and Swatara cops were still examining the car for clues, checking on the identity of the victim and questioning the Host Inn people for leads, the body itself was already en route to Community General Osteopathic Hospital in Harrisburg.

When it arrived, a routine autopsy would be performed by Dr. Robert Bear, a clinical pathologist, and the autopsy would ultimately be certified by Dr. William Bush, the veteran coroner of Dauphin County.

Bear would determine what circumstances or trauma within the body had caused the victim's mechanisms to shut down, with the resultant death. It was not his job to decide what the specific physical cause of death had been. Still, after this preliminary autopsy, "homicide by asphyxiation" would be mistakenly entered on the official report. Six months later, a minute sample of frozen tissue taken at that preliminary autopsy would reveal belatedly the real cause of death.

As far as a good homicide cop is concerned, medical information like that obtained by Dr. Bear might be interesting, but irrelevant. What *is* vitally important is the evidence unearthed, not by a clinical but by a forensic pathologist, whose specialty it is to describe the probable cause of death—the *reason* for the clinical shutdown of the body.

In most cases, that would be the first and only way that the cops would know exactly what kind of doer they were dealing with—a shooter, a stabber, a poisoner, a junkie, etc.

Without the information supplied by a forensic pathologist, it would be practically impossible for a homicide investigation to proceed quickly and professionally.

Yet, within a matter of hours, these were precisely the circumstances in which the police would find themselves on that lovely summer day in central Pennsylvania. No sooner had their investigation begun than their corpse disappeared.

County Coroner Bush insists that nothing improper took place. So does the spokesman for Community General Hospital. Charges were never filed, and they are probably right. It's just that, as the investigation into the body in the parking lot continued, very little would turn out to be as it had originally appeared.

The first break for the police came when they realized that the victim had actually been dumped into her own car—a 1978 Plymouth Horizon, registered to Susan Reinert, 37, of 662 Woodcrest Avenue, Ardmore, a small suburb on Philadelphia's exclusive Main Line.

What Susan Reinert had been doing in Swatara Township, near Harrisburg, in a motel parking lot more than 100 miles from her home, was anyone's guess.

Reinert's family was immediately contacted, including an ex-husband, Kenneth Reinert, who lived near her home outside Philadelphia; and a brother, W. Patrick Gallagher, a chemist, who worked in Pittsburgh.

While the police were just beginning to ask themselves who and what Susan Reinert was, and how and why she had turned up lifeless and naked in the tire well of her own car, her family was making arrangements to claim her remains.

In fact, her brother had immediately contacted an undertaker who was already in the process of removing her body from Community General in Harrisburg. The family had decided on cremation, and he was there later that morning to carry out their wishes. All of this was happening only hours after the body had been discovered.

Once the preliminary autopsy was completed, Coroner Bush ordered her body released to the family. He did this before the police had even begun their medical detective work.

In the meantime, before noon, the state police had taken over the investigation and Sergeant Joseph Van Nort of the Criminal Investigation Unit in Harrisburg was on the phone to Coroner Bush. Hold on to the body, he told him, so that the lab could fingerprint it and conduct a more thorough examination.

After Van Nort's call, the coroner immediately notified the hospital and told them to keep the undertaker waiting. But by early afternoon the corpse had been fingerprinted and the undertaker was again requesting the remains.

No forensic pathologist had shown up yet and the hospital was under a standing order, as well as a Pennsylvania state law, *not* to release any body without the coroner's specific permission. But the undertaker was getting impatient.

By this time Coroner Bush had both okayed the removal of the body and rescinded that order after the state police intervened, but somewhere along the line somebody misunderstood—and no sooner had the corpse been fingerprinted than the undertaker was permitted to leave with the remains of Susan Reinert. He cremated her at once.

Later that afternoon, when the men from the Criminal Investigation Unit came looking for the body, the stunned personnel at Community General could only stammer, "What body?"

By the early evening of June 25th, 1979, most of the people closest to Susan Reinert were aware of what happened. Her ex-husband, Kenneth, an Employee Benefits administrator with Fidelity Bank in Philadelphia, who had been called to Harrisburg to identify the body, telephoned his parents in upstate Pennsylvania and told them that Susan, with whom they had remained very close despite the divorce, had been injured in a serious automobile accident. It wasn't until hours later that he could bring himself to tell them what had really happened.

As stunned and distraught as they were over Susan's death, both her ex-husband and his parents were even more concerned about the whereabouts and safety of the young Reinert children, Michael, 11, and Karen, 12.

By that evening, the Pennsylvania State Police, too, realized that they were confronting not simply the murder of Susan Reinert, but also the disappearance, virtually certain kidnapping, and probable demise of her children, as well.

Suddenly, the unidentified female Caucasian discovered in the parking lot at the Host Inn had all the markings of a triple murder. It was quickly dawning on them that the nuts-and-bolts case they had anticipated that morning had escalated into something far more complicated.

Governor Thornburgh's recently appointed commandant of the Pennsylvania State Police was Daniel Dunn, a former FBI special agent-in-charge from the Pittsburgh bureau, where Thornburgh himself had served for many years as western Pennsylvania's relentless United States attorney. He and Dunn understood each other quite well, and Dunn's response to the Reinert murder was instant and predictable.

He wanted his old colleagues from the bureau in on this one at once. They didn't need any jurisdictional approval to offer their assistance and lab facilities to Troop H at Harrisburg—they had done so often in the past. The mere fact that Reinert's two kids were missing was enough to raise the federal kidnapping issue. Besides, the way this case was shaping up, Dunn knew that Troop H could use all the help it could get.

One of the first FBI agents to be assigned to the Reinert investigation was Michael Wald, then 35, a nine-year veteran of the Harrisburg office and one of the most experienced agents anywhere in the bureau. The day they discovered Susan Reinert's body, Wald was vacationing in Florida.

He had no idea who Susan Reinert was or why she had been killed or what had happened to her children. In fact, when her body was discovered, a tough homicide case was the last thing on his mind. Within weeks, however, all that would change dramatically.

The last time the neighbors recall seeing Susan Reinert and her children alive was on Friday evening, June 22nd, 1979, three days before her body was discovered.

That was at approximately 9:15 p.m. Her children, Michael and Karen, were outside their home playing. There had been a sudden, savage, summer cloudburst and the kids were picking up hailstones that had pelted the quiet, family street in Ardmore.

About 15 minutes later, the neighbors claim, just after they'd heard the Reinert phone ring, Reinert and the kids rushed out of the house rather quickly, the car doors slammed, and Reinert's small Plymouth was backing out of her driveway. Some of the hailstones crunched under the tires as the car left Woodcrest Avenue.

No one knows who called Susan Reinert or why, or if, in fact, anyone did really call. If the police have any theories on this point, they aren't disclosing them. Somehow, probably by that phone call, Reinert and her kids were lured away from the safety of their home. Whoever served as the bait, most investigators agree, will one day figure prominently when and if indictments are ever handed down.

Earlier that evening Reinert's son, Michael, had spoken on the phone with his father, Kenneth, and explained that he was going away for the weekend to visit his paternal grandparents near Phoenixville. Otherwise, he would have spent much of the weekend with his father. Ever since their separation and divorce about three years before, Kenneth Reinert had managed to see the kids practically every weekend. Both he and Susan were devoted to them, and divorce or not they were determined to maintain the children's lives as normally as possible.

Susan Reinert had also been on the phone during the early evening that Friday calling John and Florence Reinert, her ex-in-laws, around 5 p.m. to check with John about whether or not a single tank of gas would get her back and forth to Allentown that weekend. Before she left Woodcrest Avenue that night, the neighbors also remember her asking other people on the street if they thought a tank of gas would do it.

The gas shortage had been gripping Pennsylvania and Governor Thornburgh had instituted the odd/even license plate rationing plan only days before. Gas lines and empty fuel tanks were common and Susan Reinert was understandably nervous about risking a long trip. Still, ever since her divorce she had gotten used to doing things on her own, and appeared to have every intention of hitting the turnpike the next day.

Reinert, an English teacher at Upper Merion High School and a very popular organizer on the faculty, had also become active recently in Parents Without Partners, a self-help group for widowed, divorced or separated parents.

The next day she was supposed to help conduct a workshop in Allentown for the group. Following the seminar, Michael was to be dropped off at his grandparents' house where he would begin a week's visit. Susan Reinert and her daughter, Karen, were then going to attend a gym clinic, since Karen was an enthusiastic gymnast. Later that week Reinert was planning to visit Valley Forge Music Fair, as well as Washington Memorial Chapel in Valley Forge with her kids. Susan and Michael's grandmother were making plans for Michael to be baptized there.

When Susan and Michael failed to show up at the elder Reinerts' home, they knew something was wrong.

In her own quiet, reserved, well-bred way, Susan Reinert had been looking—searching desperately, in fact—for Mr. Goodbar.

Privately, many investigators are convinced it could have been that very search that led to her death. Almost no one disputes the fact that ever since her divorce, the pixieish Reinert, with her big, dark eyes set behind large, round glasses and her short, bouncy brown hair, had been consumed by a sense of loneliness. She was a woman who needed a man—a woman struggling to make it with two children whom she adored and who, she hoped, would bear no lingering scars from the divorce that had shattered her life.

Over the last few years the English teacher had worked long and hard at broadening her circle of friends, at trying to meet the kind of men who measured up to her emotional and intellectual standards, and at anchoring her career on the fast-track faculty of Upper Merion High School.

She had met her ex-husband, Kenneth, when both were students at a small college in upstate Pennsylvania, then later married him and spent the first few years of that marriage traveling with him from one air base to another while he was in the Air Force. In the early 1970s they had settled down in another small Main Line suburb, just outside Philadelphia.

She rarely spoke about the divorce, and her husband, who has since remarried, routinely declines comment except through his attorney, who is deeply involved in the Susan Reinert saga even now.

Somewhere along the line, she and her husband had grown apart, had wearied of each other's temperaments and dispositions and had conceded reluctantly that the marriage just wasn't making it. Many of her friends would later claim that when the divorce finally became a reality, Susan Reinert at first embraced it as a sort of deliverance. Later, however, she would succumb, almost visibly and physically at times, to the vacuum and the loneliness that it had created.

One of the very first things the investigators did following that gruesome discovery in the parking lot of the Host Inn was to begin questioning her friends and relatives and neighbors about her boyfriends. The name that kept cropping up was William S. Bradfield, 47, now on a recovery-of-health sabbatical from the faculty of Upper Merion High School; but then, a fellow teacher of Susan Reinert's and the most charismatic figure by far, in the cliquish, pseudo-intellectual faculty community of Upper Merion High.

While other investigators were running down leads, especially about Bradfield and several other teachers at the high school, the FBI's Michael Wald was establishing a kind of beachhead for the murder probe in Philadelphia.

By early August, Wald and his partner of several years, Don Redden, now the bureau's agent-in-charge in their office in Covington, Kentucky, were working full-time on the Reinert investigation. Eventually, dozens of state troopers and more than 16 FBI agents in four separate states would attack the case. But back in August 1979, Wald was attempting to coordinate things pretty much on his own.

He'd spent the last few years on cases like official corruption in Harrisburg; a bloodthirsty ring of black Muslim bank robbers in central Pennsylvania, and interstate vice as it affected the state capital. A homicide was a distinct change of pace, and at first a not-altogether unpleasant one.

Wald's family was from the Shenandoah Valley coal country in upstate Pennsylvania, but the agent had grown up in New York. He still retained his heavy Bronx accent and didn't look anything like the prototypical FBI farmboy-turned-agent. Where they were tall, Wald was stocky; where they were light and blond, Wald was swarthy with kinky black hair and a thick, full mustache. In fact, he looked a good deal more like somebody the FBI would arrest.

In the past, this had often served Wald to good advantage as one of the bureau's top undercover men. In that capacity he had helped infiltrate and close down a cigarette-smuggling operation in North Carolina; before that, he had been involved in one of the bureau's pioneer offensives against videocassette and eight-track-tape pirates on the East Coast. As an undercover man, Wald was typecast—he always played a fast-talking hustler from New York.

That summer a Reinert command post was set up in the Pennsylvania State Police's Belmont Barracks on Belmont Avenue in West Philadelphia. The agents, like Wald, who had been dragooned in from outlying bureau offices like Harrisburg, were put up at the nearby Marriott on City Line.

Wald had actually put in for a transfer to Philadelphia before Reinert's body had been discovered. The agent-in-charge in Philadelphia, Edgar Best, had been Wald's boss or "control" on two of his previous clandestine assignments, and the two men were looking forward to working together again. The Reinert murder, however, wasn't exactly what they had in mind, and when Wald started on the case, neither he nor any of the other investigators dreamed that they would practically be making a career of it.

One of the first things that Michael Wald did was to visit the Reinert house at 662 Woodcrest Avenue in Ardmore. "It was a very child-oriented house, if you know what I mean," Wald would remember nearly two years later, still prepared to describe the interior of the home and the feelings that welled up around him there, with a vivid, detailed, almost total recall. Like most of the other state troopers and agents in on the Reinert murder, Wald had kids of his own.

"There were toys and games all over the place . . . posters up on the walls and school papers that they'd brought home had been hung up—that sort of thing. The little boy, Michael, had a race car set up upstairs, and the little girl, Karen, had her suitcases and overnight bag all packed. . . . It was a nice environment for a kid to grow up in. . . . From what we could determine, they were really nice kids, too; well-behaved. . . . I don't have to tell you what it felt like whenever we went there.

"It's hard to imagine how much more difficult those kids made the case. They were always there in the back of your mind. . . . You *wanted* to find them—it was your *job* to find them; but if you found them buried somewhere . . . in a grave in somebody's backyard or out in the woods, you couldn't tell how you'd react to that, either. . . . It was just so *damn* hard . . . one of the worst things I ever had to go through.

"It really affected everybody. Joe Van Nort, the state trooper in charge of this thing—you can't imagine what it's done to him. . . . This is his *life* now.

"When the weekend would come, when it would be Friday night and I'd hit that turnpike for Harrisburg and know that I was going home, I'd be so glad. I'd just feel the weight lifting off. Then, come Monday morning I'd hit the road again; the pressure would start building up for an hour before I even got to Philadelphia. . . . But I guess we made the same mistake that everybody else did in the beginning. We never expected that it would take this long—we started out by looking at it as a nuts-and-bolts thing."

About two months before her death, Susan Reinert purchased several hundred thousand dollars worth of life insurance which she added to an already sizable estate. Her mother had died the year before, in October 1978, leaving her approximately $30,000 in cash and about $200,000 in property near Ridgeway, Pennsylvania, in upstate Elk County. About a month after her mother died, Susan Reinert drew [up a] will naming her brother, W. Patrick Gallagher, executor, and her children, Michael and Karen, sole beneficiaries.

But those plans changed radically just seven weeks before her death. Besides purchasing a half-million-dollar life insurance policy (which included a $200,000 accidental death rider) from the United States Automobile Association of San Antonio, Texas, she also obtained a $160,000 policy from New York Life. The Great-West Assurance Company, a Canadian firm, had also written a substantial policy on her life.

At that point, in the spring of 1979, Susan Reinert's estate amounted to a little over $1.1 million.

She had amazed her friends and stunned her family by suddenly revising her will in early May, eliminating her brother as executor and also writing out her children as beneficiaries. In their place she substituted William S. Bradfield, her fellow teacher at Upper Merion High School, as both the new executor and the sole beneficiary.

A significant phrase in the revised will identified Bradfield as "my future husband."

Today, through his lawyers, big, bearded Bill Bradfield insists that that's news to him.

During his only court appearance in connection with the Reinert investigation, Bradfield stared through what one observer called "stony blue eyes" and contended that he and Susan Reinert had been merely very good friends. "She didn't take my advice very often. . . . She asked me about who she should date. She dated people I thought she ought not to, went places I thought she ought not to, lived a lifestyle I thought was not. . . ."

Bradfield was wisely interrupted at that point as he testified before Judge Francis Catania in the County Courthouse in Media, Delaware County, by his attorney, John Paul Curran.

The man questioning Bradfield then, on June 10th, 1980—almost a full year after Susan Reinert's body had been found—was Deputy District Attorney John A. Reilly of Delaware County, the court-appointed administrator of the embattled Reinert estate. Reilly would charge that all along Bradfield had been "leading her down the primrose path with a promise of marriage."

Without ever putting it in so many words, Bradfield and his defenders refuted this accusation by implying that Susan Reinert had actually been an unhappy and desperately lonely woman, perhaps neurotic, and that she had wistfully manufactured an imaginary romance with Bradfield, capped in her own mind by her naming him in her will.

However, friends of the victim, her former psychologist, police investigators speaking off the record, and a horde of aggressive reporters would eventually come up with a much different version of events.

According to that unofficial consensus, Reinert and Bradfield had been casual lovers for approximately six years, despite the fact that Bradfield had been living with another teacher at Upper Merion, Susan Myers, for much of that time. (Bradfield was also previously married.)

Just prior to her death, Susan Reinert had told friends of plans to move to England with Bradfield, along with the children, and marry him. And neighbors on Woodcrest Avenue in Ardmore told investigators that Bradfield had been a frequent visitor at Susan Reinert's house, going on trips with the murder victim, playing with her kids, and occasionally staying all night.

Bradfield, who had recently been elected head of the teachers' union at Upper Merion, claimed that this was nonsense, that he had no intention of leaving for England, and that he was looking forward to negotiating the school district's new contract.

Naturally, the police investigating Susan Reinert's murder were spellbound by all this, especially by the fact that Bradfield profited so handsomely and directly as a result of Susan Reinert's death.

Today, John Paul Curran, a top-notch, Jesuit-educated defense lawyer in center city Philadelphia, scoffs at this speculation.

"William Bradfield has never been charged with anything and has not done anything. He has become as much as victim of all this as Susan Reinert. It has ruined his health and jeopardized his career.

"The people trying to link him to this must subscribe to the 'butler always did it theory'. . . . Well, this time the butler *didn't* do it."

On the advice of Curran and his other attorneys, Bradfield has declined all comment on the case. His only public statement on it was a brief written denial of any involvement in the murder and a wish for its speedy solution, which he issued when he abruptly stepped aside as the head of the Upper Merion teacher's union. He has, according to investigators, declined to cooperate with the FBI or the state police.

Bradfield had been teaching at Upper Merion since 1963 with certifications in English and Latin. A native of Colorado, he graduated from Haverford College in 1955 and has spent much of the rest of his life either taking or giving courses.

Most considered him the premier figure at Upper Merion, academically as well as politically. Students fought to get into his classes and female teachers, like Susan

Reinert, apparently melted under the gaze of those "stony blue eyes." Stories—never really substantiated—circulated around the Upper Merion campus that in his younger days, Bradfield had fought with Castro in Cuba and lived the dashing life of a romantic scholar. While the Bradfield legend was almost certainly more fascinating than the real thing, the fact remained that among the catty, warring cliques within the faculty, Bradfield's was the predominant. In fact, the only educator in the township with as much clout as Bradfield was Upper Merion's veteran principal, Jay C. Smith. It appeared to many that together, the two actually ran the school. Bradfield has always adamantly maintained though, that because of his union activities and because he was faculty rather than administration, their relationship was adversarial.

Outside the school, Bradfield was the part owner of a craft shop in the Montgomeryville Mall, and also the holder of some choice real estate in Chester County. He was bright, charming and mesmerizing. Sometimes Bradfield's admirers couldn't help but wonder what he was doing in the English department of a high school. As one of them expressed it, "He is what a teacher should be. When you think of somebody poring over the Great Books, when you think of your typical Ivy League professor, the image that pops into your mind immediately is a guy like Bill Bradfield. It's not hard to see why a little English teacher like Susan Reinert went nuts over him."

The police, meanwhile, were singularly unimpressed with Bradfield's credentials and personality. *He* was the one who would get the money after Reinert's death, and that was good enough for them.

Bradfield's whereabouts on the night Reinert disappeared have never been confirmed by the police. However, that early summer weekend of the slaying, he and three fellow teachers from Upper Merion checked into a boarding house in Cape May, New Jersey, where they remained until Monday, the day that Susan Reinert's body was found. On that day, June 25th, 1979, Bradfield and another teacher took a night flight to Santa Fe, New Mexico, where they would spend the summer taking graduate courses. In fact, Bradfield was still in New Mexico when he contacted John Paul Curran of Curran, Mylotte, David & Fitzpatrick.

Long after Bradfield had become a central figure in the investigation—though one who, to this day, has never been charged with anything—the police determined that Susan Reinert had been killed sometime between 12:15 and 6:15 a.m. on Sunday, June 24th, 1979.

Eventually, Bradfield; his ex-roommate, Susan Myers; and Christopher Pappas, all teachers at Upper Merion, would hire Guardsman Security Systems Inc. to give them polygraph tests to determine if they were telling the truth about being in Cape May that weekend (where witnesses had seen them, anyway). A fourth teacher, Vincent Valaitis, who was also there, declined to participate, and instead, chose to cooperate with investigators. According to a spokesman for the polygraph firm, there were "no signs of any deception at all" in Bradfield's and the others' replies to questions about Susan Reinert's murder or their own whereabouts at that time.

Nearly one year after Susan Reinert's death, in June 1980, Bradfield, through his attorneys, finally moved to probate Susan Reinert's will and collect the $1.1 million estate.

Almost immediately, Reinert's brother, W. Patrick Gallagher, and her ex-husband, Kenneth Reinert, sought to block that probate. Both claimed to be acting in behalf of the missing children. According to the objection filed by Patrick Gallagher, there had been "undue influence exerted by William Bradfield, who was in a confidential relationship" with Susan Reinert, Gallagher's sister.

While a monumental will contest over the Reinert estate was taking shape— "the kind of an estate fight that comes along only about once every ten years in the entire United States," according to the fiery John Paul Curran—the cops were still searching for a murderer—and two missing kids.

After the episode of Susan Reinert's cremation before a proper forensic examination could take place, the FBI and the state police figured that things couldn't get any worse. But that was before they decided to reexamine the tape recording of the anonymous caller who had first informed the courthouse dispatcher that a sick woman was in a car in the Host Inn parking lot.

. . .

Like the corpse, the tape had also vanished. Employees in the courthouse claimed that they must have run short of tapes at some point because of the volume of incoming calls over the recent Three Mile Island scare, and accidentally reused the tape, thereby erasing one of the earliest and most promising leads.

. . .

Susan Reinert had been an excellent English teacher and a valued addition to the Upper Merion faculty. Her pet project was filmmaking and she had become *the* audio-visual lady at Upper Merion. The kids thought she was great; the administration felt fortunate to have her, and her fellow professionals held her in high esteem.

The principal at Upper Merion, Jay C. Smith, whom Bill Bradfield had characterized as his adversary, was born and bred in Chester, Pennsylvania, and had been the undisputed boss of the school for the last dozen years. Personally, according to published accounts of the situation at Upper Merion, his life was becoming a shambles, with an estranged wife dying of cancer and a daughter and son-in-law who were both beset with problems of their own. However, for most of his tenure at Upper Merion, the outside world knew Smith as a spit-and-polish colonel in the Army Reserve and a thoroughly competent administrator in a demanding school district. In the beginning the school had flourished under Smith and had attracted dedicated educators like Susan Reinert. But all that began to change for Smith and Upper Merion High about two years before the English teacher's murder.

Today, Jay C. Smith, now 52, is serving hard time at the State Correctional Institution in Dallas, Pennsylvania, one of the toughest prisons in the East.

Since May 1979, Smith has been convicted of or has pled no contest to a whole series of crimes. It all began when he was accused of trying to steal $158,000 from a Sears store in St. Davids in December 1977. Since then he has pled no contest to a weapons offense, disorderly conduct, and possession of instruments of crime. Juries found him guilty of theft by deception, attempted theft by deception, possession of marijuana, and receiving stolen property. All told he could spend the next 4 to 12 years behind bars.

His last sentencing in June 1980, before a Dauphin County judge, saw Smith plead unsuccessfully for leniency. He had, he told the judge, "made a mess" of his life over the last two years. Today, homicide investigators are still trying to determine whether that mess could possibly shed any light on the fate of Susan Reinert as well.

In the months immediately following her murder and the revelations about Smith's "secret life," as the principal himself termed it in rambling open letters to the faculty written from prison, the Upper Merion community erupted.

Allegations of everything from teen orgies to satanic cults to sex between students and teachers ripped through the neighborhood like an outbreak of herpes—and Smith's name was linked to all of it by stop-the-presses newspaper coverage. Smith was portrayed, while still principal, as having amassed a huge porno collection; as having dabbled in swingers' sex clubs, where he was known as Colonel Jay; and as having sometimes donned a devil's costume during his escapades. *Today's Post*, a local paper, published excerpts of a journal allegedly kept by Smith's estranged wife, which provided more details.

These allegations were and are vehemently contested by Jay Smith. He reacted to the massive tabloid coverage with the "open letters" to the faculty at Upper Merion and filing suits for libel against several publications, including *Today's Post*, the *Daily News* and the Philadelphia *Inquirer*. Those lawsuits are presently pending and the truth of the allegations is still in dispute, but these rumors did little to calm the parents at Upper Merion and only created more leads for the investigators of Susan Reinert's murder to track down.

Even after Smith had been arrested and removed in 1978, Upper Merion parents screamed at one public protest meeting after another that they were still afraid to send their children to school. Reinert's murder coming on top of all this less than 12 months later left them absolutely hysterical.

On top of everything else, the police soon learned that Smith's daughter and son-in-law had not been seen near their Montgomery County home for almost a year-and-a-half.

Counting the Reinert kids, that made four missing persons the police had to deal with, plus one cremated corpse.

Investigators looking hard for any possible parallels between the Smith and Reinert cases soon found one in the person of William S. Bradfield.

In May 1979, the month before Reinert's murder, Bradfield had provided Smith's alibi at the principal's trial for the attempted theft of the Sears in St. Davids in 1977. Bradfield told the court that on the day of the incident he had actually run into Smith in Ocean City, New Jersey; spent time with him there looking for a mutual friend, and even shared a meal with him.

Bradfield's alibi for Smith obviously wasn't sufficient. Smith was convicted on May 31st. His sentencing date, when he was to appear before a state judge in Harrisburg, Pennsylvania, was Monday, June 25th, 1979—the day Susan Reinert's body was discovered in the parking lot of the Host Inn in Swatara Township about eight miles from Harrisburg.

According to published reports and stories later circulated by her friends at Upper Merion, Susan Reinert was very upset over Bradfield's testimony. The psychologist who had been treating her since 1973 would say later in an interview that: "Sue Reinert had serious and deep concerns that Bradfield may have committed perjury for Smith at his trial. When she confronted him about a month before her death, he acted high and mighty, Sue said. She said he became very indignant that she would dare question his honesty."

The problem was, Reinert confided to some of her friends, that she had been with Bradfield that day in Ocean City and couldn't recall Bradfield even seeing Smith, much less spending any time with him.

Over the next few weeks, just before her death, her relationship with Bradfield became strained. Neighbors even recall seeing her start to run after him, crying, as Bradfield left her house one day. For his part, Bradfield started hinting to friends that Sue Reinert had gone off the deep end.

This wasn't the first time their relationship had been troubled. A few years before, Sue Myers, Bradfield's roommate, and Reinert had argued and even come to blows over Bradfield one day at the high school. However, her friends were very concerned about the split that was developing because Sue Reinert still insisted that she and Bradfield were to be married in England that fall.

. . .

There had been one more piece of evidence found in the Reinert car—a small, blue, plastic comb with the inscription "79th USARCOM." That happened to be the same Army Reserve unit where Jay C. Smith was a colonel.

New developments on the botched autopsy were also giving investigators like Wald still more to go on. Over five months after the body had been found, a forensic pathologist in Philadelphia, working his way backwards and using those tiny samples of frozen tissue taken at the preliminary autopsy, determined that Susan Reinert had not died of asphyxiation, as originally certified, but from an overdose of morphine. Because they no longer had the body, it was impossible to double-check it for needle marks, but the pathologist was certain that the drug overdose had been induced from the outside.

The police also attempted to determine whether fibers found in Reinert's hair could match those found in a rug in Jay C. Smith's home. Further legwork revealed that when Smith had been arrested at the Gateway Shopping Center in Devon in 1978 while allegedly attempting a holdup, the police had confiscated a hypodermic syringe—the kind that could have possibly been used to induce a morphine overdose.

Also, the police could place Jay C. Smith in Harrisburg the day Reinert's body was found. He had shown up in a judge's chamber for sentencing that day, several hours late, explaining that he had been caught in a gas line—the same kind of gas line that Susan Reinert had worried about.

The FBI and the state police spent the rest of 1979 trying to put the whole thing together. They looked for meetings between Bradfield and Smith, sought to interview Jo Ann Aitkens—a former student who had driven Bradfield's car to New Mexico—and checked phone records to determine who had called Sue Reinert the night she disappeared. Subpoenas were issued and a grand jury began investigating the case, as well.

The police were especially curious about Bradfield's and Smith's movements on the night Reinert and her children disappeared.

Bradfield claimed that he had been visiting his ex-wife, miles from the Reinert neighborhood. He had waited for her but she had never shown up. Smith declared that he, too, had been visiting his wife in Bryn Mawr Hospital, but the staff there didn't recall seeing him.

. . .

In June 1980, when William S. Bradfield quietly moved to probate the will and collect on the insurance policies that named him as executor and sole beneficiary of Susan Reinert's $1.1 million estate, interest in the case revived again.

It was later that month that Delaware County [Deputy] District Attorney John Reilly would accuse Bradfield of leading Susan Reinert down the primrose path to marriage.

That took place in Orphans Court where Reilly, as [administrator] of the estate, had forced Bradfield to take the stand to answer an accusation that shortly before her death he had taken $25,000 of Susan Reinert's money, as well as a diamond ring, to invest in some financial scheme involving a $100,000 certificate of deposit, of which Susan Reinert would have been a part owner. Now, Reilly said, the money and ring were missing and unaccounted for, and therefore owed to the estate.

What Assistant DA John Reilly really was doing was forcing *someone* to testify in open court about the Reinert case for the first time in over a year. William Bradfield denied any knowledge of the money or the ring. From law enforcement's point of view, that hearing in Orphans Court proved little, but at least it was a start—maybe even the beginning of the end.

On July 26th, 1980, William Bradfield's lawyers, who were still trying to probate the Reinert will, responded to the efforts by the dead woman's ex-husband and brother to contest it.

Running behind a legal blocking line comprised of defense attorney John Paul Curran, Charles A. Fitzpatrick, III, an expert in estate law, and Walter ReDavid, the former register of wills in Delaware County, Bradfield dramatically put the opposition on the defensive by demanding that the investigators' notes and files on the case be turned over to him to facilitate the probate. Once and for all, Bradfield had to know if he was a suspect or not. That was the only way, his lawyers insisted, that his name could be cleared, his life be put back together again and the charge that he had exerted "undue influence" on Susan Reinert be thrown out once and for all.

By now, another renowned expert in estate law, Robert Costigan, the former register of wills for Philadelphia, had also entered the case as the attorney for Kenneth Reinert. If nothing else, it seemed certain that the will fight would make judicial history with one of the most able casts of courtroom heavyweights ever assembled in the arcane field of estate law.

In the meantime, the several insurance companies involved were going to court themselves, and balking at paying anything to anybody who might conceivably be considered a suspect in Reinert's murder.

Somehow, the mystery of the Reinert children had to be cleared up, too. So much—from a legal standpoint—hinged on them.

If the will was validated as it stood, then William Bradfield could collect as the sole beneficiary and return to Upper Merion High School in triumph.

But if the will were thrown out, as Susan Reinert's brother and ex-husband wanted, then the fate of Michael and Karen Reinert, Susan's missing children, would be crucial.

If the children were somehow found alive, they would be entitled to the estate.

If the kids really were dead and the police could demonstrate that they had died prior to their mother, then Susan Reinert's brother, W. Patrick Gallagher, would stand to benefit. However, if there was proof that the children had died after Susan Reinert, then her ex-husband, Kenneth, would probably be entitled to some of the money, as party-of-interest through the estates of the children.

Then, of course, there was always the possibility that there could have been prior wills that the investigators hadn't even discovered yet. At stake was over $1 million in property and insurance.

In the event of any criminal prosecutions for the murder of Susan Reinert, then the Pennsylvania Slayer's Act would come into effect. By statute, that prevents anyone from profiting by their own misdeed.

Since the case was an ongoing investigation, the Justice Department responded to Bradfield by refusing to turn anything over to him. All along, investigators had been incensed over his refusal to cooperate on the case. At this point, they had no intention of turning over their findings to him. Instead, the feds pleaded for—and eventually all parties agreed to—six months, continuance on the request.

Sources close to the investigation claim that the work is almost completed and the case nearly closed. The identity of the murderer is known, they hint. Every detail of the investigation, however, is being checked and double-checked and made as airtight as possible. This is being done because of the double-jeopardy rule in a murder trial. The prosecution will only have one crack at whoever they name. After that, even new evidence won't make much difference.

. . .

CODED BRADFIELD NOTE: 'MY DANGER CONSPIRACY'

FBI EXPERT DECODES MESSAGE

Emilie Lounsberry

HARRISBURG, October 25, 1983—In a dramatic conclusion to the state's case against William S. Bradfield Jr., the prosecution yesterday produced a cryptic note in Bradfield's handwriting that an expert witness said was topped with the coded message: "Immunity improbable. My danger conspiracy."

Jacqueline Taschner, who analyzes codes for the FBI, said the note was deciphered by comparing it to a code listed on pages of a book owned by Bradfield, a former Upper Merion High School teacher who is charged in the June 1979 slayings of fellow teacher Susan Reinert and her two children.

The book, titled *The Works of Confucius* by Ezra Pound, and the note were obtained by police from Susan J. Myers, who lived with Bradfield until April 1980.

The note was taken from Ms. Myers' apartment in February 1981, according to testimony, and Ms. Myers gave the book to authorities this month or last.

The note and an enlarged copy viewed by the jury were the last two of 63 exhibits admitted into evidence before the prosecution rested its case against Bradfield, 50. The trial began Oct. 15.

Bradfield is charged with conspiring with at least one unnamed accomplice to plan the Reinert slayings.

The note concluded the prosecution's efforts to construct a web of circumstantial evidence showing that Bradfield had plotted the killings to inherit $900,000 in life-insurance and estate benefits.

The Dauphin County trial is expected to resume at 9 a.m. today with the defense beginning its case. Defense attorney Joshua D. Lock said yesterday that he would call Bradfield to the stand as the first witness.

In her testimony concerning the coded message, Ms. Taschner said the note also contained references to a typewriter.

The text included the following: "Does FBI have typewriter," "Does FBI know V has it" and "FBI must not get it."

A red IBM typewriter of Bradfield's has been mentioned during the testimony of several previous witnesses.

One of those witnesses, Jeffrey Olsen, 26, a former friend and student of Bradfield's, testified yesterday that Bradfield had asked him to keep the typewriter.

Bradfield, Olsen testified, said the typewriter "had produced letters to Mrs. Reinert that could be made out to be important."

Olsen, who now lives in Kansas City, Mo., testified that the conversation had occurred after the Reinert slayings, while he and Bradfield were attending summer school at St. John's College in Santa Fe, N.M.

Olsen said that during that summer, Bradfield burned a handful of documents in Olsen's fireplace in Santa Fe. He said Bradfield stirred the ashes and "made sure everything was destroyed." Olsen said that Bradfield told him, "they were just school papers of Mrs. Reinert's."

Another witness, Christopher Pappas, a former substitute teacher at Upper Merion, testified yesterday that Bradfield had discussed destroying the ball of the typewriter because he was afraid it would link him to the killings.

Joanne Aitken, an architect who said she is still romantically involved with Bradfield, testified Friday that she now has the typewriter.

Outside the courtroom, the prosecutor, Deputy Attorney General Richard L. Guida, declined to say to what, or to whom, "V" might refer in the message, except to suggest that Bradfield might have been referring to anyone who had possession of the typewriter after Mrs. Reinert's body was found on June 25, 1979.

The testimony by Ms. Taschner also suggested that "V" may have referred simply to "you."

The coded message, Ms. Taschner said, consisted largely of numbers but also contained some translations of those numbers into letters.

The words "immunity improbable, my danger conspiracy," however, were not already translated, she said.

Ms. Myers testified earlier that the code was based on numbering of lines in Bradfield's book by fives, up to 100 on several pages. Another teacher at Upper

Merion High, Vincent Valaitis, testified that he, Bradfield and others had used the book in a code system to communicate.

The coded message was the second document containing cryptic notations to be introduced into evidence during the trial. On Friday, Pappas testified that he had obtained a list in 1980 that included the notation "lured and killed kids, taped her" in Bradfield's handwriting.

The jury heard conflicting testimony yesterday about Bradfield's plans for $730,000 in life-insurance benefits from three policies in which Mrs. Reinert named Bradfield as beneficiary.

Olsen quoted Bradfield as saying, shortly after Mrs. Reinert's killing, "I don't want that goddamn money."

"He said it would be put up as a trust for the children, but he'd never keep it himself," Olsen said.

Later, representatives of two insurance companies told the jury that Bradfield had attempted to claim the $730,000 by filing lawsuits against the companies in 1980.

In each case, both witnesses said, Bradfield agreed to drop the suit in exchange for a $100 settlement.

In other testimony, Olsen said that shortly after Mrs. Reinert's death, the defendant said former Upper Merion High School principal Jay C. Smith probably had committed the killing. Olsen said Bradfield had discussed his feelings about Mrs. Reinert's death and said "how awful it was that Smith got her."

Olsen testified that Bradfield had first discussed Mrs. Reinert and Smith with him when he visited Bradfield at Upper Merion High during Christmastime 1978. At that time, he said, Bradfield appeared preoccupied and depressed.

When he coaxed Bradfield into discussing what was wrong, Olsen said, Bradfield told him that he was troubled by what he had learned about Smith, who recently had been arrested for theft, attempted theft, drug possession and weapons charges.

Smith, 55, is serving a prison term at Dallas State Prison in Wilkes-Barre as a result of his 1978 arrests.

Bradfield said Smith "was a crook, and not just a petty crook," Olsen told the court. "Smith was under suspicion for several crimes, and Bill Bradfield said they were small potatoes compared to the real truth."

Bradfield said Smith was a murderer, was trafficking in drugs and may have been involved in prostitution, Olsen said.

He said Bradfield also disclosed that he thought Smith was going to kill Mrs. Reinert.

Olsen said Bradfield had told him that "Mrs. Reinert had been Smith's mistress, and therefore she might have some of the same kind of information about Smith that Bradfield claimed to have. And therefore, Smith would have to kill her to silence her potential testimony."

After Guida rested his case yesterday, defense attorney Lock moved for the dismissal of the murder charges against Bradfield.

Lock contended that the state had not produced evidence that Bradfield had planned the deaths of Mrs. Reinert's two children, Karen, 11, and Michael, 10, and that the evidence suggests that Bradfield was in Cape May, N.J., when Mrs. Reinert was killed.

What Decoder Found

The following is the text of a message written in a numerical code and deciphered by Jacqueline Taschner, a cryptanalyst for the FBI. The prosecution and the defense agreed that the numbers in the message were in Bradfield's handwriting. Ms. Taschner said she had been able to decode the message by assigning letters to the numbers based on a numerical code found on pages of a book belonging to Bradfield.

Ms. Taschner said her analysis showed that the full message said:

Immunity probable

My danger conspiracy

Does FBI have typewriter

Does FBI know V has it

Have V remove ball or destroy it, or better claim it was stolen

Did I sell it to you

Then get rid of it

FBI must not get it

Does FBI know you mailed it

Can you think of substitute—same weight—until V claims it stolen

The children, who were last seen alive on June 22, 1979, while leaving their Ardmore home with their mother, never have been found. The statewide grand jury that recommended Bradfield's arrest concluded that they, too, had been slain.

The only evidence that placed Bradfield at the slayings, Lock told the judge, was testimony by former prison inmate Proctor Nowell, who said Bradfield had confided that he had been present when "they" were killed but that he did not kill them.

Lock said that the evidence shows that Mrs. Reinert died no earlier than around noon on Sunday, June 24, 1979, and that Bradfield had spent that weekend in Cape May, N.J.

Guida countered that Bradfield's alleged admission that he had been present when "they" were killed could have referred to the children.

Nowell testified that Bradfield had said, "'None of this was meant for the kids, only Susan, but you can't leave a stone unturned. You have to tie up all the loose ends.'"

Perhaps, Guida suggested yesterday, the children were killed because "they saw what happened to their mother."

Guida further argued that the law states that murder can be established "by complicity in the actual act."

"Whoever planned the killing is as guilty of first-degree murder under the law as the person who actually committed it," Guida said.

Lock's request to dismiss the charges was denied by Bucks County President Judge Isaac S. Garb, who was specially appointed by the state Supreme Court to preside over the trial.

THE JURY: CONVINCED OR CONFUSED?

Emilie Lounsberry and Henry Goldman

HARRISBURG, October 25, 1983—Unanswered questions in the mysterious murders of Susan Reinert and her two children could end up weighing more heavily on the minds of the jurors than the web of circumstantial evidence tying William S. Bradfield Jr. to the crimes.

Despite eight days of testimony from more than 60 witnesses, the prosecution rested its case yesterday without producing a "smoking gun." And that may pose problems in proving Bradfield's guilt beyond a reasonable doubt.

The most compelling aspect of the prosecution's case is the totality of testimony that portrays Bradfield as a manipulator capable of committing such crimes.

Witnesses testified that he was so successful in getting others to do his bidding that a friend built a gun silencer for him, others helped destroy evidence at his request, two people stored money in a safety deposit box for him, and others agreed to lie or otherwise obstruct a police investigation that Bradfield allegedly feared would center on him as the suspect.

But the question remains whether a jury will be confused by the hours of detailed, sometimes contradictory, testimony, in which subtle, seemingly unimportant facts must be woven together to support a theory of guilt.

What is the jury to make of the red IBM typewriter, for example, which was often spoken of by witnesses and was the subject of a coded message introduced yesterday in which Bradfield said: "FBI must not get it."

All they know is that the typewriter was given to Susan J. Myers, with whom Bradfield was living, as a birthday present, that it became the source of concern for Bradfield in the weeks and months after Mrs. Reinert's murder.

Bradfield tried to exchange the machine's typing ball with a friend, the jury has been told. He said "important documents" had been typed on it.

But the jurors don't know what those documents are. Even the typewriter, now in the possession of Joanne Aitken, who described herself as still romantically involved with Bradfield, has not been introduced as evidence.

The jury may also have difficulty determining guilt because of the prosecution's presentation of Bradfield's whereabouts on June 22, 1979, the night Mrs. Reinert was last seen alive.

Deputy District Attorney Richard L. Guida has tried to establish that Bradfield cannot account for his whereabouts between 8:30 and 11:30 that night.

Autopsy results concluded that Mrs. Reinert died sometime after noon on Sunday, June 24. Her body was discovered at 5 a.m. Monday, June 25, and three witnesses testified that they accompanied Bradfield to Cape May, N.J., that weekend, leaving for the shore about 11:30 p.m. Friday and returning after 4 p.m. Monday.

That time sequence would appear to make it physically impossible for Bradfield to have been present when Mrs. Reinert was killed—regardless of his whereabouts during the unexplained two hours on that Friday.

What Guida did succeed in demonstrating to the jury was a possible motive for the murders: Bradfield had been named the beneficiary of more than $900,000 in life insurance and estate benefits shortly after Mrs. Reinert's death.

The most dramatic, and perhaps the most damning, evidence in Guida's case came in the last few days, when he introduced several notes in Bradfield's handwriting that appeared to show the defendant trying to hide his complicity in the crime.

In testimony yesterday, Guida introduced a coded message, in Bradfield's handwriting, found by police on Feb. 18, 1981, in the apartment he once shared with Ms. Myers.

An FBI cryptanalyst testified that she decoded the message, and that it says, in part: "My danger conspiracy."

And on Friday, Guida introduced into evidence two lists in Bradfield's handwriting. One contained cryptic notations including "lured and killed kids, taped her."

The prosecution has presented expert testimony that said Mrs. Reinert's body showed signs of having been taped, chained and beaten.

The other list contained questions that a witness said Bradfield had compiled to coach him in answering police questions about Mrs. Reinert's death.

Among the other problems the prosecution faced in presenting its case:

- Police could not conclude with certainty where the killings took place.
- The bodies of Mrs. Reinert's children, who are presumed dead, have never been found.
- No physical evidence links Bradfield to the body or Mrs. Reinert's hatchback car, in which her body was found on June 25, 1979, in the parking lot of a motel near Harrisburg.
- Because of a bungled autopsy, officials did not learn until five months after her death that blood samples showed Mrs. Reinert had died of an overdose of morphine. The autopsy, performed by an osteopathic pathologist who was not a specialist in forensic medicine, had concluded that cause of death was suffocation. And because Mrs. Reinert's body was cremated soon after her death, it could not be reexamined for evidence.
- Much of the testimony depicting Bradfield as obsessed with the impending death of Mrs. Reinert and with ensuring himself of an alibi came from witnesses who testified only after receiving grants of immunity from the prosecution.
- The only witness to connect Bradfield to the murders of the children is Procter Nowell, a convicted felon who faces criminal charges of his own and who may have agreed to testify because of promises of leniency.
- The prosecution has sought to establish that Bradfield conspired to commit the murder—which carries the same penalty as actually committing the murder—but no other co-conspirators have been named.

As Guida pointed out yesterday while successfully arguing against a defense motion to dismiss the case, "The murder of Mrs. Reinert can be established by an actual act or complicity in an actual act. Whoever planned it is as guilty as whoever did it."

Guida pointed out that under Pennsylvania law, the prosecution need not produce other conspirators to prove a case of conspiracy.

And, it is on the hunch that he can prove conspiracy that Guida has hung his case.

Defense attorney Joshua D. Lock, relying on the remaining mysteries, will take his shot at the jury beginning today. He has said he will present plausible explanations for testimony that appeared to incriminate Bradfield.

Whether the mysteries that still surround the case are enough to create a reasonable doubt as to Bradfield's guilt is a question only the jury can answer.

Lawyers on both sides say they expect an answer to that question by early next week.

Bradfield, on Stand, Denies Any Role

Emilie Lounsberry

HARRISBURG, October 26, 1983—Testifying in his own defense, former Upper Merion High School teacher William S. Bradfield Jr. yesterday denied killing—or planning to kill—fellow teacher Susan Reinert and her two children.

He denied that he had intended to marry Mrs. Reinert, denied that he had had an affair with her and denied that he had influenced her to name him as beneficiary of $730,000 in life-insurance benefits.

"I never hurt Mrs. Reinert or her children in any way," Bradfield, 50, told a packed courtroom in Dauphin County.

Under questioning by his defense attorney, Joshua D. Lock, Bradfield insisted that he had played no role in the June 1979 deaths.

"Did you kill Susan Reinert?" Lock asked.

"No," Bradfield replied.

"Did you kill the children?"

"No."

"Did you plan to kill them?"

"I did not."

Under cross-examination by Deputy Attorney General Richard L. Guida, Bradfield said he did not know who had killed the Reinerts. But he suggested that former Upper Merion principal Jay C. Smith—or any of several men Mrs. Reinert had been dating might have committed the slayings.

Smith, 55, who is imprisoned in Dallas State Prison near Wilkes-Barre on charges including theft, drug possession and weapons offenses, was subpoenaed yesterday by the defense to testify, according to documents filed in Dauphin County Court. Lock has contended that Smith, not Bradfield, should be on trial for the Reinert slayings.

Bradfield's daylong testimony opened the defense portion of the case yesterday, the ninth day of the trial. He testified in a soft, even voice that at times was barely audible. He gave such expansive and detailed testimony that prosecutor Guida made numerous objections.

Spectators, many from the Philadelphia area, waited in line for seats in the courtroom throughout the lunchtime recess and lined up an hour early before the start of the evening session. Once inside, the spectators remained silent, straining to hear Bradfield's explanation of the months before and after the killings.

Bradfield named several men who he said Mrs. Reinert had been dating and who he thought might have killed her and her children.

One of those, he suggested, was a man named Alex who lived near Harrisburg. He also mentioned Jay, Ted and Grant.

Bradfield said Mrs. Reinert had told him that "they were into group sex and were advocates of bondage."

Earlier, Bradfield testified that he had grown concerned that Smith was going to kill Mrs. Reinert months before her death. Her body was found on June 25, 1979, stuffed in the rear of her hatchback car outside a suburban Harrisburg motel.

Bradfield testified that Smith had said a number of people "did not deserve to live." Smith's "hit list," Bradfield said, included the Upper Merion School District superintendent, the deputy superintendent and Mrs. Reinert.

Bradfield testified that he had become concerned about Mrs. Reinert's safety shortly after he began helping Smith to defend himself against the various charges he faced, all of which were unrelated to the Reinert case.

"His arrest and charges had become the gossip of the school. I had really been shocked and saddened," Bradfield said in explanation of why he offered to assist Smith.

But soon after he began meeting with the principal, Bradfield testified, Smith began telling him that he had ties with "figures of the underworld."

When Smith informed him that Mrs. Reinert was among those who did not deserve to live, Bradfield said he "expressed surprise."

"He said I didn't know Susan Reinert as well as I thought I did," Bradfield testified.

Bradfield said he discussed with friends whether Smith's threats might be real and decided "we didn't know the answer so the best thing was to keep an eye on Dr. Smith."

Bradfield said that although Smith continued to make the threats, he decided to avoid going to the authorities because "we just couldn't get ourselves to believe it was true. It was just too bizarre."

Later, when asked if he believed that he should have called the police, Bradfield replied, "Looking back, I wish at this point it was done."

He said he approached Mrs. Reinert "indirectly" [regarding the] threats, questioning her about whether she had been involved with Smith. Mrs. Reinert, he said, denied any involvement, so he continued his efforts to control Smith, whom he called an "unguided missile."

By the end of 1978, Bradfield said, he had become physically exhausted from "keeping an eye" on Smith and trying to protect Mrs. Reinert.

"I was at the point of being so concerned about Susan Reinert that I checked on her almost constantly," he said.

He said he continued to meet with Smith so he could monitor the former principal's plans. Smith continued to imply that he was going to harm someone, Bradfield testified.

At one point, Bradfield said, Smith gave him guns, chains, tape and hydrochloric acid, which Smith claimed to have used on victims.

The bottle of acid, Bradfield said Smith had told him, "was the kind of thing to remove identification marks from bodies. I recall he said the tape was useful in disarming someone."

Bradfield said that as soon as he obtained any "objects or intelligence" from Smith, he showed the items to a friend and former student, Christopher Pappas.

Bradfield said that although he and Pappas had continued to discuss approaching authorities with the information, they decided "the danger was too great to do that."

Smith, he said, had claimed to have connections with several police officers.

Bradfield further explained that he was perplexed by Smith's inferences.

"Smith spoke in a very circumspect way," Bradfield said. "Dr. Smith never said, 'I have killed somebody.' Dr. Smith never said, 'I'm going to kill somebody.'

He said, 'I've been involved in things I wish I hadn't been.'" Bradfield said Smith had claimed to have been involved as a "screen of eliminations."

"We concluded from what Dr. Smith had told me what it meant," Bradfield said. "None of us knew what screen of eliminations meant. But when used in connection with [talk about] assassinations, it sounds like he meant hit man.

"We never really knew whether to take Smith that seriously or whether he was deranged," Bradfield said.

"We became more afraid to do anything. We were prisoners of our own fear."

Under cross-examination by Guida, Bradfield testified that he and Pappas had become so terrified of Smith that they discussed killing him.

BRADFIELD AND WOMEN

Henry Goldman

HARRISBURG, October 26, 1983—Two say they still care for him. One says she parted amicably from him years ago. One, 27 years younger than he, says she was engaged to marry him. And one of them is dead.

They were the women in the life of William S. Bradfield Jr. during the days and nights in 1978 and 1979, when the prosecution contends that Bradfield plotted the killing of fellow Upper Merion teacher Susan Reinert.

In the past five days, four women who have been involved with Bradfield, 50, have taken the stand at his Dauphin County trial for the June 1979 slaying of Mrs. Reinert and her two children. In their testimony, they revealed—sometimes reluctantly—intimate details about their lives and relationships with Bradfield, 50, a handsome and imposing man.

When it was Bradfield's turn to testify yesterday, the jury heard a story that sometimes differed remarkably from what the women had said.

"Susan Myers offered me the one really comfortable home base I had had since leaving home," Bradfield testified of his relationship with the teacher who shared an apartment with him from 1973 to 1980.

"We had a warm, close relationship. I cared for her very much. I think we loved each other, but we were no longer lovers after we returned from Europe in 1973. We were not intimate."

To Ms. Myers, 40, the apartment she shared with Bradfield was anything but a "comfortable home base." She testified that Bradfield's relationships with other women, and his frequent absences from home, had taken an emotional toll on her. She said she had been forced to rely on an assortment of mind-altering drugs, including Librium, to treat her depression.

"I became unhappy when we returned from Europe, and he became involved with Susan Reinert, Wendy Zeigler and Joanne Aitken," she recalled. She said she had been about to leave Bradfield at one point in 1976 when he "begged me to stay." She did, she said, "because I loved him."

Ms. Myers testified with some sarcasm that when she asked Bradfield about his relationships with other women, he told her he was conducting "poetry research."

When Bradfield asked her in late 1978 to sign a cohabitation agreement dividing their assets in the event that they split up, she refused.

In the fall of 1980, after the Reinert killings, she changed the locks of the apartment she shared with Bradfield and refused to let him in. She said she even refused to return his high school photographs and pictures of his parents.

"I would tell him to have his attorney call my attorney, but he never did," Ms. Myers testified.

In February 1981, Ms. Myers turned over to the FBI several notes that the prosecution has introduced as evidence in an attempt to show that Bradfield was concerned about possible circumstantial evidence that might tie him to the killings.

Yet, Ms. Myers ended her testimony by saying, "I still have feelings for him."

There were others that felt, or feel, the same way.

Wendy Zeigler, 23, testified last week that she and Bradfield had become engaged in 1978 and planned to marry when she graduated from college.

Ms. Zeigler, 23, a slender woman with clear blue eyes, a creamy complexion and long brown hair, was a student of Bradfield's at Upper Merion. During his testimony, Bradfield described her as one of "my favorite students" in his English, Latin and Greek classes.

According to Bradfield, the two had "discussed marriage but never made any plans." In testimony, they both described how they would go to motels and talk intimately but never engage in sex.

Their relationship was close enough for Bradfield to entrust her with a safety deposit box in which he placed $28,500 in cash and what she said he described as "important documents."

While Bradfield discussed marriage with Ms. Zeigler, he was involved with Joanne Aitken, a Harvard graduate student in architecture now living in Philadelphia.

When Ms. Aitken, 32, testified last week, she wore no makeup, and her long brown hair was wound tightly in a bun. She smiled faintly at Bradfield as she told the court that she remained "romantically involved" with the man on trial for Susan Reinert's killing.

As Bradfield explained it yesterday, his relationship with Ms. Zeigler had been based on "mutual admiration," while his involvement with Ms. Aitken had grown since 1974, when she was director of admissions at St. John's College in Annapolis, Md.

"Ms. Aitken was a very liberated person. Certainly we had a sexual relationship, but that was not the central relationship between us," he testified. "It [sex] didn't have the importance that it might have with Wendy Zeigler, for example."

As for Mrs. Reinert, who had named Bradfield the beneficiary of about $900,000 in life-insurance and estate benefits, Bradfield adamantly denied that he had ever asked her to marry him.

"She had told me about her past, her family," he said. "It was honest on her part; it was not so honest on my part. It would have been more honest if I had told her the burden [she] was on me."

Instead, Bradfield testified, he endured several years during which Mrs. Reinert sent him love notes, sometimes in view of his students and other teachers.

Bradfield testified that in the months up to Mrs. Reinert's killing, he had established what amounted to a death watch. He said he visited her home as often as three times a week, kept one of his cars parked at her house and called her when he could not be with her. All of this, he said, was done in an effort to protect her.

Bradfield said he told his friends that Mrs. Reinert had become "increasingly insistent since 1976 or so that I could solve her personal problems as a husband and father to her children. I told them she was . . . morbidly concerned with her own death—from cancer—particularly after her mother died."

Bradfield also told his friends that Mrs. Reinert had been dating a man named Alex, who Bradfield said was interested in "bondage and discipline" and "urination during sex."

What attracted Bradfield to these women?

"Physical appearance has never been important to me," he testified yesterday. "You can see that by some of the women I've been involved with. My poor wife, Muriel, was certainly not a bathing beauty—nor did it bother me," he said.

Muriel Bradfield testified last week that Bradfield left her in 1967 and that she had obtained an "amicable" divorce from him in March 1979. They were married in 1963.

STUDY QUESTIONS

1. Explain the difference between evidence and proof.
2. What is the strongest evidence in the case against William Bradfield?
3. Do you think Bradfield is guilty of conspiracy to commit murder? Beyond a shadow of a doubt? Beyond a reasonable doubt?
4. What is it about this case that makes it so difficult to *prove*?

Summary

The Yale student killing is a good example of the concepts introduced in this chapter. There are many traces left by the suspect which less alert investigators might have missed. For instance, just because a person uses one color ink to sign his work sheets at one time of day and another color later in the day is only a trace if one notices it and it could be indicative of several different patterns—depending on the story one is telling. The best story is the one that fits well with one's background knowledge and which uses as many of the traces as possible as evidence for the story being told. Ray Clark, on the other hand, tries to lead investigators away from a story that might incriminate him. His "hiding in plain sight" suggests the behavior of someone who is not worried and certainly not guilty of a heinous crime. But some of his behavior is more suspicious.

Background knowledge enables the police to weave the traces together into a story that uses familiar patterns that indicate Mr. Clark is not so innocent. "Workplace violence," however, is not a familiar motive to most people or a very satisfying one. Our background knowledge suggests other, more interesting motives which while more exciting, may not be supported by the evidence. The prosecutor at the trial will try to convince the jury of the defendant's guilt by presenting the traces as evidence for the story she will tell of a very violent workplace crime. She will build on the jury's background knowledge to show that the story she is telling fits well with what the jurors already know about crime and human behavior.

Of course, that is exactly what the prosecutor did in the trial of Todd Willingham. While the story that prosecutor told convinced the jury of Willingham's guilt, the story cannot *prove* that Willingham was guilty. In this case the difference between confirmation and proof is clearly evident. There are at least two very different stories that can be told using the same traces but as evidence for stories with very different conclusions as to Willingham's guilt. Again we see the importance of background knowledge: the jury's, the local fire investigators', the townspeople's, the scientist's and so on. Where you sit on the verdict in this story depends in large part on your own collection of background knowledge.

As for Jay Smith and William Bradfield, they were convicted of the murders of the three Reinharts. Bradfield was sentenced to life imprisonment. He continued to deny any wrong doing and died of a heart attack while serving three life sentences in prison. Smith was given the death sentence. He appealed all the way to the Supreme Court and was released in 1992 on the technicality of evidence concealment by the prosecution. He died in 2009. To the end he protested his innocence and defended himself in a book, self-published shortly before his death at age 80.

Exercises

7–I

1. The car in front of you suddenly flashes its brake lights. Your foot automatically moves from the accelerator to the brake. Explain the inductive reasoning involved in this common act.
2. Your boyfriend (girlfriend, significant other) forgot your birthday. What is your reaction? What is this trace evidence for? Why? What is the story you tell yourself?
3. Give an example where common sense came to your rescue in a tense situation. What background knowledge was important in your success?
4. Describe a belief you hold which you know is based on little evidence. How would you go about confirming it?
5. How might you convince a friend of the guilt/innocence of Todd Wilingham?
6. Create an example to explain to a friend why not all traces are evidence.

7–II

1. You know the subject matter of the course as well as your roommate but your roommate consistently gets better grades than you do? How could background knowledge explain this difference?
2. You and your father disagree about which candidate to vote for in the coming election. How might background information play a role in this disagreement? Can you prove who is the better candidate? Why or why not?
3. Describe a belief you hold for which you have proof. Write out your proof. How has your response to this question been influenced by the material in this chapter?
4. What is the difference between beyond "the shadow of a doubt" and beyond "a reasonable doubt"?
5. Why can beliefs about the way the world is only be confirmed and never proven?
6. Two famous court cases in the 1990s—the Rodney King beating trial and the O. J. Simpson murder trial—resulted in verdicts that the American public found very hard to accept or understand. Use the Internet to review what happened in each of these trials if you are not familiar with them. How would you explain this discrepancy between what the public thought should be the trials' outcomes and the actual verdicts of the two juries? Provide as much detail as you can. Use the ideas you learned in this chapter in your explanation.

8

Standards of Inductive Reasoning

THREE BASIC FORMS

There are three especially useful forms of inductive argument that we often use when we reason inductively. Most of us are not aware that we are using one of these forms in our reasoning, but being more aware of these forms can improve our inductive reasoning and our critical thinking. These three forms of inductive reasoning are generalizations, analogies, and causal claims. Inductive reasoning is "tricky" because the answers or conclusions never follow necessarily from the evidence provided. In inductive reasoning, we are always reasoning about what is probable or likely, but never certain. All three of these forms make claims that "stretch" beyond the evidence available to us. They involve inferring from features of examined or known cases to features of unexamined or unknown cases. There is plenty of room to make mistakes; so, it is best to have guidelines to avoid potential errors. In this chapter, we will explain each of the three forms and develop some guidelines for improving how we use these forms.

We reason with probability constantly in our ordinary everyday lives. We also use this kind of reasoning in more formal situations: to formulate scientific laws, to predict the outcome of elections, to diagnose an illness and suggest its treatment, and so on. Whenever we reason inductively, we make an inference from something observed to something unobserved or even unobservable. This sort of inference is the basis of all inductive reasoning. In outline, the three common forms of reasoning with probability are

1. All Xs are Ys (generalization)
2. If Xs have the property P, then this Y, which is very much like an X, probably also has the property P (analogy)
3. X causes Y (causal claim)

We will discuss each one of these forms in detail in this chapter.

Since we cannot examine all the Xs to see if they are Ys, inductive reasoning presents many puzzles. Consider generalizations, for example. "All circles are round" is clearly a warranted generalization. So is "All humans need food to live." But we are not so certain about some generalizations, such as "All humans have ten toes" or "Small town librarians lead boring lives." It would be nice, indeed, to have a rule which told us when to generalize and when not to generalize. Our expectations for the future would be more accurate, and we would be disappointed less often. Unfortunately, it is difficult to develop such a rule, and there are some interesting reasons why. However, what is equally interesting is that—despite the absence of any such rule—we actually do fairly well with our generalizations so that most of us confidently fly in airplanes, brush our teeth to prevent tooth decay, and regularly watch our favorite shows on television without disappointment. In this chapter, we will suggest some guidelines, but not a rule or rules, for making warranted generalizations and for distinguishing warranted generalizations from unwarranted ones.

When we make generalizations, we are observing at least one or more specific case(s) and then projecting the **pattern** we have observed onto future cases. The key word here is *pattern*. We must first observe a pattern, rather than randomness. Then we must decide if it makes sense to expect that pattern always, frequently, or sometimes in the future, given what we know. We discussed patterns in the previous chapter where we pointed out that many patterns of traces frequently go unnoticed by us. We begin to see patterns, however, when we have some interest that motivates us or when the pattern has been repeated so often that we cannot avoid recognizing it. The typical American high school, with its daily class schedule marked by the ringing of bells, would be a good example of the latter where a pattern is imposed on students with such regularity that they cannot help but notice it.

The patterns we are talking about can be very complex like weather patterns or the behavior of nations at war, or they can be rather simple like ice cubes melting in a warm soft drink. The importance of these patterns to us and our ability to generalize these patterns into the future cannot be exaggerated. They help us know what to **predict** and to a certain extent how to **control** what happens to us in the future.

Because the inference from something observed to something unobserved or even unobservable is the basis of all inductive reasoning, and generalizations are a very common pattern of this kind of reasoning, let's take an example of a generalization to see how this works. Consider, for instance, "Small town librarians lead boring lives." Someone might make such a generalization on the basis of having observed the lives of several librarians living in small towns. Or someone might have conducted a survey of librarians in small towns, asking them if they found their lives boring. Or someone might have made this generalization solely on the basis of his own beliefs about the lives of librarians and his beliefs about life in a small town. The generalization also has something to do with what the speaker may find boring or not boring. The point is that not every librarian in a small town has been observed. Even if one tried to observe or survey every such librarian, one could never be sure one had and certainly there are future librarians in small towns that one cannot now survey. So the claim is broader than the evidence for it. The claim takes a pattern that is presently observed and projects that pattern onto the future or onto cases not yet observed. Moreover, it suggests a certain expectation. That is, if you should happen to observe the life of a small town librarian in the future, you should not expect it to be a life of excitement. It also suggests that if you are considering becoming a librarian in a small town, you should not expect the excitement and glamour of sailing to Monte Carlo on a luxury liner.

Now the question we are concerned with here is when should we project our observations of patterns onto the future and when should we avoid projecting them. Are we warranted in saying—and believing—"Small town librarians lead boring lives," given that we have only visited a limited number of small town libraries? The answer is, "Maybe." Indeed, you might wonder if we are justified in project- ing a past pattern onto the future at all. That is, we seem to be assuming that the future will be like the past. But what evidence do we have for that assumption? The only evidence is that in the past the future was often like the past! This evidence, of course, is no evidence at all. It is just a restatement of the very point for which it is supposed to be evidence. It's like asking your friend who is always eating yel- low gumdrops, "Why do you like yellow gumdrops?" and your friend's replying, "I like yellow gumdrops because they taste good." And when you ask what is it that he likes about the taste, he replies, "They have a good flavor." It's an answer that's a non-answer. Yellow gumdrops taste good because they taste good. This puzzle— that the future will be much like the past because the past was much like its past—is called **the problem of induction**, and it does not have a solution. It's an assumption that we humans make (and perhaps animals, too), which we cannot prove but still must make to have order and stability in our lives. Thus, we need to keep in mind that when we generalize, our reasoning rests on an unprovable assumption about the likelihood of resemblance between past and future and, therefore, one guideline for making warranted generalizations is that we should proceed with caution and not be too hasty.

It should be noted that this puzzle of inductive reasoning cannot be avoided by changing our "all" statement to a "some" statement about a certain percentage of cases. That is, you might think that while maybe we can't prove that all librarians in small towns lead boring lives, surely we are warranted in believing that some of them do. Indeed we may be. But our warrant does not mean that we can be **certain** that the cases we have not observed will be like the ones we have. If 40% of the lives of small town librarians we have observed are boring, we may be warranted in believing that 40% of all librarians in small towns lead boring lives, if we have followed the guide- lines to be suggested here. But our projection about unobserved cases still rests on the unprovable assumption that the future will be like the past. **All inductive reasoning rests on this unprovable assumption!**

As we said, despite the fact that we cannot prove that the future will be like the past, the assumption that it will be like the past guides our future thinking and enables us often to predict and sometimes control what will happen to us. The point is there are no guarantees about the future's being exactly like the past. We will sometimes make mistakes even if we are following the guidelines as best we can. These mistakes are an important part of critical thinking as well. A good critical thinker is someone who learns from his mistakes so that he does not have to repeat them, at least not very often. We learn from our mistakes by correcting the generalizations that disap- point us or that give us unwanted surprises. So critical thinking about unobserved events is an ongoing process that is never ending, and our "mistakes" become part of the evidence we use for future generalizations.

GENERALIZATIONS

Before we discuss generalizations in greater detail, it is important to distinguish between generalizations and "quasi-generalizations" which look like generalizations but are really definitions. "All circles are round" is a quasi-generalization. Quasi-generalizations are not based on past experience at all but rather on the meanings of the words used in the generalization. They are not pieces of reasoning and hence do not rest on the unprovable assumption that the future will be like the past. It should also be noted that not all generalizations begin with "all." Sometimes the "all" is understood, as in the statement "A whale is a mammal."

You may be wondering whether this last generalization is intended to be a definition (a quasi-generalization) or a regular generalization, that is, a result of inductive reasoning. What if we found a whale-like creature that was not a mammal? Would we then say, "This creature is not a whale" or would we be more willing to say, "This creature is a whale that is not a mammal"? (The contemporary philosopher Hilary Putnam has made the ambiguity of statements like these famous among philosophers.) There is no right answer to this question. We can imagine circumstances in which both responses might be warranted. Usually we defer to the scientific community, or the community of language speakers closest to the context, and the common usage within that community.

Notice, however, for the statement "a whale is a mammal" to be a statement about the world and not a definition, it must be about some possible experience. Our observations of the world cannot be irrelevant to its being a warranted or an unwarranted claim. To put the matter another way, if the statement "a whale is a mammal" is about **whales** and not about the definition of the term *whale*, then our whale-like creature must at least have the possibility of being a whale even though it is not a mammal, if it is sufficiently whale-like. What this means is that all generalizations about the world must allow the possibility of counter examples. They cannot be immune to new information gained from experience. This is one of the meanings of the old adage, "The exception proves the rule." The possibility of an exception proves that the generalization is about the world and not about words and their definitions. This possibility again suggests the important guideline to keep in mind when making warranted generalizations, which is that we must always to be ready to revise our generalizations in the light of new information. We will have more to say about this below.

Let's go back to our small town librarian and our fundamental assumption, the future will be like the past. The problem is: *Which* future will be like *which* past? Failure to give the right answer to this question leads to bigotry, phobias, and thwarted expectations! The question is both more simple and more complex than it might seem. On one hand, as human beings we are always projecting into the future. We have expectations. We make plans. We don't even think about it. We get up, we get dressed, we eat, expecting today to be like yesterday. Most of our daily life is based on these simple generalizations, projecting the past we have observed onto the future we have not yet observed. If it were not, we would have trouble surviving. We would be worn out deciding what to do and how to do it. (This is what happens to us when we are put in a new environment and must think about how to accomplish the most basic tasks. Travelers in a foreign country and first-year college students are people who feel this kind of fatigue.)

On the other hand, some of our projections onto the future are very complex. Realizing this, we worry about what to expect, what to choose, whom to believe, and we make mistakes. There are too many variables, too many uncertainties, too little time. While we want to focus on these problems here and to suggest guidelines for meeting them, we should not forget or underestimate how well we actually anticipate the future or how adept human beings are at drawing warranted generalizations.

First, let us talk about "which past." This is a much more complicated problem than is often acknowledged. Usually something motivates us to pick out a particular pattern, or to collect data on a particular issue, whose worth is considered obvious. For example, we collect data on voter preferences because we want to help a candidate get elected. We look for patterns of authoritarian behavior in ordinary people because we want to understand why so many German soldiers could have obeyed such inhumane orders during World War II. We look for patterns in the biological responses of rats to a particular chemical compound because we want to know if the compound will be helpful in the treatment of some disease in humans.

This goes back to the point made in the previous chapter about **traces**. Traces abound. We notice those that have interest for us. One could say (as some philosophers have said) that we place **value** on them. We generalize a **pattern of traces** and project it into the future when it has value for us or when we think it has value for us. To put the matter another way, data are not there in our experience to be collected by us. We create data by valuing them or by collecting them. Our experience is one big cauldron of patterns of traces, or data, which we sort out according to our interests. This is why, despite what historians say, there are no lessons in history—because there is every lesson in history! For every battle that was followed by X, there was some battle, virtually identical, which was followed by the opposite of X. History, then, is a story that people tell to understand the traces they have picked out or placed value on. When people value things differently, they tell different stories. They have different histories.

If we are talking about small town librarians, we will have to make some decisions about which patterns to generalize. We will have to decide how small is a small town, for example. We will also have to consider who is a librarian. Are we considering only those who are librarians by occupation or anyone who works in a library? Perhaps we should limit our pattern to only librarians with blond hair or only bald, six-foot-tall librarians who speak with a Russian accent. How do we decide whether hair, height, weight, and all the many other features librarians could have are relevant to our generalization or to some other pattern worth generalizing? For example, maybe our focus should be the lives of bald librarians living in big cities. Why pick out only the feature of living in a small town? Which past, it becomes clear, is determined by us, by our interest, by what we value—and by the **background knowledge** which we bring to these experiences. Our background knowledge tells us, for example, that hair color or height have little to do with the amount of excitement in one's life, whereas living in a small town often precludes certain activities which might make life more interesting and exciting. We cannot emphasize too much the importance of background information in helping us decide "which past" to generalize.

Background knowledge is the key here but there are some very specific ways to use our background knowledge in determining when and what to generalize. When we make a generalization, we are projecting features of a sample population, or a certain number of observed cases, to a larger population. This sample population needs to meet certain criteria for our projections to be warranted. First, it needs to be **random** or **representative**. Second, it must be of **sufficient magnitude**.

To say that a sample population needs to be random means that, strictly speaking, any member of the **target population** could have been among our sample, the target population being simply the group that we are interested in the future, such as all small town librarians or all whales. For instance, if you gave everything or person or event in the target population a name and put all the names in a hat and then drew names from the hat, the sample of the target population would be a random sample. Of course, this is often not possible or would be very time-consuming, so we make compromises such as choosing every tenth name on a list (like a telephone book or a class roster).

Truly random samples are hard to come by and so we often opt for a **representative sample**. A representative sample is a more deliberate selection of the target population that contains individuals (things or people or events) with a range of particular features similar to the range of particular features in the target population and in the same proportion so that the representative sample mimics a random sample. Which particular features are picked out to make a representative sample, again, depends on background information. If our target population is small town librarians in the United States, then our sample population must be representative of the United States as a whole. It cannot just include librarians from Vermont or from the outskirts of Las Vegas. The proper selection of representatives is what allows presidential pollsters to predict national elections on samples as small as 1500 responses! This last comment brings up the issue of the magnitude of the sample. A sample of 1500 doesn't seem like a sample of enough voters to predict a national presidential election. But pollsters know on the basis of their background knowledge, namely, their past successes and failures, how large their representative sample must be. Generally, the larger the sample, the more warranted we are in projecting into the future. Too often we can cite instances where a generalization or a prediction was not warranted because the sample was too small with respect to the target group. (For example, "I don't like people who go to State University. I met someone from there once and he was extremely stuck-up.")

The *Literary Digest*'s prediction of Alf Landon's victory in the presidential election of 1936, which you are about to read, is a classic violation of one of these guidelines. The *Digest* sent out a lot of ballots relative to the size of the target population. They also had a good track record using their method of presidential-voter sampling. But the *Digest,* among other things, had to rely on the ballot recipients to return their ballots. Thus, its sample was not random but rather self-selected by the respondents themselves. (Surveys of sexual habits sent out by popular magazines have this same bias.) Clearly, more Republicans returned ballots than Democrats. Although the *Literary Digest* may not have had a bias toward either candidate, its straw polling procedure did!

We can see from the *Digest* example that the magnitude of the sample is only part of the story. In fact, there are times when one instance is enough for us to be warranted in drawing a generalization, and there are times when after any number of instances we would not be willing to project the pattern into the future.[1] **In general, the better the resulting generalization fits in with other beliefs we consider warranted, the smaller the sample necessary to warrant making that generalization and vice versa; that is, the poorer the fit between a generalization and other beliefs we hold, the larger the sample we should seek before considering it warranted.**

From the discussion above and the examples we have looked at it is clear that background knowledge plays a big role in how successful we are at reasoning with probability. Not only does background knowledge help us see traces and patterns of traces as we saw in Chapter 7, but it also helps us in judging whether to project these patterns into the future and in determining what guidelines to use in the process of generalizing or projecting.

Remember: Our generalization can be warranted; that is, we can be justified in projecting from our sample of observed cases to future unobserved cases, but there is no guarantee that the outcome will be as predicted. When we project into the future, we are always reasoning with probability, not with necessity.

There is something we can do, however, that can help us avoid disappointments and unpleasant surprises which is fundamental to our making warranted generalizations. That is **we must always revise our store of background knowledge in light of new information.** Our store of background knowledge is not fixed. Each new case and each new mistaken generalization goes into our collection of observed cases and changes the warrant for making future projections. The person who is a good critical thinker is the person who is open to the increasing number of relevant cases and who does not become fixed on a certain set of background knowledge and beliefs which he refuses to change.

As individuals, our background knowledge is constantly growing. When we are children, it is growing exponentially. As we grow older, its growth rate slows down. Sometimes as we get old, we get stubborn and then it may not grow at all and we deteriorate as critical thinkers and, consequently, as movers and shakers in the world. There is no guaranteed protection from warranted generalizations that disappoint us in the future. What we can do is protect ourselves from being disappointed by that **same** future projection. We do this by continually revising our background knowledge and, consequently, the patterns of traces that we project.

We perform these revisions in the patterns we have noted all the time. After being bitten by a dog, we are more careful the next time we encounter an unfamiliar canine. If we find ourselves underprepared for Dr. Smith's exam, we study harder for the next exam. If Joe is a practical joker who likes to pull the chair out from under people when they sit down, we sit down slowly when Joe is around. But sometimes we become lazy or even stubborn and refuse or fail to revise our generalizations in the light of new experiences. Many smokers are like this. They refuse to revise their background knowledge in light of the warning of the U.S. Surgeon General and are prone to cite some acquaintance who smoked and still lived to 90 and died of old age.

---

[1]This point was recognized by David Hume, the philosopher who has most influenced our understanding of reasoning with probability. See, for example, his *A Treatise of Human Nature,* Book I, Part III, Section VIII.

We are fortunate that our background knowledge is continually growing. As critical thinkers we must grow and adjust our thinking accordingly.

Before looking at a classic mistake in generalizing that occurred in 1936, let's review the guidelines mentioned in this section that can help us to reason well. These guidelines are general and apply to all forms of reasoning with probability. Statistics and probability theory are sources of more specific guidelines for this kind of reasoning and are useful tools for physical scientists and social scientists.

Guidelines for good reasoning with probability:

1. Proceed with caution. Remember, there are no guarantees that the future will be like the past.
2. Be open to the world around you. Look for traces and patterns of traces. The storehouse of background knowledge you bring to the reasoning process is crucial to the success of your projections.
3. The sample on which your projections are based must be appropriate. Generally, this means that it must be either random or representative and it must be of sufficient magnitude relative to the size of the target group.
4. Continually revise your projections (generalizations) in light of your increasing storehouse of background knowledge, paying particular attention to past errors.

Think of these guidelines as you read this collection of excerpts from *The Literary Digest,* an American magazine which was very popular in the 1930s. It shows a familiar use of generalization: predicting the victors in elections or at least trying to predict the victor. As you read this classic election poll *faux pas*, look for reasons why the *Digest*'s prediction that Alf Landon would win the 1936 Presidential election over Franklin Roosevelt was not a good generalization to make! Today, of course, pollsters do a better job than *The Literary Digest* did. We can, however, learn a lot from looking at its mistakes.

THE LITERARY DIGEST PREDICTS VICTORY BY LANDON, 1936 "DIGEST" POLL MACHINERY SPEEDING UP

FIRST FIGURES IN PRESIDENTIAL TEST TO BE PUBLISHED NEXT WEEK

Swinging into higher speed, THE LITERARY DIGEST's great Presidential Poll machinery of 1936 is now settling into the steady, certain, increasingly-swifter pace that will carry it to a country-shaking climax just before Election Day.

Who will win—Roosevelt or Landon? Will the country repudiate the New Deal or give its leader a new, four-year mandate? To-day, nobody knows. But THE DIGEST is seeking the answer—in the same way that has enabled it, time after time, to tell the country exactly what was going to happen when the voters went to the polls.

Hints of what the voters will do this year began trickling into DIGEST Poll Headquarters last week. This week the volume increased. Next week—and in next week's issue the first figures to be tabulated will be published—the volume of returning

---

"Landon to Win" (articles). From *The Literary Digest,* Volume 122. No. 9, August 29, 1936; No. 11, September 12, 1936; No. 14, October 3, 1936; No. 18, October 31, 1936; No. 20, November 14, 1936.

votes will be even larger. Thereafter it will rise steadily to avalanche proportions, with scores of thousands of ballots weekly.

Figures

Finally, the last of the more than 10,000,000 secret ballots which now are being broadcast to every State, county, city, town and hamlet will be in the mails; the last of the voted ballots will have been returned, checked and tallied.

In that great mass of post-card votes, representing the opinions of every section, class, age and occupation, will be found the answer as to the political fate of Franklin D. Roosevelt, Alfred M. Landon, William Lemke, Earl Browder, Norman Thomas.

In election after election, as the public so well knows, THE LITERARY DIGEST has forecast the result long before Election Day. For this journalistic feat and public service it has received thousands of tributes during many years. To-day the praise is continuing. For instance, Percy B. Scott, Editor, writes in the September issue of *The American Press*, "a magazine for makers of newspapers":

> "With the advent of the Presidential election campaign comes THE LITERARY DIGEST Poll—that oracle, which, since 1920, has foretold with almost uncanny accuracy the choice of the nation's voters. . . .
>
> "Nothing which could be construed as bias has ever been permitted to crop into the stories or operation of the Poll. No matter what the returns may have indicated, those indications must be given to the public without qualification or color.
>
> "Political leaders have praised and damned the Poll—depending upon whether or not it coincided with their hopes and prayers—but, like the brook, it has gone merrily on its way, confounding its critics and accurately forecasting the hitherto unpredictable."

Tempers Lost

That is correct. There never has been a DIGEST Poll that was not sharply criticized. Frequently there have been charges that it had "sold out" to this, that or the other interest. Such criticism may be expected again, as the campaign grows hotter and this or that faction, seeing the tide running against them, find themselves losing their tempers.

But THE DIGEST would like to mention in advance that such criticism will be as unfounded in 1936 as it was in every other poll. Most of our readers know that it costs a "king's ransom" to conduct a Poll. But THE DIGEST believes that it is rendering a great public service—and when such a service can be rendered no price is too high.

In 1924 the first large Presidential Poll was launched. Coolidge, Davis and La Follette were the candidates. That poll predicted the Electoral College result within three votes—more than 99 per cent. right—and the popular vote for Coolidge within 1 per cent.—99 per cent. correct.

This extraordinary performance attracted the attention of the press of the world. To many papers it was "amazing." "Here," said the Cincinnati *Post*, "is the way to economy and comfort in elections." But its very accuracy made the Poll machinery a target for political sharpshooters. Ever since, each poll has been watched meticulously to guard against the slightest chance of error.

It was in 1928 that THE DIGEST Poll met perhaps its greatest test. When the returns began to pour in, some Poll observers began to suffer a slight case of jitters. It was not so astonishing that the Hoover Republicans should be shown carrying such States as Kentucky, Tennessee and West Virginia, for they were considered border States. But when the voters began to indicate firmly that Alfred E. Smith would not carry such States of the "Solid South" as Virginia, Texas, North Carolina and Florida—would not even carry his own State, New York—the experts began to wonder about the accuracy of the Poll.

But the election showed that the Poll had forecast the popular vote with an error of only 4.4 per cent. and had predicted the first break-up of the "Solid South" since the War between the States.

During earlier Presidential Polls, the Democrats had consistently hammered at them because they predicted Republican victories. In 1932 the tables were turned. Republicans became critical. The Poll that year indicated that Roosevelt would win by pretty much of a landslide; it was over 99 per cent. correct.

By the spring of 1934 there appeared to be a sharp division of opinion on the New Deal. THE DIGEST asked the voters what they thought, on the whole, of Roosevelt's acts and policies. The response showed about 61 per cent. for the New Deal.

Again, in the fall of 1935, when rumblings of criticism of the New Deal became louder, THE DIGEST, using virtually the same list, sent out 10,000,000 ballots to find out what the country then thought. As many readers will remember, that Poll showed more than 63 per cent. of the total vote registered against the Administration's acts and policies.

To the casual observer, this might mean that a Republican landslide is due this fall. But it must be remembered that that Poll was taken on policies and not on personalities.

And so the great question remains: Who will win the election next November? To repeat: To-day, nobody knows. But THE DIGEST is seeking the answer—in the same way that has enabled it, time after time, to tell the country exactly what was going to happen when the voters went to the polls.

LANDON, 1,293,669; ROOSEVELT, 972,897

FINAL RETURNS IN THE DIGEST'S POLL OF TEN MILLION VOTERS

Well, the great battle of the ballots in the Poll of ten million voters, scattered throughout the forty-eight States of the Union, is now finished, . . . we [have recorded] . . . the figures received up to the hour of going to press.

These figures are exactly as received from more than one in every five voters polled in our country—they are neither weighted, adjusted nor interpreted.

Never before in an experience covering more than a quarter of a century in taking polls have we received so many different varieties of criticism—praise from many; condemnation from many others—and yet it has been just of the same type that has come to us every time a Poll has been taken in all these years.

A telegram from a newspaper in California asks: "Is it true that Mr. Hearst has purchased THE LITERARY DIGEST?" A telephone message only the day before these lines were written: "Has the Republican National Committee purchased THE LITERARY DIGEST?" And all types and varieties, including: "Have the Jews purchased THE LITERARY DIGEST?" "Is the Pope of Rome a stockholder of THE LITERARY DIGEST?" And so it goes—all equally absurd and amusing. We could add more to this list, and yet all of these questions in recent days are but repetitions of what we have been experiencing all down the years from the very first Poll.

Problem

Now, are the figures in this Poll correct? In answer to this question we will simply refer to a telegram we sent to a young man in Massachusetts the other day in answer to his challenge to us to wager $100,000 on the accuracy of our Poll. We wired him as follows:

"For nearly a quarter century, we have been taking Polls of the voters in the forty-eight States, and especially in Presidential years, and we have always merely mailed the ballots, counted and recorded those returned and let the people of the Nation draw their conclusions as to our accuracy. So far, we have been right in every Poll. Will we be right in the current Poll? That, as Mrs. Roosevelt said concerning the President's reelection, is in the 'lap of the gods.'

"We never make any claims before election but we respectfully refer you to the opinion of one of the most quoted citizens to-day, the Hon. James A. Farley, Chairman of the Democratic National Committee. This is what Mr. Farley said October 14, 1932:

"'Any sane person can not escape the implication of such a gigantic sampling of popular opinion as is embraced in THE LITERARY DIGEST straw vote. I consider this conclusive evidence as to the desire of the people of this country for a change in the National Government. THE LITERARY DIGEST poll is an achievement of no little magnitude. It is a Poll fairly and correctly conducted.'"

WHAT WENT WRONG WITH THE POLLS?

NONE OF STRAW VOTES GOT EXACTLY THE RIGHT ANSWER—WHY?

In 1920, 1924, 1928 and 1932, THE LITERARY DIGEST Polls were right. Not only right in the sense that they showed the winner; they forecast the *actual popular vote* with such a small percentage of error (less than 1 per cent. in 1932) that newspapers and individuals everywhere heaped such phrases as "uncannily accurate" and "amazingly right" upon us.

Four years ago, when the Poll was running his way, our very good friend Jim Farley was saying that "no sane person could escape the implication" of a sampling "so fairly and correctly conducted."

"Landon to Win" (articles). From *The Literary Digest,* Volume 122. No. 9, August 29, 1936; No. 11, September 12, 1936; No. 14, October 3, 1936; No. 18, October 31, 1936; No. 20, November 14, 1936.

Well, this year we used precisely the same method that had scored four bull's-eyes in four previous tries. And we were far from correct. Why? We ask that question in all sincerity, because *we want to know*.

"Reasons"

Oh, we've been flooded with "reasons." Hosts of people who feel they have learned more about polling in a few months than we have learned in more than a score of years have told us just where we were off. Hundreds of astute "second-guessers" have assured us, by telephone, by letter, in the newspapers, that the reasons for our error were "obvious." Were they?

Suppose we review a few of these "obvious reasons."

The one most often heard runs something like this: "This election was different. Party lines were obliterated. For the first time in more than a century, *all* the 'have-nots' were on one side. THE DIGEST, polling names from telephone books and lists of automobile owners, simply did not reach the lower strata." And so on. . . .

"Have-Nots"

Well, in the first place, the "have-nots" did not reelect Mr. Roosevelt. That they contributed to his astonishing plurality, no one can doubt. But the fact remains that a majority of farmers, doctors, grocers and candlestick-makers *also* voted for the President. As Dorothy Thompson remarked in the New York *Herald Tribune*, you could eliminate the straight labor vote, the relief vote and the Negro vote, and *still* Mr. Roosevelt would have a majority.

So that "reason" does not appear to hold much water. Besides—

We *did* reach these so-called "have-not" strata. In the city of Chicago, for example, we polled *every third registered voter*. In the city of Scranton, Pennsylvania, we polled every *other* registered voter. And in Allentown, Pennsylvania, likewise other cities, we polled *every* registered voter.

Is that so? chorus the critics, a little abashed, no doubt. Well, they come back, you must have got the right answer in *those* towns, anyway.

Well, we didn't. The fact is that we were as badly off there as we were on the national total.

Cities

In Allentown, for example, 10,753 out of the 30,811 who voted returned ballots to us showing a division of 53.32 per cent. to 44.67 per cent. in favor of Mr. Landon. What was the actual result? It was 56.93 per cent. for Mr. Roosevelt, 41.17 per cent. for the Kansan.

In Chicago, the 100,929 voters who returned ballots to us showed a division of 48.63 per cent. to 47.56 per cent. in favor of Mr. Landon. The 1,672,175 who voted in the actual election gave the President 65.24 per cent., to 32.26 per cent. for the Republican candidate.

What happened? Why did only one in five voters in Chicago to whom THE DIGEST sent ballots take the trouble to reply? And why was there a preponderance of

Republicans in the one-fifth that did reply? Your guess is as good as ours. We'll go into it a little more later. The important thing in all the above is that all this conjecture about our "not reaching certain strata" simply will not hold water.

Hoover Voters

Now for another "explanation" dinned into our ears: "You got too many Hoover voters in your sample."

Well, the fact is that we've *always* got too big a sampling of Republican voters. That was true in 1920, in 1924, in 1928, and even in 1932, when we *over*estimated the Roosevelt popular vote by three-quarters of 1 per cent.

In 1928 in Chicago, we underestimated the Democratic vote by a little more than 5 per cent., overestimated the Republican vote by the same margin.

We wondered then, as we had wondered before and have wondered since, why we were getting better cooperation in what we have always regarded as a public service from Republicans than we were getting from Democrats. Do Republicans live nearer mail-boxes? Do Democrats generally disapprove of straw polls?

We don't know that answer. All we know is that in 1932, when the tide seemed to be running away from Hoover, we were perturbed about the disproportion of Republican voters in our sampling. Republican and Democratic chieftains from all points in the country were at the telephones day after day for reports of what the Democrats called our "correctly conducted" system. And then the result came along, and it was so right, we were inclined to agree that we had been concerned without reason, and this year, when it seemed logical to suppose that the President's vote would be lighter, even if he won (hadn't that been the rule on reelections for more than a hundred years?) we decided not to worry.

Figures

So the statisticians did our worrying for us on that score, applying what they called the "compensating-ratio" in some cases, and the "switch-factor" in others. Either way, for some of the figure experts, it didn't matter; interpret our figures for 2,376,523 voters as they would, the answer was still Landon. Then other statisticians took our figures and so weighted, compensated, balanced, adjusted and interpreted them that they showed Roosevelt.

We did not attempt to interpret the figures, because we had no stake in the result other than the wish to preserve our well-earned reputation for scrupulous bookkeeping. So we sent out more than ten million ballots, exactly as we had sent them out before. We don't know what proportion went to persons who had voted for Roosevelt in 1932 or what proportion went to persons who had voted for Hoover, because our polls are secret always, and the ballots come back with no signatures, no identifying characteristics of any sort except the post-marks.

Basis

However, since the basis of the 1936 mailing-list was the 1932 mailing-list, and since the overwhelming majority of those who responded to our Poll in 1932 voted for

Mr. Roosevelt, it seems altogether reasonable to assume that the majority of our ballots this year went to people who had voted for Mr. Roosevelt in 1932. There simply was no way by which THE DIGEST could assure itself or the public that the marked ballots would come back in the same proportion. We couldn't very well send duplicate ballots to indifferent Democrats, or personal letters prodding them into action, because we didn't know which were Democrats and which were Republicans, let alone which would vote for Roosevelt and which for Landon.

If any of the hundreds who have so kindly offered their suggestions and criticism can tell us how we could get voters to respond proportionately, and still keep the poll secret, as we believe it ought always to be, then we wish these critics would step up and do so. And with arguments more convincing than the familiar ones about our not reaching the "lower strata" and "sampling too many Republicans." Because those two theories explain nothing; they only add to the multiplicity and confusion of words—words—words.

Too Many

And there's another "explanation" that doesn't seem to hold much water, when you examine it closely. That's the one that argues that we polled too many voters, that cites the experience of another poll that sent out less than a fourth as many ballots and came closer to being right. The answer here is that the Baltimore *Sunpapers* polled more persons per square mile in Maryland than we did anywhere except in the cities—and the *Sunpapers* were a lot nearer right than this "model poll" for Maryland. Also, the man who came nearer the right answer than all the polls put together was Jim Farley, and Jim based his prediction on reports from tens of thousands of precinct leaders in every city, town and hamlet in the country.

So—what?

So we were wrong, although we did everything we knew to assure ourselves of being right.

We conducted our Poll as we had always done, reported what we found, and have no alibis. We drew no special satisfaction from our figures, and we drew no conclusions from them. The result was disappointing only in the sense that it threw our figures out the window, and left us without even the satisfaction of knowing why.

Future

As for the immediate future, THE DIGEST feels that in truth "the Nation has spoken." THE DIGEST hails a magnificent President against whom it never uttered one word of partizan [sic] criticism. THE DIGEST can not support him, in the sense that newspapers support a President editorially, because THE DIGEST does not editorialize. But it can obtain genuine satisfaction from the knowledge that its several Editors, as American citizens, and its millions of readers, as American citizens, will stand behind the First Citizen.

Speaking of the President, there is a spot of comfort for us in the knowledge that he himself was pretty badly off on his Electoral total, and that he "laughed it off" in his genial way. His last guess was 360 votes to Mr. Landon's 171. (On June 5 he had estimated his margin at 315 to 216.)

As for the more distant future, the questions have been asked: Will THE DIGEST conduct another Poll? Will it change its methods?

The answer to the first question we phrase in others: Should the Democratic Party have quit in 1924, when it reached a modern low-ebb in power and confidence, instead of going on to the greatest triumph in its history? Should the Republican Party have quit in 1912, when it carried only two States? Should the University of Minnesota, with the greatest record in modern football, give up the sport because it finally lost one game, after a string of twenty-one victories?

The answer to the second question is: We'll cross that bridge when we come to it.

STUDY QUESTIONS

1. In 1936, Americans were shocked to wake up the day after the presidential election to find that Roosevelt, not Landon, had won. Why should they not have been so surprised? What suggestions would you make to *The Literary Digest* for its future predictions of elections given what you have learned about making warranted generalizations?

2. *The Literary Digest* had a very large number of responses in its informal poll, many more than current pollsters use to predict election results. Why wasn't that sufficient to avoid its embarrassing misprediction of the election results? Be specific in your answer.

3. The year 1936 was the height of the Depression when millions of Americans were unemployed. How might this have been a factor in *The Literary Digest*'s prediction failure? What does this suggest about background knowledge?

ANALOGIES

Analogies are important form of inductive reasoning. Reasoning using analogies is always "tricky." Since no two things in the world are identical, for every analogy or similarity we see in the world, there is always a disanalogy or dissimilarity. That is, no matter how much alike two (or more) individuals (things) are, there is always some way in which they are not alike. Consider, for example, identical twins. No matter how much alike they are, people who know them well can usually find something that can be used to distinguish them. Or, consider two identical automobiles just off the assembly line. If they have no other difference, they at least have the difference of occupying different spaces. Hence, our reasoning using analogies or similarities is always probable, never certain.

We talked about argument by analogy in Chapter 4 in the argument where Melchizedek draws an analogy between the world's three great religions and the three rings. The underlying principle is the same here as in that argument. The principle is that it is reasonable to assume that if two things share a number of features, they also have additional properties in common. You can see that analogies are like generalizations in that they are a projection of a **pattern**. Here, we are projecting from a set of observed cases possessing a certain **pattern** of properties to some additional cases where some properties have yet to be observed. When we reason with analogy, we are assuming that the pattern of properties will be the same for both the cases whose properties we have observed and for the cases whose pattern we have only partially observed. For example, if every time Professor Smith has given a pop quiz in the past, he has urged the class "to be sure to do their homework," then you might assume that there will probably be a pop quiz tomorrow since Mr. Smith reminded the class today not to forget to do their homework.

The pattern for reasoning using analogies generally looks like this:

If case A has the properties P_1, P_2, P_3, P_4, P_5

And if case B has the properties P_1, P_2, P_3, P_4,

Then case B probably also has the property P_5.

The more cases like A with that particular set of observed properties including the one (or more) not yet observed in B, the more likely B also has that unobserved property. In addition, the greater the number of properties cases of A have in common with B (P_1–P_n), the more likely that B has the property not yet observed. For example, suppose you want to buy some basil, and at the store you find a shelf with plants labeled "basil." A little while later you come upon a shelf of plants that look like the plants with the basil label, but with no label. You would prefer to buy the plants on the unlabeled shelf because they look a bit fresher but you are not sure if they are basil. You might create a little argument from analogy for yourself. You would see how many properties the labeled plants have in common with the unlabeled plants—color, leaf shape and size, and smell! You conclude that if it smells like basil, then it must be basil. That is, even though the plants on the second shelf do not have the observed property of being labeled "basil," you assume that they must also deserve that label.

This is a very common form of reasoning. It is often used in medicine when making a diagnosis from a set of symptoms but it is just as fundamental to law (treating like cases alike), to grading tests, papers or products, and to testing the effectiveness of new drugs, where we often reason from the effectiveness in rats to the effectiveness in humans. There is also a well-known theological argument which uses reasoning from analogy to support the claim that God exists. The nineteenth-century British theologian William Paley proposed a version of this argument in his book *Natural Theology*. There he argues that the universe is like a great big watch, filled with careful design and order. Just as the watch must be made by a watchmaker, so the universe must be made by a super watchmaker, namely God.[2]

Reasoning by analogy presents us with some of the same reasoning puzzles that generalizations do. We have already talked about patterns and how some people see patterns that others do not. This raises the problem when dealing with analogies of whether to focus on the analogous features or on the points of disanalogy. The example of testing drugs (and other products) on rats to see if the drugs are safe for humans is a good example of this problem. How meaningful such a test is depends on whether rats are sufficiently analogous to humans physically so that it makes sense to say they will both have analogous reactions to the same product.[3]

---

[2]For another view of the analogy between the universe and a watch, look at the philosopher David Hume's (mentioned above) reply to Paley. This can be found in his *Dialogues Concerning Natural Religion,* Parts II, V, and VII.

[3]A well-known controversial case here was a study that showed that laboratory rats exposed to large amounts of saccharine developed cancer in significant numbers. Some people argued that the amount of saccharine consumed by the rats was so great that the results had little relevance for humans who would be consuming only small amounts in diet sodas, etc. That is, they argued since humans would be consuming only small amounts in diet sodas, the two situations were not sufficiently analogous for the test results to be taken seriously for humans.

Whether we focus on similarities or dissimilarities depends on our interest or what we value at the time. It's like the situation with twins. Sometimes, you focus on the ways they are alike. Other times you note, or try to figure out for purposes of identification, how they are different. Neither focus is better all the time. It depends on your goal. Again, background knowledge is important. Background knowledge tells us which features to focus on, given our interest. Like reasoning with generalizations, we need to keep in mind guidelines for reasoning with analogy to avoid disappointment and too much surprise and disappointment in our lives.

Guidelines for good reasoning using analogies:
1. Keep in mind that reasoning by analogy is always probable, never certain.
2. Remember that reasoning by analogy depends on background knowledge and how well the reasoning fits in with that background knowledge.
3. The reasoning becomes more warranted with increasing numbers of cases. That is, the more cases of A having properties P1–P5, the more likely it is that cases like B with properties P1–P4 will also have property P5. Also, the more properties A and B have in common, the more likely they will have the property in question in common. (They can have many more than five!)
4. We must constantly revise the conclusions we draw on the basis of analogy as we encounter more and more cases and add them to our storehouse of background knowledge.

The reading which follows is part of the continuing dialog about racial and ethnic profiling in the United States. In this excerpt from his article, Malcolm Gladwell, a regular contributor to *The New Yorker* magazine and the author of several popular books about how we think about current issues, draws an analogy between the popular prejudice about pit bulls and the prejudices that lead to racial profiling. He argues that just as we have wrongly indicted all pit bulls for the bad behavior of a few (who often have been mistreated or poorly bred), so we often indulge in racial profiling and assume that all members of a particular ethnic group are likely to be terrorists or drug dealers or so on. Thus, just as the prejudice against pit bulls is misguided, he argues, so is the popular mistrust of members of minority groups who are stereotyped by the behavior of a few members of the group. This is a clear argument based on an analogy. (Note the words "just as" here.) Besides giving us this good example of an argument from analogy, Gladwell also raises the question of when a generalization becomes a stereotype. This, in effect, is also an argument from analogy. That is, if the members of group X, for example, have the properties P_1, P_2, P_3, P_4, and P_5 where P_5 is "commits acts of terrorism," then does someone similar to members of that group who also has properties P_1, P_2, P_3, P_4 have the further property P_5? This is a very difficult issue, and you will have to pay close attention to Gladwell's examples to evaluate his argument. It's like drawing generalizations about small town librarians: What are the important features (the Ps here) which make generalizations warranted or unwarranted? The importance of this critical thinking skill cannot be overestimated: While we do not want to categorize people (or breeds of dogs) unfairly, we do want to pick out the relevant features of potential terrorists.

WHAT PIT BULLS CAN TEACH US ABOUT PROFILING

Malcolm Gladwell

One afternoon last February, Guy Clairoux picked up his two-and-a half-year-old son, Jayden, from day care and walked him back to their house in the west end of Ottawa, Ontario. They were almost home. Jayden was straggling behind, and, as his father's back was turned, a pit bull jumped over a back-yard fence and lunged at Jayden. "The dog had his head in its mouth and started to do this shake," Clairoux's wife, JoAnn Hartley, said later. As she watched in horror, two more pit bulls jumped over the fence, joining in the assault. She and Clairoux came running, and he punched the first of the dogs in the head, until it dropped Jayden, and then he threw the boy toward his mother. Hartley fell on her son, protecting him with her body. "JoAnn!" Clairoux cried out, as all three dogs descended on his wife. "Cover your neck, cover your neck." A neighbor, sitting by her window, screamed for help. Her partner and a friend, Mario Gauthier, ran outside. A neighborhood boy grabbed his hockey stick and threw it to Gauthier. He began hitting one of the dogs over the head, until the stick broke. "They wouldn't stop," Gauthier said. "As soon as you'd stop, they'd attack again. I've never seen a dog go so crazy. They were like Tasmanian devils." The police came. The dogs were pulled away, and the Clairouxes and one of the rescuers were taken to the hospital. Five days later, the Ontario legislature banned the ownership of pit bulls. "Just as we wouldn't let a great white shark in a swimming pool," the province's attorney general, Michael Bryant, had said, "maybe we shouldn't have these animals on the civilized streets."

Pit bulls, descendants of the bulldogs used in the nineteenth century for bull baiting and dogfighting, have been bred for "gameness," and thus a lowered inhibition to aggression. Most dogs fight as a last resort, when staring and growling fail. A pit bull is willing to fight with little or no provocation. Pit bulls seem to have a high tolerance for pain, making it possible for them to fight to the point of exhaustion. Whereas guard dogs like German shepherds usually attempt to restrain those they perceive to be threats by biting and holding, pit bulls try to inflict the maximum amount of damage on an opponent. They bite, hold, shake, and tear. They don't growl or assume an aggressive facial expression as warning. They just attack. "They are often insensitive to behaviors that usually stop aggression," one scientific review of the breed states. "For example, dogs not bred for fighting usually display defeat in combat by rolling over and exposing a light underside. On several occasions, pit bulls have been reported to disembowel dogs offering this signal of submission." In epidemiological studies of dog bites, the pit bull is overrepresented among dogs known to have seriously injured or killed human beings, and, as a result, pit bulls have been banned or restricted in several Western European countries, China, and numerous cities and municipalities across North America. Pit bulls are dangerous.

Of course, not all pit bulls are dangerous. Most don't bite anyone. Meanwhile, Dobermans and Great Danes and German shepherds and Rottweilers are frequent biters as well, and the dog that recently mauled a Frenchwoman so badly that she was given the world's first face transplant was, of all things, a Labrador retriever. When we say that pit bulls are dangerous, we are making a generalization, just as insurance companies use generalizations when they charge young men more for car insurance than the rest of us (even though many young men are perfectly good drivers), and doctors use generalizations when they tell overweight middle-aged men to get their cholesterol checked (even though many overweight middle-aged men won't experience heart trouble). Because we don't know which dog will bite someone or who will have a heart attack or which drivers will get in an accident, we can make predictions only by generalizing. As the legal scholar Frederick Schauer has observed, "painting with a broad brush" is "an often inevitable and frequently desirable dimension of our decision-making lives."

Another word for generalization, though, is "stereotype," and stereotypes are usually not considered desirable dimensions of our decision-making lives. The process of moving from the specific to the general is both necessary and perilous. A doctor could, with some statistical support, generalize about men of a certain age and weight. But what if generalizing from other traits—such as high blood pressure, family history, and smoking—saved more lives? Behind each generalization is a choice of what factors to leave in and what factors to leave out, and those choices can prove surprisingly complicated. After the attack on Jayden Clairoux, the Ontario government chose to make a generalization about pit bulls. But it could also have chosen to generalize about powerful dogs, or about the kinds of people who own powerful dogs, or about small children, or about back-yard fences—or, indeed, about any number of other things to do with dogs and people and places. How do we know when we've made the right generalization?

In July of last year, following the transit bombings in London, the New York City Police Department announced that it would send officers into the subways to conduct random searches of passengers' bags. On the face of it, doing random searches in the hunt for terrorists—as opposed to being guided by generalizations—seems like a silly idea. As a columnist in *New York* wrote at the time, "Not just 'most' but nearly every jihadi who has attacked a Western European or American target is a young Arab or Pakistani man. In other words, you can predict with a fair degree of certainty what an Al Qaeda terrorist looks like. Just as we have always known what Mafiosi look like—even as we understand that only an infinitesimal fraction of Italian-Americans are members of the mob."

But wait: do we really know what mafiosi look like? In "The Godfather," where most of us get our knowledge of the Mafia, the male members of the Corleone family were played by Marlon Brando, who was of Irish and French ancestry, James Caan, who is Jewish, and two Italian-Americans, Al Pacino and John Cazale. To go by "The Godfather," mafiosi look like white men of European descent, which, as generalizations go, isn't terribly helpful. Figuring out what an Islamic terrorist looks like isn't any easier. Muslims are not like the Amish: they don't come dressed in identifiable costumes. And they don't look like basketball players; they don't come in predictable shapes and sizes. Islam is a religion that spans the globe.

"We have a policy against racial profiling," Raymond Kelly, New York City's police commissioner, told me. "I put it in here in March of the first year I was here. It's the wrong thing to do, and it's also ineffective. If you look at the London bombings, you have three British citizens of Pakistani descent. You have Germaine Lindsay, who is Jamaican. You have the next crew, on July 21st, who are East African. You have a Chechen woman in Moscow in early 2004 who blows herself up in the subway station. So whom do you profile? Look at New York City. Forty percent of New Yorkers are born outside the country. Look at the diversity here. Who am I supposed to profile?"

Kelly was pointing out what might be called profiling's "category problem." Generalizations involve matching a category of people to a behavior or trait—overweight middle-aged men to heart-attack risk, young men to bad driving. But, for that process to work, you have to be able both to define and to identify the category you are generalizing about. "You think that terrorists aren't aware of how easy it is to be characterized by ethnicity?" Kelly went on. "Look at the 9/11 hijackers. They came here. They shaved. They went to topless bars. They wanted to blend in. They wanted to look like they were part of the American dream. These are not dumb people. Could a terrorist dress up as a Hasidic Jew and walk into the subway, and not be profiled? Yes. I think profiling is just nuts."

Pit-bull bans involve a category problem, too, because pit bulls, as it happens, aren't a single breed. The name refers to dogs belonging to a number of related breeds, such as the American Staffordshire terrier, the Staffordshire bull terrier, and the American pit bull terrier—all of which share a square and muscular body, a short snout, and a sleek, short-haired coat. Thus the Ontario ban prohibits not only these three breeds but any "dog that has an appearance and physical characteristics that are substantially similar" to theirs; the term of art is "pit bull-type" dogs. But what does that mean? Is a cross between an American pit bull terrier and a golden retriever a pit bull-type dog or a golden retriever-type dog? If thinking about muscular terriers as pit bulls is a generalization, then thinking about dangerous dogs as anything substantially similar to a pit bull is a generalization about a generalization. "The way a lot of these laws are written, pit bulls are whatever they say they are," Lora Brashears, a kennel manager in Pennsylvania, says. "And for most people it just means big, nasty, scary dog that bites."

. . .

Then which are the pit bulls that get into trouble? "The ones that the legislation is geared toward have aggressive tendencies that are either bred in by the breeder, trained in by the trainer, or reinforced in by the owner," Herkstroeter says. A mean pit bull is a dog that has been turned mean, by selective breeding, by being cross-bred with a bigger, human-aggressive breed like German shepherds or Rottweilers, or by being conditioned in such a way that it begins to express hostility to human beings. A pit bull is dangerous to people, then, not to the extent that it expresses its essential pit bullness but to the extent that it deviates from it. A pit-bull ban is a generalization about a generalization about a trait that is not, in fact, general. That's a category problem.

. . .

Before Kelly became the New York police commissioner, he served as the head of the U.S. Customs Service, and while he was there he overhauled the criteria that border-control officers use to identify and search suspected smugglers. There had been a list of forty-three suspicious traits. He replaced it with a list of six broad criteria. Is there something suspicious about their physical appearance? Are they nervous? Is there specific intelligence targeting this person? Does the drug-sniffing dog raise an alarm? Is there something amiss in their paperwork or explanations? Has contraband been found that implicates this person?

You'll find nothing here about race or gender or ethnicity, and nothing here about expensive jewelry or deplaning at the middle or the end, or walking briskly or walking aimlessly. Kelly removed all the unstable generalizations, forcing customs officers to make generalizations about things that don't change from one day or one month to the next. Some percentage of smugglers will *always* be nervous, will *always* get their story wrong, and will *always* be caught by the dogs. That's why those kinds of inferences are more reliable than the ones based on whether smugglers are white or black, or carry one bag or two. After Kelly's reforms, the number of searches conducted by the Customs Service dropped by about seventy-five per cent, but the number of successful seizures improved by twenty-five per cent. The officers went from making fairly lousy decisions about smugglers to making pretty good ones. "We made them more efficient and more effective at what they were doing," Kelly said.

Does the notion of a pit-bull menace rest on a stable or an unstable generalization? The best data we have on breed dangerousness are fatal dog bites, which serve as a useful indicator of just how much havoc certain kinds of dogs are causing. Between the late nineteen-seventies and the late nineteen-nineties, more than twenty-five breeds were involved in fatal attacks in the United States. Pit-bull breeds led the pack, but the variability from year to year is considerable. For instance, in the period from 1981 to 1982 fatalities were caused by five pit bulls, three mixed breeds, two St. Bernards, two German-shepherd mixes, a pure-bred German shepherd, a husky type, a Doberman, a Chow Chow, a Great Dane, a wolf-dog hybrid, a husky mix, and a pit-bull mix—but no Rottweilers. In 1995 and 1996, the list included ten Rottweilers, four pit bulls, two German shepherds, two huskies, two Chow Chows, two wolf-dog hybrids, two shepherd mixes, a Rottweiler mix, a mixed breed, a Chow Chow mix, and a Great Dane. The kinds of dogs that kill people change over time, because the popularity of certain breeds changes over time. The one thing that doesn't change is the total number of the people killed by dogs. When we have more problems with pit bulls, it's not necessarily a sign that pit bulls are more dangerous than other dogs. It could just be a sign that pit bulls have become more numerous.

STUDY QUESTIONS

1. What arguments does Gladwell use to defend pit bulls from their stereotype? Critically evaluate these arguments.
2. What are some of the analogies and disanalogies between canine profiling and human profiling?
3. How does background knowledge play a role in the kinds of generalizations one draws with respect to dogs? With respect to ethnic groups?

CAUSAL CLAIMS

One of the **patterns** we observe and then use to our advantage is the pattern of correlation. If two events or properties occur together frequently or even constantly, we say there is a correlation between them. For example, the property of having 10 toes is highly correlated with the property of being human. The correlation is probably not constant, since people do lose toes to injury or genetic abnormalities, but the correlation is very high. On the other hand, the properties of being human and of being over six feet tall are not highly correlated. Thus, if you picked a human being at random from the world's population, there would be only a small likelihood that the person you picked would be over six feet tall, but a very high likelihood that the person would have 10 toes. For us to notice a correlation between events or properties, they generally have spatial proximity to one another in addition to their temporal proximity, but not always. The behavior of the tides and the position of the moon are known to be highly correlated, despite their spatial distance. Statisticians study correlations and use them to make predictions of future correlations of events and properties.

Some correlations are considered coincidental; that is, the events or properties occur together by chance or accident. Being a sports car and being red is a coincidental correlation. While there may be a high correlation between being a sports car and being red, if we were describing a sports car, there would be no necessity that we describe it as red. Other correlations, we believe, are causal in nature. For example, most people believe that if you drop a glass on a marble floor, that event has to be followed by the event of the glass's breaking. Although dropping the glass may be an accident, the relation between dropping the glass and the glass's breaking is not a coincidence but something that we think has to happen. Our experience tells us that these two events are so highly correlated with one another as to be constantly conjoined; one event cannot happen without the other event following. Consequently, we claim that the first **causes** the second. We believe they **have** to happen that way—together.

Causal connections are of great interest to us since they help us expect and control future events in our lives. As with warranted and unwarranted generalizations, we are usually very good at distinguishing coincidental correlations from causal connections. However, we have the same problem of having no perfect rule for drawing a firm distinction between coincidental correlations and causal connections because, again, we are judging from observed events and making projections about unobserved events. Thus, we can have only guidelines to help us distinguish warranted causal claims from unwarranted ones.

Consider the well-known example of the correlation between cigarette smoking and the incidence of lung cancer. The two are known to be significantly correlated. A much higher percentage of people who smoke cigarettes end up with lung cancer than in the general population or in the population of nonsmokers. Is this just a coincidence? Have smokers just had bad luck? Have they tended to live in environments with other pollutants which cause lung cancer? Or, does the correlation indicate a causal relation? After all, not all smokers develop lung cancer. As you know, the cigarette industry refused for years to acknowledge that this higher-than-expected correlation indicates a causal connection. We will return to this issue below.

Let's consider two other cases of correlations about which there is little disagreement. If you let go of your pencil in mid air, it falls to the ground. Every time you let go of it, it falls to the ground. Letting go of it and its falling to the ground are so highly correlated that you certainly believe a causal relation is involved. It **has to** fall to the ground. On the other hand, suppose every time you reach in your pocket for a coin, the coin you come up with is a penny. Even if this happened time after time, you would never believe that if a coin is in your pocket it **has** to be a penny. You observe constant conjunction but refuse to attribute a causal connection! This is the puzzle of causal reasoning: How do we distinguish between causation and mere correlation if all we have to go on is our experience of the world, namely, our experience of constant conjunction?

The philosopher Hume noted that when it comes to causation there is a gap between what we experience and what we believe on the basis of that experience. What we experience is constant conjunction. The pencil's being let go has been constantly conjoined with the pencil's falling to the floor. Lightning has always been followed by thunder. Salt dropped in water has always dissolved. This constant conjoining of events leads us to expect that in the future if the first event occurs it will be followed by the second event; in fact, it leads us to say that the second **has** to happen. It leads us to believe that the connection between the events is a necessary one because the first event is **causing** the second. Notice that this necessary connection is **not** something we observe (What would it look like?) but rather is something we attribute to our experience. **There is always a gap between our experience and what we say about it when we talk about causation.**

Sometimes we fill in the gap with technological descriptions, so the gap seems to get filled in. This filling in, however, is never complete. What happens is the big gap gets divided into smaller sections with gaps within the sections. Gaps remain. For example, for the ordinary person pushing on the brake pedal causes the car to stop. The mechanic can fill in this causal gap with a number of mechanical connections, but each one of the causal connections in the mechanic's causal chain contains a gap. Similarly, to say that gravity causes the pencil to fall does not eliminate the gap between what we experience and what we say about it. In many ways, introducing gravity makes the gap wider for what is gravity but a name for a force, which, like a cause, is something else we do not observe but which is part of our description of the world.

To put this point another way, there is no mark on experience, that is, no regularly occurring feature of the experience itself that tells us whether a correlation between events is coincidental (of low probability or "accidental") or necessary (of high probability or "causal").[4] Somehow we know that the glass falling on the marble floor *has* to break, but we do not see or in any way sense a property or mark which we might call the "must-break" property. Consequently, we sometimes make mistakes and attribute causal connections where there are none (e.g., "That teacher gave me a bad grade because he doesn't like me."), and sometimes we fail to see causal connections where we ought to (e.g., "I don't know why I didn't see the red light. I've only had a few beers. . . ."). What is truly surprising—and fortunate—is that we make

---

[4]The situation is similar to the difference between dreaming and being awake. While these two states are certainly different, there is nothing in the dream itself, while you are having it that tells you "You are only dreaming." Everything happens as if you were wide awake. Generally you know you were dreaming only afterwards—when you wake up.

relatively few mistakes in attributing causal connections where there are causal connections. That is, our expectations of necessary connections between events are usually born out in practice, so we are not generally disappointed and we are very good at using those expectations to control, to some extent at least, our environment.

Since there is no mark on our experience of causation, there is no way to confirm the distinctions we draw between necessary and accidental connections. The only experiential difference we have is that, with connections we deem necessary connections, we have a psychological process of expectation, which we do not have with accidental connections (correlations). We cannot set down any rules to guarantee that we are always right in our expectations. The best we can do in this case is to suggest some guidelines for causal reasoning based on the logical concepts of **necessary and sufficient conditions**. In our ordinary usage of the term *cause,* we sometimes mean a sufficient condition, sometimes a necessary condition, and sometimes the set of both necessary and sufficient conditions. Necessary and sufficient conditions are **logical patterns** we impose on our experience of constant conjunction and our psychological experience of expectation to give that experience more order.

Let X and Y stand for two events. Then we could say, **X is a sufficient condition for Y, if every time X occurs, Y occurs.** That is, X is always followed by Y (or is simultaneous with Y). For example, if you drop salt in water, it will dissolve. The salt's being dropped in water (event X) is a *sufficient* condition for the salt's dissolving (event Y). Dropping salt in water *causes* it to dissolve.

But we might also say that the water *causes* the salt to dissolve. Water—that is, water or some not already saturated liquid—is a *necessary* condition for dissolving salt. **Y is a necessary condition for X, if whenever X occurs, Y occurs, or X cannot occur without Y.** (See Chapter 6 for a discussion of these formal logical relations.) And in some contexts it is appropriate to list both the necessary and sufficient conditions of an event as its cause: Dropping salt in ordinary water *causes* it to dissolve.

To be clear about this point, consider another example. You strike a match and the match lights. What caused the match to light? Striking it caused it to light. Striking the match was sufficient, in that context, to cause it to light. But striking is not a necessary condition of a match's lighting. It could have ignited by being touched by another flame, by the rays of the sun focused on it with a magnifying glass, and so on. Also, we know that other conditions are necessary for the match's lighting. The match must not be wet. There must be oxygen. There must be a scratch pad to create friction. If we state all the necessary and sufficient conditions for the match's lighting, we could have quite a long list. (In fact, the list could go on and on. Usually we just aren't interested in the whole causal chain.) Most commonly we speak of the cause as the last event (striking the match) to complete a set of conditions sufficient for bringing about the effect (the match's lighting). Background knowledge comes into play. It is our background knowledge and our knowledge of the context which enable us to select from among the set of necessary and sufficient conditions for an event, one condition which we speak of as *the cause* of that event.

The nineteenth-century British philosopher John Stuart Mill set out some guidelines for determining the cause of an event in his *System of Logic.* These guidelines have become known as *Mill's methods.* These methods are suggested by common sense. You have probably used them yourself at times when trying to figure out the cause of an event in your experience. Mill himself laid out five different methods for determining causes. Philosophers since Mill have criticized and amended these methods, but they continue to refer to them because we use them so frequently in our everyday life. We will look at three of the methods here.

The first is called **the Method of Agreement**. You have probably used this method for determining a cause many times. For example, you may have tried to figure out why your face broke out so badly before the big dance. You might try to determine the cause by thinking back to other times that your face broke out, looking for some common factor that was present in all the cases. Perhaps the common factor is stress, a new face cream, or something you ate. The success of your search for the cause will depend on how many cases you examine and the thoroughness with which you look for a common element, discarding elements which only appear in some of the cases. Suppose you determine that the common factor in all these episodes is eating peanut butter the day before. You would then call peanut butter the cause of your complexion distress. Since you have determined that no episodes of complexion trouble occur except when you have eaten peanut butter, peanut butter is a *necessary condition* for your face to break out. On the other hand, if your research reveals that your face breaks out at other times besides those when you have eaten peanut butter but always when you have eaten peanut butter, then peanut butter is a *sufficient condition*, but not a necessary condition, for your bad complexion. This is Mill's Method of Agreement: Some single condition that is present in all the cases which concerned you.

"Has it ever occurred to anyone that if we stopped wearing these damned skirts we wouldn't have to march off to defend our manhood every five minutes?"

Perhaps the relevant common factor is wearing a kilt.

Mill's **Method of Difference** can be illustrated by the all-too-common experience of trying to figure out why the computer lost your history paper. You would try to determine what you did this time while you were using the computer that you did not do before when you used it successfully. That is, you would try to find some relevant difference between this occasion that went awry and the other past times you successfully used the computer to prepare your paper. You may have hit a wrong key and accidentally erased it, there may have been a power surge that wiped it out, or someone may have handed you a highly magnetized object that interfered with the electrical circuitry of the computer. For your determination of the cause to be successful in this case, you must not jump to conclusions too quickly. There may be several apparent differences which you may have to eliminate as possibilities, and you will have to be careful to consider only relevant differences. That you were wearing your new blue sweater for the first time is not relevant. That you were wearing an awkward bangle bracelet that caught on the keyboard might be relevant. Your bracelet in this case may be a *sufficient condition* for the computer destroying your history paper.

A third method of Mill for determining causes is the **Method of Concomitant Variation**. In this method, variations in one condition are matched (either positively or negatively) with variations in another. Let's go back to the problem of determining the cause of your bad complexion. One possibility is that the state of your bad complexion is influenced by the amount of stress you are feeling. Stress-free days are days without a blemish. Days of moderate stress—say, only one exam—are days with moderate blemishing. And on days of high stress, your face is a mess! One might conclude, then, that stress is a cause of your complexion troubles because the variation of the stress is correlated with the variation in your complexion. One would have to be careful here to make sure that there is no third condition which is the cause of both the stress and your poor complexion. For instance, suppose you were suffering from some illness which was causing both the stress and the poor complexion.

Just because two properties are highly correlated with one another does not necessarily mean that they are causally related. There must be some way that the one property can affect the other. There may be a high correlation between the population growth in Manhattan and the population growth in Shanghai, but that does not mean that the former is the cause of the latter. Such a correlation is simply accidental. There is no way that these two properties can affect one another. There is no known mechanism that connects the populations of these two cities. This distinction between accidental correlations and necessary connections is the issue in the third reading in this chapter. It is a comment on the controversy about the cancer-causing effects of cigarettes. Scientists have long claimed that the high correlation between cigarette smoking and lung cancer indicates a causal relation, that is, a necessary connection. The tobacco industry, on the other hand, long maintained that the correlation is accidental, not necessary.

Making causal statements is an awful lot like making generalizations. A lot of our success depends on our **background knowledge**. There is no way, for instance, that the word *relevant* can be eliminated from the discussion of the above example, nor can it be characterized in a noncircular way which would help us avoid every mistake. Our background knowledge is what keeps us from making a lot of mistakes. It enables us to be selective in our choices of causal factors. Our background knowledge tells us that the color of our clothing is irrelevant to the operation of a computer. It also tells us that computers are directly responsive to the keys we hit on the keyboard. If we mistype, we get what we typed.

Our background knowledge is actually quite sophisticated. For all of our background knowledge is not alike. Some parts of our background knowledge are more fundamental to our ways of looking at the world than other parts. In the words of the philosopher Nelson Goodman, some of the beliefs that make up our background knowledge are more **entrenched** than others.[5] A simple understanding of what Goodman means is that these beliefs lie deeper and more centrally in our web of belief than do other beliefs and, therefore, if we try to change them or remove them from our web of belief, we disturb many other beliefs that are connected to them. Consequently, the more entrenched a belief is, the less willing we are to give it up because giving it up means giving up on a great many other beliefs as well. Some beliefs are easy to give up. For example, suppose you believe that it is cold outside. Then you go out and find that the day is balmy. Other beliefs are much harder to give up. Your beliefs about what happens to a pencil when someone lets go of it in mid air are very entrenched. Just think how shocked you would be if you let go of a pencil and it just stayed there, somehow suspended in space! We are not conscious of the pattern of entrenchment of our beliefs until one of them gets challenged. But it is there all the same. The pattern of entrenchment is not the same for everyone, but similarities of patterns will tend to characterize different groups of people, for example, family members, Americans, Asians, Catholics, Muslims, and so on.

Entrenchment is a very important factor in our ability to distinguish accidental correlations from necessary connections or causal connections. To see how entrenchment works in causal reasoning, let's go back to the example above of pennies in your pocket. Although you might pull 100 (or even 200!) pennies from your pocket, you would continue to believe that this correlation between being a penny and being in your pocket is an accidental one, not a necessary one. Although you are experiencing constant conjunction between these two events, nothing else in your past experience or background knowledge supports a causal connection between being in your pocket and being a penny. It is a well-entrenched belief of yours that coins don't change their denomination by being in a certain place. And this belief is connected with other well-entrenched beliefs about metals, the nature of pockets, etc., all of which would have to be altered to **fit** with a new belief in a causal connection between being in your pocket and being a penny.

On the other hand, if you let go of your pencil and it stayed suspended in mid air, you would suspect some unanticipated causal factor. A magician's string, perhaps. Or a stream of air blowing up beneath it. Your belief that there is a necessary connection between the pencil's being let go of and the pencil's falling is so well entrenched that you are already expecting the sound of the pencil hitting the floor before you hear it! So we can see that background knowledge and well-entrenched beliefs about causal connections enable us most of the time to distinguish between accidental correlations and necessary connections. **It is important to remember, however, that even our well-entrenched beliefs are still only based on the experience of constant conjunction.**

---

[5] *Fact, Fiction and Forecast*, 1955.

Not only does entrenchment help us distinguish accidental correlations from causal connections, it also helps us avoid a common error of causal reasoning, namely, the fallacy of *post hoc, ergo propter hoc*. This is a fallacy of thinking that just because X is followed by Y, X caused Y. While it is true that causes always precede their effects, it does not follow that whatever precedes an event is the *cause* of that event. Just because the last thing you did before the computer lost your paper was to eat a candy bar, it would be poor causal reasoning to attribute the loss of your paper to the eating of the candy bar. It does not fit in with other well-entrenched beliefs you have about the nature of computers—unless, of course, you happened to have dropped some candy on the end of your flash drive before trying to print out your paper. It is easy to fall into *post hoc* reasoning because, again, there is no mark or distinguishing feature of experience which distinguishes necessary connections from accidental ones. While preceding the effect is a *necessary* condition for being a cause, it is not a *sufficient* condition for being a cause.

The first reading of this section on causal claims reviews the continuing argument about the connection between cigarettes and cancer. The second reading in this section is from a contemporary philosopher, Hilary Putnam. In this short excerpt, Putnam worries about how we might teach computers to think and, in particular, how we might teach them to deal with evidence that leads to conflicting beliefs. Putnam is marveling at the ability of human beings to sort out conflicting inductive hypotheses in ways which don't always seem to be explicable through experience alone. That is, just because we know from our background knowledge that something always happened a certain way in the past, lying still more deeply in our web of belief may be other beliefs that allow us to believe, or even force us to accept a belief, which contradicts that background knowledge. Our webs of belief are so complex that it is hard to imagine how to convey all of their many relationships to an artificial intelligence.

It should be clear from this discussion of causal reasoning that many of the guidelines for good causal reasoning are similar to those for the other forms of reasoning with probability. The importance of background information is again quite clear. We cannot be good critical thinkers without having knowledge of the world around us. This is why we must be open and willing to watch and listen to that world.

The guidelines for good causal reasoning are

1. Proceed with caution. Remember that our experience is only of constant conjunction, not of necessary connection, so it is easy to make mistakes when reasoning about causes.
2. Since mistakes are likely, we should always be ready to revise our causal claims. (This is true even for scientific, laboratory-tested claims as we will show in the next chapter.)
3. Our causal claims must always be evaluated by how well they fit together with the background knowledge we bring to our experience. When we have conflicting causal beliefs or are uncertain, we should look to our most well-entrenched beliefs and look for the best fit with those beliefs. Since there is no mark on experience which would enable us to distinguish necessary connections from accidental correlations, this fitting in with our well-entrenched beliefs is our best guide in causal reasoning.

4. We should look for the relevant common factor when we have a number of similar occurrences. When we have one unique case (or unusual correlation), we should look for the relevant specific difference in that case. When we have a similar variation of two correlated events, we should look for a possible causal connection between them or for some third factor which may be the cause of the concomitant variation.

So, Smoking Causes Cancer: This Is News?

Denise Grady

Was it *really* news to anybody, as headlines proclaimed a little more than a week ago, that smoking causes lung cancer?

The discovery behind the news stories was a report by a team of scientists showing that benzo[a]pyrene, a chemical in cigarette smoke, causes genetic mutations in lung cells that are identical to those found in many patients with lung cancer.

That this unsurprising discovery made such a big splash illustrates a curiously unintuitive idea: When it comes to proof, sometimes scientists are easier to please than ordinary people.

Benzo[a]pyrene has been recognized as a carcinogen for 20 years, but its exact mechanism was unknown. And the tobacco industry exploited that seed of doubt to the fullest, arguing that although scientists had shown an association between smoking and cancer, they had not proved cause and effect. The new study was seen as the proof that would silence the tobacco industry. It was the first proof, on the cellular and molecular level that a chemical in smoke could damage lung cells in a way that could eventually lead to cancer. But who was actually swayed by the study?

"From the point of view of scientists and doctors, and many people who are reasonably educated in medicine, this finding will make virtually no difference at all," said John Banzhaf, a professor of law at Georgetown University and the director of Action on Smoking and Health, an anti-smoking group.

"There are so many different studies of so many different kinds which establish about as conclusively as anything we know in medicine that smoking causes cancer in human beings, that this doesn't really help," Mr. Banzhaf said. "We already have 50,000 studies. Why do we need 50,001?"

Living with Uncertainty

This last bit of proof is for ordinary people. Scientists and lay people have different ideas about what constitutes proof, Mr. Banzhaf said. Part of scientific training involves learning to deal with uncertainty.

If a statistical analysis shows that there is a 5 percent or smaller chance that two events—say, smoking and cancer—are linked purely by coincidence, then most scientists would accept the idea that the association between them has at least a 95 percent chance of being real and likely to repeat itself, even if the nature of the link is not fully understood.

But non-scientists, less familiar with statistics, may not be able to let go of that 5 percent, or the lack of an explanation. They may insist that proof does not exist until all competing possibilities have been eliminated. Their notions of "reasonable doubt" in criminal cases, or of the "preponderance of evidence" that is required in civil court, may be colored by their discomfort with uncertainty.

This Causes That

Pinning down a mechanism—being able to say, this molecule causes this change in this cell, which is known to lead to cancer—eliminates some of the uncertainty. People are more likely to believe in things that they can understand.

But some may never be persuaded. The Tobacco Institute said it wasn't ready to comment. R.J.R. Nabisco, the cigarette manufacturer, called the study "preliminary rather than conclusive." Philip Morris said it is "extremely interesting and merits careful review."

One of the nagging issues, and a favorite of the defenders of smoking, is the question of why not all smokers get lung cancer. Knowing the mechanism may help provide an answer. Scientists may one day be able to say that people may differ in the tendency of their cells to convert benzo[a]pyrene to a highly carcinogenic form, or in the ability of their cells to repair the sort of genetic damage that the chemical inflicts, said one of the authors of the study, Dr. Gerd Pfeifer, an associate professor at the Beckman Research Institute at the City of Hope in Duarte, Calif.

The availability of an explanation has made the connection between smoking and cancer less of an abstraction for some people. Idee Fox, a Philadelphia judge who quit smoking a month ago and who still craves cigarettes, said, "This report really meant something to me as a smoker. I had been thinking, not everybody who smokes gets cancer, they don't really understand it, so maybe it won't happen to me. This explained how it works, and it made it more real."

People who want to rationalize smoking may now have to turn to philosophy for solace.

"Theoretically, you can never prove anything," said Dr. Bert Vogelstein, a Johns Hopkins expert in cancer genetics. "No one will ever be able to prove that smoking causes cancer, or that anything causes anything."

RENEWING PHILOSOPHY

Hilary Putnam

One huge problem might be described as the existence of *conflicting inductions*. To use an example from Nelson Goodman: as far as I know, no one who has ever entered Emerson Hall in Harvard University has been able to speak Inuit (Eskimo). Thinking formalistically, this suggests the induction that if any person X enters Emerson Hall, then X does not speak Inuit. Let Ukuk be an Eskimo in Alaska who speaks Inuit. Shall I predict that if Ukuk enters Emerson Hall, then Ukuk will no longer be able to speak Inuit? Obviously not, but what is wrong with this induction?

Goodman answers that what is wrong with the inference is that it conflicts with the "better entrenched" inductively supported law that people do not lose their ability to speak a language upon entering a new place. But how am I supposed to know that this law *does* have more confirming instances than the regularity that no one who enters Emerson Hall speaks Inuit? Background knowledge again?

As a matter of fact, I don't believe that as a child I had any idea how often either of the conflicting regularities in the example (conflicting in that one of them must fail if Ukuk enters Emerson Hall) had been confirmed, but I would still have known enough not to make the "silly" induction that Ukuk would stop being able to speak Inuit if he entered a building (or a country) where no one had spoken Inuit. Again it is not clear that the knowledge that one doesn't lose a language just like that *is* really the product of induction—perhaps this is something we have an innate propensity to believe or, if that seems unreasonable, something that we have an innate propensity to conclude on the basis of only a little experience. The question that won't go away is *how much what we call "intelligence" presupposes the rest of human nature.*

Moreover, if what matters really is "entrenchment" (that is, number and variety of confirming instances), and if the information that the universal statement "one doesn't lose one's ability to speak a language upon entering a new place" is better entrenched than the universal statement "no one who enters Emerson Hall speaks Inuit" is part of my background knowledge, it isn't clear how it got there. Perhaps this information is implicit in the way people speak about linguistic abilities; but then one is faced with the question of how one "decodes" the implicit information conveyed by the utterances one hears.

The problem of conflicting inductions is a ubiquitous one even if one restricts attention to the simplest inductive inferences. If the solution is really just to give the system more background knowledge, then what are the implications for Artificial Intelligence? It is not easy to say, because Artificial Intelligence as we know it doesn't really try to simulate intelligence at all; simulating intelligence is only its notional activity, while its real activity is just writing clever programs for a variety of tasks. This is an important and useful activity, although of course, it does not sound as exciting as "simulating human intelligence" or "producing artificial intelligence." But if Artificial Intelligence existed as a real rather than a notional research activity, there would be two alternative strategies its practitioners could follow in the face of the problem of background knowledge.

(1) One could simply try to program into the machine *all* of the information a sophisticated human inductive judge has (including the tacit information). At the least it would require generations of researchers to formalize this information (probably it could not be done at all, because of the sheer quantity of information involved); and it is not clear that the result would be more than a gigantic "expert system." No one would find this very exciting; and such an "intelligence" would be dreadfully unimaginative, unable to realize that in many cases it is precisely background knowledge that needs to be given up.

(2) One could undertake the more exciting and ambitious task of constructing a device that could *learn* the background knowledge by interacting with human beings, as a child learns a language and all the cultural information, explicit and tacit, that comes with growing up in a human community.

STUDY QUESTIONS

1. How would you argue with the tobacco company spokesperson who said, "Smoking increases the risk factors of getting lung cancer but there is no proof that smoking causes lung cancer"?
2. Why would Putnam—or any person or computer—believe that if Ukuk enters Emerson Hall, then Ukuk will no longer be able to speak Inuit? What better entrenched beliefs conflict with this belief? What is the evidence for each of these conflicting beliefs?
3. What are some of your entrenched causal beliefs?
4. Why do some people doubt that the six beers they had at the party caused their hangover?

Summary

These last two readings are very useful because they call attention to two of the most interesting puzzles of inductive reasoning or reasoning with probability. To review: Induction is a prediction of the future based on past experience. It is reasoning from observed cases to unobserved cases. If one is trying to program a computer to reason inductively, what rules for drawing generalizations would one give it? Consider the case posed by Putnam. In the past, thousands of people have entered Emerson Hall, none of whom could speak Inuit. Should one conclude that any future person entering Emerson Hall, including Ukuk, would not speak Inuit? If one goes on the basis of past experience alone, then given the many cases of individuals who have entered Emerson Hall, none of whom could speak Inuit, a computer programmed to base its generalizations on past evidence would draw that conclusion. Yet Putnam believes this is the wrong conclusion for the computer to draw. Why? Because he believes that if an Inuit-speaking person would enter Emerson Hall, that Inuit-speaking individual would retain his Inuit language skills. That is, there are beliefs in his web of belief about how people retain their language skills regardless of what building they enter. These unarticulated, entrenched beliefs are very important to our success in inductive reasoning and somehow they have to be acquired by the computer even though they do not seem to have any relevance to the generalization at hand.

Now we can see how amazing and sophisticated human inductive reasoning is! Human beings are very good at knowing when a high number of cases are not sufficient to justify projecting a generalization into the future because to do so would be inconsistent with some belief or beliefs that are much better entrenched in our webs of belief. Yet, we are generally not conscious of how much background knowledge we have and are using in our ordinary anticipation of the future. And we are usually not conscious of the depth of entrenchment of our beliefs until we find that we hold conflicting beliefs or are being threatened by conflicting beliefs. This is puzzle number one. Why are human beings so good at inductive reasoning?

Many smokers and people in the tobacco industry are examples of people faced with conflicting beliefs. For example, the cigarette smoker may believe (1) since many of those who die from lung cancer have been heavy smokers, there is causal link between tobacco and cancer, and (2) since Uncle Joe smoked two packs a day and died of heart failure at age ninety, like Uncle Joe he will also live to ninety—or at least die of something else. The smoker's ability to maintain these nearly inconsistent beliefs often rests on a mistaken understanding of causality. That is, they can hold these two beliefs because they hold a third belief about the nature of causation. They mistakenly believe that for cigarettes to cause cancer there must be a mechanism that *completely closes the gap* between our experience of the cause and the effect and that this mechanism must be either a necessary or sufficient condition for lung cancer. It is, of course, well known that cigarettes are neither a necessary nor a sufficient condition for lung cancer. People who have never smoked do get lung cancer and many people who smoke cigarettes do not get lung cancer (before they die). Both of these points misunderstand the nature of cause.

We must return to the point made by the philosopher David Hume that our experience of cause is always the experience of constant conjunction, never of the necessity of the connection between the cause and its effect. No matter how much we might fill in the details of the chemical process resulting from cigarette smoke inhalation which damages the cellular and molecular structure of the body, there would still be a gap between our experience of the events and the causal connection we attribute to them. We experience the exposure of cells to benzo[a]pyrene (as the scientists now claim) and then we experience (cancerous) cell mutation. We cannot see the benzo[a] pyrene bring about the cancer. We just see the cancer developing.

Furthermore, just because not all people who smoke die of lung cancer, it does not follow that cigarette smoking is not a sufficient cause of lung cancer. A gunshot wound can be a sufficient cause of death but not all gunshot wounds result in death. Not even all gunshot wounds to the heart are fatal. The human body is a very complex organism with many variables that are hard to account for. Some bodies are able to resist the same causal forces that other human bodies cannot. So it is with cigarettes. Some people's bodies resist the causal effects of nicotine smoke, and others succumb all too easily. And some resist long enough to die of something else.

The situation is similar to the match's lighting. Striking a match doesn't always cause it to light. The match may be damp, the scratch pad too worn, the wind too strong, and so on. No one would say, however, that it is yet to be proven that striking a match causes it to light. By the same token, when study after study reveals a high correlation between cigarette smoking and lung cancer (and other serious diseases), a reasoning person can no longer claim that these high correlations are accidental. The connection between cigarettes and cancer must be a necessary one. This necessary connection—like all causal connections—can never be proven. But it is very well confirmed. This is puzzle number two!

In sum, from the guidelines for determining causation and from the guidelines set out above for the other forms of reasoning with probability, we see that our projections are warranted if our projections are effective. By the same token, our projections are effective if they are warranted. There is no noncircular warrant for our reasoning with probability. We can avoid a *vicious* circle, however, if we continue to increase our background knowledge and adjust our projections in light of new experience. **To make sense out of our own experience together with others' reports of their experiences, we must continually test our reasoning against future experience and adjust our background knowledge and projections in light of the results of those testings.**

Exercises

8–I

1. Explain what a phobia is using concepts you have learned in this chapter. How can a phobia be seen as a failure of reasoning with probability?
2. Why is a telephone book not a good source for a random sample?
3. You may have heard the generalization "Everyone always acts in his own self-interest." How would you argue for or against this generalization? Are there better or worse ways of arguing here?
4. Pick one of the three forms of inductive reasoning described in this chapter, and explain how "Success is in the details."

8–II

1. Explain why a bigot is not a good critical thinker.
2. When would it be more appropriate to use a random sample as opposed to a representative sample? When would it be more appropriate to use a representative sample instead of a random sample?
3. Critically evaluate the warning found on cigarette packages.
4. The *Literary Digest* articles continually talk about the assumptions one could make in analyzing the straw ballot it conducted. Are there any assumptions they made or failed to make that could have saved them from embarrassment?
5. Distinguish between a necessary connection between two events and a necessary condition for an event.
6. Do you know what the experience of *déjà vu* is? (If not, look it up in the dictionary.) How could *déjà vu be seen as* an instance of reasoning by analogy?
7. Explain the following quotation from Bertrand Russell: "The whole problem with the world is that fools and fanatics are always so certain of themselves, but wiser people so full of doubts."

9

Fallacies

THE NATURE OF FALLACIES

Errors in our reasoning occur with more frequency than we would like to believe. These errors hinder our daily activities and often prevent us from fully enjoying life. Sometimes they even threaten life itself. One way to avoid errors in reasoning is to learn and understand what *good* reasoning is and to practice using good reasoning skills in our daily activities. Learning and understanding has been the focus of the previous chapters in this book. Another way to avoid reasoning errors is to become familiar with some of the errors people commonly make in their reasoning. By recognizing these errors, we can avoid making them ourselves and also not be misled by the errors of others.

Erroneous reasoning is usually called *fallacious* reasoning. Like sound and cogent reasoning, fallacious reasoning often occurs in patterns. These fallacious reasoning patterns are referred to simply as **fallacies**. One approach to critical thinking focuses exclusively on recognizing fallacies and being able to name them and distinguish one from the other. Good critical thinking does not require that you should be able to recognize and name each of the very large number of patterns of fallacious reasoning you might come across. It is helpful, however, to be familiar with some common patterns, so you can spot them in your own and in other people's reasoning and can avoid being misled.

Philosophers of the Middle Ages spent a lot of time identifying and naming patterns of fallacious reasoning, and many fallacies still have the Latin names they were given at that time. Fallacies give us trouble, not because they have Latin names that are hard to remember, but because they often seem like pieces of good reasoning and, therefore, we tend to accept the reasoning and to give more warrant to the conclusions they purport to support than we should.

Philosophers usually distinguish two kinds of fallacies, the formal fallacies and the informal fallacies. The formal fallacies

As we all do when we commit a fallacy.

are mistakes in deductive reasoning. Several of these have already been described in Chapter 6 and will not concern us here. The informal fallacies are mistakes in inductive reasoning, that is, in reasoning with probability. In this chapter, we will look at a few of the more commonly found informal fallacies, so you can recognize them when you encounter them.

A fallacy, for our purposes in this chapter, is a piece of inductive reasoning which gives the mistaken impression of conferring greater probability on the conclusion than is warranted by the evidence. To put it another way, the information offered as evidence only *seems* to increase the likelihood of the conclusion; when we take a closer look at the evidence offered, the apparent probability of the conclusion on the basis of the evidence offered lessens or even melts away.

Fallacies are tricky because they give the appearance of being good reasoning and supplying information (**traces**) we should count as sufficient evidence for the conclusion. If we use our **background knowledge**, however, we soon find that there is not enough of a **story** connecting the information to the conclusion. Consequently, we should *not* consider the information as strong evidence, or even as support, for the conclusion. For example, consider the case of a man who applies for a job and when asked about his qualifications, offers his wife and six needy children as evidence for the wisdom of employing him. From our background knowledge we know that these are not what an employer means by *job* qualifications. As much as someone might want to help the poor man by giving him a job, the question of whether or not he is qualified for the job still remains.

Fortunately, most fallacies fall into three primary categories, which makes it easier to learn and remember them. Understanding the general principles of each grouping will help you recognize the fallacies which make up the group. Sometimes fallacies are very much alike so that it is hard to distinguish instances of each specific fallacy. Being able to distinguish between fallacies that closely resemble one another is not as important to being a good critical thinker as being able to recognize pieces of reasoning as fallacious. A good way to remember the individual fallacies is to focus on a clear instance of the fallacious pattern and then use that instance as a model by which to recognize the fallaciousness of future instances. We will help you do this by suggesting clear instances of the fallacies covered in this chapter to use as models.

FALLACIES OF IRRELEVANCE

One common form of fallacious reasoning is offering irrelevant material as evidence for a conclusion. In Chapter 7, we stressed the importance of recognizing traces and patterns of traces. To be able to do this it is helpful to have a large store of background knowledge which helps us see connections and patterns. We also saw in Chapter 7 that there is a difference between traces and evidence, so that not all information or traces provide evidence for a conclusion. **Fallacies of irrelevance** are examples of this latter situation. They imply connections where there are none. They draw us into believing a conclusion is warranted by suggesting considerations which may seem to be evidence for the conclusion but which are not. It is always possible to weigh these considerations against our background knowledge to see that the information is irrelevant to the conclusion at hand.[1] This critical thinking skill can be aided, however, by learning these common patterns of using irrelevant evidence.

Appeal to Sympathy

One common pattern has already been introduced in our example above, namely, the pattern the Medieval philosophers called *ad misericordiam* or **appeal to sympathy or pity**. Although a person may have need for a job or a good grade or for mercy and so on, need is not the proper criterion for judgment in these situations. It is not a relevant quality for hiring, grading, or legal decisions. So, when someone appeals to your sympathy in a particular situation, a little red flag should go up warning you that you should question carefully the relevance of that appeal to the question at hand.

Ad Hominem

Ad hominem is another common pattern of offering irrelevant information as evidence for a conclusion. A person who commits the *ad hominem* fallacy offers information about another's character as evidence against the content of that other person's ideas or point of view. For instance, if a politician is making a case for a particular stance on an issue, and her opponent in the discussion offers an irrelevant comment about the speaker's family life, then the opponent has committed the *ad hominem* fallacy. This pattern occurs frequently in politics. Of course, sometimes character is important. Character is important in leaders like presidents and teachers and police. In an *ad hominem* argument, however, character is irrelevant as evidence to the topic

---

[1]While we have used the commonly used designation of "fallacies of irrelevance" for this group of fallacies, they might better be called "fallacies of suppressed insupportable premises." Careful examination of these arguments reveals that the information in the premises is not irrelevant to the conclusion but rather is connected to the conclusion by an implicit premise, which most people would not accept as factual if it were explicitly expressed.

under discussion or dispute. Suppose the baseball umpire says, "You're out," and when you ask why she says, "Because I don't like your face" or "I don't like your team's uniforms." Then she would be committing the *ad hominem* fallacy. (Lucy in the classic comic strip "Peanuts" argued this way when she was losing an argument to Charlie Brown!)

The character of a witness on the witness stand is relevant to whether the jury takes the words of the witness as evidence. But the statement that witness' grandmother wears army boots is not relevant. If you are arguing with a friend about whether God exists or not and your friend is offering reasons for her position, it is *ad hominem* to respond with an attack on her character, or ancestry, or appearance; for example, "You're just the believing/doubting type."

You probably can remember when you heard or read an *ad hominem* argument. You probably can remember when you uttered one yourself. ("You're going to vote for Joe for student body president? You're just a creep.") *Ad hominem* arguments are very common, but they are not very helpful. They shift the focus of a discussion from reasons that are evidence for a conclusion to information that is irrelevant, thereby avoiding or subverting the critical thinking that the topic deserves. They also often play to biases and prejudices. Consequently, they should be avoided in discussion or dialogue, and you should be on guard not to be pulled in by them. If you are arguing with someone who offers an *ad hominem* argument, it is usually a good idea to point out that this is not a good form of reasoning and that the information is irrelevant as evidence for the conclusion. An easy model of *ad hominem* to keep in mind here is the umpire who says, "You're out because I don't like your face."

Appeal to False Authority

Advertisements are a good source of fallacies of irrelevance. The most common fallacy exploited by advertisers is the **appeal to false authority**. The authority often cited by advertisers is a sports figure that is held up as an expert on underwear or cereal or automobiles, and so on. Appeals to false authority occur in other situations as well. Two little children on the playground arguing might try to settle their argument by appealing to the authority of one of their parents. For example, one child might claim that Willy Mays is the best baseball player ever. The other might claim that that honor belongs to Babe Ruth "Oh, yeah? Who says?" "My father says, that's who!" In general, an appeal to false authority occurs when we attribute to someone, who has expertise in one area (like baseball), expertise in another area (like the quality of an automobile) for which there is no reason to think that person has expertise.

Judging who has expertise in an area and who does not is often very difficult. In our modern technological age, many court cases rest on the credibility of expert testimony, and often conflicting expert testimony is presented. Even experts may disagree about who has the most expertise and, hence, who should have the most authority in a particular situation. You will have to use your background knowledge in making judgments of this kind. The key point to keep in mind in recognizing the fallacy of appeal to *false* authority, however, is that expertise is the basis of authority and not some other irrelevant feature of an individual, such as good looks, celebrity, or physical power.

Slippery Slope

Another fallacy of irrelevance that you surely have encountered is the fallacy called **slippery slope**. Political arguments often take this form; for example, "Some politicians want to ban cigarettes. Will alcohol be next? Will caffeine be next? Will high-fat foods be next?" The slippery slope argument generally comes in two varieties. According to one variety, once you take one step down the slope, whatever it is, you might as well keep on going until you reach the end of it. There's no obvious resting place or way to stop along the way once you have started—so you might as well just enjoy the journey. The other variation of this argument is that since there's no obvious stopping place until you reach the bottom, you should not even take one step down the slope.

The person who commits the slippery slope fallacy uses the generally accepted claim that there is no obvious or fixed place to draw a line between two conditions or properties to make the further claim that no line can reasonably be drawn. Dieters are fond of both versions of the slippery slope argument. The "loose diet" version: "Since I ate one piece of cake, I might as well ruin my diet some more and have a second." Or the "strict diet" variation on this theme: "I won't even eat one peanut because if I do, I'll eat the whole bowl." The implication is that once we start down that slope, there's no place to stop. But there are many places to stop on the slope, and good reasoning will help us determine which is the most desirable for us. Just because beer is sold in six-packs does not mean that one has to consume the whole six-pack in one evening. There are six obvious stopping points, depending on whether one is driving, partying, thirsty, and so on and one could create others at will.[2]

Part of the apparent effectiveness of this kind of slippery slope reasoning stems from the nature of language. Many words have no obvious dividing line or point between themselves and their opposite. This leads the erring reasoner to conclude that there is no difference between the two extremes. For instance, it is certainly not clear when a person becomes bald. There is no clear dividing line between being bald and not bald. Will two more lost hairs be the deciding factor? Three? Although we cannot say just how many more hairs John will have to lose before we consider him bald, we do know the difference and can usually distinguish between bald and non-bald. Many opposites have no fixed line between them. When, for example, does a person become rich, or poor, or white haired, or old, or tall?

In many cases we have to make a decision and say this person is rich and that one poor, and so on. That this distinction always contains an element of arbitrariness does not mean that the line cannot be reasonably drawn. The open Socratic dialogue is the best way to determine the best place for drawing the line. There is still a difference between being rich and being poor, and we all know which one we would rather be. Borderline cases will always be troublesome, especially when other goods or benefits are determined by where the line is drawn. For example, if people below a certain income level are entitled to a governmental support program, then where the line is drawn between poverty and non-poverty takes on considerable importance.

---

[2]If a person truly has a compulsion about something, then from a *psychological* point of view, it may be a good thing not to expose her to the danger of that compulsion. Many people, however, use their "compulsive personality" as an excuse to justify doing what they want to do when reason tells them they should not.

Because the line is arbitrary, it is open to rational discussion and possible adjustment. It does not mean, however, that no line can be drawn or that once it is drawn it has no significance.

The abortion debate is an area where slippery slope arguments are common—from partisans on both sides of this issue. The pro-life proponent sometimes argues that since there is no way of saying when a fetus becomes a person, that is, no non-arbitrary line between being a fetus and being a person, we must accept the view that life begins at conception. (The argument might take the form "If you are willing to abort impaired fetuses, then what is to stop you from killing impaired infants?") The pro-choice advocate sometimes also argues the same way, namely, since there is no point before birth when a fetus becomes a person, the mother should always have freedom of choice and may choose abortion at any time during her pregnancy. Both of these arguments are guilty of the slippery slope fallacy. The dialogue about the moral legitimacy of abortion suffers because of this poor reasoning pattern and often becomes a stalemate, leading sometimes even to the use of force to express beliefs.

Although slippery slope arguments are tempting, we should avoid them in our discussions with others and with ourselves. That there is no non-arbitrary way of drawing a line does not mean that there is no line or difference between two opposite properties. Keep in mind the model of the dieter who will never lose weight thinking that there is no difference between eating and overeating, between one piece of cake or two!

False Dichotomy

False dichotomy (also called the fallacy of false alternative or bifurcation) is another fallacy of irrelevance. Perhaps it might better be called a fallacy of missing relevance. The arguer committing this fallacy assumes an either/or hypothesis or situation when there are more than two relevant alternatives and then argues against one of the possibilities, leaving the one she prefers. For example, the young lover might threaten, "Either we go to the dance or you don't love me." A very common use of false dichotomy to make a point is when someone says, "Jason wins the election or I'll eat my hat." Since we know the speaker will not eat his hat, we are pushed to believe the speaker strongly believes that Jason will win. Or consider the policy often advanced in politics, "Either you are for us or you are against us." Again, we can think of other alternatives, and we hope our politicians can too.

Red Herring

Sometimes an arguer will try to divert the attention of his opponent in the argument with an argument or claim that is not to the point and then draw some conclusion based on this claim. This effort at distraction is called a **red herring**. Politicians often try to get away with red herring arguments. If an opponent is criticizing a politician's policy on health care, rather than responding to the criticism the politician is apt to respond with some anecdote about poor so-and-so who was ill-served under his opponent's policy. Or consider the practice resorted to in some recent State of the Union addresses, where the President invites recent heroes to sit in the Presidential box and then acknowledges them during his speech as if to claim them for his administration and its policies. While it is splendid to acknowledge heroes, their heroism is rarely the result of something the sitting President has done and his taking credit for them is a red herring.

Begging the Question

A common mistake in a discussion is to offer an argument that is **begging the question**. Instead of distracting the reader or listener by focusing on irrelevant points as in a red herring argument, the person who commits the fallacy of begging the question assumes that which she is claiming to show and then claims to have shown it. Sometimes this can be very inadvertent, especially when different vocabularies obscure the similarity between the offending premise and the conclusion. For example, suppose someone says, "The new presidential administration will usher in a new world," and when asked why, replies, "Because it's a new administration." This person has begged the question and has not answered it. It's as if she said, "It's a new world because it's a new world." That is why this fallacy is often referred to as circular reasoning. We are all guilty of it at times, and there are some puzzles of reasoning where circularity is hard to avoid. We discussed one of these puzzles when we talked about the problem of induction.

A good example of begging the question is the television announcer (as in Chapter 2) commenting on figure skating who says something like, "The second skater clearly didn't skate as well as the first." When asked why he thinks she did not skate as well, he replies, "She got a lower score from the judges. She must have made some mistakes. If she hadn't made some mistakes she would have gotten a higher score." The viewer is thus left to wonder what the skater did wrong. Such instances of begging the question are frustrating and reinforce our earlier point that no statement is self-warranting, even if it is repeated or repeated in different words, giving the false appearance of warranting.

Subjunctive Fallacy

One final fallacy of irrelevance that we will mention here is the **subjunctive fallacy** (or hypothesis contrary to fact). These fallacies usually begin with "what if . . ." or "if only . . ." For example, "If only I had practiced my backhand more, I would have won the tournament." Practicing one's backhand more would probably help to make one a better player, but it is certainly no guarantee that one would win the tournament. Or the all-to-familiar: "I could get good grades, too, if I studied as hard as Mary does." Many students argue this way, including some who are afraid to make the effort for fear they might fail. Perhaps you know some people like that. In the reading which follows this section the humorist Russell Baker makes clear the fallacious nature of a popular instance of an argument of this type. While we all cannot be as clever as Baker, his technique for making the fallacy clear is one that can be copied. What he does is construct an argument in the same form as the argument in question and draw some ridiculous conclusion from it so that it is clear that the reasoning pattern is fallacious.

There are many other fallacies of irrelevance. The eight we have discussed here are very common and, in their own way, rather fun to know. It is good to keep the general category of irrelevance in mind as well as the specific named fallacies.

LOST GENIUS

Russell Baker

Do you ever feel sad about all the geniuses who might exist, but don't?

Of course not, and I wouldn't either if antiabortion people didn't keep talking about Beethoven. One of their most provocative arguments against abortion is that Beethoven might never have existed if abortion had been available in his mother's day.

They note that the economic and physical health of the Beethoven family and of Ludwig himself were the sort that bode ill for a well-rounded life and are commonly used to justify abortion today. Given easy access to abortion, might Mother Beethoven not have ended her pregnancy before Ludwig's birth?

Possibly so, and the possibility is sad to contemplate. Think how much drearier the world would be without Beethoven's Sixth Symphony and Fourth Piano Concerto. Or those fantastic quartets.

Well, fortunately abortion was discouraged in Mother Beethoven's day and Ludwig came into existence. I am still saddened, however, because the line of thought opened by the antiabortionists makes me think of all the other geniuses the world has lost without knowing it.

I am reasonably certain for instance that, good as Beethoven was, an infinitely greater composer was due to be born in Europe early in the 19th century. "Reasonably certain?" you ask. "How so?" My answer is that there is always somebody better coming along. The first problem is to bring him into existence.

As we know, the composer destined to top Beethoven failed to appear. What became of him? It's unlikely his mother denied us his genius by a trip to the abortionist. As we know from the Beethoven example, abortion was relatively rare in the late 18th century and no more commonplace by the early 19th century, when our new musical genius was scheduled for birth.

I suspect the mother either contracted smallpox or was killed during pregnancy when she was caught in the cross fire of a minor skirmish during the Napoleonic wars.

Of course, you can't prove conclusively that this extraordinary genius would have cast Beethoven's name in the shadow if musket fire hadn't cut down his mother. But then if Beethoven's mother had had an abortion, we couldn't prove that the abortionist deprived the world of the Sixth Symphony, either.

What's worse about Beethoven's case, we wouldn't care. If Beethoven hadn't existed, how many people today would be sitting around saying, "Isn't it sad that the world doesn't have Beethoven's Sixth Symphony"?

That would seem as silly to a lot of people as sitting around saying, "What a pity that a poor woman's death in a minor musket skirmish in 1809 should have deprived us of the magnificent Tuttlekinder Concerto."

Well, there's nothing silly about mourning the fact that the world will never hear the Tuttlekinder concerto, the most moving music never composed. The world is a poorer place because genius was silenced in the womb.

I become especially depressed about all the geniuses who don't exist in our present century. We need geniuses badly nowadays, and about the best we get are technicians.

Is this because our geniuses are being aborted by a society indifferent to its own fate? I doubt it. Oh, maybe we've lost a half-dozen geniuses or so to abortion, and admittedly that's a terrible loss, but I suspect it's negligible compared with the hordes we've lost to wars and automobile accidents.

I have in mind two dozen brilliant European political personalities with the genius to weld Europe from Moscow to the Atlantic into one great peaceful, productive political system between 1919 and the present day. The names of these geniuses will never be known.

The first generation of them was killed in its youthful entirety in the trenches of World War I, leaving Europe under the management of commonplace politicians incapable of anything but getting on with World War II.

The second generation, who would by now have turned Europe into a dazzling model of civilization, failed not only to be born, but also to be conceived. The fathers essential to their existence had been killed in World War I.

And so we live in a world denied its rightful geniuses, and it is sad how wantonly we squander them, and it's good to have the antiabortionists reminding us of how cavalierly we ignore the genius shortage.

I am sorry they can't get beyond Beethoven though and persuade people to mourn for all the great composers, writers, artists and statesmen who would have made the world so much more beautiful and wise but whose names we will never know because their mothers or potential fathers were terminated suddenly by bullets, bombs and bayonets.

On the other hand, thinking too powerfully along these lines leads to moral dilemma. Of course abortion is sad when it leads Mother Beethoven to deny us Ludwig. But suppose it is Mother Hitler denying us Adolf? Genius, alas, also has its dark side.

STUDY QUESTIONS

1. Construct the argument about Beethoven that Baker has in mind. Write out the premises and the conclusion.
2. Construct your own subjunctive argument that has an air of plausibility and then show it to be fallacious by constructing another argument in the same form which is clearly fallacious.

FALLACIES OF FAULTY GENERALIZATION

Another category of frequently committed fallacies is the category of **generalization fallacies**. We have already seen that generalization is one of the common forms of reasoning with probability—so it is not surprising that there are some common patterns of *poor* reasoning associated with this type of reasoning.

Hasty Generalization

Hasty generalization is one of the fallacies of generalization that occurs frequently. A person who commits this fallacy draws a generalization from too small a sample. We saw in Chapter 8 that appropriate sample size is not something that can be specified without reference to background knowledge. There is no general rule that can be stated as to when a generalization is made too hastily. Consequently, the error of hasty generalization is a mistake that we must be acutely aware of and take care to avoid.

It is rather commonplace, for example, to decide on the basis of one bad meal in a restaurant not to go back to that restaurant or from owning one automobile of a particular brand that needs frequent repairs not to buy that make of automobile again. We human beings are often "jumping to conclusions." A good model of hasty generalization to keep in mind is, "I don't like people who go to State University. I met someone from there once and he was very stuck on himself." But how many times have you met someone that you reacted to negatively on the first meeting only to find on future encounters that you genuinely like that person! And how representative of all students at State University could one student be?

Hasty generalizations can be rather sophisticated errors as we saw in *The Literary Digest* misprediction of the 1936 Presidential election. The *Digest* thought long and hard about how to generalize from its sample results to the nationwide election. Since four previous predictions had been accurate, it assumed that the 1936 prediction would also be accurate. Unfortunately, we sometimes cannot know that our generalization has been hasty until it has been tested and found to be so.

Unrepresentative Sample

The mistake *The Literary Digest* made could also be called the fallacy of **unrepresentative sample**. One can get into drawing finer distinctions between fallacies and their labels than we choose to do here, but this does not help one become a better critical thinker. The discrimination between a sample that is too small, unrepresentative, or nonrandom can sometimes be a difficult matter of judgment, one best left to the experts. What is important is that you realize that sampling errors can be made despite the best of intentions not to be hasty.

Sometimes we use faulty generalizations on purpose, knowing that our reasoning is weak but hoping to convince someone of our point of view. Advertisements are notorious in this regard. "Try it, you'll like it" or "Doctors recommend. . . ." The best way to avoid committing the fallacies of hasty generalization and unrepresentative sample or to avoid being taken in by them is to build up a good storehouse of background knowledge. The generalizations you draw and the generalizations you accept should fit in well with other beliefs that you hold, especially the beliefs which are more fundamental or well entrenched.

Anecdotal Evidence

A variation of hasty generalization that deserves special mention is the fallacy called **anecdotal evidence** or **vivid data**. We commit this fallacy when we allow the last or most vivid of our experiences to outweigh all the previous experiences we have had. We cease looking at all the evidence and focus on a small part of it. Consequently, we project the wrong conclusions into the future. A rather common example of this kind of reasoning is the person who has a bad experience flying and insists, therefore, on driving by car to every destination or on staying home. While we may sympathize with that person's fear, the overall safety record for long-distance traveling is much better for flying than it is for riding in a car. The person has given too much weight to her vivid experience and not enough weight to the less vivid but, nevertheless, overwhelming evidence that flying a long distance is safer than driving it.

This is not to suggest that being wary of something after one has had a bad experience is unreasonable. Unfortunately, there are many things to be afraid of in our world. But a fear that is based on one isolated personal experience needs to be put in perspective with the fuller picture so that reasonable judgments can be made in the future. Similarly, one should not let the most recent or most vivid experience override all previous experience, either his own or the collective experience of the larger group.

These three fallacies—hasty generalization, unrepresentative sample, and anecdotal evidence—are closely related to one another. In effect, unrepresentative sample and anecdotal evidence are more specific types of hasty generalizations. You will need to examine the context of the fallacious reasoning to make the best discrimination and designation.

Equivocation

Sometimes, people draw faulty generalizations because they equivocate on the use of a word and thereby draw more individuals under the umbrella of their generalization. Equivocation can also make arguments hard to resolve because the discussants may use the same word but each has assigned the word a different meaning, so they end up talking about two different things. The fallacy of **equivocation** is rather common in political arguments. *Democracy,* for example, is often used equivocally. It means one thing to an American and quite another to an elected dictator. One individual can also use a word equivocally, leading to an erroneous conclusion. For instance, suppose a teenager is arguing with a parent about being allowed to have the car for the night and the parent replies, "You're not old enough to have the car out at that hour." The teen then reminds the parent that her older brother Tommy was allowed to take the car out at night at that age. And the parent replies, "Well, Tommy was more mature at your age." The parent in this argument has equivocated on the word *old. Old* has been used to mean both chronological age and emotional maturity.

Definitional Fallacy

A somewhat similar fallacy is the **definitional fallacy**. People commit this fallacy when they make a claim based on a generalization and make the generalization into a definition so that their claim becomes unarguable. For example, "Taxation is theft. Therefore, taxation should be illegal." By defining taxation as theft, the arguer is precluding any further discussion about the fairness or unfairness of taxation, thereby "winning" the argument. Arguments like these rest on the confusion between empirical generalizations and definitions, which often look alike in their grammatical structure. This confusion was discussed in Chapter 8. "All whales are mammals" could be considered an empirical generalization or it could be considered a definition. Usually, however, when we are arguing about a specific instance, we are not arguing about definitions. For arguments about definitions we turn to the dictionary. A very common instance of the definitional fallacy comes up in arguments about whether human beings are capable of doing unselfish acts or whether they always act in their own self-interest. The person who takes the latter side usually wins this argument by defining self-interest in such a way that *all* acts become acts of self-interest. The hypothesis under debate, then, is no longer an empirical generalization and is no longer interesting.

Post Hoc/Propter Hoc

Another important area of overzealous generalization are the causal fallacies; that is, the fallacies of attributing a causal relation where the relationship is simply coincidental. The most common of these fallacies is the one mentioned in Chapter 8, namely, *post hoc*, *ergo propter hoc* or *post hoc*, for short. This is the fallacy of thinking that just because X is followed by Y, X causes Y. For instance, many people buy insurance when flying and then attribute their safe arrival to prior act of buying insurance. Analogously, surely you have heard someone say that she is bringing her umbrella to make sure that it doesn't rain.

We are all guilty of *post hoc* reasoning at times. As in reasoning about generalizations, the only way we can protect ourselves from *post hoc* reasoning is by using our background knowledge and relying on those beliefs which are well entrenched to guide us in distinguishing causal connections from accidental connections. This entrenchment is usually more reliable if it characterizes the webs of belief of people who are recognized experts on the subject, people who have used Mill's methods to test for the constancy of the conjunction. For instance, there are many well-entrenched old wives' tales about what causes the common cold. Doctors tell us, however, that colds, like many other diseases, are caused by a virus and not by getting caught in the rain without a raincoat or going barefoot too early in the spring, and so on.

FALLACIES OF EMOTIONAL MANIPULATION

These fallacies provoke emotions through language and encourage us to substitute emotional reactions for reason. It's not that emotions are illegitimate or unimportant to critical thinking. It is perfectly all right to indicate that you feel strongly about something. What is not all right, however, is to use emotional language to manipulate others—to inhibit them from using their powers of reason—or to preclude rational discussion altogether. From emotionally manipulating a discussion to preclude rational thought it is only a small step to getting one's way by threatening someone with a punch in the jaw.

Poisoning the Well

The fallacy of **poisoning the well** is a common method of emotional manipulation. Someone who poisons the well says something derogatory before the discussion has even started. This has the effect of precluding further discussion, open rational discussion being the most important ingredient in critical thinking. Calling your opponent in a discussion a liar before the discussion has even started, for instance, has the effect of casting suspicion on whatever she might say thereafter, no matter how cogent and well argued. Name calling, ethnic and racial slurs, and derogatory comments all have the effect of limiting or even precluding discussion of the actual merits of what a person has said or is about to say. They influence how we think about what is being said but without proper warrant.

Emotionally Loaded Language

In general, **emotionally loaded language** precludes discussion. When an author uses heavily emotionally loaded language, she doesn't really want you to argue with her. She only wants you to believe her. She only wants you to accept what she says. This is why it is a form of fallacious reasoning. It carries the *pretense* of rational dialogue, but its primary goal is to *preclude* rational dialogue. It is not that people should not be allowed to use emotional language or to express strong feelings—as long as that expression is not dangerous to others. But such emotionally charged language should not be passed off as rational dialogue or presented as a substitute for thinking critically about difficult controversial issues. When carried to extreme, it becomes dogmatism, which is the charade of reason. We shall have more to say about dogmatism in chapters which follow.

Political campaigns and political candidates often try to appeal to emotions rather than make the more complex arguments they need to support their positions. While there is always a certain amount of emotional appeal in politics, when politicians use "zingers" to stop the discussion, critical thinking has been abandoned. In her campaign for the Republican nomination for President of the United States in 2012, Michele Bachmann, Congresswoman from Minnesota, often used emotionally loaded language to persuade people to her candidacy. One example of her use of this tactic appears below in a news article about that campaign. Notice, as you read the excerpt from the article, the source of her information and the power of her example. Notice also that she provides no scientific data and cites no studies to back up her claim.

BACHMANN FINDS AN ISSUE WITH HPV DEBATE

Trip Gabriel

Representative Michele Bachmann seems to have found the issue she believes will allow her to distinguish herself from Gov. Rick Perry in their fight for the Republican presidential nomination—the vaccination of young girls against a sexually transmitted virus.

In Monday night's debate, Mrs. Bachmann seized on an executive order that Mr. Perry issued requiring sixth-grade girls in Texas to be vaccinated against the human papillomavirus, or HPV, criticizing him for an overreach of state power in a decision properly left to parents.

On Tuesday she expanded her criticism, suggesting that Mr. Perry had potentially put young girls at risk by forcing "an injection of what could potentially be a very dangerous drug."

Mrs. Bachmann said on NBC's "Today" show on Tuesday that after Monday night's debate in Tampa, Fla., a tearful mother approached her and said her daughter had suffered "mental retardation" after being vaccinated against HPV. "It can have very dangerous side effects," Mrs. Bachmann said.

With her statements, Mrs. Bachmann thrust herself into an issue that pushes many buttons with social conservatives: abuse of executive authority, suspicion that sex education leads to promiscuity and the belief—debunked by science—that childhood vaccinations cause mental disorders.

STUDY QUESTIONS

1. Use the Internet to find out what scientists have said about the relationship between vaccinations and mental retardation.
2. Why is Bachmann's example appealing? What emotional buttons does it reach?

Summary

The fallacies discussed in this chapter are only a sampling of the many fallacies that have been singled out and given names by philosophers as examples of faulty reasoning. Recognizing fallacies can be helpful in improving your reasoning skills. To make it easier to recognize fallacies, we have grouped them into three categories which can be more easily remembered. These categories are **fallacies of irrelevance, fallacies of faulty generalization,** and **fallacies of emotional manipulation.** If you have trouble remembering the specific fallacies, remembering these general categories can help you examine the reasoning in question to see whether the evidence is relevant, the generalizations sound, and the language not emotionally manipulative.

Fifteen specific fallacies have been discussed in this chapter. We could list many more. Most fallacies have more than one name, often a Latin name and then several translations of that Latin name. Don't let this confuse you. Examine the reasoning, not the name. Some fallacies very closely resemble one another and, therefore, different people may analyze the reasoning differently and come up with a different label for the fallacy. What is important is that you recognize fallacious reasoning when you see it. Being able to put a label on it gives you confidence that your analysis is correct. The best way to remember these fallacies is to keep a model for each one in mind. Then, when you come across a piece of reasoning that resembles that model, a little red flag should go up telling you that the reasoning looks suspicious and that you should examine it carefully to make sure that no fallacy is being committed. Here is a list of fallacies discussed and a simple model of each one to help you remember the pattern and the name.

FALLACIES OF IRRELEVANCE:

appeal to sympathy — "I think I deserve an A on that paper. I want to go to medical school and I need As to get in."

ad hominem — Lucy: "You're wrong, Charlie Brown. Anyone with a face like yours cannot be right."

appeal to false authority — Little Boy: "The Dodgers are the best team in baseball. My daddy says so."

slippery slope — "Now that I've opened this bag of potato chips, I might as well finish it."

false dichotomy — "If you're not for me, then you're against me."

red herring — "Don't vote for that candidate for President. The President is Commander and Chief of the armed forces. This man was never even in the military."

begging the question — Student A: "I'm sick." Student B: "What's wrong with you?" Student A: "I don't feel good."

subjunctive fallacy — "If only I had practiced my backhand longer, I would have won the tournament."

FALLACIES OF FAULTY GENERALIZATION:

hasty generalization — "I ate in the cafeteria once. The hamburger tasted like shoe leather. The food there is lousy."

unrepresentative sample — "I wanted to see how students at State feel about this issue, so I polled the people in my fraternity. Students at State are against eliminating frats."

anecdotal evidence — "I used to like that pizzeria but the last time I ate there I got sick afterwards. I wouldn't eat there again."

equivocation — "She's not short. She's just vertically challenged."

definitional fallacy — "It's inhuman to murder. If somebody murders someone, then she's not a human being."

post hoc, ergo propter hoc — "Every time I plan a picnic, it rains. I don't think I'll plan any picnics for a while. We don't need any more rain."

FALLACIES OF EMOTIONAL MANIPULATION:

poisoning the well — "You like Bill? That funny looking kid with the big ears and thick glasses?"

emotionally loaded language — "Don't be misled by the bombastic, overblown oratory of my opponent."

Exercises

9–I

1. Name the fallacies in each of the following. Note: Where there are several possible choices, pick the one you consider to be the *best* one.
   a. I don't respect Bill Clinton. He's such a lousy saxophone player.
   b. Did you know Elvis is still alive? It's true. There's a brand new picture of him on the front of the latest issue of the *National Star*. I saw it at the supermarket while I was checking out.
   c. Don't buy that make car. We had one once. It was always breaking down. That company really builds poor cars.
   d. If we let 18-year-olds drink, then we might as well let 16-year-olds drink. And if we let 16-year-olds drink, then, before you know it, 14-year-olds are going to be drinking. And that will make 12-year-olds want to drink, too. But it's crazy for 12-year-olds to be drinking. So we might as well leave the drinking age at 21.
   e. It's just not right that I'm going to be laid off. I just bought a new house and spent the rest of my savings on a vacation. I won't be able to survive two weeks without a job.
   f. Let's decide together which movie to see tonight. Of course, you'll probably want to go see that stupid new Batman movie at the Ritz.
   g. This was my first week in French I. All the teacher does is speak French. I haven't understood a single word in three classes. I'll never understand French.
   h. Most college students drink too much. A recent survey reported in the Psi Psi Psi fraternity journal found that 80 percent of the respondents get drunk every weekend at college.
   i. I bowled a perfect game last week! I was wearing my new purple socks. I'm going to wear them again this week for the big tournament!
   j. The assault-weapons ban is just one more example the government's efforts to disarm and ultimately enslave the American people.
2. Collect five examples of fallacies from hard copy media (newspapers, journals, magazines, printed advertisements, etc.).
3. Suppose your friend is training for the marathon. She's becoming a fanatic about running 12 miles every day even though her knees are aching and her times are getting slower. What would you suggest she do? How would you argue your case?
4. You have probably heard someone argue in the following fashion, "I never wear my seat belt. A friend of mine was in an accident and luckily was thrown from the car before it rolled down a cliff. If he'd been wearing his seat belt, he'd have been killed." What's wrong with this bit of reasoning?
5. If you were the opposing lawyer, how would you argue with the woman on the witness stand who is suing her employer for damages, including pain and suffering, because a piece of ceiling tile fell on her head at work after which she came down with an appendicitis?
6. In the confirmation hearings for Justice Clarence Thomas, Thomas was accused by at least one witness of sexual harassment. Is this an instance of *ad hominem*? Defend your answer.

9–II

Identify the fallacies, if any, in the following pieces of reasoning taken from the newspaper and other familiar sources. In some cases there may be more than one fallacy, and in some cases there may be more than one possible way to characterize the fallacy being committed. Sometimes the writer is not the culprit but is accusing someone else of having committed a fallacy. Name the fallacy or fallacies you think best characterize the errant reasoning and be prepared to defend your answer.

1. "While the cameras focused on flowers, candles, and old photos, and while sentimentality and sorrow flowed, criticisms of John Kennedy, Jr., were uttered sotto voce. One whispered condemnation was that 'he took too many risks.'" *Janna Malamud Smith, New York Times*

2. "I hope this correspondence finds you well. I intended to write you earlier but was very ill and needed surgery. . . . The purpose of this letter is to share my devastation upon receiving a grade of B in your course. I am asking your kind thoughtfulness in reconsidering it. The B prevents me from graduating with honors, making my GPA a 3.734 instead of the required 3.75.

   "I know you are unaware that I am foreign born and have English as my second language. I have had to make many sacrifices to receive an education.

   ". . . I respectfully request your reconsidering my grade, enabling me to graduate with honors." *From a student letter to a professor*

3. "A candidate's war service record is important, not just whether they served but also how they served. Did they have a desk job in the US or a well-protected, behind-the-lines duty abroad? A candidate for the position of Commander and Chief of the Armed Forces should have served in a leadership post, preferably among the front lines, assuming there's a war going on." *Letter to the Editor*

4. "For children of suburban boomers the sport is soccer. As we fathers help our sons strap on shin guards, we imagine a scrawny young bird venturing just beyond the nest, bravely flapping its wings to stay aloft. But the image ends there. No father wants his son playing for a team called the Robins.

   ". . . As the season kicked off I didn't let Charlie know what his wise Daddy knew: a bad name means a bad season. I was proved right. The Robins lost ten in a row. On successive weekends, September through November, the Robins scored only one goal." *William Sorenson, New York Times*

5. ". . . If we allow parents to choose the sex of their child today, how long will it be before they order up eye color, hair color, personality traits, and I.Q.?" *Lisa Nelkin, New York Times Magazine*

6. "In Leonard Rohrbach's letter to the editor, he wants to say that there is no connection between religion and good deeds. In other words, there is no real difference between the things a Christian would do and those a Godless heathen would do. As an example, Mr. Rohrbach claims that Hitler always said he was a Christian. Well, Hitler may have called himself a Christian but his actions clearly show otherwise. How could a Christian kill or order the killing of millions of innocent people? The answer is obvious. No, Mr. Rohrbach. Hitler cannot possibly have been a Christian. Religion makes a difference in how people act." *Adapted from a Letter to the Editor*

7. "Mrs. Dickerson's criticisms of the survey research industry may not be indicative of how other Americans feel about the process. A 1998 paper I co-wrote with W. Bradford Fay of Roper Starch Worldwide found that a large majority of Americans believe that polls work in the best interests of the public, that respondents are generally honest in interviews, and that polls play an influential role in society." *Letter to the Editor*

8. "In 1999, law professors John J. Donohue and Steven D. Leavitt said they had proved a statistical link between legalization of abortion and lower crime rates. They said five states that had allowed abortion earlier than the rest of the nation in the 1970s also saw their crime rates decline earlier than the nation's. . . . Their explanation: More abortions had led to fewer "unwanted" children, and "unwanted-ness" was a risk factor for becoming a criminal." *Philadelphia Inquirer*

9. "Serial killers [according to FBI agents John Douglas and Robert Ressler] fall into one of two categories. Some crime scenes show evidence of logic and planning. Douglas and Ressler call that kind of crime "organized." In a "disorganized" crime, the victim isn't chosen logically. She's seemingly picked at random. . . . Each of these styles, the argument goes, corresponds to a personality type. The organized killer is intelligent and articulate. He feels superior to those around him. The disorganized killer is unattractive and has a poor self-image. . . . Not long ago, a group of psychologists at the University of Liverpool decided to test the FBI's assumptions. . . . When they looked at a sample of a hundred serial crimes, however, they couldn't find any support for the FBI's distinction. Crimes don't fall into one camp or another." *Malcolm Gladwell, The New Yorker*

10. "You couldn't have it if you did want it," the Queen said. "The rule is, jam tomorrow and jam yesterday—but never jam today"

"It must come sometimes to jam today," Alice objected.

"No, it can't," said the Queen. "It's jam every other day: today isn't any other day, you know."

Lewis Carroll, Through the Looking Glass and What Alice Found There

9–III

1. If someone could take one of your cherished beliefs and show that it is based on faulty reasoning, would you abandon it?
2. What kind of issues do you tend to look at in black-and-white (either/or) terms?
3. Do you hold beliefs which you recognize to be inconsistent with one another? Name a few.

10

Scientific Reasoning

SCIENCE AND GOOD REASONING

It is instructive in trying to become a better critical thinker to take a close look at scientific reasoning because science has a well-deserved reputation as a very successful approach to predicting and controlling the world around us, enabling us to survive and even prosper. Hence, science is often taken as **the** model of good reasoning. Other disciplines, in fact, have tried to copy what they perceive as the pattern of scientific reasoning, even going so far as to call themselves "sciences" (e.g., "the social sciences"). Scientific reasoning is supposed to be better somehow, yielding accurate descriptions of the world, where other forms of good reasoning are supposed to be distorted by assumptions and human biases, thereby producing less accurate results.

Scientific reasoning, however, is not radically different from other forms of good reasoning. The scientist makes decisions about theories much the same way the good historian determines the best description of past events or the good shopper decides what to buy. This similarity can be seen by looking at the history of science—a history that is often ignored by both scientists and historians. The history of science can also give us a clearer picture of the methods that science actually uses. These methods are somewhat different from what is often labeled "the scientific method" in science textbooks. Indeed, the history of science reveals that science is much like other disciplines and other forms of reasoning in its use of assumptions and its reliance on background information. This is because scientific reasoning is simply a branch of inductive reasoning and, therefore, science also relies on the general principle we discussed in Chapter 8, namely, the principle that the future will be much like the past (the principle of induction). Hence, science is subject to all the uncertainties of reasoning with probability that we have already discussed.

COPERNICUS AND KEPLER

You are familiar with our solar system and the revolution of the planets around the sun, so the accomplishment of Copernicus probably seems a bit old hat. Of course, the sun is the center of the solar system—that's the way it is! The earth goes around the sun. Everybody knows that! And you have seen pictures or models of the solar system showing the planets and their proximity to the sun and to each other. What we tend not to realize, however, is that this picture does not exist—except as a drawing or representation in a book. That is, there is no "correct" point in space, from which, if only we could get to it, we could take this "accurate" picture of our immediate solar system.

Think about this for a minute. Our naive view, encouraged by science teachers and science books, suggests that there is some privileged position in space, marked with a sign saying "stand here," where we could see our solar system with the sun in the center and the nine planets (if you count Pluto) revolving around it. But how without such a sign would we know it? What would tell us that *this* is the right spot to make our picture? There are no signs in space, no Xs saying "Stand here." And why should any particular place be *the* place? What would make a view from one location in space any more "correct" than a view from some other place? Just as we realize that there are no

"There goes one strange cow."

Even cows cannot avoid the problem of induction.

privileged positions on the earth's surface, there are no privileged positions in space in general. For instance, if you stood still in space relative to the earth, then the earth would take the position of being the center of motion. However, if you stood still in space relative to Venus, then Venus would be the center of motion. Of course, we human beings see everything from our position on the earth. From our position, we see that the stars move. They change position over time. That could be because they are moving, or that could be because we are moving. (Scientists believe we are both moving.)

What Copernicus did is realize that if he assumed that no position in space, including his position on earth, was considered privileged, the picture of the motions of the heavenly bodies that scientists in his day were using could be simplified. That is, if no position in space was privileged, then he might just as well assume the sun was in the center of the system of moving bodies, not the earth as had been assumed. This assumption yielded a picture or **pattern** of the motions of the heavenly bodies that was less complicated and made the calculations for plotting the positions of the stars much easier.

The earth-centered Ptolemaic theory used prior to Copernicus' work to calculate the positions of the heavenly bodies was complex but not inaccurate. It required 77 epicycles to account for the motions of the planets. An epicycle is a circle on a circle, or a loop. These epicycles were necessary because sometimes the motion of a planet or star would appear to be in a backward direction and the epicycle captured this retrograde motion. Copernicus saw that by placing the sun in the center and the earth in motion around this center he could reduce the number of epicycles to 34. He still needed epicycles in his picture, however, because he assumed the planetary motions were circular motions.

It is important to see here that the Copernican picture is not more accurate than the Ptolemaic picture. At the time they both accurately predicted the past and future motions of the heavenly bodies. There was no observation of the heavenly bodies which would tell an observer that one of the theories was right and the other wrong. There were, however, plenty of observations of everyday phenomena that suggested that Copernicus's view was wrong, like the fact that, from the ordinary perspective of human experience, everything happens as if the earth is stationary! The main reason that led Copernicus and others to prefer his view to the Ptolemaic or geocentric view was that it was **simpler**. The simplicity was in the mathematics. With fewer epicycles it was easier to calculate future (or past) positions of the heavenly bodies. Simplicity suggested the harmony and symmetry of a divine design to Copernicus and appealed to his strong religious convictions.

Kepler, an astronomer who followed Copernicus, reasoned similarly. He, too, firmly believed that there must be some pattern for describing the motions of the planets that was simple and elegant because God would only design a world of mathematical harmony. He discovered that if he took the sun as one of the two foci of an ellipse, he could describe the motions of the planets around the sun as ellipses. By doing this, he eliminated epicycles altogether and could also account for new observations that had been collected since the time of Copernicus. He also found that the planets do not move with constant velocity along their orbital paths but that they sweep out equal areas of the ellipse during equal times. He was led to this (his second) law of planetary motion because of his firm belief that there must be an order and harmony in the pattern, since he believed that it was created by God.

Clearly, Copernicus and Kepler made many assumptions in coming to their discoveries about our solar system. For both of them, the primary assumption was religious. They both believed in an all-powerful and all-rational God who would only create a world of rational design. They then set out to discover that design or pattern. They also made assumptions about what would constitute a rational design. Here they turned to the **values of simplicity, harmony, symmetry, and order**. We think of these as aesthetic values, values associated with our sense of **beauty**.

We see these same aesthetic values of Copernicus and Kepler in the fundamental assumptions of contemporary scientists. For example, one of the heroes of modern biology, James Watson, who with Francis Crick won the Nobel prize for his discovery of the structure of DNA, in summing up the main points of his DNA model was said to have gazed at the model and said, "It's so beautiful, you see, so beautiful."[1] And Paul Dirac, Nobel Prize winning physicist, was well known for his strong belief in the connection between mathematical beauty and physical laws. "A theory with mathematical beauty," said Dirac, "is more likely to be correct than an ugly one that fits some experimental data."[2]

It is not hard to see why science is so intimately connected with values, such as beauty, simplicity, harmony, and symmetry. The scientist tries to make order out of experience. If there were no order in the universe, we would not be able to predict the course of future events and we would have little control over the world around us. (Just think what it would be like if everything happened by chance or accident.) Making order out of apparent disorder means making things simpler. It means construing events in **patterns** that can be remembered and used for future reference. In general, scientists have tried to describe these patterns in the language of mathematics. And mathematics is precisely that, a language. Mathematics is a very useful language because it allows us to use symbols to stand-in for a range of individuals (numbers, people, things), so we don't have to write down all those individuals. That is, even by its very nature mathematics simplifies. So the scientist and the mathematician have similar values which are fundamental to their respective enterprises. These values are aesthetic. They include simplicity, harmony, symmetry, and elegance.

The scientist makes other assumptions as well. For instance, the scientist must assume he does not occupy a unique position in the universe. The laws of nature should be the same in China as they are on the moon or in the United States. The regularities discovered in one laboratory will be like the regularities discoverable in any other laboratory. Just to get started, scientists must "take on faith" certain laws of nature which cannot be proven, such as the law that matter is always conserved. Scientists could never prove this law with certainty because they would be stuck in a vicious circle of assuming the conservation of the matter making up the instruments they were using to test the conservation of matter.

Science, then, is not "value-free," nor does it rest totally on observation. Scientists do make assumptions which they cannot prove by experiment. Some of these assumptions are necessary to the whole enterprise of collecting experimental

---

[1] Quoted by Crick in *What Mad Pursuit: A Personal View of Scientific Discovery,* 1988.

[2] Quoted in R. Corby Hovis and Helge Kragh, "P.A.M. Dirac and the Beauty of Physics," *Scientific American,* May 1993.

data. The most fundamental assumptions of science are aesthetic in nature and represent **values** like simplicity that every scientist brings to his work.

The reading in this chapter has been chosen to show that science has many controversies about what is real in our world. You probably have not heard of whiptail lizards, and you probably are not that concerned about their sex life. But some scientists spend their lifetimes studying animal behaviors and making generalizations about them. Besides showing that scientists have arguments and do not all agree, the reading also shows that observation itself is influenced by the observer's expectations, a point made in Chapter 2 above and worth noting again and again. Here, the scientists do not "see" the same thing. Nor do they accept the same reasoning about patterns. The reading also suggests that scientists may be influenced by the biases and controversies around them. There has been much discussion in the United States about homosexuality among humans and whether sexual orientation is something one chooses or an orientation one is born with. Hence, some people are eager to find answers to this question in the behavior of other animal species.

THE SEX LIFE OF THE WHIPTAIL LIZARD

Harry Collins and Trevor Pinch

Introduction

David Crews, a professor of zoology and psychology at the University of Texas, might be thought of as a sexual voyeur. This is because he spends much of his time observing the bizarre sex lives of reptiles such as lizards and snakes. His work is of great interest to biologists. It is sometimes controversial. Our focus in this chapter is on one particular set of observations which Crews made of the mating behaviour of a particular species of whiptail lizard. However, by way of introduction to the sexual world of reptiles which Crews studies, we will first look at his less controversial work on the red-sided garter snake.

The Arctic environment of western Canada provides perhaps the harshest conditions encountered by any vertebrate on the planet. It is here that the red-sided garter snake lives. In order to survive the long Arctic winter, snakes have learnt the trick of cryopreservation. Their blood becomes extremely thick, and crucial bodily organs stop functioning almost completely, exhibiting barely detectable levels of activity. However, when Spring arrives, they undergo rapid transformation in preparation for mating.

Mating occurs over a short, intense period. The males emerge first from their long winter deep-freeze and spend from three days to three weeks basking in the sun near the entrance to the den. When the females emerge, either alone or in small groups, the males are attracted by a pherome (a messenger substance) on their backs. Up to 100 males converge and form a 'mating ball'. Once a male succeeds in mating, the others immediately disperse. The mated female, who has been rendered unattractive to other males as a result of a pheromone which she has received from the mating male, now leaves the locale. The males regroup, waiting by the entrance of the den for the emergence of other females with which to mate.

Why are biologists interested in such a curious ritual? Crews is a behavioural neuroendocrinologist. He studies the evolution of the systems in the body that control reproduction and sexual behaviour. He uses a variety of techniques, including observations of behaviour, examination of organs, and analyses of substances in the blood. Comparisons are made with other species. The garter snake is of particular interest to Crews because of the way that its sexual behaviour and its physiology are synchronised with the demands of the environment. The snakes' sexual activities may seem strange to us, but they have adapted perfectly to the extreme conditions under which they live. For Crews the behaviour of the garter snakes was a particularly powerful illustration of how environmental factors may influence the evolution and development of various aspects of reproduction. By emphasising the role of the environment, Crews can be thought of as taking sides in one of the oldest debates in biology: nature versus nurture.

Crews' interest in reproductive physiology is somewhat at odds with the traditional fields of reptile study. His work falls between the interests of herpetologists who study snakes and lizards from a natural history standpoint and neuroendocrinologists who compare various hormonal control systems without necessarily linking their work to the sexual behaviour of the species. With his interest in evolution and in comparing more than one species, Crews also finds audiences for his work among evolutionary theorists, comparative biologists, zoologists and psychologists. Like many scientific innovators, Crews brings together approaches from a variety of areas that traditionally have gone their separate ways. It is partly because of this that his work has been tinged with controversy. By asking new questions of aspects of the behaviour and physiology of species that have already been well studied, Crews was posing a challenge to the established experts.

Of course, just because a scientist's work challenges that of his or her colleagues, does not mean that it will necessarily lend itself to controversy. Many contentious findings or approaches within science are simply ignored. For instance, numerous papers have been published challenging the foundations of quantum mechanics or relativity theory which scarcely cause a ripple on the surface of physics. Turning a blind eye in the no-nonsense way to deal with potentially troublesome ideas. Indeed, obtaining a controversial status for a set of ideas such that other scientists feel compelled to reject them in an explicit manner is a substantial achievement in itself.

By the time Crews produced his controversial work on the whiptail lizard he was too important a figure to ignore. In the early stages of his career at Harvard there was no inkling of the controversy to come. His approach and findings did not challenge the fundamentals of his field. By the time he moved to Texas University (after seven years at Harvard) he was a highly respected, visible, and well-connected scientist. It was only now, after having established himself, that he started to stress the radical quality of his ideas. The most sharply focussed controversy in which Crews has become involved has not centred on the grander issues of evolutionary theory but on some rather specific claims that he made concerning the sexual behaviour of the whiptail lizard. It is his observations of this vertebrate and their reception which form the backbone of our story.

In what follows we shall be particularly concerned to follow the twists and turns of this one scientific controversy. It may seem perverse to go into such detail. However, we would remind the reader that it is exactly in the detailed arguments that we find the rough diamond of science.

'Leapin' Lesbian Lizards'

This heading was used by *Time* magazine to introduce Crews' observations of the sexual habits of *Cnemidophorus*, the whiptail lizard. *Cnemidophorus* is unusual in the reptile world because it breeds 'parthenogenetically'. That is to say it can reproduce from the eggs of the female without needing a male to fertilise them. This makes the species ideal for studying aspects of the evolution of sexuality that cannot be separated and analysed in normal sexual species, where the complicating factor of male heredity is always present.

As soon as Crews started work on *Cnemidophorus* he noticed what at first sight was a bizarre pattern of behaviour. These non-sexual lizards, who did not need to mate, sometimes mounted each other, behaving just like other sexual lizards. It was this observation which previous researchers had ignored, or chosen to ignore, which lies at the heart of the controversy.

The behaviour of significance to our story is reproduced in the series of illustrations shown in figure 6.1[*]. The sequence appears to be simple enough. One active female climbs onto the back of another passive female, curves its tail around its partner's body so that their sexual organs come into contact, strokes the neck and back, and rides on top of the other for one to five minutes. All biologists agree that this is what happens. They disagree over the meaning to be given to the observations.

For Crews and his co-worker Fitzgerald, the lizard's strange behaviour (repeatedly observed with different lizards) was clearly sexually related. Indeed, they thought that what they had seen was so significant that they presented it as a new and important scientific discovery about parthenogenetic species. The courtship routine followed by the copulatory behaviour seemed remarkably similar to ordinary mating which Crews had observed in other closely related sexual species. Furthermore, dissection and palpation (examining by touch), of the lizards revealed its sexual significance. The courted animal appeared to be reproductively active, 'having ovaries containing large, preovulatory follicles, while the courting animal was either reproductively inactive or postovulatory, having ovaries containing only small undeveloped follicles'. This difference raised general questions about the function of the pseudo-copulatory behaviour for sexuality, such as its possible role in priming reproductive mechanisms.

If Crews thought he had made a major discovery, other biologists were not so sure. Some were outright sceptics. Two of the best-known researchers into this genus of lizard, Orlando Cuellar of the University of Utah, who in the early 1970s had shown the chromosomal mechanisms of parthenogenesis, and C. J. Cole of the American Museum of Natural History, who pioneered the physiological study of the genus, soon disputed Crews' claims. For these scientists, who had spent years studying *Cnemidophorus* and in particular learning how to maintain them in captivity, Crews was an inexperienced upstart. Rather than carefully observing the lizards over lengthy periods, he had, in their view, immediately seized upon a peculiar piece of behaviour, noticed in a very few animals, and blown it up into a sensational claim. Cuellar and Cole may have been particularly irked that *Time* magazine had picked up on the story; the sexual exploits of lizards made for compelling media coverage.

---

[*]Omitted

The first response of Cuellar and Cole was to attempt to play down the aberrant behaviour. They claimed that there was nothing particularly novel or surprising going on, since others (including themselves) had observed such activity among lizards before. Also Crews was simply wrong in claiming any general significance for the study of parthenogenetic species. The behaviour he had observed was trivial: it was unnatural and a product of captivity. Moreover a more experienced worker would not have been led astray and would have chosen to ignore it for the artefact it undoubtedly was. The key issue, then, was whether the lizard's behaviour was an artefact, produced by the overcrowded conditions of captivity, as the critics asserted, or an essential and previously neglected part of reproductive behaviour.

One feature of scientific controversies is that they bring into sharp focus the competence of the protagonists. Normally in science ability is taken for granted. However, in a controversy the specific scientific issues at stake and the abilities of the scientists involved are difficult to disentangle. In the ensuing debate between Crews and his critics the need for all the researchers to establish their skill became paramount.

Much of the controversy has taken place in the published scientific literature and one indication of the increasing importance attached to the establishment of competence is the expansion of the normally brief methods' sections of the papers. In Crews and Fitzgerald's original paper the method section was simply a few lines which accompanied photographs of the lizards. However, by the time it comes to rebutting their critics five years later, there is a remarkable amount of detail concerning the regimen of care of the lizards, the observational procedures followed and so on. As the controversy develops, the skills and competence necessary to make these sorts of observation also become an issue. For instance, in his published attack on Crews, Orlando Cuellar refers to his own long experience (over a decade) observing captive *Cnemidophorus* produce eggs, and his 'precise knowledge' of the reproductive cycle. He states that, although he has seen behaviour such as that observed by Crews sporadically on and off for fifteen years in the laboratory, it is insignificant.

In the same way, Cole and Townsend, in a rebuttal of Crews and Fitzgerald, emphasise their own skills as observers, stressing the detail and duration of their observations (in contrast to the short period of Crews and Fitzgerald's work), and the fine-grained nature of their behaviour categorisation system. They even mention where the lizards were kept (in their offices), and that they cared for the animals personally. Again such details never normally appear in routine research reports.

Such personal appeals to a scientist's own skills and reconstructions of the details of everyday work in the lab produce, however, an unintended effect. They make science look more like other areas of activity which are carried out in the mundane world of offices and which depend on skill.

It is no accident that the routine scientific paper plays down such factors. It is the absence of these discussions which makes science look like a special activity; scientists become merely mediators or passive observers of Nature. Because the establishment of skill and competence becomes important during a controversy we start to see better what goes into the making of science. Processes which are normally hidden become visible.

Ironically when Crews and his colleagues responded to Cuellar they made his appeal to his own diligence and experience count against him. They took his admission that he had indeed seen the pseudo-copulatory behaviour as a confirmation of their own observations. They then went on to treat his failure to realise its significance as stemming from his own preconceptions. This is part of a general strategy which Crews has used against his critics whereby he portrays them as being stick-in-the-mud, paradigm bound, and caught up in the old traditions, rather than seeing what is there to be seen. This 'young Turks' strategy is not unfamiliar in scientific controversy.

Part of the argument concerning competence centres on the carefulness of the observers. In this case the critics claim that Crews and Fitzgerald simply have not been careful enough in their observations. The argument about carefulness, however, like most arguments in a controversy, can cut both ways. This line is taken by Crews and his group in their response to Cole and Townsend; they pick upon an apparent lack of rigour in the methods followed. They note that Cole and Townsend assess the reproductive state of the lizards from a visual inspection of abdominal distension. This, they claim, is inadequate as it is well known that palpation is also needed. In an ingenious move, they actually cite Crews' other critic, Cuellar, in support of this requirement.

Accusations of carelessness are ineffective in resolving disputes because they tend to circularity. Everyone knows that the careful scientist will find the 'truth', while the careless observer gets it wrong. But what there is to find is exactly the point at issue. If you believe pseudo copulation is a genuine phenomenon then Crews appears to have been careful and his critics careless; conversely if pseudo-copulation is taken to be an artefact then it is his critics who have been careful and Crews careless. Care, in and of itself, like most such factors in a controversy, cannot provide an independent means to settle the issue. We are back in the experimenter's regress with a vengeance.

If general attributions of skill and competence cannot settle the controversy, what about matters of fact? As we have argued above, matters of fact are inseparable from the skills of the scientist used to produce them. Thus when the critics make a specific claim in an attempt to refute Crews, it is no surprise to find again that issues of competence are never far from the surface. The claim made by Cuellar, and Cole and Townsend, that the copulatory-like behaviour of the lizards stems from overcrowded conditions lies at the core of the controversy. It is answered by Crews in the following way. In his later articles, as mentioned above, he goes into great detail concerning his methods. The exact conditions under which his lizards are kept are given. Having done this, he is able to turn the tables on his critics by claiming that they present no specific data themselves to show that crowded conditions will lead to the artefactual copulation. 'They do not give the dimensions of the cages used, nor the number of animals housed per cage' (quoted in Myers, 1990, p. 125). With this move, it is Crews who appears to have been painstakingly careful in the very area where his critics have chosen to make their attack; the critics, on the other hand, are made to look cavalier in their accusation.

One way in which this controversy in biology appears to differ from the controversies in physics examined in this book is that very few new data are generated during the course of the controversy. The grounds of the debate seem to be constantly switching in the process of trying to find the right interpretation for previous observations. In physics, experiments serve as a way of focusing the debate. In this area of biology, experiments are seldom possible. Rather, attention is constantly drawn to evidence that is missing from the rival side's position—such as the evidence on crowded conditions leading to pseudo-copulation as mentioned by Crews in response to Cole and Townsend.

The most salient piece of negative evidence in the whole debate is simply that no-one, including Crews and Fitzgerald, has ever seen pseudo-copulation of lizards in the field. Cole and Townsend make much of this point, mentioning that the most thorough study of *Cnemidophorus* in the wild does not include it. As might be expected, Crews' and his group's response is up to the job. Again they turn the tables on the critics. They point out that such behaviour might well occur, but are observations in the wild capable of documenting it? It is well known that *Cnemidophorus* is a very shy species and that even matings in the ordinary sexual lizard are observed infrequently. So where better to observe such delicate phenomena than in captivity!

Love Bites and Hand Waving

Often in the course of a scientific controversy previously ignored minutiae become highly relevant and hotly debated. As both sides try to cast doubt upon the others' arguments, more and more additional pieces of evidence get brought in. In the present case the number of 'love bites' the lizards underwent and whether or not they wave their hands as a sign of sexual submission both became important.

Cuellar argued that in species he had collected in the wild he had rarely seen any 'copulation bites' and more would be expected if pseudo-copulation was routine. The answer Crews and his group gave was again to reverse the argument by pointing out that if Cuellar was right then it would mean that normal sexual lizards were not mating either! The answer, they suggested, was that such bites are not a natural inscription of mating. To try to substantiate their point they examined the corpses of 1000 dead female lizards from a sexual species and found only 3% had marks on their backs and sides and, further, that the same frequency of males possessed such marks. So in this way Crews managed to turn the evidence produced by Cuellar back against him. Marks are most certainly found on dead lizards, but as they are found on males as well they are probably produced by aggressive behaviour.

Hand waving became significant in a postscript added by Cole and Townsend to their rebuttal of Crews. They criticise Crews for 'erroneously' relying on the lizards' lifting of the hand as an indication of submissiveness. Instead, according to them, it is merely a sign that the lizard is basking. Again it is the competence of the researchers which is under attack. A researcher who cannot tell basking from hand waving has a credibility problem. Although Crews does not seem to have responded in public to this particular criticism, from what has gone above the reader can speculate about the possible lines of argument Crews could have adopted in defence.

An Honourable Draw

So where does this controversy stand today? The current consensus is that Crews and his critics have battled to an honourable draw. Both sides have given their version of the endocrinology of *Cnemidophorus* in separate articles in the *Scientific American* and both continue to work within their rather different approaches.

The even-handed view which we have presented as we have followed the twists and turns of the debate is not likely to be shared by the protagonists. Their own arguments and positions are, of course, compelling, indeed irresistible to them. In presenting a neutral account we risk disappointing both sides.

Many scientists are wary of getting entangled in controversies and perceive them to be the repository of shoddy science. This can mean that denying you are party to a controversy can itself be a tactic in such disputes. We see it happening in the lizard controversy. In writing their articles in *Scientific American* both sides avoided any explicit reference to the controversy at all.

One way to close down a controversy is to rewrite history such that the dispute seems premature: an over-reaction of an under-developed field. Crews, in particular, in his later writing has presented his first paper and the reaction to it as having this character. For Crews it was an unfortunate debate which was characterised by a lack of firm experimental tests and decisive evidence. By appealing to the rhetoric of experiment and testing, something to which his methodology of working with lizards in captivity is ideally suited, Crews can appear to have found a way to have advanced beyond the earlier controversy. Whether this rhetoric succeeds remains to be seen.

One question has been left unanswered. Do *Cnemidophorus* lizards indeed exhibit pseudo-copulatory behaviour which is relevant to their reproduction? Despite five years of research and debate the answer appears to be that we do not know. According to one group of respected scientists they do; according to another group they do not. As always the facts of nature are settled within the field of human argument.

STUDY QUESTIONS

1. What differences do you see between how science is often practiced and how it is usually taught?
2. Why do scientists have arguments among themselves about such things as the behavior of whiptailed lizards?

HYPOTHETICAL-DEDUCTIVE REASONING

So far in *Thinking Socratically* we have stressed the close relation between good reasoning and common sense. And, indeed, they are very close to being one and the same. When we turn to science, however, a few words of caution are necessary. For the world described by science is quite different from the world of our common sense experience. We live in a world of rather medium-sized objects, while the world described by science is composed of microphysical particles or of large macrophysical systems. Much of the scientific description of the world doesn't seem very commonsensical, just as Copernicus's description of the solar system didn't seem very commonsensical to people in his day. We must be clear about the distinction between common sense, which can be thought of as the lowest theoretical level for making sense of experience, and the experience of the world through our senses. The latter often leads to very naive descriptions of our experience which we then correct by using common sense reasoning. For example, if you take a straight stick and immerse part of it in water, the stick will appear to be bent at the water's surface. If we were to describe this observation on the basis of sense experience alone, we would say that the stick was bent by the water. We know from our background knowledge, however, that water does not bend sticks, and so we reason to the conclusion that this visual experience is a kind of optical illusion. That is, we use reason as well as sensory experience to arrive at our description of the world.

Similarly, the scientist also uses reason and sensory experience to arrive at a description of the world. This description is often quite different from our everyday description of events. We describe the sun as "coming up" in the morning while the scientist talks about the earth turning on its axis. We talk about "solid" tables and chairs while the scientist may talk about the atoms and molecules that make up these objects—and the great spaces within and between them. It is important to see that the scientist's description of the world is just one description among many possible descriptions of the world. It is the appropriate description in some contexts but not in others. It is not better or more correct than others except in certain circumstances. For example, if someone asks you for a description of your significant other, he does not want a description of that person's physical chemistry. On the other hand, if a doctor asks for a description of a patient, he may want precisely that.

The scientific description of the world includes many entities which are not directly known through sense experience—like atoms, electrons, entropy, DNA, and so on. How, you may ask, does the scientist get information about *this* world of unobservable objects? This is a good question and one to which we will offer only a partial answer in this text. (Whole textbooks are devoted to answering this question.) The first point that should be noted is that scientists do not generally follow the method often described in science textbooks as "the scientific method." According to the textbook method, what scientists do is collect information about the world by observing it or by performing experiments and observing the results. They then organize this information into generalizations. These generalizations are considered law-like if they are based on a large number of observations, if the observations have been repeated under a variety of different circumstances, and if the generalization—now a "law of nature"—does not conflict with any known observations. These generalizations are then used to predict future occurrences and to explain past events.

For example, the generalization that all metals conduct electricity is based on past observations of the behavior of metals. According to the scientific method, for this generalization to be considered law-like, these observations must have been made in a variety of circumstances and under a variety of conditions, using a variety of different kinds of metals. Furthermore, there should be no observation of a metal that does not conduct electricity. Scientists then use this law to predict that in the future any specific piece of metal will conduct electricity.

There are several problems with this version of the method of science, some of which may be obvious to you already from the previous reading and from the discussion of Copernicus and Kepler. New observations were not the cause of their discoveries. If you were to review the history of science, you would find that the Copernican model is typical of scientific discovery. Second, in the discussion of forms of reasoning with probability in Chapter 8, it was clear how important **background knowledge** is in making warranted generalizations and warranted causal claims. Yet, the "popular" version of the scientific method takes no account of its importance. Nor does it acknowledge the problem of induction.

Finally, this description of the method of science makes observation central to the scientific enterprise—but it ignores the problematic character of observation which we saw in Chapter 2. There we pointed out that the same events can be described in different ways by different observers, as also happens in the case of the sex life of whiptail lizards. Our **descriptions** of our experience are not neutral. In science, observation and experiment are guided by theory as much as the other way around. To see this, consider what would happen if they were not. What observations would the scientist gather? What experiments would he perform? He must already have an idea of what is important to know what to pay attention to. As we said in Chapter 8, there are too many **traces** and too many **patterns** of traces for us to pay attention to all of them. So we use theory (or a story) to guide us in our collection of information. (We should not be surprised, then, when our theory fits the information!) Consequently, the usual account of the scientific method is rather limited in its usefulness to scientists.

A pattern of reasoning that scientists *do* use frequently, which is rather interesting and useful in everyday affairs as well, is the hypothetical-deductive pattern. This reasoning pattern enables scientists to find evidence for claims that they cannot support by direct observation—claims about electrons, forces, chemical composition, psychological complexes, and so on. When a scientist has a hypothesis that cannot be tested directly (there is no direct observation evidence), he deduces (using deductive, not inductive, reasoning) an observable consequence from the hypothesis which is very specific and therefore testable. If the observable result is as anticipated, then the scientist has evidence for the hypothesis. If the observable result is not as anticipated, then there is *not* evidence for the hypothesis. It is important to note that in neither case is the hypothesis proven nor disproven. Let's look at some examples, again from the history of science.

In the late eighteenth century, Edward Jenner, an English country doctor working in the dairy region, discovered the first effective inoculation against the scourge of the English countryside, smallpox. It was a well-known fact that milkmaids got cowpox but not smallpox, cowpox being a milder, much weaker form of the disease. Jenner formulated the hypothesis that exposure to cowpox gives immunity to smallpox. Assuming this hypothesis is true, Jenner reasoned, if I take some pus from the cowpox sore of an infected milkmaid and expose another individual to cowpox by scratching the cowpox germs into his skin, then that individual will not get smallpox even if exposed to it. In 1796, he persuaded the parents of a young neighbor boy (by paying them money) to allow him to scratch pus from a cowpox sore of a milkmaid into his arm. Two months later the boy was injected with smallpox but did not develop the disease.

Jenner's result confirmed his hypothesis, as do all the ensuing smallpox vaccinations. Today most American school children must be vaccinated for smallpox before they can attend school, and smallpox has been eradicated from the United States. These are observable results which provide evidence for a hypothesis which cannot itself be directly verified. At this point, we would say that the hypothesis is well confirmed and, consequently, well entrenched in the set of beliefs of American pediatricians. In Jenner's day, however, his claim to have discovered a method for preventing smallpox was scoffed at. He had to postpone publishing his results for two years to avoid being thought a quack.

The hypothetical-deductive method of reasoning also played a role in the confirmation and eventual acceptance of the Copernican world view. Astronomers reasoned that if the Sun is in the center of the universe (a hypothesis whose truth is not directly observable), then Venus should appear to change size during the year as it is closer and farther from the Earth. Also, Venus should exhibit phases. Like the moon, it should wax and wane. (Both of these are observable consequences of the theory.) But in this case, observations at the time could confirm neither of these! This inability to confirm his hypothesis did not lead Copernicus to change his mind, however, nor did it deter Galileo from adopting the Copernican world view. Rather Galileo was spurred on to find and develop an instrument—the telescope—that could observe the change in size and the phases of Venus, thereby confirming Copernicus's hypothesis.

This last historical example is interesting because it points out the role that background knowledge and entrenchment play in science, both of which are ignored by the usual discussion of the "scientific method." Copernicus and Galileo were steadfast in their belief in a solar system. Others of their contemporaries, such as Andreas Osiander and Tycho Brahe, were just as adamant in their support of the Ptolemaic view. Although it is not possible to give a rigorous comparison of the background knowledge of these scientists, it is possible to see that, for Copernicus and Galileo, what weighed most heavily was the mathematical attractiveness of the heliocentric or sun-centered theory. On the other hand, what was more important to Osiander and Brahe were the physical observations they made, namely, that Venus continued to look the same no matter what time of year they viewed it. There was *no* observational evidence they could point to that confirmed the heliocentric hypothesis, and many observations disconfirmed it.

That is, for Copernicus and Galileo the belief that the universe is simple, harmonious, and capable of being described by elegant mathematical formulae led them to discount the failure of observation to confirm the Copernican hypothesis. This belief was more entrenched than their belief in the information given by their senses. (After all, the senses often mislead us.) Osiander and Brahe, on the other hand, were more committed to observation and its dictates. Eventually, we know, the Copernican hypothesis acquired a large body of confirming evidence so that today it is firmly entrenched in the world view of contemporary scientists.

The hypothetical-deductive method is clearly a method used by scientists to gather support for hypotheses which are not directly verifiable, that is, when no direct observations are possible. A person using this method uses deductive reasoning to derive a consequence from the hypothesis that can be observed. The scientist then sets up the proper conditions for making this observation(s) and tests to see if he gets the predicted results.

It should be clear from these two examples that the hypothetical-deductive method does not prove or disprove a hypothesis. What it does is provide **evidence** for or against that hypothesis. Consequently, scientists may differ on whether to accept a hypothesis. Whether or not a scientist accepts an observation as evidence (either for or against) depends, in part, on his background knowledge and which of his beliefs are more fundamental than others—or, in the language of Chapter 8, which beliefs are better **entrenched**. This is very clear in the example of the whiptail lizards. Both scientists hold very entrenched beliefs about the whiptail lizards and consequently explain the behavior of the lizards quite differently. Scientists are no different from the rest of us. They find hypotheses acceptable which fit in well with the beliefs they already hold and which are well entrenched in their webs of belief. They tend to reject hypotheses that would upset or require them to change any well-entrenched belief. So how well a hypothesis fits into the scientist's web of belief is also a factor in accepting a hypothesis. Since, as we have already seen, scientists (at least most of them) tend to admire simplicity and order, they prefer hypotheses which are powerful but also economical. By this we mean that the hypothesis can explain a large number of observations but is itself rather simple. For example, Newton's second law of motion was thought to be very powerful, because it could explain all motion that results from the action of an external force, and at the same time it is very simple: $F = ma$ (force equals the mass multiplied by the acceleration).

A scientific hypothesis may become so well accepted that it is called a law of nature, but even so-called laws of nature are only part of our description of the world and are, therefore, only confirmed, not proven. The history of science is littered with "laws of nature" which have been discarded or altered. The Ptolemaic universe is one such discard.

Summary

Much can be learned about the good reasoning skills and the nature of science by looking at the history of science. We have looked at only a few examples of that history, but we have seen some very important features of science and of scientific reasoning. Despite all the credit we give to scientific reasoning, science has a long history of failed and discarded hypotheses. These hypotheses failed over time to stand up to the demands of testing and confirmation. Moreover, many of our most significant scientific hypotheses concern the behavior of unobservable entities, which can only be tested by the hypothetical-deductive method. Values have also played a role in the acceptance of hypotheses, with most scientists favoring those hypotheses which are simple, mathematically elegant, and which at the same time have broad explanatory power.

But, wait a minute, you might say. There's a world out there that is fixed, that is not our creation. Isn't our description getting closer and closer to that fixed world, that "real" world? Unfortunately, neither we nor the scientists can answer that question because there is no way of knowing. We have only our experience and our description of that experience. The scientist examines the **traces** and tells us a **story** about those traces. The scientist tries to include more and more detail in the story while at the same time keeping it neat and economical. The scientist tests the story by the hypothetical-deductive method and confirms or disconfirms it, adjusting the story accordingly. The story has no end and no proof. The story of modern science is an exciting and useful story, but, in the end, it is only a story! The scientific description of our world that we have today will not be the scientific description of the world tomorrow.

In sum, modern science presents us with one way, among many, of describing our experience. This way of describing the world has been very helpful to us, enabling us to predict and sometimes control events in our lives, generally making life more pleasant and fruitful. It is important to remember that this mode of description rests on implicit assumptions, not often acknowledged, and on unarticulated values, particularly the aesthetic values of simplicity and beauty and the rational values of coherence and consistency.

Exercises

10–I

1. What is hypothetical-deductive reasoning? What role does the hypothetical-deductive method play in science?
2. Describe a recent case of scientific discovery or controversy. Examine it for its implicit assumptions.

10–II

1. Formulate a hypothesis which cannot be directly verified, and test it by deducing a consequence which can be directly observed. Collect your evidence. Was your hypothesis confirmed or disconfirmed? Describe in detail what you did.
2. Why is the hypothetical-deductive method a kind of reasoning with probability rather than a form of reasoning with necessity, although it has the word *deductive* in it?
3. The "scientific method" as it is usually taught could be said to be naive. How would you critique this method, given the insights you have gained in this chapter?
4. Observation is said to be "theory-laden." What do you think this means? What insights for thinking critically do you see as a consequence of this claim? (Hint: you might want to review Chapter 2.)
5. List five of your most well-entrenched beliefs. What kind of evidence would lead you to give up one of them?
6. How has your view of science changed from reading about the history of science? What consequences for good reasoning do you see?

11

Pseudoscience

DISTINGUISHING SCIENCE FROM PSEUDOSCIENCE

Scientific reasoning, as noted in the last chapter, is a very important part of critical thinking. The hypothetical-deductive method, which is a primary reasoning tool of science, is a model of good reasoning that we all use at times. It is also good critical thinking, however, to realize the limits of scientific reasoning and to see that science is one way among many of describing our experience.

Pseudoscience is a way of reasoning that sometimes competes for our attention as an alternative description of the world. Pseudoscience uses neither critical thinking skills nor the methods of science. If anything, it asks that we suspend common sense and abandon our critical thinking skills. Pseudoscientists purport to be scientists. That is why it is very important to distinguish between science and pseudoscience. We don't want to be misled and disappointed by pseudoscience. We want to continue to use good common sense and our critical thinking skills.

You are already familiar with pseudoscience. Astrology is a common pseudoscience. The astrologer who provides the newspaper with the daily horoscopes claims to have good reasons for the predictions she makes (she claims that the predictions are warranted by the movements of the stars and the planets) and urges us to make decisions on the basis of those predictions. Most people take the astrologer's predictions with a grain of salt. Some people, however, are very committed to their favorite astrologer (President Reagan's wife, Nancy, former first lady, was a well-known devotee) and consult their horoscopes before making decisions. It is important to understand why this is not good critical thinking so that you can avoid taking a pseudoscience more seriously than is warranted.

One of the characteristics of a pseudoscience is that it cannot be refuted. Not only do the adherents of a pseudoscience refuse to admit any evidence as refuting their position, the hypotheses of a pseudoscience are such that they cannot be refuted. They are compatible with every outcome and every observation!

"Hobart, this is Merlin, my science adviser."

Many people have their "Merlins," even a recent President's wife.

Horoscopes are an excellent example of this. Most horoscopes are written in such broad terms that no matter what happens to you that day, it would be compatible with what is predicted for you. A typical example might be: "You must be careful today because you are headed for bad luck." When it appears that the horoscope was inaccurate—for instance it foretold that something was going to happen to you which didn't (e.g., bad luck)—adherents will dismiss the contrary evidence by saying that, because you were forewarned, you changed your behavior and avoided the negative outcome that had been headed your way. The prediction wasn't wrong, they say. Rather your behavior altered the circumstances. It turns out, then, that it is impossible to refute astrology. There are no consequences of the hypotheses of astrology that can be observed that would be considered by its adherents as disconfirming evidence. Other pseudosciences similarly rest on irrefutable hypotheses.

A scientific hypothesis, on the other hand, in order to be considered scientific, must be capable of refutation. That is, although we can never absolutely prove a scientific theory, it must be possible for us to refute (or "falsify") it. A theory is capable of refutation if it is possible to derive an observational consequence from the theory that would refute or contradict the theory if it were actually observed. For instance, "All substances expand when heated" is falsifiable, while "The planets move in elliptical orbits because God prefers ellipses" is not.

Moreover, scientists are expected to regard scientific hypotheses with a certain amount of skepticism and must always be willing to change their assumptions in light of new evidence. If we look at the history of science, we see that it is a history of the replacement of one theory by another, just as the Copernican theory replaced the Ptolemaic, as we discussed in the last chapter.

If we studied this particular piece of scientific history in greater detail, we would learn that Copernicus' theory was not consistent with all the known evidence at the time. According to the theory, if the planets revolved around the Sun then the planet Venus should appear to wax and wane like our moon. Copernicus and Galileo, however, did not accept the observational evidence of the constancy of the appearance of Venus as refuting Copernicus's hypothesis of a heliocentric universe. They continued to believe in the heliocentric universe despite the fact that they could not observe any change in the size of Venus or its waxing and waning. You might ask, then, how is this situation different from the situation of astrologers, who refuse to accept evidence against their hypotheses? That is a good question.

The difference is that the observations of Venus as unchanging in size and neither waxing nor waning *did* count as evidence against the Copernican hypothesis. These were certainly disconfirming observations. It was only that other considerations in the background knowledge of Copernicus and Galileo weighed more heavily than the observational evidence. If future refinements of the telescope had not revealed the phases of Venus, its changing size, and so on, other scientists would have eventually put the Copernican theory where scientists put other discredited scientific hypotheses—into the trash can of the history of science.

Astronomers, unlike astrologers, are *always* ready to revise their hypotheses in the light of new information. This process of revision is sometimes slow but is always a possibility. So **scientific theories are always refutable**, while pseudoscientific theories are never refutable. (This probably sounds like a strange thing to say. We generally think of science as the home of those theories which are not refutable. What we mean, however, is that science contains those theories which are refutable but which have not been refuted.) We can see this when we look at what happened to the Copernican hypothesis. It was first revised by Kepler who changed the shapes of the orbits of the planets around the sun from circles to ellipses. Then in the twentieth century, it was revised by Einstein and his theory of general relativity. Today scientists describe the planets as following straight line paths in curved space which they call geodesics.

Another important difference between science and pseudoscience is that a scientific hypothesis must **fit in** with other scientific hypotheses. There is a **connectedness** in the story that science tells. One piece fits in with another piece, so the connecting pieces get larger and larger over time, like a big jigsaw puzzle. Pseudosciences do not connect with one another or with other beliefs that we hold. The story each pseudoscientist tells is unique. Although she may use the language of science, the story doesn't fit into a larger picture. Again, consider astrology. Your horoscope depends on the position of the planets, moon, and stars on the day you were born. How does that causal mechanism—whatever it is—fit in with what we believe about gravity or human biology and psychology? What are the connections?

This leads us to a third major difference between science and pseudoscience and that is there is always an appeal to mystery or mysterious forces in pseudoscience. Of course, there are forces in science, too, and the very idea of a force is somewhat mysterious in that we can only describe the effects of forces. But the scientist does not really want to stop at that point. She wants to learn more and eliminate mystery whenever possible. The pseudoscientist, on the other hand, is happy with mystery. She may even be said to glory in it! "That's just the way it is," she says. For example, the astrologer doesn't know and doesn't care to know why the positions of the stars and planets are supposed to exert such power in our earthly lives. She is content with the story as is.

Before leaving this topic, we should draw one more distinction that is helpful in understanding the difference between science and pseudoscience and that is the distinction between a would-be science and a pseudoscience. A would-be science is a new story that is beginning to be told that may not fit well with the current story told by scientists. The difference between a would-be science and a pseudoscience is in the methodology used. The scientist of the potential new science uses the methods of critical thinking and is willing to test her hypotheses in the same way the established scientist is. Sometimes, it is not clear whether an enterprise is a potential science or a spurious pseudoscience. An example here is parapsychology. Some parapsychologists have used the critical thinking techniques of science to examine the possibility of extra-sensory ways of communicating. Some parapsychologists, on the other hand, refuse to admit possible refutations of their hypotheses. Currently there are more pseudoscientists in parapsychology than scientists.

The reading in this chapter is by Martin Gardner who was for a long time the editor of *Scientific American*'s mathematical puzzle page. In this article, Gardner debunks a very popular pseudoscience, biorhythms. The article shows why biorhythms are a pseudoscience.

FLIESS, FREUD, AND BIORHYTHM

Martin Gardner

At Aussee I know a wonderful wood full of ferns and mushrooms, where you shall reveal to me the secrets of the world of the lower animals and the world of children. I am agape as never before for what you have to say—and I hope that the world will not hear it before me, and that instead of a short article you will give us within a year a small book which will reveal organic secrets in periods of 28 and 23.

Sigmund Freud, in a letter to Wilhelm Fliess, 1897

One of the most extraordinary and absurd episodes in the history of numerological pseudo-science concerns the work of a Berlin surgeon named Wilhelm Fliess. Fliess was obsessed by the numbers 23 and 28. He convinced himself and others that behind all living phenomena and perhaps inorganic nature as well there are two fundamental cycles: a male cycle of 23 days and a female cycle of 28 days. By working with multiples of those two numbers—sometimes adding, sometimes subtracting—he was able to impose his number patterns on virtually everything. The work made a considerable stir in Germany during the early years of this century. Several disciples took up the system, elaborating and modifying it in books, pamphlets, and articles. In recent years the movement has taken root in the United States.

Although Fliess's numerology is of interest to recreational mathematicians and students of pathological science, it would probably be unremembered today were it not for one almost unbelievable fact: For a decade Fliess was Sigmund Freud's best friend and confidant. Roughly from 1890 to 1900, in the period of Freud's greatest creativity, which culminated with the publication of *The Interpretation of Dreams* in 1900, he and Fliess were linked in a strange neurotic relationship that had—as Freud himself was well aware—strong homosexual undercurrents. The story was known, of course, to the early leaders of psychoanalysis, but few laymen had even heard of it until the publication in 1950 of a selection of 168 letters from Freud to Fliess, out of a total of 284 that Fliess had carefully preserved. (The letters were first published in German. An English translation entitled *The Origins of Psycho-Analysis* was issued by Basic Books in 1954.) Freud was staggered by the news that these letters had been preserved, and he begged the owner (the analyst Marie Bonaparte) not to permit their publication. In reply to her question about Fliess's side of the correspondence Freud said: "Whether I destroyed them [Fliess's letters] or cleverly hid them away I still do not know." It is assumed that he destroyed them. The full story of the Fliess-Freud friendship has been told by Ernest Jones in his biography of Freud.

When the two men first met in Vienna in 1877, Freud was thirty-one, relatively unknown, happily married, and with a modest practice in psychiatry. Fliess had a much more successful practice as a nose and throat surgeon in Berlin. He was two years younger than Freud, a bachelor (later he married a wealthy Viennese woman), handsome, vain, brilliant, witty, and well informed on medical and scientific topics.

Freud opened their correspondence with a flattering letter. Fliess responded with a gift; then Freud sent a photograph of himself that Fliess had requested. By 1892 they had dropped the formal *Sie* (you) for the intimate *du* (thou). Freud wrote more often than Fliess and was in torment when Fliess was slow in answering. When his wife was expecting their fifth child, Freud declared it would be named Wilhelm. Indeed, he would have named either of his two youngest children Wilhelm but, as Jones put it, "fortunately they were both girls."

The foundations of Fliess's numerology were first revealed to the world in 1897 when he published his monograph *Die Beziehungen zwischen Nase und Weibliche Geschlechtsorganen in ihrer biologischen Bedeutungen dargestellt* (*The Relations between the Nose and the Female Sex Organs from the Biological Aspects*). Every person, Fliess maintained, is really bisexual. The male component is keyed to the rhythmic cycle of 23 days, the female to a cycle of 28 days. (The female cycle must not be confused with the menstrual cycle, although the two are related in evolutionary origin.) In normal males the male cycle is dominant, the female cycle repressed. In normal females it is the other way around.

The two cycles are present in every living cell and consequently play their dialectic roles in all living things. Among animals and humans both cycles start at birth, the sex of the child being determined by the cycle that is transmitted first. The periods continue throughout life, manifesting themselves in the ups and downs of one's physical and mental vitality, and eventually determine the day of one's death. Moreover, both cycles are intimately connected with the mucous lining of the nose. Fliess thought he had found a relation between nasal irritations and all kinds of neurotic symptoms and sexual irregularities. He diagnosed these ills by inspecting the nose and treated them by applying cocaine to "genital spots" on the nose's interior. He reported cases in which miscarriages were produced by anesthetizing the nose, and he said that he could control painful menstruation by treating the nose. On two occasions he operated on Freud's nose. In a later book he argued that all left-handed people are dominated by the cycle of the opposite sex, and when Freud expressed doubts, he accused Freud of being left-handed without knowing it.

Fliess's theory of cycles was at first regarded by Freud as a major breakthrough in biology. He sent Fliess information on 23- and 28-day periods in his own life and the lives of those in his family, and he viewed the ups and downs of his health as fluctuations of the two periods. He believed a distinction he had found between neurasthenia and anxiety neurosis could be explained by the two cycles. In 1898 he severed editorial connections with a journal because it refused to retract a harsh review of one of Fliess's books.

There was a time when Freud suspected that sexual pleasure was a release of 23-cycle energy and sexual unpleasure a release of 28-cycle energy. For years he expected to die at the age of 51 because it was the sum of 23 and 28, and Fliess had told him this would be his most critical year. "Fifty-one is the age which seems to be a particularly dangerous one to men," Freud wrote in his book on dreams. "I have known colleagues who have died suddenly at that age, and amongst them one who, after long delays, had been appointed to a professorship only a few days before his death."

Freud's acceptance of Fliess's cycle theory was not, however, enthusiastic enough for Fliess. Abnormally sensitive to even the lightest criticism, he thought he detected in one of Freud's 1896 letters some faint suspicions about his system. This marked the beginning of the slow emergence of latent hostility on both sides. Freud's earlier attitude toward Fliess had been one of almost adolescent dependence on a mentor and father figure. Now he was developing theories of his own about the origins of neuroses and methods of treating them. Fliess would have little of this. He argued that Freud's imagined cures were no more than the fluctuations of mental illness, in obedience to the male and female rhythms. The two men were on an obvious collision course.

As one could have predicted from the earlier letters, it was Fliess who first began to pull away. The growing rift plunged Freud into a severe neurosis, from which he emerged only after painful years of self-analysis. The two men had been in the habit of meeting frequently in Vienna, Berlin, Rome, and elsewhere, for what Freud playfully called their "congresses." As late as 1900, when the rift was beyond repair, we find Freud writing: "There has never been a six months' period where I have longed more to be united with you and your family. . . . Your suggestion of a meeting at Easter greatly stirred me. . . . It is not merely my almost childlike yearning for the spring and for more beautiful scenery; that I would willingly sacrifice for the satisfaction of having you near me for three days. . . . We should talk reasonably and scientifically, and your beautiful and sure biological discoveries would awaken my deepest—though impersonal—envy."

Freud nevertheless turned down the invitation, and the two men did not meet until later that summer. It was their final meeting. Fliess later wrote that Freud had made a violent and unprovoked verbal attack on him. For the next two years Freud tried to heal the breach. He proposed that they collaborate on a book on bisexuality. He suggested that they meet again in 1902. Fliess turned down both suggestions. In 1904 Fliess published angry accusations that Freud had leaked some of his ideas to Hermann Swoboda, one of Freud's young patients, who in turn had published them as his own.

The final quarrel seems to have taken place in a dining room of the Park Hotel in Munich. On two later occasions, when Freud was in this room in connection with meetings of the analytical movement, he experienced a severe attack of anxiety. Jones recalls an occasion in 1912, when he and a group that included Freud and Jung were lunching in this same room. A break between Freud and Jung was brewing. When the two men got into a mild argument, Freud suddenly fainted. Jung carried him to a sofa. "How sweet it must be to die," Freud said as he was coming to. Later he confided to Jones the reason for his attack.

Fliess wrote many books and articles about his cycle theory, but his magnum opus was a 584-page volume, *Der Ablauf des Lebens: Grundle-gung zur Exakten Biologie* (*The Rhythm of Life: Foundations of an Exact Biology*), published in Leipzig in 1906 (second edition, Vienna, 1923). The book is a masterpiece of Teutonic crackpottery. Fliess's basic formula can be written $23x + 28y$, where x and y are positive or negative integers. On almost every page Fliess fits this formula to natural phenomena, ranging from the cell to the solar system. The moon, for example, goes around the earth in about 28 days; a complete sun-spot cycle is almost 23 years.

The book's appendix is filled with such tables as multiples of 365 (days in the year), multiples of 23, multiples of 28, multiples of 23^2, multiples of 28^2, multiples of 644 (which is 23×28). In boldface are certain important constants such as 12,167 [23×23^2], 24,334 [$2 \times 23 \times 23^2$], 36,501 [$3 \times 23 \times 23^2$], 21,952 [28×28^2], 43,904 [$2 \times 28 \times 28^2$], and so on. A table lists the numbers 1 through 28, each expressed as a difference between multiples of 28 and 23 [for example, $13 = (21 \times 28) - (25 \times 23)$]. Another table expresses numbers 1 through 51 [$23 + 28$] as sums and differences of multiples of 23 and 28 [for example, $1 = (1/2 \times 28) + (2 \times 28) - (3 \times 23)$].

Freud admitted on many occasions that he was hopelessly deficient in all mathematical abilities. Fliess understood elementary arithmetic, but little more. He did not realize that if any two positive integers that have no common divisor are substituted for 23 and 28 in his basic formula, it is possible to express *any positive integer whatever*. Little wonder that the formula could be so readily fitted to natural phenomena! This is easily seen by working with 23 and 28 as an example. First determine what values of x and y can give the formula a value of 1. They are $x = 11$, $y = -9$:

$$(23 \times 11) + (28 \times -9) = 1$$

It is now a simple matter to produce any desired positive integer by the following method:

$$[23 \times (11 \times 2)] + [28 \times (-9 \times 2)] = 2$$
$$[23 \times (11 \times 3)] + [28 \times (-9 \times 3)] = 3$$
$$[23 \times (11 \times 4)] + [28 \times (-9 \times 4)] = 4$$

...

As Roland Sprague recently pointed out in problem 26 of his *Recreation in Mathematics*, 1963, even if negative values of *x* and *y* are excluded, it is still possible to express all positive integers greater than a certain integer. In the finite set of positive integers that *cannot* be expressed by this formula, asks Sprague, what is the largest number? In other words, what is the largest number that cannot be expressed by substituting nonnegative integers for *x* and *y* in the formula $23x + 28y$? The answer: $xy - x - y$.

Freud eventually realized that Fliess's superficially surprising results were no more than numerological juggling. After Fliess's death in 1928 (note that obliging 28), a German physician, J. Aelby, published a book that constituted a thorough refutation of Fliess's absurdities. By then, however, the 23–28 cult was firmly established in Germany. Swoboda, who lived until 1963, was the cult's second most important figure. As a psychologist at the University of Vienna he devoted much time to investigating, defending, and writing about Fliess's cycle theory. In his own rival masterwork, the 576-page *Das Siebenjahr* (*The Year of Seven*), he reported on his studies of hundreds of family trees to prove that such events as heart attacks, deaths, and the onset of major ills tend to fall on certain critical days that can be computed on the basis of one's male and female cycles. He applied the cycle theory to dream analysis, an application that Freud criticizes in a 1911 footnote to his book on dreams. Swoboda also designed the first slide rule for determining critical days. Without the aid of such a device or the assistance of elaborate charts, calculations of critical days are tedious and tricky.

Incredible though it may seem, as late as the 1960s the Fliess system still had a small but devoted band of disciples in Germany and Switzerland. There were doctors in several Swiss hospitals who determined propitious days for surgery on the basis of Fliess's cycles. (This practice goes back to Fliess. In 1925, when Karl Abraham, one of the pioneers of analysis, had a gallbladder operation, he insisted that it take place on the favorable day calculated by Fliess.) To the male and female cycles modern Fliessians have added a third cycle, called the intellectual cycle, which has a length of 33 days.

Two books on the Swiss system have been published here by Crown: *Biorhythm*, 1961, by Hans J. Wernli, and *Is This Your Day?*, 1964, by George Thommen. Thommen is the president of a firm that supplies calculators and charting kits with which to plot one's own cycles.

The three cycles start at birth and continue with absolute regularity throughout life, although their amplitudes decrease with old age. The male cycle governs such masculine traits as physical strength, confidence, aggressiveness, and endurance. The female cycle controls such feminine traits as feelings, intuition, creativity, love, cooperation, cheerfulness. The newly discovered intellectual cycle governs mental powers common to both sexes: intelligence, memory, concentration, quickness of mind.

On days when a cycle is above the horizontal zero line of the chart, the energy controlled by that cycle is being discharged. These are the days of highest vitality and efficiency. On days when the cycle is below the line, energy is being recharged. These are the days of reduced vitality. When your male cycle is high and your other cycles are low, you can perform physical tasks admirably but are low in sensitivity and mental alertness. If your female cycle is high and your male cycle low, it is a fine day, say, to visit an art museum but a day on which you are likely to tire quickly. The reader can easily guess the applications of other cycle patterns to other common events of life. I omit details about methods of predicting the sex of unborn children or computing the rhythmic "compatibility" between two individuals.

The most dangerous days are those on which a cycle, particularly the 23- or 28-day cycle, crosses the horizontal line. Those days when a cycle is making a transition from one phase to another are called "switch-point days." It is a pleasant fact that switch points for the 28-cycle always occur on the same day of the week for any given individual, since this cycle is exactly four weeks long. If your switch point for the 28-cycle is on Tuesday, for instance, every other Tuesday will be your critical day for female energy throughout your entire life.

As one might expect, if the switch points of two cycles coincide, the day is "doubly critical," and it is "triply critical" if all three coincide. The Thommen and Wernli books contain many rhythmograms showing that the days on which various family people died were days on which two or more cycles were at switch points. On two days on which Clark Gable had heart attacks, the second fatal, two cycles were at switch points. The Aga Kahn died on a triply critical day. Arnold Palmer won the British Open Golf Tournament during a high period in July, 1962, and lost the Professional Golf Association Tourney during a triple low two weeks later. The boxer Benny (Kid) Paret died after a knockout in a match on a triply critical day. Clearly it behooves the Fliessian to prepare a chart of his future cycle patterns so that he can exercise especial care on critical days; since other factors come into play, however, no ironclad predictions can be made.

Because each cycle has an integral length in days, it follows that every person's rhythmogram will repeat its pattern after an interval of $23 \times 28 \times 33 = 21,252$ days, or a little more than 58 years. This interval will be the same for everybody. For example, 21,252 days after every person's birth all three of his cycles will cross the zero line simultaneously on their upswing and his entire pattern will start over again. Two people whose ages are exactly 21,252 days apart will be running on perfectly synchronized cycle patterns. Since Fliess's system did not include the 33-day cycle, his cycle patterns repeat after a lapse of $23 \times 28 = 644$ days. Swiss Fliessians call this the "biorhythmic year." It is important in computing the "biorhythmic compatibility" between two individuals, since any two persons born 644 days apart are synchronized with respect to their two most important cycles.

Postscript

George S. Thommen, president of Biorhythm Computers, Inc., 298 Fifth Avenue, New York, is still going strong, appearing occasionally on radio and television talk-shows to promote his products. James Randi, the magician, was moderator of an all-night radio talk-show in the mid-sixties. Thommen was twice his guest. After one of the shows, Randi tells me, a lady in New Jersey sent him her birth date and asked for a biorhythm chart covering the next two years of her life. After sending her an actual chart, but based on a *different* birth date, Randi received an effusive letter from the lady saying that the chart exactly matched all her critical up and down days. Randi wrote back, apologized for having made a mistake on her birth date, and enclosed a "correct" chart, actually as wrongly dated as the first one. He soon received a letter telling him that the new chart was even *more* accurate than the first one.

Speaking in March, 1966, at the 36th annual convention of the Greater New York Safety Council, Thommen reported that biorhythm research projects were under way at the University of Nebraska and the University of Minnesota, and that Dr. Tatai, medical chief of Tokyo's public health department, had published a book, *Biorhythm and Human Life*, using the Thommen system. When a Boeing 727 jetliner crashed in Tokyo in February, 1966, Dr. Tatai quickly drew up the pilot's chart, Thommen said, and found that the crash occurred on one of the pilot's low days.

Biorhythm seems to have been more favorably received in Japan than in the United States. According to *Time*, January 10, 1972, page 48, the Ohmi Railway Co., in Japan, computed the biorhythms of each of its 500 bus drivers. Whenever a driver was scheduled for a "bad" day, he was given a notice to be extra careful. The Ohmi company reported a fifty percent drop in accidents.

Fate magazine, February, 1975, pages 109–110, reported on a conference on "Biorhythm, Healing and Kirlian Photography," held in Evanston, Ill., October, 1974. Michael Zaeske, who sponsored the conference, revealed that the traditional biorhythm curves are actually "first derivatives" of the true curves, and that all the traditional charts are "in error by several days." Guests at the meeting also heard evidence from California that a fourth cycle exists, and that all four cycles "may be related to Jung's four personality types."

Science News, January 18, 1975, page 45, carried a large ad by Edmund Scientific Company for their newly introduced Biorhythm Kit ($11.50), containing the precision-made Dialgraf Calculator. The ad also offered an "accurate computerized, personalized" biorhythm chart report for 12 months to any reader who sent his birthdate and $15.95. One wonders if Edmund is using the traditional charts (possibly off three days) or Zaeske's refined procedures.

A ridiculous book, *Biorhythm: A Personal Science*, by Bernard Gittelson, was published in 1975 by Arco, and later by Werner books as a paperback. Pocket Books jumped into the action with Arbie Dale's *Biorhythm* (1976). *Reader's Digest* (September 1977) gave the "science" a major boost with Jennifer Bolch's shameless article, "Biorhythm: A Key to Your Ups and Downs."

By 1980 biorhythm had become so popular among the gullible that half a dozen firms were manufacturing mechanical devices, electronic computers, and even clocks that told true believers what to expect each day. See *Fate* for advertisements. *Science 80*, in its January/February 1980 issue, ran an article by Russell Schoch called "The Myth of Sigmund Freud," which included a good photograph of Freud and Fliess together as young men.

STUDY QUESTIONS

1. Why do you think people are drawn to a pseudoscience?
2. What gives biorhythms its credibility; that is, what makes it seem believable?
3. What other pseudosciences can you name?

Summary

Clearly Gardner has no patience with biorhythms. His attack on the spurious scientific nature of biorhythms discredits the reasonableness of the theory, so we do not need to critically evaluate biorhythms here. We do need to be clear, however, about the general characteristics of pseudosciences and what distinguishes them from genuine sciences, so we are not led to unfulfilled expectations and disappointments by other false "sciences." After all, pseudosciences resemble sciences well enough that some people are misled into believing that they have the same authority that sciences do.

Scientists and pseudoscientists both tell stories but the methods they use to arrive at that story are different, and consequently the value of the stories to us is different. The scientist uses the methods of critical thinking. She tests her story and changes her story in light of the evidence she finds. She is open-minded and in constant dialogue with other scientists, listening to their stories, and trying to make her hypothesis or story fit in with theirs. The pseudoscientist is locked into her story. Contrary evidence is ignored. The story is never revised. No effort is made to connect the story to a larger world picture. The dialogue is only among adherents or disciples. And the story always ends with a mystery which precludes further dialogue and discussion. The story told by the scientist helps us predict and control events in our lives. The story told by the pseudoscientist suggests that we are at the mercy of forces which we cannot understand and can only accept.

Exercises

11–I

1. Bring in a recent horoscope.
   a. Are these predictions refutable?
   b. Suppose you were to take these predictions seriously. What view of the universe would you have to accept to accept these predictions?
2. Describe the marks of pseudoscience you see in biorhythms.
3. Choose another pseudoscience (the paperback book shelf can give you ideas here) and use its own examples to show why it is a pseudoscience.
4. Can you think of any other would-be sciences besides parapsychology?

11–II

1. What differences do you see between the unproven assumptions of Copernicus and the unproven assumptions of Fliess?
2. Why is it next to impossible to convince a firm believer in astrology that the astrologer's predictions are not warranted?
3. a. Develop an argument to show that the study of UFO sightings is a pseudoscience.
   b. Develop an argument to show that the study of UFO sightings is a scientific enterprise.
4. We often look to the words and deeds of past heroes for inspiration to help us resolve problems in our own lives. Former First Lady Hillary Rodham Clinton employed the services of New Age psychic Jean Houston to talk to the spirits of her heroes, Eleanor Roosevelt and Mohandas Gandhi. Critically evaluate Clinton's search for inspiration in light of what you have learned about pseudoscience.

IV

Reasoning About Values

You may be surprised to find a critical thinking text ending with a whole section on moral reasoning. But what could be more important? "How ought I to live?" is one of the most important questions a person can ask. Critical thinking ought to be helpful in answering that question.

In the previous three parts of the text, you have seen that our beliefs about the world form a web of connections. This web, of course, will contain moral beliefs as well as non-moral beliefs. From what you already know about this web of belief, it should be clear to you that our non-moral beliefs have connections with our moral beliefs and, therefore, influence our moral beliefs and attitudes. We cannot separate them. So, it is only appropriate that this book end with a discussion of moral reasoning.

We have also seen that it is vitally important to good critical thinking that we keep our dialogues with friends open, so we can improve our own thinking about the world and so we can avoid fisticuffs. This is particularly important when we discuss our moral beliefs! Our ideas about what is good and what is just too often are the beliefs we are the most closed-minded about and the least willing to put to the test in open rational dialogue with others. Too many people draw lines in the sand—or walk away—when there is moral disagreement. This means that moral reasoning, particularly, can profit from the application of critical reasoning skills and open dialogue. We may not always arrive at consensus but we hope not to arrive at a fight!

In Part VI, you will learn how to bring the concepts and techniques of critical thinking you have learned to thinking about morality. It will help you answer the question above: "How ought I to live?"

The Nature of Morality

It is a common view—one that we think is mistaken—that reasoning about questions of value, and especially about moral values, is different from reasoning about the non-moral aspects of the world. Some of the people who hold this view claim that talk about values doesn't use much reasoning at all. They think that when we talk about values, we are mostly expressing our emotions. From this point of view, reason enters into talk about non-moral features of the world, but because values are irrational there isn't much to say about them. They believe about morality what many people believe about beauty—that it is entirely in the eye of the beholder. What is important in moral matters, they say, is simply the sincerity of one's belief or the degree of one's commitment.

Sometimes, people who hold this view support it with an argument about the logic of moral arguments. The philosopher David Hume is often cited as the source of this argument. Hume argued, in a now very famous passage in his *Treatise of Human Nature,* that one cannot reason (he meant reason deductively) from statements about the way a thing *is* to statements about the way it *ought* to be without taking a jump that has no logical justification. Some people have thought, on the basis of Hume's argument, that critical thinking has no place in discussions of moral values. Since the topic of this part of our book is the use of critical thinking skills in moral discourse, it is important for us to take a closer look at Hume's argument:

> In every system of morality which I have hitherto met
> with, I have always remark'd, that the author pro-
> ceeds for some time in the ordinary way of reasoning,
> and establishes the being of a God, or makes observa-
> tions concerning human affairs; when of a sudden I
> am supriz'd to find, that instead of the usual copula-
> tions of propositions, *is,* and *is not,* I meet with no
> proposition that is not connected with an *ought* or an

ought not. This change is imperceptible; but is, however, of the last consequence. For as this *ought* or *ought not*, expresses some new relation or affirmation, 'tis necessary that it should be observ'd and explain'd; and at the same time that a reason should be given, for what seems altogether inconceivable, how this new relation can be a deduction from others, which are entirely different from it. But as authors do not commonly use this precaution, I shall presume to recommend it to the readers; and am persuaded that this small attention wou'd subvert all the vulgar systems of morality, and let us see, that the distinction of vice and virtue is not founded merely on the relations of objects, nor is perceiv'd by reason.[1]

In this passage Hume makes a very good point, namely, that value statements (*ought* statements) cannot be logically derived from factual statements (*is* statements). It follows from this that there is no logical or deductive necessity when we use statements about the non-moral features of the world to support moral claims. But this should not be surprising or disheartening. We have already seen there is no logical or deductive necessity in our everyday reasoning about matters of fact or matters of scientific thought either.

This is because most of our everyday reasoning is reasoning with probability. So, does Hume also mean (as he is sometimes interpreted to mean) that reasoning with probability (or inductive reasoning) is also irrelevant to moral discourse? If we look closely at the passage, we see that Hume does not say that claims about what is the case are irrelevant to claims about what ought to be the case. He simply says that the latter do not logically follow (with necessity) from the former. This does not mean that statements about non-moral features of the world cannot be used to give **rational support** to claims about values.

We will see that critical thinking is very important in discussions of value, perhaps more important than in discussions of non-moral matters because we tend to have more disagreement when we deal with values and less evidence that we can offer to support our moral beliefs. **Our moral dialogues can profit from the same critical thinking skills that we should use in discussions of matters of fact: being open to discussion and being a good listener, having a large storehouse of background knowledge, being able to recognize patterns of traces and see a story that weaves those patterns in ever larger patterns, recognizing the limits of evidence and proof, and so on.** Let's face it, the alternatives to rational dialogue about moral beliefs are not attractive or helpful: seeing who can outshout the other, giving the other person a sock in the jaw, or as happens between nation states, going to war![2]

SUPPORTING MORAL CLAIMS

You probably hold a set of moral beliefs to which you are quite committed. But chances are that you are unsure about how to justify them. As a consequence, you probably have avoided some moral discussions not to anger someone else or because

---

[1]Book III, Part I, Section I.

[2]A classical ethics that takes a similar view of the role of reason in ethics is Aristotle's model of the man of practical reason, Aristotle's analogue to our critical thinker.

you were not sure how to argue successfully for what you believe. These chapters on reasoning about values do not argue for any particular moral point of view. They are intended to help you sort out some of your confusions about how moral beliefs connect with beliefs about the world and help you support the beliefs you hold. We all need to learn how we can better support our point of view in a moral argument, whether "all" refers to toddlers in the sandbox or professional diplomats. Fisticuffs and war are not attractive alternatives.

Moral statements do appear to be different from statements about matters of fact in at least one respect. Moral statements have words in them like *ought, good, right, duty, should.* Something different is being said when we talk what ought to be the case from when we talk about what is the case. This apparent difference makes us think that we have to support these two types of statements differently. Most of the time we think we know how to support non-moral claims and how to dispute them. We give evidence from experience. We cite other non-moral claims. Part III has discussed a variety of ways we use to reason about matters of fact, including those which go beyond the evidence available and project into the future. Although we generally know how to support factual claims, we often do make claims that we later have to revise.

When it comes to supporting or disputing moral claims, however, we are often not so sure about how to go about it. Either we argue for or against moral statements with non-moral statements—which do not convey or confer moral value—or we argue about them using other moral statements—which suggests that the reasoning is circular. An example of the first alternative is "You ought not to steal because you might get arrested." Here the moral force of *ought* seems to get lost. It makes stealing sound like just a matter of imprudence, something with unpleasant consequences like eating too much or getting caught in the rain. An example of the second alternative is "You ought not to steal because stealing is wrong." This is like saying you ought not to steal because you ought not to steal, which is clearly circular reasoning.

This puzzle of justifying moral claims is not new. It has bothered philosophers for over 2000 years! We saw it earlier in the dialogue *Euthyphro* where Socrates asks Euthyphro why the gods love piety. ("Do the gods love piety because it is pious, or is it pious because they love it?")

What we would like are some objective features of the world which we could point to, which we could use as evidence to support our belief that someone's behavior is morally incorrect. Such objective features would enable us to decide who is right. We could settle moral disputes the same way we settle disputes about the height of the flag pole or the color of the neighbor's new car.

For instance, we might use the words 20 *feet tall* to describe the height of the flag pole, or we might say the car is *midnight blue*. These expressions are usually taken as describing objective features of the world. We generally know when to use them correctly. We know that we know how to use them correctly because there is consensus about when to use them. We say the pole is 10 feet tall when the tape measure reads 240 inches. We describe the car as midnight blue when it looks blue but almost black to us. There are publicly observable criteria for the proper usage of these words.

Of course, sometimes there is ambiguity about the use of words. We are not sure if the car is blue—maybe it is a black car that we're looking at. To avoid ambiguity, we sometimes convert qualitative features of the world into quantitative features, as for example, when we agree to determine length by feet and inches or by meters. Even the ambiguity about the proper usage of *blue* or *black,* however, is guided by consensus. That is, there is general agreement that it is difficult sometimes to distinguish dark blue from black. It is very important to remember that the general consensus of language users guides us in describing the "objective features" of experience.

Similarly, many philosophers have established objective criteria for the proper use of moral terms (or for the appropriate moral evaluation of an act or agent), based on what they claim is the general consensus of moral language users. Jeremy Bentham, for instance, thought that what people mean when they call an act *right* is that it promotes the greatest amount of happiness for the greatest number of people. Perhaps you have heard of this view which is called **utilitarianism**. Bentham, in the reading below, tries to make this criterion for *right* very clear by making it quantitative—in the same way that the tape measure makes height quantitative. He says that *happiness* means pleasure and pleasures are measurable by their intensity, duration, and so on. Hence, one can determine which acts should be performed and which acts should not, just by calculating the amount of pleasure which can be derived from them.

CHAPTER I: OF THE PRINCIPLE OF UTILITY

Jeremy Bentham

I. Nature has placed mankind under the governance of two sovereign masters, *pain* and *pleasure.* It is for them alone to point out what we ought to do, as well as to determine what we shall do. On the one hand the standard of right and wrong, on the other the chain of causes and effects, are fastened to their throne. They govern us in all we do, in all we say, in all we think: every effort we can make to throw off our subjection, will serve but to demonstrate and confirm it. In words a man may pretend to abjure their empire: but in reality he will remain subject to it all the while. The *principle of utility* recognizes this subjection, and assumes it for the foundation of that system, the object of which is to rear the fabric of felicity by the hands of reason and of law. Systems which attempt to question it, deal in sounds instead of sense, in caprice instead of reason, in darkness instead of light.

But enough of metaphor and declamation: it is not by such means that moral science is to be improved.

II. The principle of utility is the foundation of the present work: it will be proper therefore at the outset to give an explicit and determinate account of what is meant by it. By the principle of utility is meant that principle which approves or disapproves of every action whatsoever according to the tendency it appears to have to augment or diminish the happiness of the party whose interest is in question: or, what is the same thing in other words to promote or to oppose that happiness. I say of every action whatsoever, and therefore not only of every action of a private individual, but of every measure of government.

III. By utility is meant that property in any object, whereby it tends to produce benefit, advantage, pleasure, good, or happiness, (all this in the present case comes to the

From *An Introduction to the Principles of Morals and Legislation* by Jeremy Bentham.

same thing) or (what comes again to the same thing) to prevent the happening of mischief, pain, evil, or unhappiness to the party whose interest is considered: if that party be the community in general, then the happiness of the community: if a particular individual, then the happiness of that individual.

IV. The interest of the community is one of the most general expressions that can occur in the phraseology of morals: no wonder that the meaning of it is often lost. When it has a meaning, it is this. The community is a fictitious *body,* composed of the individual persons who are considered as constituting as it were its *members.* The interest of the community then is, what is it?—the sum of the interests of the several members who compose it.

V. It is in vain to talk of the interest of the community, without understanding what is the interest of the individual. A thing is said to promote the interest, or to be *for* the interest, of an individual, when it tends to add to the sum total of his pleasures: or, what comes to the same thing, to diminish the sum total of his pains.

VI. An action then may be said to be conformable to then principle of utility, or, for shortness sake, to utility, (meaning with respect to the community at large) when the tendency it has to augment the happiness of the community is greater than any it has to diminish it.

VII. A measure of government (which is but a particular kind of action, performed by a particular person or persons) may be said to be conformable to or dictated by the principle of utility, when in like manner the tendency which it has to augment the happiness of the community is greater than any which it has to diminish it.

VIII. When an action, or in particular a measure of government, is supposed by a man to be conformable to the principle of utility, it may be convenient, for the purposes of discourse, to imagine a kind of law or dictate, called a law or dictate of utility: and to speak of the action in question, as being conformable to such law or dictate.

IX. A man may be said to be a partizan of the principle of utility, when the approbation or disapprobation he annexes to any action, or to any measure, is determined by and proportioned to the tendency which he conceives it to have to augment or to diminish the happiness of the community: or in other words, to its conformity or unconformity to the laws or dictates of utility.

X. Of an action that is conformable to the principle of utility one may always say either that it is one that ought to be done, or at least that it is not one that ought not to be done. One may say also, that it is right it should be done; at least that it is not wrong it should be done: that it is a right action; at least that it is not a wrong action. When thus interpreted, the words *ought,* and *right* and *wrong* and others of that stamp, have a meaning: when otherwise, they have none.

XI. Has the rectitude of this principle been ever formally contested? It should seem that it had, by those who have not known what they have been meaning. Is it susceptible of any direct proof? it should seem not: for that which is used to prove every thing else, cannot itself be proved: a chain of proofs must have their commencement somewhere. To give such proof is as impossible as it is needless.

XII. Not that there is or ever has been that human creature at breathing, however stupid or perverse, who has not on many, perhaps on most occasions of his life, deferred to it. By the natural constitution of the human frame, on most occasions of their lives men in general embrace this principle, without thinking of it: if not for the ordering of their own actions, yet for the trying of their own actions, as well as of those of other men. There have been, at the same time, not many perhaps, even of the most intelligent, who have been disposed to embrace it purely and without reserve. There are even few who have not taken some occasion or other to quarrel with it, either on account of their not understanding always how to apply it, or on account of some prejudice or other which they were afraid to examine into, or could not bear to part with. For such is the stuff that man is made of: in principle and in practice, in a right track and in a wrong one, the rarest of all human qualities is consistency.

XIII. When a man attempts to combat the principle of utility, it is with reasons drawn, without his being aware of it, from that very principle itself. His arguments, if they prove any thing, prove not that the principle is *wrong*, but that, according to the applications he supposes to be made of it, it is *misapplied.* Is it possible for a man to move the earth? Yes; but he must first find out another earth to stand upon.

XIV. To disprove the propriety of it by arguments is impossible; but, from the causes that have been mentioned, or from some confused or partial view of it, a man may happen to be disposed not to relish it. Where this is the case, if he thinks the settling of his opinions on such a subject worth the trouble, let him take the following steps, and at length, perhaps, he may come to reconcile himself to it.

1. Let him settle with himself, whether he would wish to discard this principle altogether; if so, let him consider what it is that all his reasonings (in matters of politics especially) can amount to?
2. If he would, let him settle with himself, whether he would judge and act without any principle, or whether there is any other he would judge an act by?
3. If there be, let him examine and satisfy himself whether the principle he thinks he has found is really any separate intelligible principle; or whether it be not a mere principle in words, a kind of phrase, which at bottom expresses neither more nor less than the mere averment of his own unfounded sentiments; that is, what in another person he might be apt to call caprice?
4. If he is inclined to think that his own approbation or disapprobation, annexed to the idea of an act, without any regard to its consequences, is a sufficient foundation for him to judge and act upon, let him ask himself whether his sentiment is to be a standard of right and wrong, with respect to every other man, or whether every man's sentiment has the same privilege of being a standard to itself?
5. In the first case, let him ask himself whether his principle is not despotical, and hostile to all the rest of human race?
6. In the second case, whether it is not anarchial, and whether at this rate there are not as many different standards of right and wrong as there are men? and whether even to the same man, the same thing, which is right today,

may not (without the least change in its nature) be wrong tomorrow? and whether the same thing is not right and wrong in the same place at the same time? and in either case, whether all argument is not at an end? and whether, when two men have said, "I like this," and "I don't like it," they can (upon such a principle) have any thing more to say?

7. If he should have said to himself, No: for that the sentiment which he proposes as a standard must be grounded on reflection, let him say on what particulars the reflection is to turn? if on particulars having relation to the utility of the act, then let him say whether this is not deserting his own principle, and borrowing assistance from that very one in opposition to which he sets it up: or if not on those particulars, on what other particulars?

8. If he should be for compounding the matter, and adopting his own principle in part, and the principle of utility in part, let him say how far he will adopt it?

9. When he has settled with himself where he will stop, then let him ask himself how he justifies to himself the adopting it so far? and why he will not adopt it any farther?

10. Admitting any other principle than the principle of utility to be a right principle, a principle that it is right for a man to pursue; admitting (what is not true) that the word *right* can have a meaning without reference to utility, let him say whether there is any such thing as a *motive* that a man can have to pursue the dictates of it: if there is, let him say what that motive is, and how it is to be distinguished from those which enforce the dictates of utility: if not, then lastly let him say what it is this other principle can be good for?

STUDY QUESTIONS

1. Bentham links happiness and pleasure. What do you see as the differences between them?

2. Are all pleasures alike? Or, are some pleasures "better" than others? What does this say about Bentham's pleasure calculus?

OBJECTIVISM AND SUBJECTIVISM

People frequently use Bentham's criteria—or some modification of them—in reasoning about values. It is not uncommon to hear, for instance, a legislator argue that a particular bill will promote more happiness for more people than an alternative or that the severe punishment of an individual today for a crime will have a deterrent effect on would-be criminals in the future, thereby promoting the future happiness of more people. Probably all of us have used utilitarian reasoning at some time. There is not the same kind of universal consensus, however, about these criteria as about the criteria for the height of flag poles. Both philosophers and non-philosophers have proposed different objective criteria for the rightness of an act which are at times inconsistent with the criteria of promoting happiness.

One of these alternatives was proposed by the philosopher Immanuel Kant. Kant claimed that the key objective criterion of a moral imperative is that it is non-contradictory. (This would presumably be an objective feature of the world, although it is not one directly experienced. Rather, it is a logical feature, a feature which all rational people are capable of recognizing.) Kant examined the way people use moral language and then determined that our common usage presupposes that beings that are rational and moral must act from rationally consistent principles. He interpreted this to mean that a person performs a right act when he acts on the basis of a principle that he can universalize without contradiction. That is, according to Kant, each of us must do what we think every other rational being should do in similar circumstances. We cannot make exceptions for ourselves. That would be logically inconsistent and not living up to our potential as rational human beings. What is important, then, on Kant's account, is the principle from which one acts, not the consequences and the good (or lack thereof) the act produces, and that principle must apply to everyone in like circumstances.

You can see from these brief accounts of utilitarianism and Kantian ethics that each uses different objective criteria for the rightness of an action. Consequently, they do not always agree on which acts are right. Let's look at one more effort to establish objective criteria for making moral claims, namely, the view often proposed by religious believers (although not usually by theologians) that an act is good if God wills it. There are many versions of this account of morality. We already saw one in *Euthyphro*. They refer to some divine being who approves, wills, is pleased by, and so on, the act in question. You may not have thought of these views as proposing objective criteria for making moral judgments but they do. That is, holders of this belief consider it as an objective feature of the world that God wills an act or does not will an act, just as it is an objective feature of the world whether you will an act or not. You will that the car turns to the right when you turn the steering wheel to the right. You do not will that the car turns to the right when you hit a slick patch in the road and skid toward the right. Of course, we may have a harder time knowing what God wills than what our neighbor wills but not always. Historically, religious groups have offered many and diverse ways of determining the will of God, ranging from reliance on the utterances of inspired individuals to reliance on the natural reason of the believer.

These three objectivist views—the utilitarian, the Kantian, and the religious—about the nature of morality have attracted many followers because they generally make it much easier to make moral judgments. When in doubt, one can find objective answers by calculating the total amount of pleasure, or determining whether the moral principle is universalizable, or consulting a religious minister, priest, rabbi, imam, or text. As a consequence, all three of them have many adherents. There are several problems, however, that these objectivist views face. One obvious one is that they all do not pick out the same features of reality as the important criteria for making moral judgments. One has focused on features of human experience, one has focused on the nature of human rationality, and one has focused on the viewpoint of some divine being. This leads to conflicting moral judgments—and sometimes even fisticuffs and war. It also suggests that maybe the right objective features of experience are not being singled out since there is sometimes so little agreement.

There is a more fundamental problem here as well, one which we have already encountered and which makes the objective account of moral reasoning less attractive than it initially appears. This is the problem encountered with many of our statements about experiences, even non-moral ones, namely, that our statements of the "objective criteria" do not always agree. It is not just that people pick different objective criteria—like Bentham and Kant and the various religions have done—but we do not always experience the same "objective features" of the world. Where one person sees fog, another sees a fine mist. Where one person sees the brownstone houses of New York as "palaces," another sees them as intolerable ugly.[3] The objectivist account seems to assume that we have certainty about the features of our experience and that this certainty can be used as the basis for certainty with regard to moral beliefs. We have already seen, however, that our descriptions of our experiences often vary, and we can have disagreements about the "objective features" of experience. Even scientific descriptions of our experience are simply part of a largely unprovable story which rests on some unproven assumptions. Thus, grounding moral judgments on the objective features of our experience does not provide moral judgments with an unquestionably firm base, and certainly not as firm a base as many of the adherents of these views would like. Consequently, objectivist views of the nature of moral judgments cannot, for the critical thinker, provide a final answer to the question of who is morally right.

These weaknesses of objectivism have led many people to think that moral judgments are *subjective.* According to the subjectivist account, moral judgments are the product of each individual subject's conscious deliberation, and they are morally correct for that subject provided the judgment is a result of a process which is rational, impartial, and deliberate—and not simply a casual decision. On this view, there are no objective features of the world which serve as criteria for moral judgments unless a particular subject decides to rely on some feature as a criterion.

A number of philosophers have argued for a subjectivist view of moral statements. The seventeenth-century philosopher Spinoza is a good example of someone with a subjectivist view of morality. According to Spinoza, the world and God are identical so that everything that happens happens necessarily as a product, or function, of God's nature. Consequently, the world is neither good nor bad. It just is as it has to be. *Good* and *bad,* then, can only be terms used by human beings to reflect their own reactions to events in the world. They are not descriptive of objective features of the world. People like Spinoza, who see events in the world as happening of necessity through the unfolding of a fixed nature, for example, or as governed by fixed mechanical laws, generally hold subjectivist views of moral statements.

More contemporary subjectivist accounts of morality come from philosophical viewpoints that see the world as having no order or fixed nature at all. On these accounts, the world just *is* and human beings give it shape and form by describing it and by valuing certain aspects of it. Existentialists like Jean Paul Sartre are subjectivists of this type. They hold that morality is an individual matter since there is no "human nature" which is fixed which would determine how human beings should behave.

The subjectivist viewpoint has much to recommend it. For one thing, it helps to explain why we have such differences of opinion and why we find it so hard to agree when it comes to making moral judgments. Since each of us is a separate subject, we are likely to have different views of the same events, and because the factors which

---

[3]Remember the two quotations describing New York in Chapter 2.

enter into the judgment are particular to each of us as subjects, it is hard to have much agreement. The subjectivist viewpoint is also appealing in that it suggests a way to resolve moral disagreements: When the argument reaches a stalemate, we should just agree to disagree. We should avoid unpleasantness and not keep arguing—or fighting— because continued argument is useless. If the two arguers are arguing from considered judgments (judgments which are rational, impartial, and deliberate), then each disputant holds a view which is a morally correct view for him.

On the other hand, subjectivism seems counterintuitive to our ordinary moral sentiments in several important ways. For example, most people find deliberate cruelty morally unjustifiable if not morally blameworthy. It seems inexcusable, no matter what one's subjective beliefs. On the subjectivist view, however, it makes no sense to argue with the person who deliberately chooses to act in order to harm. It does make sense, on the subjectivist view, for us to tell that person that we think his behavior is too harsh— because we seek to influence his opinion. But as long as the decision is construed as a considered judgment and not hasty, is very deliberate and thought out, and considered just and right by the agent, it does not make sense to say it is morally wrong or hold him responsible for a morally blameworthy act. The subjectivist view also leads to the counterintuitive view that two people can both be morally correct, even though they judge the same act very differently. Some moral subjectivists attempt to solve these problems by claiming that we, as communities through consensus, establish inter-subjective values which all members of community are bound to respect.

The second reading in this chapter is a small selection from *The Brothers Karamazov* by Fyodor Dostoevsky. The justification of moral values is one of the main themes of this very rich and rewarding novel. As part of the exploration of this theme, Dostoevsky tells a story, within the larger story of the Karamazov family, about a general and a serf boy. This story is very short and will make you think long and hard about the nature of morality.

THE BROTHERS KARAMAZOV

Fyodor Dostoevsky

There was in those days a general of aristocratic connections, the owner of great estates, one of those men—somewhat exceptional, I believe, even then—who, retiring from the service into a life of leisure, are convinced that they've earned the power of life and death over their subjects. There were such men then. So our general, settled on his property of two thousand souls, lives in pomp, and domineers over his poor neighbors as though they were dependents and buffoons. He has kennels of hundreds of hounds and nearly a hundred dog-boys—all mounted, and in uniform. One day a serf boy, a little child of eight, threw a stone in play and hurt the paw of the general's favorite hound. 'Why is my favorite dog lame?' He is told that the boy threw a stone

From *The Brothers Karamazov*, A Norton Critical Edition by Fyodor Dostoevsky, edited by Ralph E. Matlaw, translated by Constance Garnett, revised by Ralph Matlaw. Copyright © 1976 by W.W. Norton & Company, Inc. Used by permission of W.W. Norton & Company, Inc.

that hurt the dog's paw. 'So you did it.' The general looked the child up and down. 'Take him.' He was taken—taken from his mother and kept shut up all night. Early that morning the general comes out in full pomp, mounts his horse with the hounds, his dependents, dog-boys, and the huntsmen, all mounted around him. The servants are summoned for their edification, and in front of them all stands the mother of the child. The child is brought from the lockup. It's a gloomy cold, foggy autumn day, a capital day for hunting. The general orders the child to be undressed; the child is stripped naked. He shivers, numb with terror, not daring to cry. . . . 'Make him run,' commands the general. 'Run! run!' shout the dog-boys. The boy runs. . . . 'At him!' yells the general, and he sets the whole pack of hounds on the child. The hounds catch him, and tear him to pieces before his mother's eyes!

STUDY QUESTIONS

1. The general believes he has done a morally correct act. Do you agree or disagree? How would you argue with him?
2. As the general, how would you argue for the moral correctness of your action?
3. Is the general's action morally correct in nineteenth-century Russia but not in the twenty-first century in the United States? Focus on the moral value of the act, not the legality of it.
4. Are there moral facts in the world? What do they look like?
5. Are moral values in the eye of the beholder?
6. When we come to argue about moral values, why can we not just "agree to disagree"?

MORALITY AND REASONING

Most people who read about the general's choice of punishment for harming his favorite hound believe this choice is morally wrong. While all punishments involve harming another person, here the punishment seems too severe for the nature of the crime. A child's life has more moral worth than a hound's injured paw. The general, of course, does not see it this way. From the general's point of view, good hounds are hard to come by. The children of serfs are plentiful and so without much value. Besides, all assembled will learn an important moral lesson which will help to avoid harm in the future to both hounds and serf boys. So, he thinks, the sacrifice of one serf boy is out-weighed by the future good that his punishment will bring about. The general does not think himself an evil person. He believes he is doing the morally correct thing.

What are we to say to this general? Or, should we just keep silent? Some people would argue that the general's behavior is morally all right (at least not evil), given that it happened in Russia in the nineteenth century, but they would claim that times have changed and such behavior today is no longer morally acceptable but rather is morally blameworthy. Morality, on this view, would be a function of social values or cultural norms and would vary over times and places. This response is unsatisfying for two reasons. First, the general's action offends our moral sensibilities so much that it is hard to accept any claim about its being a morally acceptable act. Second, the

Statements about moral matters are often clearly warranted (even if we would *want* to deny them).

view that behavior is morally blameless as long as it is acceptable within the cultural community in which it occurs allows the possibility of all sorts of atrocities, and it removes them from moral criticism as long as the relevant social community accepts them. This would put headhunting, terrorism, torture, slavery, wife burning, human gas chambers, and so on outside the realm of moral criticism which, again, offends our ordinary moral sentiments.

Neither the objectivist nor the subjectivist seems to offer us much help here. While both have some attractive features and both make claims about the nature of moral judgments that fit well with our ordinary experiences in dealing with moral issues, both also lead to consequences which conflict with our ordinary moral sentiments, and neither appears able to resolve our moral differences. In this section we will present an alternative way of approaching moral judgments, showing how the ideas of good reasoning that we have already developed in preceding chapters can help us to support our moral judgments and become better moral reasoners.

Part of the difficulty in understanding the nature of moral judgments comes from a mistaken belief, encouraged by a misunderstanding of the Hume passage with which this chapter begins, that there are two different kinds of statements which are always distinguishable from one another, statements about matters of fact and statements about values. This distinction, if we examine it closely, collapses under scrutiny and cannot be maintained.

Factual statements, as we pointed out in Chapter 2, **are simply those statements which have been found to be the most warranted.** Factual statements are statements that are rarely questioned, statements for which support is rarely demanded. The usage "statements about matters of fact" tends to imply, however, that "matters of fact" are somehow separate from our statements about them. While the world itself is not identical with our statements about it or even with our perceptions of it, we have seen that the world is describable in a variety of ways, no one of which can be said to be the single correct description. What we can say is that some descriptions are more **warranted** than others and that some descriptions are **better** than others. We warrant a statement or show that it is a better description than another statement by supporting it with **other** statements.

For example, to call an apple "red" (usually called "fact") is much the same as calling an apple "good" (usually considered "value"). Both statements could be warranted or unwarranted and the warranting takes place in much the same way. We warrant "This apple is red" generally by comparing it with other red things. We warrant "This apple is good" by comparing it with other tasty things or perhaps with other nutritious things. Like detectives in the courtroom, we offer evidence to support our description, and this is the only proof we can offer. Whether others accept our description sometimes depends on how well we have supported it with other statements, other times on how well it is seen to work, and most of the time it depends on both.

It is important to remember that even scientific statements do not rest on neutral descriptions of experience. The scientist, like the rest of us, uses a theory or story to organize the myriad of traces in the world into a pattern that can be described and tested. Hence, the statements he chooses to describe the objective features of the world rest on certain assumptions. Some of these assumptions are about the efficacy of inductive reasoning and making causal claims, some are about the warrant for the theoretical framework from which the scientist works, and some are "value loaded," like the assumption that simple theories and mathematically elegant formulas are better than complex and untidy ones. Thus even in science, the human enterprise thought to be the most value neutral, we are often faced with alternative descriptions of the objective features of the world (like the sex life of whiptail lizards).

A distinction which can be drawn, although not in every case, is the distinction between moral and non-moral statements. Some statements are clearly non-moral, for example, "The cat is on the mat." Some statements are clearly moral, for example, "It is wrong to steal." Some statements, however, do not fall neatly into one category or the other. Consider, for example, the statement, "John is anemic." Most people would think that it is not good to be anemic. Most people would not choose to be anemic. Although *anemic* refers to a non-moral feature of the world, namely, a quantitatively low hemoglobin level in the blood, it also carries evaluative content. It is not a value-neutral word. Many putatively descriptive words are like *anemic*. They are both descriptive and evaluative. Statements about the non-moral features of the world and statements about values, then, are best thought of as being on a continuum. Some statements are clearly at one end of the continuum, and some are clearly at the other. But there is also a grey area between the two ends where many statements about the world belong.

What this means is that the fact/value distinction that has bothered many people, including many philosophers, is not a distinction which can be clearly drawn. It certainly cannot be drawn in every case. Some statements about the world have both descriptive and evaluative content. Even scientific statements, while usually on the descriptive end of the continuum, rest in part on assumptions of value, namely the aesthetic values of beauty and simplicity and the rational values of coherence and consistency. While there is a difference between "is" statements and "ought" statements, when the difference between them is seen as a continuum, it can be seen as much more a difference of degree, not a difference of kind. Hence, it is reasonable to support moral statements in the same way that statements about the non-moral features of the world are supported—by warranting them with other statements. Moreover, just as there are factual statements about the non-moral features of the world (i.e., statements that have been found to be the most warranted and for which support is rarely demanded), so, too, there are moral factual statements, that is, moral statements that are rarely questioned.

To support moral statements, then, we need to offer evidence for them in the same way we support non-moral statements with evidence. We use reason and descriptions of our experience. We use a story (a theory) to guide our selection of evidence, and we give it a pattern that makes sense in relation to our background knowledge and the background knowledge of the people with whom we are reasoning. Some of the statements we offer in support of our moral claims will be statements about non-moral features of the world, and some will be statements with moral content.

If we are reasoning inductively (with probability), and not deductively (with necessity), there is no logical problem in offering (only) non-moral statements in support of moral ones. If we are reasoning deductively, however, we must have at least one moral statement among our premises to derive a moral statement as our conclusion. This is what Hume means in the passage that introduces this section. From a formal logic point of view, we cannot draw an "ought" statement as the conclusion of an argument with only "is" premises. There is no logical error, however, in drawing a moral statement as the conclusion of a formal argument with a combination of moral and non-moral premises. For example, "People ought not to take other people's property. Mary is taking Paul's book. Therefore, Mary's act is wrong." Of course, the first premise of this argument is a moral prescription with which everyone may not agree. A Marxist might disagree, for instance. A strict Marxist believes that no one should own private property or that only small items should be privately held.

It is harder to have moral "facts" than it is to have non-moral "facts" because there is less agreement about prescriptive statements like these. There are no obvious non-moral features of the world that one can point to support them, no scientific instruments to provide quantitative results that can be used as evidence. But we must be careful not to overstate the difference between statements about the non-moral features of the world and moral statements. The **success of the vocabulary we use in both moral and non-moral statements depends upon the consensus of language users for its efficacy.** For example, to know the meaning of the words *midnight blue* is to be able to use it in the appropriate circumstances, that is, at the times when other English speakers would choose to use the words *midnight blue*. The situation is the same when using moral words like *good* and *right*. To know the meaning of these words is to be able to use them in circumstances in which other language users would use them. If someone told you that *right* refers to all acts done east of the Mississippi and *wrong* refers to all acts performed west of the Mississippi, you would say that that person does not know the language, that the person does not know the meaning of the words *right* and *wrong*.[4]

Note, this does not mean that the consensus of the members of the language speakers is the *defining* characteristic of *good* and *bad* or *right* and *wrong*. Just as it is possible for a group of language users to make a mistake about the non-moral features

---

[4]This excellent example comes from Sam Gorovitz. (*Doctors Dilemmas,* Macmillan, 1982).

of the world, it is also possible for them to be mistaken in a particular moral judgment. For example, we have already seen how people in the fifteenth century thought
the sun went around the earth. Today we believe that the earth goes around the sun
and call their belief a mistake. Similarly, until the Civil War it was the consensus in
the American south that one person could own another person as private property.
Today Americans, north and south, see slavery as immoral and call this earlier view
a mistake. (We will have more to say about what it is for a moral view to be mistaken
in Chapter 13.)

Let's look at how the consensus of language users functions in the example of
the general and the serf boy. There are obviously more serfs than generals in the assembled group, so one might think that the consensus of the language users present
would support the mother's belief that the punishment is too harsh and, therefore,
conclude that the general's action is morally wrong. What is right or wrong in a particular case, however, is not something that can be determined in isolation. Rather, our
judgments of right and wrong—just like our judgments of blue and black—must fit in
with other beliefs we hold about the world. Each of our moral pronouncements entails
a wide-ranging set of beliefs about the world, including non-moral and moral beliefs.
In the example above about Mary's taking of Paul's book, for instance, the belief that
Mary's action is wrong entails, among other things, belief that there is such a thing as
private property and that books are appropriate kinds of private property. We could
imagine a world where this is not the case. In a world where books are scarce, for
instance, all books might be considered communal property to be held in libraries for
the benefit of the few scholars able to read them—as in the Middle Ages.

In the example of the general and the serfs, there is an interesting ambiguity
about what is property. Moreover, it is not clear whether the general and his serfs
form a community of language users or not. It is highly likely that the general regards
"his" serfs as private property, much like his hunting dogs, and believes that he has
command over them, including the right to do with them as he sees fit. The serfs,
given their upbringing and experience, may not disagree with him. That is, they may
see their fate as being at the mercy and whim of famous old generals whose land they
work. After all, they watch without remonstrance as the boy is pursued and torn apart.
We readers, on the other hand, are a different community of language users and do
not see the serf boy as the general's property. We have such a different world view
from that of the general that we would probably have a hard time trying to convince
him that his act is wrong. But surely we would have to try. The only way we could
convince him would be by using language, trying to connect our world view with his.
Of course, we could use fists or a weapon but using these tools of persuasion would
be inconsistent with our own world view. Among contemporary American language
users it would probably be fairly easy to warrant the view that the general's action is
unjust, so much so that this judgment might be regarded as a moral "fact."

It is important to note that all language, moral and non-moral, has borderline
cases. A borderline case is one where it is not clear which description is the most appropriate, and people well versed in the language may disagree about the proper use
of the language. The words *midnight blue* are a good example of descriptive words
that readily admit of borderline cases. Whether the car is blue, black, or midnight
blue is not always decidable. Similarly, there are borderline cases in the use of moral

language. People who know the language, who are morally normal (not perverse), and who share similar world views, may still disagree about the morally best course of action in some circumstances. Capital punishment is a moral issue of this sort. On the other hand, it is morally wrong to boil babies for bouillon is a moral statement for which support is rarely demanded.[5] It can be regarded as a factual moral statement.

Summary

Reasoning about moral values is like reasoning about the non-moral features of the world. These are not two different types of reasoning or reasoning about two different types of statements. While some statements are clearly about non-moral features of experience, many of the statements which describe our experience presuppose implicit value assumptions (as in the fundamental assumptions of science), and many statements which describe non-moral features of the world are not value neutral (e.g., "anemic"). It is a matter of degree, not a difference in kind. Some statements belong on one end of the descriptive-prescriptive continuum, for example, "The cat is on the mat," and some statements belong on the other end of the continuum, for example, "Stealing is wrong." What we have seen is that the so-called fact/value distinction is a distinction which does not reflect our actual language usage and which, consequently, does not change the nature of good critical thinking and reasoning whether we are reasoning about moral matters or about the non-moral features of the world.

Most statements, either about the non-moral features of the world or about moral values, are not self-warranting nor are they warranted individually. Each statement is part of a larger world view and is warranted by offering other statements from reason or experience. Some statements, moral and non-moral, have come to be accepted as factual. These are statements for which warrant is rarely sought. These are statements which are rarely questioned. All statements, moral and non-moral, are uttered within a community of language users who are the arbiters of that language. Sometimes, the community will not agree about a particular usage. Perhaps there is no community or the case is a borderline case where knowledgeable, well-meaning people will differ. Sometimes, the community makes a mistake which it later admits and corrects. Like beliefs about the non-moral features of the world—which are usually the product of inductive reasoning, not deductive reasoning—beliefs about values are not fixed but change over time both on the community level and on the individual level. Some beliefs are more fundamental than others and thus are changed, if at all, more slowly and with reluctance. Some beliefs are very peripheral and are readily changed. In the United States, for example, it would take the equivalent of a Copernican Revolution to change our fundamental beliefs about the inviolability of private property, while beliefs about the immoral or amoral nature of alcohol consumption have fluctuated over time.

Thus, the skills we need to critically evaluate statements about the non-moral features of the world and moral statements are the same. These are the skills that enable us to reason together so that we can enjoy life with friends and have pleasant

---

[5]Another good Sam Gorovitz example!

experiences and avoid intractable differences of opinion about moral matters. To reason together we need to be open to the world around us so that we are aware of traces, see patterns, and continually increase the storehouse of background knowledge we bring to experience. We need to be aware of the limits of the evidence for our beliefs, both moral and non-moral, so that we are willing continually to test those beliefs against present and future experience. **Most of all, we need to make the effort that reasoning together requires. Moral arguments try our patience even more than arguments about the nature of experience, but they also lead to more hostile consequences if the participants are unwilling to make the effort to reason together.**

Exercises

12–I

1. Why is there no sharp line of demarcation between moral matters and non-moral matters?
2. List 10 (or more) words like *anemia* that describe non-moral features of the world which also would generally be considered value loaded.
3. Can you think of any historical examples of Copernican-like changes in moral beliefs?
4. What arguments could you present to the general in Dostoevsky's story to try to persuade him not to kill the serf boy? Hint: Are there potential beliefs in his world view that might be in conflict with his choice of punishment?
5. What kinds of non-moral features of the world do **you** think are most important in making moral judgments or in reasoning about moral values?

12–II

1. What are the fundamental beliefs and differences in world view that make the abortion issue such an intractable one in the United States?
2. Some very strict Islamic courts have sentenced women accused of adultery to death by stoning. Most Americans find this punishment abhorrent and immoral. Are there any possibilities for resolving such large differences of moral viewpoint?
3. Why can *right* not be defined as "an act performed east of the Mississippi" and *wrong* defined as "an act performed west of the Mississippi"?
4. How much open-mindedness, when it comes to moral arguments, can one allow?

13

Reasoning About Good and Bad

MAKING MORAL DECISIONS

It is important to realize that when we reason about values, we do not reason about them in isolation from other beliefs. Our moral beliefs, like our non-moral beliefs, are part of a larger world view which each of us brings to experience. Within this world view there are beliefs which we consider to be factual—that is, we rarely question them—and there are beliefs for which we would like more evidence. There are also beliefs which we cannot clearly classify as moral or non-moral. They have both evaluative and descriptive content. **However, none of our beliefs—no matter now factual—stand alone.** Even the belief you have that you are presently reading this text at a certain time, on a certain day of the week, in a certain place is part of a larger web of beliefs—about the nature of reading, of what it is for something to be a text, and even who, or what, you think you are.

Similarly, what we think is good, bad, right, wrong, beautiful, ugly is dependent on other beliefs we hold about what there is in the world, about human nature, and about what we can know about these things. For instance, if you believed that flowers when picked feel excruciating pain—pain of the same sort you would feel if someone cut off your arm—you would probably have strong moral beliefs about the immorality of picking flowers. Since most people don't have such beliefs about flowers, picking a flower is not generally thought to involve us in a moral problem. There is less agreement, however, when it comes to the sentience of animals, especially the sentience of what are called the higher order animals. It is extremely likely that these animals do feel pain (and possibly other emotions of the sorts that humans feel), and so many people think that it is immoral to kill such animals for human consumption. People who choose vegetarianism on moral grounds do so because they have a world view that includes beliefs they consider factual about the sentience of higher order animals.

In Chapter 12, we emphasized the importance of reasoning together about values. When we reason about values, however, we must look at the larger world view that those moral values are part of. Some of most heated and violent moral disagreements rest on differences of belief about the non-moral features of the world rather than on differences of values. Our moral dialogues must include this larger world picture if we are to be able to reason together about moral values.

What can we say about resolving the moral problems or puzzles we all face as individuals? Are there any insights to be gained from the description of moral reasoning offered here? First, it should be clear that not all moral decisions fall into the category of moral problems. Many of our moral beliefs are beliefs we rarely if ever question. We consider them moral facts. That it is wrong to kill another person other than in self-defense, for example, would be such a belief for most of us. Moral beliefs that we consider factual are beliefs that fit in well with other things we believe, notably with our world view and our background knowledge. They are part of a larger story which we tell about what it is to be a human being and the place of human beings in the universe. If questioned, we could give some reasons or an argument why one should not kill except in self-defense, but this belief is so fundamental in our world view that it is rarely questioned. It is like the Copernican view of the earth's rotation around the sun. We consider it factual and in need of no further warrant. It is important, however, to remember what we learned from our study of scientific reasoning above, namely, no matter how well entrenched a scientific belief is, it can only be well-confirmed but not "proven." We are continually testing that belief against experience. The same is true for moral beliefs.

You may have noticed, for instance, that our well-entrenched belief that it is wrong to kill another person except in self-defense is beginning to be questioned because of recent advances in medicine. Because modern medicine has found so many ways of keeping the human body functioning at least at a minimal level, some people are beginning to ask whether "mercy killing" to end pain and suffering might also be an exception to the prohibition against killing. In this case, changes in technology have brought about changes in the background knowledge we bring to our experience. They make us reconsider the meaning of what death is and when death comes to a person. They may even lead to changes in fundamental beliefs about what it is to be a person.

Moral beliefs that are considered morally factual can also be troublesome when we seek to apply them to specific cases. We are often not so sure whether this or that instance of killing is in self-defense. For example, if an intruder enters your house or apartment in the middle of the night and is discovered putting your possessions into a bag, are you justified in shooting that intruder? How big does the threat to your life have to be to justify shooting the intruder and possibly killing him?

Still more troublesome, and unfortunately quite common in our lives, is the kind of moral problem where we must choose between two evident goods or two obvious bads ("the lesser of two evils"). Many people believe, or at least hope, that if they wait long enough and think "harder" about a moral dilemma a *perfect* solution to the problem will arise. This is rarely the case. Life does not present us with perfect solutions. Nor does it present us with only one right solution. There may be several morally justifiable solutions to a moral problem. **One choice, however, could be better than another.** Also, life does not allow us to wait. Not to choose is to choose because not choosing is a choice for the status quo.

To resolve these problems of moral reasoning we need good reasoning skills, the same good reasoning skills we use when dealing with non-moral matters. Like all good reasoning, moral reasoning is best when conducted as an **open dialogue**. This dialogue is often just with yourself because ethical issues are personal and individual, but it can also include others. However, others are not responsible for our moral decisions; only we are. We are the ones who decide how much to credit the advice of others. This open dialogue needs to be continual and not confined to situations of moral deliberation. In a moral emergency (when the intruder is on your doorstep), there may be no time for discussion. Also, it should be noted that too much talk can be a way of not deciding, of choosing not to choose. It is important to think and talk about possible moral dilemmas before being faced with them.

Background knowledge is also important in making moral decisions. We have already seen the importance of background knowledge in good reasoning. The larger our store of background knowledge, the better judgments we will be able to make. Background knowledge will be particularly helpful in determining the right course of action in a specific situation. This is because part of the success of our decision will rest on the strengths of our generalizations, analogies, and causal inferences. Our background knowledge is our biggest help in anticipating the possible consequences of our actions. This is not to suggest, however, that resolving a moral problem is simply a function of knowledge. Knowing more does not make the *moral* issue go away. One still has to choose. Knowledge of the risk factors in a situation, for example, does not determine how much risk is morally acceptable.

We also need to be **open to the world**. Our moral beliefs, like our non-moral beliefs, cannot be proven, only warranted or disconfirmed; we need to be aware of the limitations of the evidence we have for our beliefs and the unproven assumptions of our world view. Therefore, we need to be ready to revise our moral beliefs in light of new information, such as the changes in modern medicine. And we need to be ready to change our behavior in light of the successes and failures of past decisions. While we are responsible for our past moral mistakes, we do not have to repeat them. We are not bound by them. Moral reasoning, like non-moral reasoning, is open ended. We test our expectations against future experiences and adjust our background knowledge and our moral reasoning accordingly.

Good reasoning of the kind we have described here is important for ethical decisions from both the objectivist and the subjectivist viewpoints. From the objectivist point of view, good reasoning helps us *discover* the right moral behavior and avoid mistakes. When we do make mistakes, it helps us recognize them and correct them. While a staunch subjectivist holds that every choice we make is the right choice as long as it results from a considered judgment, good reasoning is important for the subjectivist because it helps us *coordinate* our goals and develop a *consistent* self. It enables to us to avoid choices which would thwart us from the things we as individuals think are important for us. On both accounts, the objectivist and subjectivist, reason helps us continue the **story** of who we are and what we think is valuable. Ethical decisions are difficult because they are complex and because, in deciding, we are deciding who we are. We are making ourselves. It's a daunting task and no one can do it for us. **It takes a lot of effort.**

REASONABLE OBJECTIVISM
AND REASONABLE SUBJECTIVISM

The passage from Dostoevsky in the last chapter has probably left you with some confusion about how moral beliefs can be supported. You would like to argue with the general about the morality of his actions. To help you get started in developing your own moral arguments, we will look at two examples of successful moral reasoning, one from Immanuel Kant and one from Jean-Paul Sartre. Both of these readings are classic examples of moral reasoning. They clearly set out their assumptions, or premises, and then show how, if one accepts those assumptions, certain conclusions follow. They have been very influential in our collective understanding of our moral experiences. It is important to observe as you read the selections that the reasoning is not different in kind from reasoning about non-moral issues.

These two readings were chosen to illustrate the interconnectedness of moral and non-moral beliefs in a larger world view. The first reading is from Kant's famous work on ethics, *Grounding for the Metaphysics of Morals.* This short excerpt can only give you a small piece of the very powerful reasoning that Kant uses to support his moral beliefs. You may find the style of reasoning a little different from what you are used to. Kant is trying to develop a moral theory which can be used in all moral situations much as a mathematical formula might be used. Try to follow his reasoning, not just his conclusions. You will find it amply rewarding, and you will probably find yourself agreeing with him.

Actions speak louder than words?

The second reading, from the French philosopher Sartre, is part of a lecture that he gave in 1946. Clearly Sartre has a very different world view from Kant's. The vocabulary and the issues of concern are very different. Sartre, who lived through the Nazi invasion of France and who spent time as a POW and later as a member of the French Resistance, is concerned primarily with human actions and not with deliberations about what is right. As you read this very powerful piece about human responsibility, think about Sartre's view of moral decision making and the very different concerns he has from those of Kant.

GROUNDING FOR THE METAPHYSICS OF MORALS

Immanuel Kant

There is no possibility of thinking of anything at all in the world, or even out of it, which can be regarded as good without qualification, except a *good will*. Intelligence, wit, judgment, and whatever talents of the mind one might want to name are doubtless in many respects good and desirable, as are such qualities of temperament as courage, resolution, perseverance. But they can also become extremely bad and harmful if the will, which is to make use of these gifts of nature and which in its special constitution is called character, is not good. The same holds with gifts of fortune; power, riches, honor, even health, and that complete well-being and contentment with one's condition which is called happiness make for pride and often hereby even arrogance, unless there is a good will to correct their influence on the mind and herewith also to rectify the whole principle of action and make it universally comfortable to its end. The sight of a being who is not graced by any touch of a pure and good will but who yet enjoys an uninterrupted prosperity can never delight a rational and impartial spectator. Thus a good will seems to constitute the indispensable condition of being even worthy of happiness.

Some qualities are even conducive to this good will itself and can facilitate its work. Nevertheless, they have no intrinsic unconditional worth; but they always presuppose, rather, a good will, which restricts the high esteem in which they are otherwise rightly held, and does not permit them to be regarded as absolutely good. Moderation in emotions and passions, self-control, and calm deliberation are not only good in many respects but even seem to constitute part of the intrinsic worth of a person. But they are far from being rightly called good without qualification (however unconditionally they were commended by the ancients). For without the principles of a good will, they can become extremely bad; the coolness of a villain makes him not only much more dangerous but also immediately more abominable in our eyes than he would have been regarded by us without it.

A good will is good not because of what it effects or accomplishes, nor because of its fitness to attain some proposed end; it is good only through its willing, i.e., it is good in itself.

The concept of a will estimable in itself and good without regard to any further end must now be developed. This concept already dwells in the natural sound understanding and needs not so much to be taught as merely to be elucidated. It always holds first place in estimating the total worth of our actions and constitutes the condition of all the rest. Therefore, we shall take up the concept of *duty*, which includes that of a good will, though with certain subjective restrictions and hindrances, which far from hiding a good will or rendering it unrecognizable, rather bring it out by contrast and make it shine forth more brightly.

I here omit all actions already recognized as contrary to duty, even though they may be useful for this or that end; for in the case of these the question does not arise at all as to whether they might be done from duty, since they even conflict with duty. I also set aside those actions which are really in accordance with duty, yet to which men have no immediate inclination, but perform them because they are impelled thereto by some other inclination. For in this [second] case to decide whether the action which is in accord with duty has been done from duty or from some selfish purpose is easy. This difference is far more difficult to note in the [third] case where the action accords with duty and the subject has in addition an immediate inclination to do the action. For example, that a dealer should not overcharge an inexperienced purchaser certainly accords with duty; and where there is much commerce, the prudent merchant does not overcharge but keeps to a fixed price for everyone in general, so that a child may buy from him just as well as everyone else may. Thus customers are honestly served, but this is not nearly enough for making us believe that the merchant has acted this way from duty and from principles of honesty; his own advantage required him to do it. He cannot, however, be assumed to have in addition [as in the third case] an immediate inclination toward his buyers, causing him, as it were, out of love to give no one as far as price is concerned any advantage over another. Hence the action was done neither from duty nor from immediate inclination, but merely for a selfish purpose.

On the other hand, to preserve one's life is a duty; and, furthermore, everyone has also an immediate inclination to do so. But on this account the often anxious care taken by most men for it has no intrinsic worth, and the maxim of their action has no moral content. They preserve their lives, to be sure, in accordance with duty, but not from duty. On the other hand, if adversity and hopeless sorrow have completely taken away the taste for life, if an unfortunate man, strong in soul and more indignant at his fate than despondent or dejected, wishes for death and yet preserves his life without loving it—not from inclination or fear, but from duty—then his maxim indeed has a moral content.

To be beneficent where one can is a duty; and besides this, there are many persons who are so sympathetically constituted that, without any further motive of vanity or self-interest, they find an inner pleasure in spreading joy around them and can rejoice in the satisfaction of others as their own work. But I maintain that in such a case an action of this kind, however dutiful and amiable it may be, has nevertheless no true moral worth. It is on a level with such actions as arise from other inclinations, e.g., the inclination for honor, which if fortunately directed to what is in fact beneficial and accords with duty and is thus honorable, deserves praise and encouragement, but not esteem; for its maxim lacks the moral content of an action done not from inclination but from duty. . . .

Thus the moral worth of an action does not lie in the effect expected from it nor in any principle of action that needs to borrow its motive from this expected effect. For all these effects (agreeableness of one's condition and even the furtherance of other people's happiness) could have been brought about also through other causes and would not have required the will of a rational being, in which the highest and unconditioned good can alone be found. Therefore, the pre-eminent good which is called moral can consist in nothing but the representation of the law in itself, and such a representation can admittedly be found only in a rational being insofar as this representation, and not some expected effect, is the determining ground of the will. This good is already present in the person who acts according to this representation, and such good need not be awaited merely from the effect.

But what sort of law can that be the thought of which must determine the will without reference to any expected effect, so that the will can be called absolutely good without qualification? Since I have deprived the will of every impulse that might arise for it from obeying any particular law, there is nothing left to serve the will as principle except the universal conformity of its actions to law as such, i.e., I should never act except in such a way that I can also will that my maxim should become a universal law. Here mere conformity to law as such (without having as its basis any law determining particular actions) serves the will as principle and must so serve it if duty is not to be a vain delusion and a chimerical concept. The ordinary reason of mankind in its practical judgments agrees completely with this, and always has in view the aforementioned principle.

For example, take this question. When I am in distress, may I make a promise with the intention of not keeping it? I readily distinguish here the two meanings which the question may have; whether making a false promise conforms with prudence or with duty. Doubtless the former can often be the case. Indeed I clearly see that escape from some present difficulty by means of such a promise is not enough. In addition I must carefully consider whether from this lie there may later arise far greater inconvenience for me than from what I now try to escape. Furthermore, the consequences of my false promise are not easy to foresee, even with all my supposed cunning; loss of confidence in me might prove to be far more disadvantageous than the misfortune which I now try to avoid. The more prudent way might be to act according to a universal maxim and to make it a habit not to promise anything without intending to keep it. But that such a maxim is, nevertheless, always based on nothing but a fear of consequences becomes clear to me at once. To be truthful from duty is, however, quite different from being truthful from fear of disadvantageous consequences; in the first case the concept of the action itself contains a law for me, while in the second I must first look around elsewhere to see what are the results for me that might be connected with the action. For to deviate from the principle of duty is quite certainly bad; but to abandon my maxim of prudence can often be very advantageous for me, though to abide by it is certainly safer. The most direct and infallible way, however, to answer the question as to whether a lying promise accords with duty is to ask myself whether I would really be content if my maxim (of extricating myself from difficulty by means of a false promise) were to hold as a universal law for myself as well as for others, and could I really say to myself that everyone may promise falsely when he finds himself in a difficulty from which he can find no other way to extricate himself. Then I immediately become aware that I can indeed will the lie but can not at all will a universal law to lie. For by such a law there would really be no promises at all, since in vain would my willing future actions be professed to other people who would not believe what I professed, or if they over-hastily did believe, then they would pay me back in like coin. Therefore, my maxim would necessarily destroy itself just as soon as it was made a universal law.

Therefore, I need no far-reaching acuteness to discern what I have to do in order that my will may be morally good. Inexperienced in the course of the world and incapable of being prepared for all its contingencies, I only ask myself whether I can also will that my maxim should become a universal law. If not, then the maxim must be rejected, not because of any disadvantage accruing to me or even to others, but because it cannot be fitting as a principle in a possible legislation of universal law, and reason exacts from me immediate respect for such legislation.

EXISTENTIALISM IS A HUMANISM

Jean-Paul Sartre

As an example by which you may the better understand . . . [human responsibility], I will refer to the case of a pupil of mine, who sought me out in the following circumstances. His father was quarreling with his mother and was also inclined to be a "collaborator"; his elder brother had been killed in the German offensive of 1940 and this young man, with a sentiment somewhat primitive but generous, burned to avenge him. His mother was living alone with him, deeply afflicted by the semi-treason of his father and by the death of her eldest son, and her one consolation was in this young man. But he, at this moment, had the choice between going to England to join the Free French Forces or of staying near his mother and helping her to live. He fully realized that this woman lived only for him and that his disappearance—or perhaps his death— would plunge her into despair. He also realized that, concretely and in fact, every action he performed on his mother's behalf would be sure of effect in the sense of aiding her to live, whereas anything he did in order to go and fight would be an ambiguous action which might vanish like water into sand and serve no purpose. For instance, to set out for England he would have to wait indefinitely in a Spanish camp on the way through Spain; or, on arriving in England or in Algiers he might be put into an office to fill up forms. Consequently, he found himself confronted by two very different modes of action; the one concrete, immediate, but directed towards only one individual; and the other an action addressed to an end infinitely greater, a national collectivity, but for that very reason ambiguous—and it might be frustrated on the way. At the same time, he was hesitating between two kinds of morality; on the one side the morality of sympathy, of personal devotion and, on the other side, a morality of wider scope but of more debatable validity. He had to choose between those two. What could help him to choose? Could the Christian doctrine? No. Christian doctrine says: Act with charity, love your neighbour, deny yourself for others, choose the way which is hardest, and so forth. But which is the harder road? To whom does one owe the more brotherly love, the patriot or the mother? Which is the more useful aim, the general one of fighting in and for the whole community, or the precise aim of helping one particular person to live? Who can give an answer to that *à priori?* No one. Nor is it given in any ethical scripture. The Kantian ethic says, Never regard another as a means, but always as an end. Very well; if I remain with my mother, I shall be regarding her as the end and not as a means: but by the same token I am in danger of treating as means those who are fighting on my behalf; and the converse is also true, that if I go to the aid of the combatants I shall be treating them as the end at the risk of treating my mother as a means.

If values are uncertain, if they are still too abstract to determine the particular, concrete case under consideration, nothing remains but to trust in our instincts. That is what this young man tried to do; and when I saw him he said, "In the end, it is feeling that counts; the direction in which it is really pushing me is the one I ought to choose. If I feel that I love my mother enough to sacrifice everything else for her—my will to be avenged, all my longings for action and adventure—then I stay with her. If, on the contrary, I feel that my love for her is not enough, I go." But how does one estimate the strength of a feeling? The value of his feeling for his mother was determined precisely by the fact that he was standing by her. I may say that I love a certain friend enough to sacrifice such or such a sum of money for him, but I cannot prove that unless I have done it. I may say, "I love my mother enough to remain with her," if actually I have remained with her. I can only estimate the strength of this affection if I have performed an action by which it is defined and ratified. But if I then appeal to this affection to justify my action, I find myself drawn into a vicious circle.

Moreover, as Gide has very well said, a sentiment which is play-acting and one which is vital are two things that are hardly distinguishable one from another. To decide that I love my mother by staying beside her, and to play a comedy the upshot of which is that I do so—these are nearly the same thing. In other words, feeling is formed by the deeds that one does; therefore I cannot consult it as a guide to action. And that is to say that I can neither seek within myself for an authentic impulse to action, nor can I expect, from some ethic, formulae that will enable me to act. You may say that the youth did, at least, go to a professor to ask for advice. But if you seek counsel—from a priest, for example—you have selected that priest; and at bottom you already knew, more or less, what he would advise. In other words, to choose an adviser is nevertheless to commit oneself by that choice. If you are a Christian, you will say, Consult a priest; but there are collaborationists, priests who are resisters and priests who wait for the tide to turn: which will you choose? Had this young man chosen a priest of the resistance, or one of the collaboration, he would have decided beforehand the kind of advice he was to receive. Similarly, in coming to me, he knew what advice I should give him, and I had but one reply to make. You are free, therefore choose— that is to say, invent. No rule of general morality can show you what you ought to do: no signs are vouchsafed in this world. The Catholics will reply, "Oh, but they are!" Very well; still, it is I myself, in every case, who have to interpret the signs. While I was imprisoned, I made the acquaintance of a somewhat remarkable man, a Jesuit, who had become a member of that order in the following manner. In his life he had suffered a succession of rather severe setbacks. His father had died when he was a child, leaving him in poverty, and he had been awarded a free scholarship in a religious institution, where he had been made continually to feel that he was accepted for charity's sake, and, in consequence, he had been denied several of those distinctions and honours which gratify children. Later, about the age of eighteen, he came to grief in a sentimental affair; and finally, at twenty-two—this was a trifle in itself, but it was the last drop that overflowed his cup—he failed in his military examination. This young man, then, could regard himself as a total failure: it was a sign—but a sign of what? He might have taken refuge in bitterness or despair. But he took it—very cleverly for him—as a sign that he was not intended for secular successes, and that only the attainments of religion, those of sanctity and of faith, were accessible to him. He interpreted his record as a message from God, and became a member of the Order. Who can doubt but that this decision as to the meaning of the sign was his, and his alone? One could have drawn quite different conclusions from such a series of reverses—as, for example, that he had better become a carpenter or a revolutionary. For the decipherment of the sign, however, he bears the entire responsibility. That is what "abandonment" implies, that we ourselves decide our being. And with this abandonment goes anguish.

As for "despair," the meaning of this expression is extremely simple. It merely means that we limit ourselves to a reliance upon that which is within our walls, or within the sum of the probabilities which render our action feasible. Whenever one wills anything, there are always these elements of probability. If I am counting upon a visit from a friend, who may be coming by train or by tram, I presuppose that the train will arrive at the appointed time, or that the tram will not be derailed. I remain in the realm of possibilities; but one does not rely upon any possibilities beyond those that are strictly concerned in one's action. Beyond the point at which the possibilities under consideration cease to affect my action, I ought to disinterest myself. For there is no God and no prevenient design, which can adapt the world and all its possibilities to my will. When Descartes said, "Conquer yourself rather than the world," what he meant was, at bottom, the same—that we should act without hope.

STUDY QUESTIONS

1. Are you surprised by Kant's claim that the only thing good in itself is a good will? Why? Why not?

2. What does it mean to say that something is good in itself?

3. How would you explain the difference Kant draws between doing an act *from* duty and doing an act *in accordance with* duty?

4. Why does Sartre refuse to give advice to his former student?

5. Human beings, according to Sartre, are given to anguish and despair. Can you see a brighter side to this human condition? Explain.

6. What moral assumptions do you see Kant making? What moral assumptions do you see Sartre making?

KANT

The selection from Kant which you have just read begins with one of the most well-known claims in the history of ethical thought, namely, that nothing ". . . can be regarded as good without qualification, except a *good will.*" While not everyone agrees with this statement, it is still a very powerful claim because of the boldness with which it is stated and because, as human beings, our ears perk up when we hear that something is an unqualified good. We would like to have or be, or at least be thought to have or be, that good. What could Kant possibly mean by a good will?

As the reading makes clear, Kant has something very specific in mind by "a good will." A will is good, according to Kant, if it acts *from* duty and not just *in accordance with* duty. We begin to see that the kind of *good* that Kant is talking about is moral good, not other goods like pleasant surroundings, love of friends, or personal content-ment. All of these other "goods" are worth having, says Kant, but as rational beings we would have to admit that even if a person has all these other goods, without a good will something is missing. A murderer who is intelligent, brave, and wealthy is just a more formidable murderer. We do not, and cannot, grant her our highest esteem.

And, indeed, this is familiar to all of us. We all know people who seem "to have it all" but whom we are not willing to call good, because they lack moral good. Similarly, probably all of us have asked ourselves at least once after someone has done something nice for us, "Did she really mean it or did she expect to get something out of it for herself?" Somehow, if the person does an act which accomplishes a desir-able end but does the act for personal gain, that doesn't seem as worthy to us as the same act done because it was the right thing to do—and for no other reason. Acts done because they are the right things to do are what Kant means by acts done from duty. Kant believes that he is making clear what all of us intend when we say that an act is good or that a person is good; that is, we mean that the act was done from duty or the person acted from duty.

The next step of Kant's reasoning is just as you might guess. If to be good is to act from duty, then we need to know what it is to act from duty. When we act from duty, says Kant, we do not act from inclination or from selfishness. Sometimes incli-nation (or desire) and selfishness may lead us to do the same act that duty demands of us (i.e., we act in accordance with duty)—but not always, so they are not possible guides in moral action. Moral action is too important to leave to chance. A good will chooses what it chooses primarily because it believes the act to be good.

This means, according to Kant, that the will must be determined by a rule or "law" which expresses the duty of any rational being. The most general law—which serves as the basic principle of duty—is that "I should never act except in such a way that I can also will that my maxim should become a universal law." This is the famous *categorical imperative* of Kant. By a "maxim" Kant means the specific principle that applies to the case at hand, such as "I ought to preserve my life" or "I ought not to make a promise I do not intend to keep."

What Kant is saying is that moral acts are acts done from duty, and acts done from duty are acts which are done on the basis of maxims that rational beings could will to be universal laws. It would be inconsistent for a rational being to will that he do something he would not will every other rational being to do. For example, he could not will that everyone lie or make false promises because of what would happen to the whole institution of talking to other people or contracting in some way about future acts if everyone lied! Kant's point is not that his lying could lead to bad consequences like destroying the institution of promising (Kant thinks the morality of an act should not rest on the consequences of the act), but rather that he is putting his will in conflict with itself. That is, he is both willing that promising be universal law and not willing that promising be a universal law, namely, in this case. Such self-contradiction is inconsistent with his rational nature as a human being.

Let us review Kant's reasoning. A good person is a person who wills an action primarily because she believes that action to be her duty. Her duty comes from the nature of human beings as rational creatures, and her duty is that she should act in conformity with a maxim which can be universalized for all other rational beings without contradiction. This categorical imperative is like a mathematical formula which can be used to determine one's duty in a particular situation. Kant does not simply claim that certain acts are right and others wrong, but rather gives us careful and clear arguments to support his thesis about the nature of a good will.

Although much has been written about how to interpret this moral reasoning of Kant, this short synopsis is sufficient for us to see that Kant can be considered as a moral objectivist, although perhaps an unusual one, who rests morality on what he considers an objective feature of the world. He believes that there is a procedure for discovering the right answer about what to do in a moral situation, and this procedure is an objective feature of a world inhabited by rational beings. This does not mean, however, that we will not make moral mistakes or not have misunderstandings and disagreements about how to apply this procedure or formula. Even though there are right answers, we may not always be able to uncover them. Again, morality is similar to mathematics. Just because we have a mathematical formula to resolve a particular puzzle does not mean that we will not make mistakes or have disagreements about the proper use of that formula.

Kant's account of what it is for an act to be morally good, then, gives us a way to reason together about what acts are morally good. Could such reasoning be used to persuade Dostoevsky's wealthy landowner not to kill the offending serf boy? Certainly. Would it be successful in persuading him? Perhaps—but perhaps not.

Kant's reasoning in the *Grounding* goes on to show that "man and, in general, every rational being exists as an end in himself and not merely as a means to be arbitrarily used by this or that will." Kant reasons that since each of us regards herself as an end, we would put our wills in contradiction with themselves if we failed to recognize that all other rational beings should likewise be treated as ends. Clearly bad actions follow, for Kant, when we make exceptions of ourselves. Then we are acting on the basis of an unjustifiable double standard.

One might use this reasoning and its conclusion to try to persuade the general that the boy is an end in himself who has "absolute worth" (Kant's terminology), and therefore he should not be killed as a means to some end like setting an example to others or giving vent to (the general's) anger. We can guess that the general might respond that the boy, being merely a serf, is less than a rational being. One might try to reason further with the general, showing him that he is being inconsistent, on the one hand arguing that the boy is morally responsible for his act, and therefore a rational human being, and, on the other, that the boy is not a rational being and therefore can be used as a means to an end. Of course, whether or not the general is persuaded by this argument depends on many factors. Most of all, it depends on whether he is willing to listen to any moral argument at all. Some people will not. They are called *dogmatists*. We will have more to say about dogmatists in the next chapter. The main point we want to make here is that there are good reasons which can be offered in support of a moral point of view. Reasoning—good reasoning—can be used to support our moral beliefs. We should treat moral disagreements the same way we treat disagreements about who is going to win the next Presidential election or whether Shakespeare is the author of a poem. We gather evidence from our experience, and we present it in as cogent a form as we can.

We sometimes fail to persuade other people in moral arguments because they begin from very different assumptions; they have very different world views from ours. For instance, you yourself may or may not be convinced by Kant's argument that moral acts are acts done primarily because a person believes they are the right things to do. Kant does have a particular world view which allows him to make certain assumptions in developing his ethical theory. You may not share that world view. Let's take a look at some of those assumptions.

One of Kant's important assumptions is about what it is to be a human being. We have seen that, according to Kant, humans are rational beings (if not abnormal) and have a will which chooses a course of action. Our rationality is our essential feature. It is what makes us different from other things in the world. Our reason gives us our special worth and our dignity (as ends), and it also gives us freedom to act from reason and not from inclination or desire. Notice that we cannot act from duty, which is to act from the universal law given by reason, if we are beings whose wills can only act from inclination. Although these ideas probably have some familiarity for us, certainly not everyone shares Kant's world view that human beings have a special nature because of their rationality and that their wills are free to determine themselves according to laws given by reason alone.

This is not to diminish Kant's powerful argument for his moral point of view but only to point out that disagreements about specific moral issues may have their roots in an individual's larger world view and the assumptions which are part of that world view. The situation is not unlike what we saw earlier when we talked about differences of background knowledge and how those differences influence what we experience. Our world view includes our background knowledge, but it also includes assumptions which most people do not consider knowledge. These assumptions are sometimes so fundamental that we would not even think of offering evidence to support them. For instance, whether a person sees human beings as creatures with individual souls (a traditional Western view), or as parts of a common world soul (a traditional Eastern view), or as machines without souls (a modern Western view) would be an important assumption within a person's world view. Background knowledge, on the other hand, is much more specific and is generally supported with evidence and argument. The various schools of Western psychology (Freudian, Skinnerian, Gestalt, etc.) might be part of a person's background knowledge.

Most of us assume that the people with whom we are having a dialogue share much the same world view that we do. If they are our friends and neighbors, this is not a bad assumption to make. We are less surprised when our friends have different background knowledge from ours. We know that our friends have not had all the same experiences that we have had. They may have studied economics while we studied chemistry, and so on. When we disagree with someone, we need to find out where the differences lie. We have a better chance of working out our differences and coming to an agreement if we do. However, it is not always so important to distinguish world view from background knowledge. What is important is that you realize that *there is a difference between them* and are aware of the important roles they both play in both our moral and non-normal discourse.

Kant is very helpful as a philosopher because he tells us a lot about his world view. This makes it easier for us to decide whether we agree with him or not. Probably many people agree with him that human beings have an essential nature which is their rationality. This agreement makes Kant's claims about acting from duty very persuasive. Our next philosopher, however, has quite a different world view, as you have already noticed from your reading.

SARTRE

According to Sartre, most moral decisions are like the one faced by the student in the passage you read. Seldom are moral choices between some obvious good and some obvious bad. Indeed, it is often the case that by choosing one good, we are prevented from doing something else good. We are forced to choose between two goods—or two evils. The student wants to be a loving son. He also wants to be a patriot and to avenge his brother's death. How to choose—that is the question!

Surely you have faced similar situations even if not so life determining. For example, Grandpa loves chocolate covered pretzels and asks you bring him some. You know that they are bad for his high blood pressure. Do you bring him some anyway, making him happy but less healthy—or do you arrive without them, leaving him sad but healthier? Life is full of such choices, some more agonizing than others, but all of them determinative of who we are as individuals.

Although Sartre like Kant is concerned with choosing a course of action and with being free to choose, unlike Kant he denies that there is any law which will tell us the right way to choose in particular circumstances. Laws and guidelines become laws and guidelines **for us**, says Sartre, because we **choose** to follow or be guided by them. We choose how to interpret them. Similarly, we choose someone as an advisor. We decide to adopt that adviser's guidance. Each of us is free to choose a course of action and therefore bears full responsibility for that act. No formula, no ethic, no other person can take that responsibility from us. As Sartre says, ". . . we ourselves decide our being."

Clearly, then, freedom has a very different significance for Sartre than it does for Kant. For Kant, freedom means that we are free not to act from inclination and can, therefore, follow a rule given by reason which tells us how we ought to act in a given situation. For Sartre, on the other hand, our human freedom means that we have to make choices ourselves—without benefit of guidelines and without any way of sharing responsibility for our moral (and non-moral) choices. The individual, and only the individual, can make the considered judgment that is an authentic moral choice. It cannot be any other way, so one must accept it and bear responsibility for the choice. There is no direction for the choice.

How, then, are we to choose? You choose, says Sartre, and in choosing you confer value on that choice—not the other way around! When you choose, you are saying by your choice, "This is good." Therefore, you must choose what you can endorse. Your choice says that you are the kind of person who values this. When you make a choice, you are choosing your identity, the person you want to be. To go back to the story of the young man again, in choosing he is deciding whether he is a person whose life is directed by the needs of one individual (his mother) or a person who serves the needs of the collective society. In choosing, he chooses which person he will be.

The key moral problem for Sartre is accepting responsibility. We are responsible for our choices. There are no excuses. The young man cannot put the responsibility for his decision on his mother and her needs. If he stays with her, it is because *he* has decided that that is the kind of son he wants to be. If he joins the Free French Forces, it is because *he* has decided that he must serve his countrymen. He cannot claim to have been overwhelmed by a need to avenge his brother's death. If he acts on that need, he is responsible for choosing to act on that need.

Since you are the person who is choosing, says Sartre, you are what you do. There is no "self" that is somehow different from the agent acting in the world. If you act in a selfish way, then you are a selfish person. The pose that many people adopt that they are not "really" the person who is acting so selfishly is just a very common way of avoiding responsibility for one's actions, according to Sartre. For example, you have probably heard someone say "I don't know why I said that mean remark. It just came out. I'm not that kind of person." Sartre would say that person is kidding herself. Of course, she is that kind of person who says mean things. She just did. Such a person is guilty of self-deception. So is Sue who claims to be generous and loving but who never seems to have time to show generosity and love. And so is Dave, the bank robber, who believes that only dire financial straights caused him to choose to rob the bank while the real Dave is not a bank robber at all.

When we recognize our responsibility for our actions, says Sartre, we feel *abandonment, anguish, and despair*. We feel abandonment (*forlornness* is perhaps a better translation) because we feel so alone. There is no one, no group, no fellow citizens on whom we can blame our faults and weaknesses. We feel anguish because only we can choose and the choices are so difficult—often between two goods or two evils. There is no right way to choose that dictates itself to us that avoids having to choose between a rock and a hard place. And we feel despair because there is no moral order outside ourselves. We are forced to give meaning to our own lives through our own choices.

All is not negative, however. Because we are free to choose, we can choose differently today from the way we chose yesterday. We are constantly making our identity with our choices. Our identity is not something that is fixed. One is not a success or failure, a hero or a coward, and so on, except by how one chooses—the next time. The person who has acted shyly in the past, for instance, need not choose to act shyly in the future. And, says Sartre, that person cannot excuse her future shy behavior by saying that she is a shy person or shy by nature. She can always choose to act otherwise. Sartre gives an example in the reading of this freedom for the future to be what one chooses when he describes the case of the young man who had failed at business and at the military. Instead of seeing himself as a failure, he sees that the future holds other possibilities for him and chooses to become a priest. So while there is despair, there is also hope. One can be what one chooses to be.[1]

Sartre's view of morality is a *subjectivist* view. Clearly for Sartre, there are no objective features of the world which can be used for discovering the right choice in a moral situation. Not only must each person decide for herself what to do but there are no guidelines or procedures for making that decision. There is only the choice and the chooser, who places value in the world by choosing. Could Sartre's view of morality have anything to say to Dostoevsky's wealthy landowner? Again, the answer is yes and no.

Certainly on such a subjectivist position, one cannot argue with the landowner that he is violating a law or rule by killing the serf boy. This does not mean, however, that one cannot argue with him. Whether he chooses to be influenced by the argument, however, is something only he can decide. One might try to persuade him to choose a different alternative by making clear to him that he is choosing to kill the boy and that he has sole responsibility for this act. He cannot claim that he is forced to do it because of the boy's behavior or because of his position as landowner. Those would be excuses and would constitute a failure to recognize the freedom he has in choosing a course of action.

If you were to argue with the landowner and fail to persuade him to choose another course of action, then *you* would be the one facing a choice. You could stand by and watch the serf boy meet his fate or you could try to intervene in the punishment. Of course, your intervention may come to naught (it may even cost you your life) but you would have the choice! And not to choose is to choose.

Like Kant, Sartre also has a world view that informs his beliefs about morality. Since his moral theory is quite different from Kant's, we would expect his world view to differ and it does. For one thing, Sartre is an existentialist. This is a term that is familiar to most people but, surprisingly, the philosophers who are most often referred to as "existentialists" have been rather uncomfortable with the term and what it might mean. Sartre himself sums up existentialism in an earlier portion of the essay excerpted here ("Existentialism is a Humanism") as the belief that "*existence* comes before *essence*." [Italics in the original.] Although this phrase and his elucidation of it in the essay do not do justice to the rich philosophical meaning of existentialism, it does give us a starting point for understanding the existential world view.

"We must begin from the subjective," says Sartre. That is, we begin from our subjective experience of the world and its objects. We first experience ourselves as beings in the world and only later come to define ourselves—by what we do. We have no essence which is the "real" human being or "real" person. "Man [sic] simply is. . . . Man is nothing else but that which he makes of himself." What this means for Sartre (and other existentialists) is that there is no human nature. A person

---

[1]Obviously there are some limitations on our choices. Our physical bodies limit us in some ways. Our time and place of birth limit our options as well. Sartre calls this our *facticity,* and we deceive ourselves if we ignore it. But, in general, says Sartre, we tend to see limitations where there are none. Being six feet tall is part of one's facticity. Being shy or a coward is not.

is what she wills and, consequently, does. There is no human nature to provide a standard or guideline for how one should will. Sartre disagrees with Kant and other philosophers who believe that the essence of "man" is to be rational and that this essence can be seen as a standard by which to measure one's success or failure as a human being or to establish a rule of moral law. This world view, that there is no human nature, underlies Sartre's view of human freedom, which is so different from Kant's, and leads Sartre to a wholly different view about human choice and moral decision making.

Summary

Both Kant's and Sartre's world views and their different views of human nature have much to recommend them. They both present well-reasoned accounts of our human experience. Yet, they result in quite different ethical perspectives. Kant's ethical theory is an objectivist view, although a rather unusual one, in that he argues that right answers to moral questions can be discovered if one follows the right procedure and that this procedure is an objective feature of a world inhabited by rational beings. Sartre's moral point of view, on the other hand, is strongly subjectivist. But his subjectivism is very demanding. We cannot simply follow our feelings or desires. Each time we act we bring value into the world so that each of us bears the moral weight of the world on our shoulders.

Our own common sense view of moral decision making probably includes some of the features of morality emphasized by both Kant and Sartre. Somehow morality implies consistency, for example, as Kant suggests. To be a morally good person is to exhibit consistency in one's moral behavior. One generous act does not make someone a generous person. Universality also seems to characterize our ordinary moral thinking. It does not seem fair for a person to expect everyone else to keep his or her promises while she does not. Similarly, Sartre's emphasis on personal commitment and responsibility for our choices fits in well with our ordinary beliefs about morality. Society, for example, did not accept the claims of the Nazi war criminals that they were "just following orders" and therefore were not responsible for the atrocities they committed.

Whether either of these two ethical views is persuasive for you depends, as we have seen, on other beliefs you hold about the world and about human nature. This does not mean that morality is simply "in the eye of the beholder"—any more than most of our non-moral beliefs can be said to be in the eye of the beholder. What these two views do show is that our moral judgments are capable of being supported by good reasoning, reasoning that makes sense if we are willing to listen to it. They also show that, like the theories of modern science which rest on fundamental claims which are assumed and not proven, ethical beliefs and theories are also part of a larger world view, which includes fundamental assumptions for which no proof is offered. When we have ethical disagreements, it is helpful to keep in mind that we may be dealing with differences that originate in differences in world views or background knowledge, rather than in differences of values. We will have more to say about resolving moral disagreements in the next chapter.

Exercises

13–I

1. What does *freedom* mean for Kant? What does *freedom* mean for Sartre?
2. What does Kant mean when he says that all rational beings ought to be treated as "ends in themselves"?
3. Kant and Sartre end up in such different places morally, Kant being a staunch objectivist and Sartre being a strong subjectivist. Yet in many ways, their ethical views are more alike than different. Describe some of the similarities you see between the ethical views of Kant and Sartre.
4. The moral fact that one should not kill except in self-defense has begun to be questioned because of changes in modern medicine. Describe other moral facts which are currently undergoing the same sort of questioning.
5. Explain how Sartre's subjectivism in ethics follows from his belief that there is no human nature.
6. Describe a moral belief which you once took to be morally factual but no longer consider to be such. How did your change of belief come about?

13–II

1. Do you think ethical disagreements are more common than scientific disagreements? If so, why? If not, why not?
2. Kant describes someone who is good as someone who acts from duty. Is there a difference between Kant's good person and what is commonly known as a "goody-goody"? Defend your answer.
3. What are some of the most important features of your world view? Where did they come from? How would you defend them against someone who does not share the same world view?
4. How would Sartre or someone who subscribes to Sartre's view of freedom and personal responsibility respond to this excerpt from a letter written by O.J. Simpson after his purported suicide attempt soon after being accused of having murdered his wife? Do you think the Sartrian response adds moral insight in this situation? Explain.

   To whom it may concern:

   > First, everyone understand, I have nothing to do with Nicole's murder. I loved her, always have and always will. If we had a problem, it's because I loved her so much.
   >
   > Recently we came to the understanding that for now we were not right for each other, at least for now. Despite our love, we were different and that's why we mutually agreed to go our separate ways.
   >
   > It was tough splitting for a second time but we both knew it was for the best. Inside I had no doubt that in the future we would be close friends or more. Unlike what has been written in the press, Nicole and I had a great relationship for most of our lives together. Like all long-term relationships, we had a few downs and ups.
   >
   > I took the heat New Year's 1989 because that's what I was supposed to do. I did not plead no contest for any other reason but to protect our privacy and was advised it would end the press hype.
   >
   > I don't want to belabor knocking the press, but I can't believe what is being said. Most of it is totally made up. I know you have a job to do, but as a

last wish, please, please, please, leave my children in peace. Their lives will be tough enough.

. . .

I think of my life and feel I've done most of the right things. So why do I end up like this? I can't go on. No matter what the outcome, people will look and point. I can't take that. I can't subject my children to that. This way, they can move on and go on with their lives.

Please, if I've done anything worthwhile in my life. Let my kids live in peace from you, the press.

I've had a good life. I'm proud of how I lived. My mama taught me to do unto others. I treated people the way I wanted to be treated. I've always tried to be up and helpful, so why is this happening?

I'm sorry for the Goldman family. I know how much it hurts.

Nicole and I had a good life together. All this press talk about a rocky relationship was no more than what every long-term relationship experiences. All her friends will confirm that I have been totally loving and understanding of what she's been going through.

At times I have felt like a battered husband or boyfriend but I loved her, make that clear to everyone. And I would take whatever it took to make it work.

Don't feel sorry for me. I've had a great life, great friends. Please think of the real O.J. and not this lost person.

Thanks for making my life special. I hope I helped yours.

Peace and love, O.J.

From a report by Associated Press, 6/18/94.

14

Moral Dialogue

DOGMATISM AND RELATIVISM

Moral disagreements are often painful, sometimes are downright nasty, and may even have dire consequences for some or all of the participants. We try to avoid them. We walk away from them. We "agree to disagree." Moral disagreements, however, are too important to ignore. They are about how we ought to live. Nothing could be more important for an individual than answering the question, "How ought I to live my life?" While we cannot answer that question for you, we can take another look at moral disagreements to discover ways they can be more profitable to us as individuals—and sometimes to us as members of a group or nation.

One of the problems with moral disagreements is that they often seem to be dominated by two types of arguers: on the one hand, people who are absolutely certain about the right course of action and who, therefore, want everyone else to agree to it and, on the other, people who argue that there is no certainty in moral matters and, therefore, whatever an individual says is right is right for him, regardless of what others believe. Those who are sure that they are right are called **dogmatists**. Those who insist that morality varies from individual to individual and that moral differences of opinion are arbitrary and cannot be bridged by reason are called **relativists**. There is a tendency to believe that people are either dogmatists or relativists. If you are not a dogmatist, you must be a relativist, and vice versa. This "either/or" kind of thinking gets people confused and even more eager to stay away from moral arguments. In this chapter, we will show that neither dogmatism nor relativism is an appropriate stance to take in moral arguments and that there is a middle ground between these two poles of moral reasoning.

We all know people who are dogmatic about what they believe. All of us are dogmatic about some beliefs we hold, or at least we have argued dogmatically at times. We become so excited about something which we consider factual that we want everyone else to consider it factual also. We cannot imagine anyone's questioning it. We also all know people who are relativists in their beliefs. They couldn't care less what other people believe and only want to be left alone with their own beliefs. They generally shrink from defending their beliefs, except their belief that beliefs are personal and that each person has "a right" to his beliefs. You probably have argued this way sometimes—perhaps when you thought a belief was warranted but felt at a loss to defend it.

Neither the dogmatist nor the relativist is willing to participate in dialogue about moral disagreement because they both see such dialogue as fruitless. The dogmatist does not want to discuss morality because he sees most moral issues as settled, with no further discussion necessary. The relativist does not want to discuss morality because he believes moral beliefs are arbitrary and cannot be rationally warranted. Moral dialogue on this view is only an exchange of rationalizations and, therefore, pointless.

This dichotomy between dogmatists and relativists ignores a whole range of alternative moral stances between them. It rests on a misunderstanding of certainty and of what can or cannot be warranted. Before we take a look at some alternative moral stances, it will be helpful to explore some of the reasons for this misunderstanding which has led so many to focus on the dogmatist/relativist stand off as the model of moral argument.

While there are certainly dogmatists and relativists in science[1] and other areas, dogmatism and relativism are less associated with scientific discourse, for example, than they are with moral discourse. One possible explanation for this is that there is a higher degree of consensus in the use of scientific vocabulary than there is in the use of our ethical vocabulary. The criteria for use of our scientific vocabulary are fairly clear which means it is easier to get other people (scientists) to accept claims as warranted. There is less need for taking a dogmatic stand and less appearance of taking a dogmatic stand.

The question then becomes why there is an apparent greater consensus of usage for the vocabulary of scientific discourse than for the vocabulary of moral discourse. One explanation for this apparent consensus is that the scientific community is not nearly as large as the ethical community. To be admitted to the community of scientists one must learn to speak the language of physics, chemistry, biology, and so on. These languages are difficult; not everyone can learn them, and not everyone needs to learn them. Moreover, their difficulty generally precludes nonscientists from entering into the scientific dialogue so that experts are left to carry on the dialogue alone.

On the other hand, all of us must make ethical decisions. We do not and cannot leave ethical decisions to the experts the same way we leave scientific decisions to the scientists. We all must speak the language of ethics. Moreover, because we all have

---

[1]See, for example, Paul Feyerabend, *Against Method,* New York: Verso, 1988, or some of the criticisms of Thomas Kuhn's *The Structure of Scientific Revolutions,* Chicago: University of Chicago Press, 1962, such as Imre Lakatos, "Falsification and the Methodology of Scientific Research Programmes," in I. Lakatos and A. Musgrave. eds., *Criticism and the Growth of Knowledge,* Cambridge: Cambridge University Press, 1970.

had ethical experiences, we like to believe that we have some expertise ourselves. We are not as willing to listen to others or to allow someone to act as an "expert" in moral matters as we are in scientific matters. Consequently, there is less consensus in the use of our ethical vocabulary than in the use of the vocabulary of science and less consensus in our ethical discourse.

Given that we are all "experts" in morality, it is surprising that there is even as much consensus in moral matters as there is. We have this consensus because we are all part of an ethical community and a community of ethical language speakers. As members of that community, we share in its traditions, laws, and customs. They are part of our background knowledge. They inform our ethical beliefs. Consequently, we do have consensus about much of our moral life. We have already seen that there are factual statements about moral matters, that is, statements with moral content that are rarely questioned and are considered warranted in the same way that statements with non-moral content are. Of course, sometimes there is no consensus in the community, and sometimes the consensus is "soft" as, for example, when the old consensus is weak but no new consensus has emerged. The belief that killing another human being is wrong, except in cases of self-defense, is a possible example of a moral belief for which the consensus is soft. There is as yet, however, no new consensus about the rightness or wrongness of euthanasia.

This consensus, while less than the consensus of science, means that we **can** discuss moral issues. Moral discussion need not deteriorate into a battle between the dogmatists, on one hand, and the relativists, on the other. We do not use the moral vocabulary so differently that we do not understand each other. It is just that we do not always agree and a lot of us are in on the disagreement.

Both dogmatism and the relativism, however, rest on mistaken understandings of consensus and certainty. The dogmatist is certain of his belief. His certainty, he believes, entitles him to forego any further dialogue either with himself (as in thought) or with others. He wants only that others believe the same way. To achieve consensus he presents his views dogmatically—with little room for further thought or discussion. The relativist, on the other hand, believes that because no moral argument is ever conclusive, in the sense of resting on premises that are entirely free of assumption, moral conclusions are always arbitrary and without rational warrant. Consensus is unlikely. Hence, the relativist thinks moral dialogue is pointless because in the end there is only rationalization—merely the appearance of rational support for moral beliefs. The dogmatist errs in thinking that we human beings can be so certain that no further dialogue is necessary, and the relativist errs in demanding the possibility of that same kind of certainty and in giving up the discussion because it is not possible. Neither is willing to carry on the dialogue that can lead to consensus.

This kind of certainty that the dogmatist thinks he possesses and the relativist thinks is impossible does not characterize any of our reasoning about matters of fact. We, therefore, should not expect it to characterize our moral discourse. It is helpful here to review the idea of science as a story and to look at the similarities between the science story and the moral discourse story. The scientist tells a story which weaves the traces we note in our experience into a pattern that helps us explain the past and predict the future. Moral discourse is similar. We weave together a story from our experiences which helps us evaluate the past and make choices about the future. Each discourse has its appropriate style. The style of science generally is quantitative. The style of moral discourse is generally qualitative. Consequently, these two stories look different from each other. They tend to look different in kind. If we recall the underlying structure, however, we see that they are much more alike than different.

For example, we have seen that scientific discourse rests on assumptions that cannot be proven, which are taken as fundamental. We have also seen that science rests in part on unarticulated values, particularly aesthetic values like simplicity and beauty. Also, scientific discourse is open-ended. The scientist is continually testing his hypotheses to see if they work, often adjusting his story to accord with his results. Moral discourse is similar. Like science, it rests on assumptions—usually about human nature—which are fundamental and unproven. Moral discourse also contains value assumptions, both moral and aesthetic. And it is also open-ended. It is subject to revision in light of new insights and changes in background knowledge. Of course, moral discourse is not quantitative (except for versions of utilitarianism which adopt the quantitative methods of science), but quantitative discourse is just a different way of talking. It is just a different way of telling a story.

In many ways there is *less* certainty in science than in moral discourse. There have been more changes in the story told by scientists in the last 2000 years than in the story of moral discourse. Aristotle's *Nicomachean Ethics* still tells a helpful story about how to live a good life. On the other hand, Aristotle's *Physics* describes the physical world in terms that we would find woefully out of date and not at all helpful. Even today science textbooks are very quickly obsolete. An old ethics textbook is much more likely to be useful than an old science textbook of the same vintage. The story told by the former tends to change much more slowly than the story told by the latter.[2]

You have already encountered one moral dogmatist in this text. Euthyphro is such a person. Remember that Euthyphro is on his way into court to bring charges against his own father for murder, and Socrates is going there because he has been charged with corrupting the morals of the youth of Athens with his teaching. So morality is a primary theme in the dialogue. One of the surprising things about a Platonic dialogue is that each time you read it, you discover new insights that you did not notice before and the *Euthyphro* is no exception. The critical thinking skills you have already acquired will help you as you reread the following passages of the dialogue.

The second reading is an example of moral relativism. It is reconstructed from an actual dialogue that took place in a college classroom. Such moral relativism is quite a common feature in moral discussions among college students. It will probably sound rather familiar.

---

[2]It is interesting to note that despite this uncertainty and the rapid pace of change, science teaching and science textbooks tend to be characterized by dogmatism. They both treat their subject matter as unquestionable and highly warranted.

	EUTHYPHRO AS DOGMATIST

Plato

SOCR.   And what is this suit of yours, Euthyphro? Are you suing, or being sued?

EUTH.   I am suing.

SOCR.   Whom?

EUTH.   A man whom people think I must be mad to prosecute.

SOCR.   What? Has he wings to fly away with?

EUTH.   He is far enough from flying; he is a very old man.

SOCR.   Who is he?

EUTH.   He is my father.

SOCR.   Your father, my good man?

EUTH.   He is indeed.

SOCR.   What are you prosecuting him for? What is the accusation?

EUTH.   Murder, Socrates.

SOCR.   Good heavens, Euthyphro! Surely the multitude are ignorant of what is right. I take it that it is not everyone who could rightly do what you are doing; only a man who was already well advanced in wisdom.

EUTH.   That is quite true, Socrates.

SOCR.   Was the man whom your father killed a relative of yours? But, of course, he was. You would never have prosecuted your father for the murder of a stranger?

EUTH.   You amuse me, Socrates. What difference does it make whether the murdered man were a relative or a stranger? The only question that you have to ask is, did the murderer kill justly or not? If justly, you must let him alone; if unjustly, you must indict him for murder, even though he share your hearth and sit at your table. The pollution is the same if you associate with such a man, knowing what he has done, without purifying yourself, and him too, by bringing him to justice. In the present case the murdered man was a poor laborer of mine, who worked for us on our farm in Naxos. While drunk he got angry with one of our slaves and killed him. My father therefore bound the man hand and foot and threw him into a ditch, while he sent to Athens to ask the priest what he should do. While the messenger was gone, he entirely neglected the man, thinking that he was a murderer, and that it would be no great matter, even if he were to die. And that was exactly what happened; hunger and cold and his bonds killed him before the messenger returned. And now my father

---

Excerpt from Plato, *Euthyphro, Apology, and Crito,* translated by F. J. Church. © 1957. Reprinted by permission of Prentice-Hall, Inc., Upper Saddle River, NJ.

and the rest of my family are indignant with me because I am prosecuting my father for the murder of this murderer. They assert that he did not kill the man at all; and they say that, even if he had killed him over and over again, the man himself was a murderer, and that I ought not to concern myself about such a person because it is impious for a son to prosecute his father for murder. So little, Socrates, do they know the divine law of piety and impiety.

SOCR.   And do you mean to say, Euthyphro, that you think that you understand divine things and piety and impiety so accurately that, in such a case as you have stated, you can bring your father to justice without fear that you yourself may be doing something impious?

EUTH.   If I did not understand all these matters accurately, Socrates, I should not be worth much—Euthyphro would not be any better than other men.

SOCR.   Then, my dear Euthyphro, I cannot do better than become your pupil and challenge Meletus on this very point before the trial begins. I should say that I had always thought it very important to have knowledge about divine things; and that now, when he says that I offend by speaking carelessly about them, and by introducing reforms, I have become your pupil. And I should say, "Meletus, if you acknowledge Euthyphro to be wise in these matters and to hold the correct belief, then think the same of me and do not put me on trial; but if you do not, then bring a suit, not against me, but against my master, for corrupting his elders—namely, myself whom he corrupts by his teaching, and his own father whom he corrupts by admonishing and punishing him." And if I did not succeed in persuading him to release me from the suit or to indict you in my place, then I could repeat my challenge in court.

EUTH.   Yes, by Zeus! Socrates, I think I should find out his weak points if he were to try to indict me. I should have a good deal to say about him in court long before I spoke about myself.

SOCR.   Yes, my dear friend, and knowing this I am anxious to become your pupil. I see that Meletus here, and others too, seem not to notice you at all, but he sees through me without difficulty and at once prosecutes me for impiety. Now, therefore, please explain to me what you were so confident just now that you knew. Tell me what are righteousness and sacrilege with respect to murder and everything else. I suppose that piety is the same in all actions, and that impiety is always the opposite of piety, and retains its identity, and that, as impiety, it always has the same character, which will be found in whatever is impious.

EUTH.   Certainly, Socrates, I suppose so.

SOCR.   Tell me, then, what is piety and what is impiety?

EUTH.   Well, then, I say that piety means prosecuting the unjust individual who has committed murder or sacrilege, or any other
such crime, as I am doing now, whether he is your father or
your mother or whoever he is; and I say that impiety means
not prosecuting him. And observe, Socrates, I will give you a
clear proof, which I have already given to others, that it is so,
and that doing right means not letting off unpunished the sacrilegious man, whosoever he may be. Men hold Zeus to be the
best and the most just of the gods; and they admit that Zeus
bound his own father, Cronos, for wrongfully devouring his
children; and that Cronos, in his turn, castrated his father for
similar reasons. And yet these same men are incensed with me
because I proceed against my father for doing wrong. So, you
see, they say one thing in the case of the gods and quite
another in mine.

SOCR.   Is not that why I am being prosecuted, Euthyphro? I mean,
because I find it hard to accept such stories people tell about the
gods? I expect that I shall be found at fault because I doubt those
stories. Now if you who understand all these matters so well
agree in holding all those tales true, then I suppose that I must
yield to your authority. What could I say when I admit myself
that I know nothing about them? but tell me, in the name of
friendship, do you really believe that these things have actually
happened?

EUTH.   Yes, and more amazing things, too, Socrates, which the multitude do not know of.

SOCR.   Then you really believe that there is war among the gods, and
bitter hatreds, and battles, such as the poets tell of, and which the
great painters have depicted in our temples, notably in the pictures which cover the robe that is carried up to the Acropolis at
the great Panathenaic festival? Are we to say that these things
are true, Euthyphro?

EUTH.   Yes, Socrates, and more besides. As I was saying, I will report
to you many other stories about divine matters, if you like,
which I am sure will astonish you when you hear them.

SOCR.   I dare say. You shall report them to me at your leisure another
time. At present please try to give a more definite answer to
the question which I asked you just now. What I asked you,
my friend, was, What is piety? and you have not explained it
to me to my satisfaction. You only tell me that what you are
doing now, namely, prosecuting your father for murder, is a
pious act.

EUTH.   Well, that is true, Socrates.

SOCR.   Very likely. But many other actions are pious, are they not,
Euthyphro?

EUTH.   Certainly.

SOCR.   Remember, then, I did not ask you to tell me one or two of all the many pious actions that there are; I want to know what is characteristic of piety which makes all pious actions pious. You said, I think, that there is one characteristic which makes all pious actions pious, and another characteristic which makes all impious actions impious. Do you not remember?

EUTH.   I do.

SOCR.   Well, then, explain to me what is this characteristic, that I may have it to turn to, and to use as a standard whereby to judge your actions and those of other men, and be able to say that whatever action resembles it is pious, and whatever does not, is not pious.

EUTH.   Yes, I will tell you that if you wish, Socrates.

SOCR.   Certainly I do.

EUTH.   Well, then, what is pleasing to the gods is pious, and what is not pleasing to them is impious.

SOCR.   Fine, Euthyphro. Now you have given me the answer that I wanted. Whether what you say is true, I do not know yet. But, of course, you will go on to prove that it is true.

EUTH.   Certainly.

SOCR.   Come, then, let us examine our statement. The things and the men that are pleasing to the gods are pious, and the things and the men that are displeasing to the gods are impious. But piety and impiety are not the same; they are as opposite as possible— was not that what we said?

EUTH.   Certainly.

SOCR.   And it seems the appropriate statement?

EUTH.   Yes, Socrates, certainly.

SOCR.   Have we not also said, Euthyphro, that there are quarrels and disagreements and hatreds among the gods?

EUTH.   We have.

SOCR.   But what kind of disagreement, my friend, causes hatred and anger? Let us look at the matter thus. If you and I were to disagree as to whether one number were more than another, would that make us angry and enemies? Should we not settle such a dispute at once by counting?

EUTH.   Of course.

SOCR.   And if we were to disagree as to the relative size of two things, we should measure them and put an end to the disagreement at once, should we not?

EUTH.   Yes.

SOCR.   And should we not settle a question about the relative weight of two things by weighing them?

EUTH.   Of course.

SOCR.   Then what is the question which would make us angry and enemies if we disagreed about it, and could not come to a settlement?

Perhaps you have not an answer ready; but listen to mine. Is it not the question of the just and unjust, of the honorable and the dishonorable, of the good and the bad? Is it not questions about these matters which make you and me and everyone else quarrel, when we do quarrel, if we differ about them and can reach no satisfactory agreement?

EUTH.   Yes, Socrates, it is disagreements about these matters.

SOCR.   Well, Euthyphro, the gods will quarrel over these things if they quarrel at all, will they not?

EUTH.   Necessarily.

SOCR.   Then, my good Euthyphro, you say that some of the gods think one thing just, the others another; and that what some of them hold to be honorable or good, others hold to be dishonorable or evil. For there would not have been quarrels among them if they had not disagreed on these points, would there?

EUTH.   You are right.

CLASSROOM SCENE

A group of students in a class on gender relations are discussing whether there are some things that women do better than men or that men do better than women. The discussions focuses on the question whether women make better supervisors than men do.

STUDENT 1 (A FEMALE):   The study in our textbook shows that women are better supervisors than men. Remember? They talked about the three important characteristics of a good supervisor. A spirit of cooperation, ability to multitask, and willingness to share the credit with others. Both the men and the women surveyed responded that they thought women performed better than men in all three of these categories. The funny thing is that when men and women were asked whether they preferred a male or a female supervisor, both males and females said they preferred male supervisors to female supervisors.

PROFESSOR: Why do you think that would be the case?

STUDENT 1:   I don't know.

STUDENT 2 (A MALE):   Because men are better leaders!

STUDENT 3 (A FEMALE):   No, they're not. Just look at the study cited by our textbook.

STUDENT 4 (A MALE):   Wait a minute! That's his opinion. Therefore, it's right for *him.*

STUDY QUESTIONS

1. Why do people take offense when they are called dogmatic?
2. Many people feel threatened by relativism. Why might someone who advocates a relativist position in ethics make ordinary moral people upset?
3. Socrates is generally considered to be Plato's hero. Why might someone consider Socrates a hero? What makes him heroic? What makes him unheroic?
4. Euthyphro is bringing his own father to trial for murder, a murder that is inadvertent at best. What kind of person would do something like this? Do you know people like Euthyphro?
5. What should Student 3 reply to Student 2?
6. What might explain the discrepancy in the textbook data, which suggest that both men and women believe women have the skills necessary for being good supervisors but both males and females say they prefer male supervisors to female supervisors?

MODERATION AS KEY

Dogmatism and relativism are related to, but not identical with, the moral viewpoints of objectivism and subjectivism that we discussed earlier. As we saw in Chapter 12, the moral objectivist is someone who believes that there are objective criteria, that is, features of the world that can be used as evidence for the use of moral terms. One would expect a dogmatist also to be an objectivist and, indeed, most dogmatists are objectivists. They believe that they have evidence from experience which justifies their claims of certainty in moral matters. For example, a Benthamite—one who uses Bentham's pleasure calculus to determine the total amount of happiness derived from one action as compared to another—has a high level of certainty about which act ought to be performed and is likely not to wish to discuss the issue further. A dogmatist, we can say, is a **certain objectivist** who believes there are objective criteria for moral statements and he knows them.

Not every objectivist, however, need be a dogmatist. One could believe, for instance, that there are objective criteria for the proper use of moral terms but also believe that he is uncertain about their particular application. This kind of **modest objectivism** allows for moral dialogue and discussion by acknowledging that evidence, even if considered an objective feature of the world, is a matter of judgment and that, consequently, moral discourse must be open-ended in the same way that scientific discourse is open-ended. Some people might consider Kant a modest objectivist, that is, someone who thinks there are moral facts which can be known but who does not claim to know what they all are.

Relativists are subjectivists. The subjectivist view, as you will recall, holds that there are no objective features of the world which serve as criteria for moral judgments, and therefore moral judgments are the product of each individual subject or person. The relativist is someone who adds to this the belief that this product is arbitrary, there being no possible deliberation sufficient for moral certainty. Hence, one moral conclusion cannot be said to be more reasonable than another.

We might say that the relativist is a **cynical subjectivist**, someone who pushes subjectivism to its limit, believing that moral decisions are so subjective that deliberation is useless. We could imagine, however, someone who is a deliberate subjectivist. A **deliberate subjectivist** would be the person who believes that, while there are no objective criteria for making moral judgments, moral judgments are not precluded from being the products of conscious deliberation, which is rational and impartial. For the deliberate subjectivist, moral judgments are subjective but can be warranted.

We can think of these moral viewpoints, then, as being on a continuum with the dogmatist as the certain objectivist on one end and the relativist as the cynical subjectivist on the other. In the middle between them are the modest objectivist and the deliberating subjectivist. Dogmatism and relativism are not attractive stances in moral discourse, and we have seen that they rest on a mistaken understanding of certainty; hence, the end points on this continuum are not very interesting moral viewpoints. Certain objectivism and cynical subjectivism do not accord with our ordinary moral sentiments and our moral discourse, and they do not accord with our understanding of facts and warranted beliefs. We have already seen that our best thinking comes from the open dialogue—with ourselves and with others—and both dogmatism and relativism resist dialogue altogether. Fortunately, there are alternative moral stances.

Moral views, like Kant's and others, which fall on the continuum in the range of modest objectivism and deliberative subjectivism, are potentially attractive moral views from the standpoint of rationality and the use of good reasoning skills. They allow for dialogue and even encourage it. They acknowledge the existence of moral facts but do not claim or require absolute certainty. They encourage the gathering of a consensus among the members of the moral community. They allow that one moral judgment can be better or worse than another and suggest ways of determining the better and the worse. They are moral views which encourage moderation in moral matters.

Moderation in moral arguments means continuing the moral dialogue as long as possible, neither jumping to fisticuffs nor walking away—"agreeing to disagree." As we have said from the beginning, **the willingness to keep the dialogue**

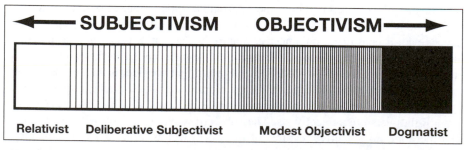

While there is no hard-and-fast dividing line where one becomes clearly either a dogmatist or a relativist, the extreme forms of both are clear and shade toward more moderate views in the center of the continuum.

open is the hallmark of the rational person. In moral matters this is particularly important. Look, for example, at what happened to Socrates not long after the episode recorded in the dialogue you read. He and the people of Athens had a moral disagreement and, like Euthyphro, the Athenians got tired of continuing the moral dialogue and executed him. **The alternative to continuing the dialogue is usually harm to someone.** Even "agreeing to disagree" can be harmful because the disagreement is still there and can fester and become violent. It can also lead to the cynical point of view that moral disagreements are irrelevant and that nothing is ever worth fighting for, even verbally. While people are talking, they cannot be harming each other. (Note: Shouting and screaming at someone is *not* having a dialogue with someone.)

There must, of course, be more to morality than moral dialogue. Moral dialogues do not always end in consensus. People refuse to listen. Sometimes there is no time for dialogue. The baby is drowning or the house is on fire. And we did say in the previous chapter that not to act is to act! How do we know when to stop talking and to start acting? Where do we draw the line between tolerating what we think is a mistaken moral view and interfering in someone else's behavior to prevent him from doing something we think is immoral? Indeed, these are tough questions which we all have worried about—and *should* worry about.

There certainly are times when we must act, even against the will and moral beliefs of another. There are times when the dialogue must stop because to continue the dialogue would allow immoral behavior to continue and harm to be done. These are not easy decisions. It would be a relief to have a rule which we could plug into a situation to determine whether or not we should act, but such a rule would be most unusual. After all, no such rule exists for making decisions in non-moral matters. This lack of a rule (or rules) in the non-moral aspects of our lives does not stop us, however, from making decisions and taking action. We have non-moral warranted beliefs, and we use them to make rational decisions on which we then act, following the guidelines of rational decision making.

Let's review decision making in the non-moral sphere by considering an example. You are about to board an airplane for a distant city. You believe, as you board, that you will arrive safely at your destination at the end of your flight. Surely this belief is warranted, and your behavior based on that belief is justified. Are you absolutely certain that you and your plane will arrive safely? No, of course not. We all know there is a risk involved in flying and that a small, very small, percentage of air travel passengers do not arrive safely. No one, however, would think your choice of a means of travel unjustified, irrational, or foolish. Indeed, we look down on people (like the late John Madden)[3] who refuse to fly as people who have "irrational" fear. The decision to fly is justified by the warranted belief that flying is a safe way to travel. Your behavior is based on good reasoning with probability.

---

[3]Former pro-football coach and television football commentator, John Madden refused to travel by airplane.

The situation is analogous for moral reasoning. We can never be absolutely certain that our decisions are morally correct. We can be justified in taking moral action, however, on the same kinds of evidence we would use in non-moral situations, using guidelines similar to the guidelines of rational decision making for non-moral decisions. Just as in non-moral decision making, there is always a certain amount of uncertainty and risk, but it is not irrational or immoral to proceed without absolute certainty if we have followed the guidelines.

Summary

Good moral reasoning, then, is like good reasoning about non-moral matters. We have moral facts and warranted moral beliefs. We recognize that our moral actions are based on moral beliefs, which are warranted but not absolutely certain, and that acting is not without risk. The certainty that the dogmatist thinks he has does not characterize either our non-moral or our moral decision making. This does not mean, however, that relativism is our only alternative. Both dogmatism and relativism get their credibility by claiming or by demanding, respectively, a kind of certainty that is not possible when reasoning about the world of our experience. Therefore, they have no place in our decision making.

The guidelines for moral decision making are similar to those of reasoning with probability:

1. We should proceed with toleration and moderation rather than haste or caprice, knowing that our moral community is large and diverse.
2. Our moral decisions should be the product of open dialogue—with ourselves and with others—since open dialogue is our best guarantee that our decisions will be the product of rational deliberation.
3. We should bring as large a store of background knowledge to the decision-making process as we can to avoid limited, uninformed judgments and possible future disappointment and regret.
4. In times of moral conflict and uncertainty, we need to know what is important to us and for us. That means we must know which of our beliefs, especially our moral beliefs, are most entrenched and look to decisions which fit in better with those beliefs which are well entrenched.
5. Like all reasoning about experience, when we make a moral decision we are always at risk of being wrong. Consequently, we must always be testing our moral reasoning against future moral experiences and be ready to revise our background knowledge and our future decisions in light of those testings.

If our goal is to maintain and improve our relationships with those around us so that we have more friends and fewer enemies, to love and be loved, to have pleasant rather than unpleasant experiences, and to enjoy as much of our lives as we possibly can, then these guidelines of rational moral thinking increase the likelihood of successfully meeting those goals. No rule or guideline, however, guarantees success. **Good reasoning can and does make for better human relationships.** It takes effort—but the rewards are great.

Exercises

14–I

1. What are the differences between dogmatism and relativism?
2. Why are dogmatism and relativism not helpful positions to take in situations of moral disagreement?
3. We talk about making moral mistakes. How would a dogmatist describe a moral mistake? A modest objectivist? A deliberate subjectivist? A relativist? Which account makes the most sense to you? Why?
4. Explain why this text is called *Thinking Socratically*.
5. Why is bumper sticker morality potentially harmful?

14–II

1. Explain how someone can avoid relativism without being a dogmatist.
2. Why is it that violence begets violence? Give some examples from history and literature to support your position.
3. We live in a culturally diverse world. Students of this cultural diversity (anthropologists, for example) often believe that, given this diversity, relativism is the only possible moral stance. How would you explain to them that respect for other cultures does not mean that one must be a moral relativist?

15

Reason and Commitment

OPEN RATIONAL DIALOGUE

This text has described what it is to be a rational thinker. Our model of the rational thinker has been Socrates. Socrates has long been revered as the epitome of the rational person. His own personal ethic he summed up as "Do no harm." The connection between rational thinking and avoidance of doing harm may not be clear to you, but they are closely connected. The final reading in this text helps to clarify this connection. It is from a commencement speech by the Pulitzer Prize-winning author, Jane Smiley. Her address was given in 1996, but it seems even more relevant today after the events of 9/11, American involvement in two wars, and the fractured politics of Washington, D.C. We believe that her words go right to the heart of the connection between reasoning together in open rational dialogue and resolving some of the difficult and divisive political and moral issues that divide people today and too often lead them to harm one another. We hope you will remember them.

KEYNOTE SPEECH MAY 18 AT SIMPSON COLLEGE'S
1996 COMMENCEMENT

Jane Smiley

In our own country, we see an unprecedented level of actual violence, and also an unprecedented level of verbal violence. Civil discourse seems to have ended in some places and [among] so many people. What is left is vows and assertions and caches of weapons and vituperation against anyone who seems different or frightening.

Jane Smiley, Keynote Speech, May 18, 1996, Simpson College commencement.

But you know what? Somehow I am no longer afraid of this lack of peace....

Many of the things that Americans argue about are worth arguing about: for example, the environment. Following the second World War, the American love affair with technology gave us many so-called innovations that turned out to be harmful. Let us take as our example "DDT."

Discussion of such a large matter as DDT and the interests and investments it represented, set off against the dangers it posed, could not fail to be significant and even acrimonious. The same goes for all sorts of environmental issues: from over-population to clear-cutting, from petroleum use to habitat destruction.

If we were not fighting over these things, we would be fools. What may emerge from our fighting, if we stick with it, is a cleaner, healthier and more beautiful world to live in. How about education, social services, health care? How about race, ethnicity, religion?

. . .

. . . Conflict is different than violence. I used to think that conflict leads to violence as pink shades into red. It was, "One was just more of the other." Now I think that violence occurs as an attempt to stop conflict, a stab at silencing the cacophony of differing opinions and divergent values.

There can come a point in an argument where one party or another just can't take it anymore. He or she leaves the room or strikes a blow. It takes courage in the face of conflict to neither leave the room nor strike a blow but to keep arguing and to keep accepting the right of the other person to argue, too.

It takes courage to realize that something, some compromise, will be hammered out, and that an interval of peace can ensue. It takes courage to accept part of, rather than all of, what you want. In other words, it takes courage to live in a diverse society where people speak up rather than shut up.

STUDY QUESTIONS

1. Do you agree that Smiley's description characterizes the contemporary world? What do you see as major contributing factors to current conflict?
2. What is Smiley's concept of courage?
3. How does Smiley's claim that moral dialogue takes **courage** relate to Socrates in the dialogue *Euthyphro*?

INDEX

Note: Page numbers followed by 'n' indicates end notes.